The Rise and Fall of the East India Company

The Rise and Fall of the East India Company

A Sociological Appraisal

Ramkrishna Mukherjee

AAKAR

The Rise and Fall of the East India Company
Ramkrishna Mukherjee

First Published in India 2011
Reprinted 2019

ISBN 978-93-5002-146-0

Published in agreement with Monthly Review Press, New York for publication and sale only in South Asia.

Published by
AAKAR BOOKS
28 E Pocket IV, Mayur Vihar Phase I
Delhi 110 091, India
www.aakarbooks.com

Printed at
D.K. Fine Art Press, Delhi

PREFACE TO THE INDIAN EDITION, 1973

When the second edition of this book went out of print in early 'sixties, I withheld its publication because I wished to revise it in light of the fresh materials available since it was last revised in 1957. Now that I have the time to do it I find that unnecessary. The new finds do not alter my thesis while to incorporate them will either make the volume unduly bulky or its structural unity will be disturbed. For the latter reason, I do not also wish to reduce its present size by omitting the details which are now well known. I may, however, state my objective in writing this book which has been succinctly put by a reviewer as to survey "a phenomenon that acted as a catalyst in the transformation of the Indian economy (and society — RM) over a period of two and a half centuries" (Tapan Raychowdhuri: "Writings on modern Indian economic history", *Contributions to Indian Economic History*, Delhi, 1960, p. 139). I believe it important to analyze the social forces manifest in the subcontinent in the pre-British and the early British period of India's history in order to appreciate her contemporary sociological issues. This is why I thank Popular Prakashan and Shri Ramdas Bhatkal for their interest in republishing it even after waiting for so many years to receive my clearance.

RAMKRISHNA MUKHERJEE

PREFACE TO THE SECOND EDITION, 1958

When the second edition of this book was called for within six months of its publication, I decided to take the opportunity to revise and enlarge it in accordance with the comments and criticisms I had received on its contents. But owing to my consistent illness the work has been delayed by a year and yet it has still not reached the point of full satisfaction. This is not merely an apology for the delay in bringing out the second edition and for the shortcomings still contained in the book, but a pointer to its limitations.

As might be expected from the nature of this study, which gives an interpretation of the facts collected by historians and other social scientists in order to explain the *social forces* behind the rise and fall of the East India Company and the effects they produced in India in particular, the book has generated extreme reactions. But whether they received it favourably or not, probably because in the first edition it was not specifically underlined that this is not a historical study but a sociological appraisal of the facts taken from authoritative sources, most of the critics have judged it from the former standpoint. In order to avoid this misunderstanding in future, a subtitle: "A Sociological Appraisal" has been added to the main title of the book in this edition. It is intended that the merits and demerits of the book should be judged from the sociological point of view only.

Ramkrishna Mukherjee

Berlin, March 1957.

ACKNOWLEDGEMENT

The present work is the result of a course of lectures which the author, as a Guest Professor of the Humboldt University in Berlin, delivered to the students of the Institute for Indian Studies during the Autumn Term of 1953–54. Thanks for its preparation are therefore due primarily to the authorities of the Humboldt University who gave full facilities for the work. The author also feels particularly grateful to Professor Walter Ruben, the Director of the Institute for Indian Studies, who took keen interest in its preparation and publication, and to Mr. Ralf D. Jung, a student of the Institute for Indian Studies, who helped in preparing the Index and other matters relating to the publication of the book.

CONTENTS

INTRODUCTORY

The present study does not claim any originality in historical materials relating to the formation of the East India Company in Britain; its activities in the mother country, vis-a-vis other European Powers, and in India; and its final decay. Very many books have been written by able historians, noting the salient points in the life of the East India Company. But scarcely any one has so far attempted a sociological analysis of the Company in the light of the *social forces* which led to its formation, its activities as they were in the course of its existence, and its eventual removal from world society. Such *social* studies, as differentiated from what are generally known as *historical* studies, are available for different phases in the life of the Company. The present study does no more than to present such a comprehensive view, covering the period from immediately before the birth of the Company until its final decay.

Since history is not the main discipline of the author, there may be some minor inaccuracies in the study, although the author has tried to gather his materials from the reliable and generally accepted historical works and documents. Though such minor inaccuracies, which do not affect the overall formulations put forward in this study, may be excusable, the author would welcome criticism to rectify them. And, in any case, in spite of such faults, if there are any, the author is inclined to consider this attempt fruitful if it can help to answer the *Whys* of the apparent behaviour of the Company, which appear to have led to fallacious views on its role in India and Europe. This he considers his duty as a sociologist.

There are in the main two views on the character of the East India

Company and the role it played in India. Firstly, there is the view that the Company always nurtured good intentions for India and her people; and if there were some cases of oppression, breach of faith, and other "ungentlemanly" behaviour on the part of the Company or its employees (which could not be completely ignored, so obvious they were), these were isolated incidents resulting either from general ignorance of the Directors of the Company in London and their servants in India, as regards peculiar "oriental" mentality and the customs of the "natives", or because of particular individuals in the employment of the Company who might have failed in prosecuting their honourable duties (as befitting the Englishman) of looking after the interests of the Company as well as of the Indian people living under British rule.

Thus, Mr. Ramsay Muir, Professor of Modern History in the University of Manchester, came to the conclusion in his well-known study on "The Making of British India"[1]:

> "Never was Empire less the result of design than the British Empire of India."

According to him, the East India Company *became* the ruler of India, even though "they struggled against it." But once having undergone the transformation, the Company "rendered immeasurable services to the peoples of India." Its "three priceless gifts" to the Indian people were:

1) "Political unity, . . . which they never in all their history possessed before";

2) "Assured peace (bringing easy intercourse)," which revealed that "the *pax Britannica* has been a yet more wonderful thing than the *pax Romana*";

3) "Reign of Law," which under the Company's rule took "the place of the arbitrary will of innumerable despots."

And, if there were some defects, they were of course unavoidable—the leaders and the servants of the Company "being human."[1]

Mr. Muir is only one of many to be still found in Great Britain and in the Continent of Europe.[2]

Besides such an appreciation of the East India Company, there is the second view that since the birth of the Company in 1600 and up to the close of the seventeenth century, the Company represented a band of peaceful traders. But the conquest of a part of India in the battle of Plassey in 1757 roused their ambition for territorial acquisition of the whole of the rich subcontinent. This ambition, which had faint expressions in the last two decades of the seventeenth century, now transformed the peaceful traders into domineering rulers; and their continued success in subjugating different parts of India, filled their heads with ideas of power and made them greedy and tyrannical.

This view has received so common an acceptance that even three reputed Indian historians—R. C. Majumdar, H. C. Raichaudhuri and Kalikinkar Datta—noted with reference to the last decades of the seventeenth century:[3]

> "The Company's policy in India also changed during this period. A peaceful trading body was transformed into a power eager to establish its own position by territorial acquisitions, largely in view of the political disorders in the country."

And, then:

> "The battle of Plassey was, ..., a great turning-point, not only in the political but also in the economic history of Bengal. Apart from the resulting misrule and confusion, which had an adverse effect upon trade and industry, several causes directly operated in impoverishing the country and ruining its rich and prosperous trade and industry."

Both the views, however, fail to take note of the *social character* of the East India Company, which was fully revealed with its assumption of political power over India. Therefore, several British writers, even though they possessed profound sympathy for the Indian people, attempted to explain this shocking revelation by abstract value-judgement. For instance, in the book of W. M. Torrens, M. P., entitled "Empire in Asia—How We came by It: A Book of Confessions," there is the attempt to account for the Company's subjugation of India by "the spirit of conquest" which "breathes so fearlessly through every page of England's history."[4] The same was also done by several Indian writers who ignored the socio-economic roots of British expansion and colonial policy and pinned their faith in the "British sense of justice," which, they thought, must prevail in the end.[5] Hence, a sociological analysis of the rise and fall of the East India Company is still called for.

Such an analysis demands not merely an assemblage of historical and economic data in relation to the East India Company, but, on the basis of these facts, an assessment of the *social forces* which led to the emergence of the Company, governed its life-course, and decided its abolition. No doubt, this is a task the full accomplishment of which demands much more work than is incorporated in this book. Nevertheless, a tentative attempt also may have some value of its own, and it is with this aim in view that the following six chapters have been written.

In order to appreciate the scope of the present study, it may be useful to state briefly the contents of the subsequent chapters. This, therefore, is given below:

Chapter 1 will deal with the social background of the rise and fall of the East India Company in England. Firstly, with special reference to England, it will give a summary account of the far-reaching changes taking place in Europe with the break-up of feudalism and the advent of a "new civilization," for the prime mover of this "new civilization" was the class of merchants and it was English merchant capital to which the East India Company owed its origin, its characteristic features and its activities. Afterwards, this chapter will examine in some detail:– (a) how from about the fourteenth century onwards conditions were created in England and some other European states for the growth of merchant capital and how from the beginning it took a monopolist charactere; (b) why trade-monopoly was a characteristic and essential demand of merchant capital and why its expansion had to be linked with of extension of commercial relations to other countries under conditions advantageous to the merchant companies; (c) why the loudly proclaimed "honest mercantile trade" of these European nations could acquire a meaning only when it was interpreted in terms of "colonial trade" and therefore led to serious rivalry between the merchant companies of different nations with regard to obtaining trading privileges in those countries with which they wanted to trade, and also raised the problem of fighting the "interlopers" or rival merchant companies and individual merchants belonging to the same country; and (d) why for such "trade relations" these companies *had* to aspire for political power in the "purchasing" countries, which the English East India Company ultimately got in India. Lastly, it will be noted why and how the English merchant bourgeoisie passed into decadence and a struggle ensued between them and the growing industrial bourgeoisie in the mother country vis-a-vis the colonies, like India; and, in consequence, when the British industrial bourgeoisie took over the reins of the society after superseding the former, they sounded the death-knell to this typical monopolist company of merchant capital.

Chapter 2 will then be concerned with a fairly detailed account of the birth of the East India Company in England, and a discussion on one of the points raised in Chapter 1, namely, since the monopolist character of merchant capital had to encounter opposition from the *have-not* merchants of the mother country, how the East India Company fared in relation to those English merchants who were barred from such a lucrative field for commercial gain as India which they all regarded as "a true mine of gold,"[6] and how the antagonism between the *have* and *have-not* merchants in England in relation to the Eastern trade was finally resolved.

Chapter 3 will examine how because of the monopolistic character of merchant capital the East India Company had to encounter another source of opposition from similar monopolist companies in other European states, and how the scramble for power in India of several mercantile interests belonging to different European states finally resolved in favour of the British, not because of their "spectacular heroism" and unflinching determination to oppose the tyranny of the Indian rulers, as has often been claimed in some quarters, but because of their best adaptation and application of the essential features of merchant capital as enunciated in Chapter 1. This chapter will thus describe the penetration of European merchant powers into India, their reaction to one another based primarily on their mercantile interests in India but also stimulated by their over-all course of rivalry as representing different European nations bidding for supreme power, and in regard to India the final resolution of their rivalry which could not be effected by internal regulations of a state and so, in the main, the Powers had to resort to open wars.

Chapter 4 will first deal with the stage of social development in India on the advent of the European Powers and until its final conquest by the English East India Company. For, as the activities of the East India Company centred in India, (where it appeared in 1608 and disappeared in 1858 when it was forced to liquidate itself after having ruled the subcontinent for about a century), in order to appreciate its life-course as well its *leitmotiv* it is necessary to have a general understanding of the social forces working in India at the time the European merchant powers appeared in the subcontinent and until the English East India Company usurped political power there. Interestingly enough, it will be seen that both in England and India the social perspective in these days was of the break-up of feudalism and the advent of a "new civilization." But, in spite of this general similarity, there were significant differences in the nature of social development of England and India. Thereby, on the one hand, having risen to power the English merchant bourgeoisie invaded India and finally brought the subcontinent under complete control, and, on the other, while striving to attain power their Indian contemporaries came under foreign rulers and were finally liquidated in the interest of these rulers. In the light of such a social background of India, it will be shown in this chapter how the East India Company manoeuvred to gain a footing in the subcontinent when its centralised power was strong, and how by taking advantage of the disintegration of this central power and the inherent weakness of the Indian feudal structure it persevered to become supreme in Indian politics and finally emerged as the strongest power in this subcontinent. Revealing some of the essential features of merchant capital in a "trading area," this chapter will thus explain the role played by the English East India Company in India in order to gain its own ends vis-a-vis the Indian rulers.

Chapter 5 will give a summary view of how the East India Company ruled India, and how the reckless extraction of her wealth and resources by the Company, its officials and underlings, and the unbearable oppression of the Indian people by the ruling authorities changed the one-time "Granary of the East" into a land of destruction and beggary. Thus briefly describing the enormous economic drain of India during the Company's rule, this chapter will point out how this phase in the life of the East India Company gave vent to the full character of merchant capital.

Finally, Chapter 6 will give a short description of the East India Company's battle against a new System—the era of industrial capital in Britain, and how the Company had to capitulate in the end to the mounting influence of British industrial capital after bleeding India white for a century. For as a social force it had spent its power and was standing as an obstruction to the full play of British capitalism in the colony.

From a sociological point of view the present study will thus endeavour to give a logical continuity to the role of the East India Company from its rise and until its decay, and show that its activities, however contradictory they might have appeared from the usual studies of history which paint it as a band of peaceful traders transforming itself into a band of oppressive rulers, were inherent in the *social character* of its genesis and development.

A note of caution is, however, necessary before the perusal of the following chapters: the reader should be fully cognisant of the scope and limitation of this course of analysis. This study is based on secondary sources for materials, and these sources do not comprise all what has been written on the East India Company or about England and India in the period under consideration. The study is therefore assuredly incomplete in character and may also contain some inaccuracies as stated at the outset. Yet, in view of the fact that new materials are now constantly forthcoming from primary researches into the history and economics of India in the pre-British as well as during the British period of her life, the sociological analysis contained in this study may serve as a pointer for subsequent undertakings to provide a fuller appreciation of the rise and fall of the East India Company. If this book has any usefulness it is in regard to such future researches.

Notes and References

1 Muir, Ramsay—*The Making of British India: 1756—1858*, Manchester at the University Press, Great Britain, 1917, pp. 2—3.

2 See, for instance, "The Man Who Ruled India" by Philip Woodruff (Jonathan Cape, London, 1953), which was dedicated:

"To the Peoples of India and Pakistan whose tranquillity was our care and whose continuance in the family of nations to which we belong is our Memorial."

3 Majumdar, R. C.; Raychaudhuri, H. C.: Datta, Kalikinkar—*An Advanced History of India*, Macmillan, London, 1953, pp. 638, 806.

4 Torrens, W. M.—*Empire in Asia—How We came by It: A Book of Confessions*, Trübner & Co., London, 1872, p. 6.

5 See, for instance, the Preface to the two books by Romesh Dutt, entitled: *The Economic History of India under Early British Rule* and *The Economic History of India in the Victorian Age*, Routledge and Kegan Paul, London, 1950.

6 Marx, Karl—*The East India Company*, New York Daily Tribune, July 11, 1853.

CHAPTER 1

ENGLISH SOCIETY AND THE EAST INDIA COMPANY

What were the *social forces* which gave rise to the East India Company in England, imparted to it its distinctive character, and finally led to its decay? This, a question which has a vital bearing on the present study, is answered by an examination of the historical development of England from about the fourteenth century onwards; from the emergence of "modern" England to her assumption of the role of the foremost power in the world by the end of the eighteenth century. Such a big canvas, however, cannot be treated here in all its details; yet, in order to appreciate properly the motivation behind the rise and fall of the East India Company, it is necessary to attend to some of the salient features in English society in this period. This, therefore, is attempted below.

1. The "New" England

How from a "backward agricultural country" of the pre-fourteenth century period Britain, which had then "little standing among the kingdoms of the world," became the foremost political and economic power by the end of the eighteenth century is a question on which there is a sharp division of opinion. To some "the astonishing expansion of British power overseas" after the defeat of the Spanish Armada in 1588 has remained an enigma. As late as in 1942, Maurice Collis, while stressing the "private enterprise, courage and audacity" of the British nation which founded their Empire, noted:[1]

"No satisfactory explanation has ever been given of the astonishing expansion of British power overseas which began immediately after the English succeeded in preventing the Spaniards from invading this country, then a poor and sparsely populated island with little standing among the kingdoms of the world. What was the secret of this extraordinary expansion and how was it that so small a maritime power, one of the smallest in Europe, grew into the vast empire which has since become something entirely new in history—namely a Commonwealth of Nations?"

To some others, again, the "secret" lay in the innate character of the British nation. Torrens, for instance, noted in his book *Empire in Asia*:[2]

"The spirit of conquest breathes so fearlessly through every page of England's history, that it would probably be reckoned by the majority of the people rather absurd to attempt, by any timid or ingenious paraphrase, to hide from view the real nature of an attribute whereof they are nationally not a little proud. From the earliest times, they appear to have cherished a longing for foreign possessions; and from the days when Edward and Henry devoted all the flower of English knighthood, and all the contributions of English trade, to 'the conquest of France', to those when the red Indian of America was proclaimed a usurper of the hunting-ground his forefathers immemorially had enjoyed, the love of territorial acquisition has been deemed by most of our distinguished, royal, and noble authorities, worth gratifying at any cost which the nation from time to time might be brought to think it could afford."

But, as will be seen in course of this chapter, the "extraordinary expansion" of British power overseas was not merely due to "private enterprise, courage and audacity" of the Britons. It was the logical outcome of the *social forces* prevailing in Europe in those days, which could be best directed and controlled by the architects of "new" England. Similarly, the "spirit of conquest" was also not a unique trait of the British nation. At the time when "new" England and a "new" Europe were coming into being, in the histories of other maritime powers in Europe also this "spirit" breathed fearlessly. For, like the desire for expansion, this was also roused by basic social forces dominating the European nation states in those days.

There is no doubt that at this stage of England's social history the Armada was an important landmark, as indicating that the new forces in English society had come to maturity. Therefore, from this time the *social values* underwent marked changes in England and in many ways the socio-spiritual life of this country as well as of many other nation states in Europe was progressively enlightened.[3] But there is also no doubt that there were some basic forces governing these changes. These forces were in the "new civilization" which in those days was spreading over Europe. This "new civilization" was characterized by "a swift increase in wealth and an impressive expansion of trade, a concentration of financial power on a scale unknown before;" and it led to "the rise, amid fierce social convulsions, of new classes and the depression of old, the triumph of a new culture and system of ideas amid struggles not less bitter."[4]

Those were the days when Europe was in the throes of an "Economic Revolution."

> "The religious revolution of the age came upon a world heaving with the vastest economic crisis that Europe had experienced since the fall of Rome. Art and scientific curiosity and technical skill, learning and statesmanship, the scholarship which explored the past and the prophetic vision which pierced the future, had all poured their treasures into the sumptuous shrine of the new civilization. Behind the genii of beauty and wisdom who were its architects there moved a murky, but indispensable, figure. It was the demon whom Dante had met muttering gibberish in the fourth circle of the Inferno, and whom Sir Guyon was to encounter three centuries later, tanned with smoke and seared with fire, in a cave adjoining the mouth of hell. His uncouth labours quarried the stones which Michael Angelo was to raise, and sank deep in the Roman clay the foundations of the walls to be adorned by Raphael.
>
> For it was the mastery of man over his environment which heralded the dawn of the new age, and it was in the stress of expanding economic energies that this mastery was proved and won. Like sovereignty in a feudal society, the economic efforts of the Middle Ages, except in a few favoured spots, had been fragmentary and decentralized. Now the scattered raiders were to be organized and disciplined; the dispersed and irregular skirmishes were to be merged in a grand struggle, on a front which stretched from the Baltic to the Ganges and from the Spice Islands to Peru. Every year brought the news of fresh triumphs. The general who marshalled the host and launched the attack was economic power."[5]

And the architects who first wielded this "economic power" and ushered in the "new civilization" were the merchant bourgeoisie, in whose course of development in England the defeat of the Spanish Armada was an important landmark.

"Up to 1588 the English bourgeoisie were fighting for existence: after that they fought for power. For this reason the defeat of the Armada is a turning-point in the internal history of England as well as in foreign affairs. It was the merchants, with their own ships and their own money, who had won the victory and they had won it almost in spite of the half-heartedness and ineptitude of the Crown and Council, whose enthusiasm diminished as the war assumed a more revolutionary character. The victory transformed the whole character of the class relations that had existed for a century. The bourgeoisie became aware of their strength and with the coming of this awareness the long alliance between them and the monarchy began to dissolve. It might still need their support but they no longer needed its protection. Even before the death of Elizabeth, Parliament began to show an independence previously unknown."[6]

How did, then, the force of merchant capital initiate changes in *social values* in England? To take a significant example, viz. the practice of usury which found great favour with the merchant bourgeoisie, while the towns in the Middle Ages in Europe "everywhere and without exception exploits the land economically by its monopoly prices, its system of taxation, its guild organizations, its direct mercantile fraud and its usury,"[7] usury is a practice which used to be sharply condemned by the Church. But now, with the mounting influence of the merchant bourgeoisie in society, as a necessary adjunct to the growth of merchant capital it came to be accepted also by several reformers whose ideas and teaching had much to do with the evolution of new forces in society. Calvin (1509–1564), who is said to have, "with all its rigour, accepted the main institutions of a commercial civilization, and supplied a creed to the classes which were to dominate the future," delivered sermons on usury and wrote a famous letter on the subject.[8] Both he and Bucer (1491–1551) were taunted "with being the first theologians to defend extortion, and it only remained for a pamphleteer to adapt the indictment to popular consumption, by writing that 'it grew to a proverb that usury was the brat of heresy.'"[9]

The result of the change in social forces was soon forthcoming. In England, where the Puritan moralists derived their teaching "most directly from Calvin" and where "the main economic dogma of the mercantilist had an affinity with the main ethical dogma of the Puritans," usury ("in the sense of payment for a loan") became "not in itself unlawful for Christians."[10] Furthermore, in 1571, "the Act of 1552, which had prohibited all interest as 'a vyce moste odyous and detestable, as in dyvers places of the hollie Scripture it is evydent to be seen,' had been repealed after a debate in the House which revealed the revolt of the plain man against the theorists who had triumphed twenty years before, and his determination that the law should not impose on business a utopian morality."[11] And, in 1692, when "the Rev. David Jones was so indiscreet as to preach at St. Mary Woolnoth in Lombard Street a sermon against usury, on the text, 'The Pharisees who were covetous heard all these things and they derided Christ,' his career in London was brought to an abrupt conclusion."[12]

Nor was it only the practice of usury by the merchant bourgeoisie that found support in the new socio-spiritual forces arising in society. Marx wrote that the "discovery of gold and silver in America, the extirpation, enslavement and entombment in mines of the aboriginal population, the beginning of the conquest and looting of the East Indies, the turning of Africa into a warren for the commercial hunting of black-skins, signalised the rosy dawn of the era of capitalist production."[13] Inaugurating this era with his discovery of America, Columbus had written that "Gold constitutes treasure, and he who possesses it has all he needs in this world as also the means of rescuing souls from Purgatory and restoring them to the enjoyment of Paradise;"[14] and new preachers, like Calvin, are said to have come forward in support of the merchant bourgeoisie who were to enjoy this "rosy dawn" of gold-hunting days. Calvin wrote to a correspondent: "What reason is there why the income from business should not be larger than from landowning? Whence do the merchant's profits come, except from his own diligence and industry?"[15] And it was "quite in accordance with the spirit of those words that Bucer, even while denouncing the frauds and avarice of merchants, should urge the English Government to undertake the development of the woollen industry on mercantilist lines."[16]

Admittedly, these reformers did not "abandon the claim of religion to moralize economic life;" but one should not also overlook the fact that, as Tawney remarked, "the life which they are concerned to moralize is one in which the main features of a commercial civilization are taken for granted, and that it is for application to such conditions that their teaching is designed."[17] Therefore, it is seen that even in its early stage Calvinism "no longer suspects the whole world of economic motives as alien to the life of the spirit, or distrusts the capitalists as one who has necessarily grown rich on the misfortunes of his neighbour, or regards poverty as in itself meritorious, and it is perhaps the first systematic body of religious teaching which can be said to recognise and applaud the economic virtues."[18] Later, while what in Calvin "had been a qualified concession to practical exigencies, appeared in some of his later followers as a frank idealization of the life of the trader, as the service of God and the training-ground of the soul," Calvinism "found favour with the English upper classes in the seventeenth century."[19]

The introduction of Calvinism in England through Presbyterianism and Puritanism, and "the growth under Elizabeth of a vigorous Puritan movement, which had its stronghold among the trading and commercial classes,"[20] marked a distinct stage in England's *social* development. It has been asserted that "Puritanism, not the Tudor secession from Rome, was the true English Reformation, and it is from its struggle against the old order that an England which is unmistakably modern emerges;"[21] and what is of further importance to note here is that the underlying force behind this all-in transformation of England was depicted by the role of the growing English merchant bourgeoisie.

"The names of the commercial magnates of the day lend some confirmation to the suggestion of that affinity between religious radicalism and business acumen, which envious contemporaries expressed in their sneers at the 'Presbyterian old usurer', 'devout misers', and 'extorting Ishban'. The four London members elected in 1661 had not only filled the ordinary civic offices, but had held between them the governorship of the East India Company, the deputy-governorship of the Levant Company, and the masterships of the Salters and Drapers Companies; two of them were said to be Presbyterians and two Independents. Of the committee of leading business men who advised Charles II's Government on questions of commercial policy, some, like Sir Patience Ward and Michael Godfrey, represented the ultra-Protestantism of the City, while others, like Thomas Papillon and the two Houblons, were members of the French Huguenot church in London. In spite of the bitter commercial rivalry with Holland, both Dutch capital and Dutch ideas found an enthusiastic welcome in London. Sir George Downing, Charles II's envoy at the Hague, who endeavoured to acclimatize Dutch banking methods in England, and who, according to Clarendon, was one of the intriguers who prepared the war of 1665–67, had been reared in the Puritan severity of Salem and Harvard, and had been a preacher in the regiment of Colonel Okey. Paterson, who supplied the idea of a joint-stock banking corporation, which Michael Godfrey popularized in the City and Montagu piloted through Parliament, was, like the magnificent Law, a Scotch company promoter, who had haunted the Hague in the days when it was the home of disconsolate Whigs. Yarranton, most ingenious of projectors, had been an officer in the Parliamentary army, and his book was a long sermon on the virtues of the Dutch. Defoe, who wrote the idyll of the bourgeoisie in his *Complete English Tradesman*, was born of nonconformist parents, and was intended for the ministry, before, having failed in trade, he took up politics and literature. In his admirable study of the iron industry, Mr. Ashton has shown that the most eminent ironmasters of the eighteenth century belonged as a rule to the Puritan connection. They had their prototype in the seventeenth century in Baxter's friend, Thomas Foley, 'who from almost nothing did get about £ 5,000 per annum or more by iron works.'

To such a generation, a creed which transformed the acquisition of wealth from a drudgery or a temptation into a moral duty was the milk of lions. It was not that religion was expelled from practical life, but that religion itself gave it a foundation of granite."[22]

Thus, "Puritanism became a potent force in preparing the way for the commercial civilization which finally triumphed at the Revolution;"[23] a force which was at first generated by "the classes who sprang to wealth and influence with the expansion of commerce in the later years of the (sixteenth) century," and which, in the first part of the seventeenth century, "with its idealization of the spiritual energies which found expression in the activities of business and industry," produced "a religious and a social philosophy" that was to carry the day.

"The new thing in the England of the sixteenth century was that devices that had formerly been occasional were now woven into the very texture of the industrial and commercial civilization which was developing in the later years of Elizabeth, and whose subsequent enormous expansion was to give English society its characteristic quality and tone. Fifty years later, Harrington, in a famous passage, described how the ruin of the feudal nobility by the Tudors, by democratizing the ownership of land, had prepared the way for the *bourgeois* republic. His hint of the economic changes which preceded the Civil War might be given a wider application. The age of Elizabeth saw a steady growth of capitalism in textiles and mining, a great increase in foreign trade and an outburst of joint-stock enterprise in connection with it, the beginning of something like deposit banking in the hands of the scriveners, and the growth, aided by the fall of Antwerp and the Government's own financial necessities, of a money-market with an almost modern technique—speculation, futures and arbitrage transactions—in London. The future lay with the classes who sprang to wealth and influence with the expansion of commerce in the later years of the century, ...

In the first forty years of the seventeenth century, on grounds both of expediency and of principle, the commercial and propertied classes were becoming increasingly restive under the whole system, at once ambitious and inefficient, of economic paternalism. It was in the same sections of the community that both religious and economic dissatisfaction were most acute. Puritanism, with its idealization of the spiritual energies which found expression in the activities of business and industry, drew the isolated rivulets of discontent together, and swept them forward with the dignity and momentum of a religious and a social philosophy."[24]

Evidently, therefore, the secret behind the emergence of modern England lay, firstly, in the growth of merchant capital and the appearance of a class of English merchant bourgeoisie.

2. Rise of the First Architects

How did, then, a class of merchant bourgeoisie come into being in England? Some authorities are of the opinion that when the town communities of western Europe succeeded in winning partial or complete autonomy from feudal domination and began their independent career, they were somewhat egalitarian in character.[25] It has been stated that "even in a great city like Paris the 128 gilds which existed at the end of the thirteenth century appear to have included 5,000 masters, who employed not more than 6,000 to 7,000 journeymen."[26] However, whether this egalitarian character of the towns in western Europe at this period was universally true or not, and whether it is not true that in some places at least, such as in Italy, the situation was complicated by the presence of feudal families within the towns, it has been asserted with some degree of certainty that "the inequalities that existed in English towns prior to the fourteenth century were not very marked."[27] In England,—

> "By the end of the Thirteenth Century almost all towns of any size, except a few under monastic rule, had won a certain measure of self-government. After gaining freedom from feudal exactions, the main object of any town was to keep its trade in the hands of its own burgesses, on the principle that only those who paid their share towards the freedom of the town had the right to share in its privileges. This object was attained through the organisation of the burgesses in the Merchant Gild. These gilds, which included all the traders in any given town (at first no clear division existed between the trader who bought and sold and the craftsman who made the goods, both functions being normally performed by the same person) were rigidly exclusive and their regulations were enforced by fines and, in extreme cases, by expulsion."[28]

Governed by these "Gild Merchants," the English towns in those days were characterized by "fewer class distinctions, more equality of wealth, and more harmony of interests;" and there—

> "The professional element was almost wholly wanting. Every man was, to a certain extent, a soldier; the chaplains were lawyers; the monks were the teachers, physicians, and *litérateurs.* Almost all the townsmen were in some way connected with trade. The few burgher proprietors of large estates who were not merchants found it advisable to join the Gild, in order that they might advantageously dispose of the produce of their lands and the manufactures of their villeins. The same would be true, though in a much less degree, of the humbler agricultural burgher. Most craftsmen, too, were concerned with the purchase and sale of wares."[29]

But, while it may be true that "all townsmen were in some way connected with trade," the question arises as to what was the character of production in the society on the basis of which the citizens obtained their income. The answer to this question is evidently that the essential basis of urban society lay in what Marx termed the "petty mode of production;" that is, under this system production was carried on by small producers who owned their instruments of production and who freely traded in their products. No doubt, as some authorities have described, in the course of time, with the growth of the towns in population and extent, the original owners of urban land enriched themselves from sales of land or from leases at a high rent, and this formed an important source of capital accumulation in the thirteenth and fourteenth century; but there also cannot be any doubt that at the outset the "petty mode of production" remained true of the handicraft body at any rate. It has been noted that at this time many of the agricultural burghers in England "devoted themselves to husbandry and to small home industries at the same time; just as, on the other hand, craftsmen were often partially occupied with agriculture;"[30] and that—

> "... even though from the earliest times there may have been some citizens who were exclusively traders, few of these in England could have been much more than pedlars travelling between the town market and neighbouring manors, and their activities could hardly have been extensive when the bulk of trade was local and took the form of an exchange of craftsmen's wares sold retail in the town market against country produce that the peasant brought to town to sell."[31]

Such a social basis of production in England in the pre-fourteenth century period leads one to the further question as to the methods by which the early bourgeoisie attained their socio-economic position. For under the system of "petty mode of production" the productivity of labour was low and the unit of production was small. Hence, savings would be meagre, and there was thus little scope for capital accumulation except from sudden luck or the increment of land values. It follows therefore that such chance gains or mere increment of land values could not fully account for the splendid riches and the accumulation of the early bourgeoisie. Also their fortune could neither be accounted for by the exploitation of the surplus labour of servile class, nor could it be realized from the surplus labour of wage-earners, as the urban bourgeoisie of the fourteenth and fifteenth centuries had neither serfs to toil for them like the feudal lords nor had they yet invested in the employment of an industrial proletariat. The "social organism" was such that—

> "There was little mobility or competition. There was very little large-scale organization. With some important exceptions, such as the textile workers of Flanders and Italy, who, in the fourteenth century, again and again rose in revolt, the mediaeval artisan, especially in backward countries like England, was a small master... In England, at any rate, more than nine-tenths were peasants, among whom, though friendly societies called gilds were common, there was naturally no question of craft organisation. Even in the towns it is a question whether there was not a considerable population of casual workers—consider only the number of unskilled workers that must have been required as labourers by the craftsmen building a cathedral in the days before mechanical cranes—who were rarely organized in permanent societies."[32]

Evidently, therefore, the growth and prosperity of the early bourgeoisie lay outside the sphere of "petty mode of production." The process unfolded itself with the formation of craft gilds in towns, was enforced with the beginning of wholesale trade in which the emergent privileged class of burghers engaged themselves after cutting themselves off from production, and was finally established with the rise of the "plutocracy of merchants" when merchant capital held sway over production.

> "The economic aspect of the development was the rise to a new position of overwhelming pre-eminence of the new interests based on the control of capital and credit. In the earlier Middle Ages capital had been the adjunct and ally of the personal labour of craftsmen and artisans. In the Germany of the fifteenth century, as long before in Italy, it had ceased to be a servant and had become a master. Assuming a separate and independent vitality, it claimed the right of a predominant partner to dictate economic organization in accordance with its own exacting requirements.
>
> Under the impact of these new forces, while the institutions of earlier ages survived in form, their spirit and operation were transformed. In the larger

cities the gild organization, once a barrier to the encroachments of the capitalists, became one of the instruments which he used to consolidate his power. The rules of fraternities masked a division of the brethren into a plutocracy of merchants, sheltered behind barriers which none but the wealthy craftsman could scale, and a wage-earning proletariat, dependent for their livelihood on capital and credit supplied by their masters, and alternately rising in revolt and sinking in an ever-expanding morass of hopeless pauperism. The peasantry suffered equally from the spread of a commercial civilization into the rural districts and from the survival of ancient agrarian servitudes. As in England, the *nouveaux riches* of the towns invested money in land by purchase and loan, and drove up rents and fines by their competition."[33]

Previously,—

". . . craftsmen were freely admitted to the Gild Merchant in the twelfth, thirteenth, and fourteenth centuries. The term merchant, as is well known, was not in those days confined to large dealers, but embraced all who traded. The line of demarcation between merchant and craftsman was not yet sharply defined. Every master craftsman was regarded as a merchant, for he bought his raw materials, and sold the products of his handiwork in his shop or at his stall, . . . Craftsmen were not only admitted to the Gild Merchant, but also, in all probability, constituted the majority of its members."[34]

But,—

"As the towns grew in size Craft Gilds came into being, in addition to, and sometimes in opposition to, the Merchant Gild. These included only the men of some particular crafts; smiths, saddlers, bakers or tailors. They aimed at regulating the whole of industry, laying down rules as to price, quality, conditions of work, and so on. They were composed of master-craftsmen, each working in his own home, usually with one or more apprentices and sometimes with journeymen or wage labourers. The latter were men who had served their period of apprenticeship but had not yet been able to become master-craftsmen.

At first the journeymen do not appear to have constituted a separate class, but were men who might expect to become masters themselves. Towards the end of the Thirteenth Century, however, clearer class divisions begin to appear. The number of journeymen increased, and many of them remained wage earners all their lives. By imposing high entrance fees and by other devices the gilds became more exclusive and harder to enter. As a result, separate gilds of the journeymen, the so called Yeoman Gilds, began to arise."[35] *

---

* The evolution of the craft gilds (and later of the merchant gilds), and their eventual domination over the old "Gild Merchant," are of interest to the present study.

"Craft gilds are first mentioned during the reign of Henry I, about a half a century after the first appearance of the Gild Merchant. The latter included merchants proper and artisans belonging to different trades; the craft gild, at first, included only artisans of a single trade. The position of these craft fraternities in the town community during the twelfth and thirteenth centuries was different from that of the Gild Merchant. They had not yet become official civic bodies, like the 'Gilda Mercatoria,' forming a part of the administrative machinery of the town. Their existence was merely tolerated in return for a yearly ferm paid to the crown, whereas the Gild Merchant constituted a valuable burghal privilege, whose continuance was guaranteed by the town charter. Still the craft gilds occupied a more important position in the community than that of a mere private association of today. For with the grant of a gild the craftsmen generally secured what in Germany was called the 'Zunftzwang' and the 'Innungsrecht', i.e. the monopoly of working and trading in their branch of industry. The craftsmen thus associated remained in the common Gild Merchant; but the strength of the latter was weakened and its sphere of activity was diminished with every new creation of a craft fraternity, though these new bodies continued subsidiary to, and under the general regulation of, the older and larger fraternity. The greater the commercial and industrial prosperity of a town, the more rapidly did this process of subdivision into craft gilds proceeded, keeping pace with the increased division of labour. In the smaller towns, in which agriculture continued a prominent element, few or no craft gilds were formed; and hence the old Gild Merchant remained intact and undiminished in power longest in this class of boroughs.

The period of the three Edwards constitutes an important epoch in the history of industry and gilds. With the rapid development and specialisation of industry, particularly under Edward III, gilds of craftsmen multiplied and grew in power. Many master-craftsmen became wealthy employers of labour, dealing extensively in the wares which they produced. The class of dealers or merchants, as distinguished from trading artisans, also greatly increased, forming themselves into separate fraternities or mysteries. When these various unions of dealers and of craftsmen embraced all the trades and branches of production in the town, little or no vitality remained in the old Gild Merchant. In short, the function of guarding and supervising the trade monopoly had become split up into various fragments or sections, the aggregate of the crafts superseding the old Gild Merchant. A natural process of elimination, the absorption of its powers by other bodies, had rendered the old organization superfluous. This transference of authority from the ancient Gild Merchant to a number of distinct bodies, and the consequent disintegration and decay of the former, was a gradual, spontaneous movement, which, generally speaking, may be assigned to the fourteenth and fifteenth centuries, the very period in which the craft gilds attained the zenith of their power...

Then,–

"One later development must be noted which accentuated the class differentiations in the towns. This was the growth of gilds of merchants and dealers who dominated the productive crafts. Thus, by the end of the Fourteenth Century, the London Drapers control the fullers, shearmen and weavers, and of the twelve great gilds from which alone the Mayor could be chosen, only two, the weavers and the goldsmiths, were productive. The same thing took place more slowly and to a less extent in other towns, and serves to remind us that it was in the form of merchant capital that the first great accumulation of bourgeois property took place."[36]

In the beginning, this emergence of an organised trading interest in the towns, as distinct from handicraft, took two parallel forms. First, a specifically trading element, "frequently drawn (at least in England) from the more well-to-do craftsmen, separated itself from production and formed exclusively trading organisations which proceeded to monopolise some particular sphere of wholesale trade;" and, second, having dominated the town government at a not very much later date, these new trading organizations began "to use their political power to further their own privileges and to subordinate the craftsmen."[37] In many areas on the Continent this process was unfolding from as early as 1200, as in the Netherlands, Italy and France; and the usual form of change in these areas vis-a-vis the form of government in their centres of commerce and manufacture was first from democracy to plutocracy, and then to oligarchy. But in the English towns,–

"these developments seem to have occurred mainly in the fourteenth century; and the growth of the 'insignificant peddling traders of the eleventh, twelfth and thirteenth centuries' into 'the important political plutocracy of the fourteenth' is a remarkable feature of the time. Here the new development involved an actual usurpation of economic privileges and political control by the new burgher plutocracy, since in England there is some evidence of the existence

In some towns where the crafts took the place of the Gild Merchant the name of the latter wholly disappeared; but in others it continued to be used, not to indicate a concrete bond of union, as of old, with distinct officers and separate administrative machinery, but only as a vague term applied to the aggregate of the crafts." (Gross, Charles—The Gild Merchant, Oxford at the Clarendon Press, 1890, Vol. I, pp. 114—118).

of an earlier urban democracy which in the fourteenth century was abolished, and also evidence that trading privileges had been more or less open (*de jure* at least, even if not *de facto*) to the general body of citizens."[38]

This usurpation of trading privileges in England took very many forms. In some cases, the traditional Gild Merchant which previously included the majority of burgesses now became a closed organization and also excluded craftsmen from wholesale trade. But in most cases the old Gild Merchants died out, and in their place appeared new mercantile gilds, or misteries, "composed entirely of traders as distinct from craftsmen and endowed by their charters with exclusive rights over some particular branch of wholesale trade."[39]

Illustrative of this development was the role of many English "Gild Merchant" from about the fourteenth century. For instance, in 1330, it was complained against the "burgesses of Derby" that—

"... certain individuals are jointly united, who assert that they are of the Gild Merchant, and do not permit others to be of the same Gild, unless they satisfy them beforehand (i.e. pay a satisfactory fine), in order that they may be in the said Gild. And by reason of this Gild the custom has prevailed among them, that if anyone brings neat's leather, wool, or wool-fells into the said town to sell, and one of the said Gild places his foot upon the thing brought, and sets a price for which he would like to buy it, no one but a member of the said society will dare buy it, nor will he to whom it belongs dare sell it to anyone save a member of the said society, nor for a higher price than that which the member of the said society offers.

... these persons do not permit foreign merchants—whatsoever wares they may deal in—to vend their merchandise in the said town except only by wholesale, and this to one of the brethren; and the profit arising therefrom does not accrue to the advantage of the community of the said town, but only to the advantage of those who are of the said society; which usages redound to the injury, oppression, and pauperization of the people."[40]

Also, referring to the role of the merchant gilds of England in that period, it has been noted[41]:

"Indeed, the desire for gain or self-advantage, which from the outset was the *raison d'être* of the Gild Merchant and many other gilds, degenerated at time into the most reprehensible forms of selfishness. The gildsmen may have been kind and loving toward those of his own fraternity, but he was too often harsh and oppressive toward non-gildsmen ... During the two centuries preceding the Reformation we frequently meet with strong condemnation of the conduct of the gilds. Their exactions 'after their own sinister mind and pleasure,' the 'outrageous hardships' to which they subject the public, the unreasonable ordinances 'for their owne singler profite and to the comen hurte and damage of the people,' etc."

Generally speaking, in England the word "merchant" passed through three stages giving significant meaning to the character of the Gild Merchant in different periods.

"At first it embraced all who, in their trade, were in any way concerned with buying and selling, including petty shopkeepers and many handicraftsmen: During the fifteenth and the greater part of the sixteenth century it applied pre-eminently to all who made a business of buying for resale—retailers as well as wholesalers—manual craftsmen not being included. It then came to have its present significance of an extensive dealer. In conception, the old Gild Merchant represents the first stage; the Companies of Merchants, the second; the Staplers and Merchant Adventurers, the third."[42]

And along with this change in the character of the Gild Merchant went on the imposition of various economic controls over the craftsmen by the merchants; the merchant gilds having the supreme authority over all commerce. Thus[43]:

"Non-gildsmen were forbidden to keep shops or sell merchandise by retail. In many cases this applied only to certain specified wares, cloth, leather, wool, fish, meat, etc., doubtless the staple commodities of the place. We frequently meet with the injunction, that strangers are not to keep wine-taverns, but they were sometimes allowed to retail wine from ships ...

In many places the unfranchised 'forinseci' were not permitted to buy certain things, wool, hides, grain, untanned leather, unfulled cloth, etc., probably for the most part, scarce articles of consumption and raw materials necessary for the production of the chief manufactures of the town. At times this enactment is particularly directed against buying for re-sale; hence provisions for one's own use, the 'parva mercimonia' were often expressly excepted ...

Various other enactments were frequently directed against merchant strangers. They were to bring their wares to 'the Common Hall' or other specified public place, and there expose them for sale, in order that their goods could be more easily examined, and their mercantile transactions more readily supervised. They were not to remain in the borough, for the purpose of selling their commodities, longer than forty days. During this time they were carefully watched, lest they should sell or buy under colour or cover of a faithless gild-brother's freedom, the latter being expelled from the fraternity or otherwise severely punished, if found guilty of this offence . . .

It is probable that already in the thirteenth and fourteenth centuries, as in later times, the officers of the Gild, in some sea-port towns, had the exclusive privilege of making the first offer for the purchase of newly arrived cargoes. The wares thus bought were then disposed of to the brethren at a small profit. . . .

The gildsman was generally under obligation to share all purchases with his brethren, that is to say, if he bought a quantity of a given commodity, any other gildsmen could claim a portion of it at the same price at which he purchased it. The aim of this law was manifestly to do away with middlemen and keep down prices: it counteracted 'regrating' and 'forestalling', offences which were regarded as especially heinous when the culprit was not in the Gild. . . .

. . . while they [gildsmen] themselves enjoyed the right 'to trade freely' ('libere mercandisare'), unfranchised merchants, when allowed to practise their vocation, were hemmed in on every side by onerous restrictions. Of these the most irksome was probably the payment of toll on all wares that they were permitted to buy or sell. From such payments the gildsmen were generally wholly exempt; even when this was not the case, they usually enjoyed discriminating rates of toll in their favour."

In short, the position of the craftsmen as well as of the unfranchised merchants became subservient to the dictates of the merchant gilds. Eventually,–

"The concentration of trading rights in these bodies meant that the ordinary craftsman, for purposes other than retail sale from his stall or shop-front in the town, was compelled to deal exclusively with members of the appropriate mercantile gild. He was precluded from selling direct to any stranger-merchant, and he could not make any contract for exporting his wares outside the town except by using one of the limited circle of well-to-do wholesale traders in the town as intermediary."[44]

Also, the political control of the towns went into the hands of the mercantile gilds, the craftsmen playing a secondary or negligible role in civic affairs.

"The expressions 'freemen' and 'being in the freedom' often became synonymous with the older terms 'gildsmen', and 'being in the Gild Merchant'. In the records of Totnes, for example, it is expressly stated that those entering the Gild were 'commonly called freemen'. The brethren of the ancient Gild Merchant... were those who enjoyed freedom of trade ('libertas emendi et vendendi'); the later freemen occupied the same position in most towns, comprehending all who were allowed to trade freely. But these freemen in many boroughs were practically co-extensive with the brethren of the craft fraternities, the freedom of the town being obtained mainly or solely through the medium of the crafts. In these places the civic freedom was in conception distinct from, and paramount to, that of the crafts; ...

To fully understand this development we must recall to mind the two great transformations that occurred in English municipalities during the fourteenth and fifteenth centuries, namely, the expansion of trade and the growth of a select governing town council. The economic development gave the crafts a more important position in the town community, and materially altered the old qualifications of burgess-ship. In the larger boroughs commerce and industry became the exclusive occupation of the townsmen, the 'rus in urbe' gradually vanishing. The ancient burgage tenure—the natural concomitant of the old burghal communities, in which agriculture rather than capital and industry played the chief role—was no longer connected with citizenship. The latter was gradually transformed into a personal privilege, without qualification of property or residence, being obtained by birth, apprenticeship, purchase, gift, or marriage. Payments of scot and lot became the pre-eminent obligation of burgess-ship; and the right to trade or exercise a craft became its pre-eminent privilege. Thus the freemen—who in many places were identical with the burgesses—were the successors of the brethren of the ancient Gild Merchant. The old popular Leet government of the borough was superseded by a select governing town council, to whose members the name 'burgess' was, in later times, often restricted. To this close corporation the crafts became a powerful and useful auxiliary often even an effective check to its extravagances; but they did not succeed in supplanting or dominating over it. The select body was an anomaly, which, with the aid of the royal prerogative, prevented the crafts from securing the paramount position to which their wealth and numbers entitled them."[45]

In this way, with "the concentration of political power in the towns into the hands of burgher oligarchy; an oligarchy which seems to have been identical with the section of richer merchants that was acquiring the monopoly of wholesale trade,"[46] the growing English merchant bourgeoisie established their position in society. In the fourteenth century, at the end of the reign of Edward III, the burgesses at large "were entirely excluded from their right of suffrage in Parliamentary elections."[47] Barring some exceptions, such as where the urban oligarchy was composed of ancient landowning elements in the town and not of commercial *parvenu*, and where usurpation of power by one group of trading interest instead of all such groups led the *have-nots* to unite with the craft-gilds to resist this monopoly power, both in the economic as well as in the political sphere merchant capital began to rule most of the towns of England from about the fourteenth century.

However, while the position of the craftsmen became subservient to the growing merchant bourgeoisie, there was one possibility open to them (and especially to the "richer master-craftsmen") to attain greater economic prosperity. This was by joining the new mercantile gilds or misteries. The procedure may appear paradoxical because in order to maintain its privileges the new merchant aristocracy formed fairly closed organizations. But these could be invaded by those who had the money to buy themselves in. For,—

> "To become a gildsman ('gildanus', 'congildanus', 'frater'), or to obtain the gildship ('gilda', 'societas'), it was necessary to pay certain initiation-fees, in some places called the 'rights' ('jura') of the house. This payment was probably proportioned to the means of the new member, or the extent to which it was likely that he would use the privileges of the society, much discrimination being shown in favour of the relatives of gildsmen. ... The new comer was also required to produce sureties, who were responsible for the fulfilment of his obligations to the Gild-answering for his good conduct and for the payment of his dues. He then took an oath of fealty to the fraternity, swearing to observe its laws, to uphold its privileges, not to divulge its counsels, to obey its officers, and not to aid any non-gildsman under cover of the newly-acquired 'freedom'."[48]

Hence it is seen that—

"... in the fifteenth and sixteenth centuries there was a fairly constant infiltration into its ranks from among the richer master-craftsmen, who tended to leave handicraft for trade, and even to become employers of other craftsmen, as soon as they had accumulated sufficient capital to enable them to scan wider horizons than the retail trade of a local market afforded them. It was inevitable that the *parvenu* ambition of such men should find the exclusive privileges of the merchant companies irksome and cramping. Two roads of advancement lay open to them. They could purchase a position in one of the privileged companies and abandon their old calling; or they could struggle to secure for their own craft gild the status of a trading body."[49]

The infiltration of ex-craftsmen into the ranks of the merchants did not however affect the solid basis of merchant capital which, as will be further explained later, was always striving for exclusive organizations (limited to a few, comparatively speaking), and for monopolistic powers. The reason was the rapid expansion of foreign trade.

"While there was some infiltration into the privileged ranks as capital accumulated among the crafts themselves, the monopolistic position of merchant capital in England was scarcely weakened thereby, and the increase of its wealth was not retarded. With the growth of the market, and especially of foreign trade, there was room for the numbers within the privileged ranks to grow without any serious overcrowding."[50]

But, in the development of foreign trade, at first the English merchants came across serious opposition from foreign merchants. For a long time "the monopoly position of England as a wool growing country" had attracted the notice of the merchants of Flanders and Italy, where merchant capital had a more rapid development, and therefore they had invaded England and established themselves with regard to the country's most precious export-trade.

"From quite early times wool was exported from this country to be woven in Ghent, Bruges, Ypres and other towns in Flanders. By the Thirteenth Century this trade had grown to large proportions, easily exceeding in bulk and value all other exports combined. In some respects England assumed a position with regard to Flanders comparable to that of Australia and the West Riding today.

There were, however, important differences. England was not politically dependent upon Flanders as countries producing raw materials usually are upon industrial countries. This was partly due to the internal situation in Flanders, politically weakened by the constant struggles between the merchants, the handicraft weavers, the counts of Flanders and the kings of France, struggles which kept Flanders divided and, in the Fourteenth Century, had important consequences in English history.

More important was the monopoly position of England as a wool growing country. Throughout the Middle Ages no other country produced a regular surplus of wool for export, and, on more than one occasion, the prohibition of the export of wool produced an instant and devastating economic crisis in Flanders. The English monopoly was the result of the early suppression of private war, noted already as one of the results of the peculiar strength here of the crown as against the barons. Sheeps are of all kinds of property the easiest to lift and the hardest to protect, and only under circumstances of internal peace not normal in the Middle Ages was sheep farming on a large scale profitable.

Besides Yorkshire, the Cotswolds, the Chilterns, Hereford and the uplands of Linconshire were important wool growing areas by the Thirteenth Century if not earlier. At first the bulk of the export trade was in the hands of Italian and Flemish merchants. The former, especially, coming from cities where banking had already made great progress, were able to conduct financial operations on a scale unknown in Northern Europe."[51]

Obviously, therefore, the "first and most important field that merchant capital found for its operation in England was the wool trade."[52] But, before the English merchants could embark upon this lucrative sphere of foreign trade, it was necessary that the special position of these merchants of the Flemish Hanse, and later Italians, be undermined and their privileges be abolished or at least drastically reduced. This, however, was not a simple task; firstly, because of the secure position these merchants had made for themselves in England with regard to the wool-trade, and, secondly, because of the privileges they had obtained from the English Crown.

"As early as the Twelfth Century the Cistercian monks had established huge sheep farms on the dry eastern slopes of the Pennines. The Cistercians were not only large scale farmers, but financiers as well, and through their hands and those of the Lombard and Florentine merchants who acted as their agents was passed much of the revenue which the Popes drew from England, a revenue stated in Parliament in the reign of Edward III to be five times that of the Crown. Much of this revenue was collected in the form of wool rather than of currency."[53]

Also, it has been noted that these foreign merchants "purchased wool direct from monasteries and landowners, often advancing loans on the security of future wool deliveries."[54] Moreover, the position of these merchants in England was "strengthened by special privileges from the English Crown," for "the English Crown was not only debtor to these foreign concessionaires, but was under the recurrent necessity of new borrowing."[55]

"It was because the Lombards were able to finance him more efficiently than the Jews that the latter were expelled from England by Edward I in 1290. This action, often represented as a piece of disinterested patriotism, was in fact the result of the intrigues of a rival group of moneylenders who could offer the King better terms."[56]

Under the circumstances it was an uphill task for the growing English merchant bourgeoisie to oust the foreign merchants from the export-trade of the country. The situation, however, began to change at the end of the thirteenth century and became more and more pronounced in the fourteenth century when the "Crown began to rely on revenue raised by an export tax on wool and on wool-loans from the English wool-exporters."[57] Now the English merchants, who had been dealing in wool, hides, tin and lead and in the reign of Henry III were organised into an association which came to be known as the Fellowship of the Staple, "were able to take advantage of the royal necessity to barter loans in exchange for monopoly-rights in the valuable export trade in wool."[58]

"The staplers were merchants who had the monopoly of exporting the principal raw commodities of the realm, especially wool, woolfels, leather, tins, and lead; wool figuring most prominently among these 'staple' wares. The merchants of the staple used to claim that their privileges dated from the time of Henry III, but existing records do not refer to the staple before the time of Edward I. Previous to this reign the export trade was mainly in the hands of the German Hanse merchants.

The staples were the towns to which the above-mentioned wares had to be brought for sale or exportation. Sometimes there was only one such mart, and this was situated abroad, generally at Bruges or Calais, occasionally at Antwerp, St. Omer, or Middleburgh. From the reign of Richard II until 1558 the foreign staple was at Calais. The list of home staples was also frequently changed. ...

The many changes in the location of the staples—especially the foreign staple, during the fourteenth century—were often due to political rather than economic considerations, the removal of the staple mart being employed by the English king as a weapon of coercion or reprisal against foreign princes. ...

It is evident that the staple was primarily a fiscal organ of the crown, facilitating the collection of the royal customs. It also ensured the quality of the goods exported by providing a machinery for viewing and marking them; and it stimulated commerce by providing alien merchants with a special tribunal and protecting them in other ways, 'to give courage to merchant strangers to come with their wares and merchandise into the realm'."[59]

Whether or not the staple system gave "courage to merchant strangers to come with their wares and merchandise into the realm," as the Statutes of Realm declared[60], there is no doubt that henceforth the English merchants began to have their way.

"With the growth of the trade English exporters began to challenge their foreign rivals. Export figures for 1273, incomplete but probably reliable enough, show that more than half the trade was in English hands. The establishment of the Wool Staple marks this stage in the growth of English merchant capital. The idea of the Staple was to concentrate all wool exports in one place or a few places, both to protect the trader from pirates and to make the collection of taxes easy. ... From the start the Staple was controlled by native merchants."[61]

The establishment of a compulsory wool staple in the Netherlands in 1313 by royal edict was one important stage in the development of the English merchant bourgeoisie. Here,—

"... all wool for export had to be brought and offered for sale 'at the orders of the Mayor and Company of Merchants'. This was regarded by the members of the English Company as a weapon against their alien competitors in the export trade, and was strenuously opposed by the latter."[62]

But while this monopoly export trade in wool resulted in "raising the price to foreign customers and in elbowing out foreign merchants from the export trade with Flanders," it depressed "the price of wool at home."[63] Therefore, since this English Company was a small and exclusive body, a demand very soon arose for the repeal of the Staple privileges, which was also taken up by those who were engaged in the internal wool trade in England. But after temporary cessation, "the privileges of the narrow circle of exporters organised in the English Merchants of the Staple were renewed."[64]

This, however, did no good to the bulk of English merchants, and "threatened to narrow the market for English wool, instead of widening it."[65] In this situation, "the very monopoly of the Staple by narrowing the channels of export and maintaining an 'immense margin between the domestic and the foreign price of wool' unwittingly assisted the growth of English cloth-making."[66] English cloth-making received "growing official encouragement" and the export trade in English cloth developed "in rivalry with the Flemish industry;" the low price of wool in England assuring that "English cloth could be sold, not only at home but abroad, much more cheaply than foreign cloth, which had to pay an immensely higher sum for the raw material."[67] The upshot was that the export of cloth became increasingly more lucrative than the export of wool.

At this juncture the Company of Merchant Adventurers, from which the East India Company could claim its birth in a way, came into great prominence in England. The soul of this Company of Merchant Adventurers, "and perhaps its original nucleus, was the Mercers' Company of London, which from a fellowship of general dealers in petty wares had developed into a body of wholesale traders, dealing mainly in silks."[68] The Company of Merchant Adventurers had come into being at the beginning of the thirteenth century, but it was definitely established and constituted into a regular company by the Royal Charter of Henry IV in 1407; and in "distinction from the staplers, who dealt in certain raw materials, the Merchant Adventurers had the monopoly of exporting certain manufactured articles, especially cloths."[69] Naturally, therefore, in the sixteenth and seventeenth centuries "frequent dissensions broke out between these two bodies regarding the exportation of cloth."[70] The Merchants of the Staple began to criticise the clothiers and the Merchant Adventurers, and joined "in the demand that the cloth industry should be confined to corporate towns."[71] But,–

> "The increase of home manufactures and the corresponding diminution in the export of wool sapped the foundations of the staple system. The prohibition of the export of wool in 1660 must have given a finishing blow to the staple as an active organism."[72]

Meanwhile, foreign trade had become the key-note of the growth of merchant capital in Europe. Although internally the market was expanding, it was "foreign trade which provided the greatest opportunities for rapid commercial advancement, and it was in this sphere that the most impressive fortunes were made."[73] Therefore,–

> "Heralded by an economic revolution not less profound than that of three centuries later, the new world of the sixteenth century took its character from the outburst of economic energy in which it had been born. Like the nineteenth century, it saw a swift increase in wealth and an impressive expansion of trade, a concentration of financial power on a scale unknown before, ..."[74]

Marching with the time, the English merchants had also moved farther; their activities having spread much beyond Europe. The middle of the sixteenth century found them solidly entrenched in foreign trade; they having ventured "sufficiently far afield, both across the North Sea and into the Mediterranean, to inaugurate some five or six new general companies, each possessing privileges in a new area."[75] It is generally agreed that a number of those belonging to the Company of Merchant Adventurers took the initiative in forming the Russia Company in 1553, which two years later received a charter giving it a monopoly, as the first company to employ joint-stock and to own ships corporately. In the same year in which the Russia Company secured its charter from the English monarch, it was successful in negotiating an agreement with the Russian Tsar, "whereby it was to enjoy the sole right of trading with Muscovy by the White

Sea route and to establish depots at Kholmogory and Vologda."[76] In 1557, an employee of the Company went to Persia and Bokhara, and in 1567 the Company "obtained the right to trade across Russia with Persia through Kazan and Astrakhan."[77]

Also, in the same year in which the Russia Company obtained its charter, the Africa Company was formed, the members of which grew fat on the lucrative enterprise they took up "to kidnap or purchase and work to death without compunction the natives of Africa."[78] About such "idyllic proceedings," as Marx described the "chief momenta of primitive accumulation,"[79] "the English and the Dutch, at that time the wisest and most religious nations of the world ... had no more scruple ... than they had about enslaving horses."[80]

Then, in 1578, the Eastland Company obtained its charter in order to "enjoy the sole trade through the Sound into Norway, Sweden, Poland, Lithuania (excepting Narva), Prussia and also Pomerania, from the river Oder eastward to Dantzick, Elbing and Konigsberg; also to Copenhagen and Elsinore and to Finland, Gothland, Barnholm and Oeland."[81] The Company also received powers "to make bye-laws and to impose fines, imprisonment, etc., on all non-freemen trading to these parts."[82] Also, in the year before the Eastland Company was formed, the Spanish Company was set-up by some members of the Company of Merchant Adventurers in order to monopolise "the lucrative trade in wine, oil, and fruit with Spain and Portugal, and to secure powers under charter to exclude competitors."[83] And, then in 1581, letters patent were granted by the English Crown to four gentlemen to trade with Turkey, which was the origin of the Levant Company. This was incorporated in 1592 as a fusion of the Turkey Company with the Venice Company, and included Queen Elizabeth as one of its leading shareholders. In 1600, this company "begat the East India Company and in 1605 had its charter of monopoly renewed in perpetuity by James I."[84]

The East India Company thus came in a logical sequence of the growth of merchant capital in England. In the earliest phase of this growth the old Gild Merchant of England "consisted mainly of small shopkeepers and artisans," lacking the "line of demarcation between merchants and manual craftsmen."[85] Afterwards, with the distinct separation of commerce from crafts, "from a fellowship of general dealers in petty wares" the Mercers' Company "developed into a body of wholesale traders." Then, with the growing importance of foreign trade, out of the womb of the Mercers' Company there emerged the Company of Merchant Adventurers, which "had to do wholly with foreign trade, and its members were forbidden to exercise a manual occupation or even to be retail shopkeepers."[86] Finally, when the English merchant capital had markedly extended its sphere of influence and several monopolist companies were already in action in order to enjoy the exclusive trade of specific areas of Europe, Western Asia, and northern and western Africa, the East India Company came into being as "the most powerful of them all."[87]

3. *Leitmotiv* of the Architects

From the preceding account of England's social development from about the fourteenth century onwards it is obvious that the class of merchant bourgeoisie which had emerged in England and was dominating her towns both in the economic and political spheres "sprang to wealth and influence" by concentrating all its energy on foreign trade. This leads one to the question as to how commerce, and especially foreign commerce, supplied the merchant bourgeoisie with enormous riches on the basis of which they built their influence in society and also effected changes in spiritual and social values in their country. In order to answer this question one should first examine the basis of the trading income of the merchant bourgeoisie. For this basis was the secret of the merchants' prosperity, and therefore it determined the *modus operandi* of merchant capital. Likewise, it shaped the characteristic form of organization of merchant capital, viz. commercial monopolies, and provided the merchant bourgeoisie with their essential traits, such as the "spirit of conquest" and the pervading desire for expansion overseas.

What then was the basis of this trading income? This is a point which has been dealt with by many renowned economists from the time economic science developed in England "as the interpreter of the practical interests of the City."[88] Mun (1571–1641), who was a director of the East India Company, declared that "moneyes exported will return to us more than trebled;"[89] and, as Marx noted, "M–M,' money which begets money, such is the description of Capital, from the mouth of its first interpreters, the Mercantilists."[90] Adam Smith (1723–1790) and other economists following the same trend of thought were of the opinion that this burgher wealth was truly "produced," instead of being "acquired;" acquired, firstly, as a share in the products of the town craftsmen and the peasant-cultivators which otherwise would have accrued to the producers themselves or would have been converted into feudal revenue, and, lately, in an increasing measure in the scarcely-veiled plunder of other lands with which these traders undertook "commercial" relations.

Adam Smith has discussed at length how the services that the spread of commerce performed for the direct producer or the aristocratic consumer produced wealth for the burgher merchants; and it is true that by extending markets and by making supplies available in greater variety in places and at seasons where no supplies were available before commerce had served to raise the standard of life of the producers, and thus obtained its reward as a share of this general increase, instead of encroaching on an unchanged standard of consumption. It is also true that, with the extension of commercial enterprise, the communities which were previously confined within the narrow limits of a local market could now raise their standards; just as at a later stage commerce created the conditions within production itself for an extended division of labour. But all such beneficial effects of commercial enterprise of a society do not explain how the vast fortunes and the great accumulations, characteristic of the merchant class at this period, were made. Granted that commerce was very useful, and enlarged the sphere of utilities in the society; but that alone does not explain why the commercial enterprise yielded such a handsome surplus which handicraft failed to produce. As has been remarked:[91]

"... it does not explain why commerce was the basis of so large a *differential* gain. Windfalls, it is true, might be expected to be more plentiful in a novel and previously unadventured sphere. But windfall gains can hardly account for a persistent and continuing income on so large a scale: in the course of time one could have expected competition in this sphere, if it were unhindered, to bring the normal expectation of gain into line with that of urban industry."

Hence, the explanation for this must be sought somewhere else, in some other features of the development of the societies of that period.

These features, in the main, were, firstly, that the bulk of commerce in those days, (and especially foreign commerce which was the most important source of accumulation to the merchant bourgeoisie), went on hand in hand with some political "concession" or it was scarcely-veiled plunder; and, secondly, that as soon as a class of merchants assumed any corporate form, they strove for monopoly powers, so as to guard themselves from competition from other merchants not included in their body, and to have the major or undisputed say in all dealings with producers and consumers. These two features were the guiding principles of all monopolist companies of Merchant Capital, including naturally the East India Company.

Of the two above features, the former pertains to what Marx called "primitive accumulation," and the latter has been characterised as "exploitation through trade"[92] Marx, in his *Historical Data Concerning Merchants' Capital,* has noted.[93]

"The rule, that the independent development of merchants' capital is inversely proportioned to the degrees of development of capitalist production, becomes particularly manifest in the history of the carrying trade, for instance, among the Venetians, Genoese, Dutch, etc., where the principal gains were not made by exportation of the products of the home industries, but by the promotion of the exchange of products of commercially and otherwise economically undeveloped societies and by the exploitation of both spheres of production.

Here the merchants' capital is pure, separated from the extremes, the spheres of production, between which it intervenes. This is one of the main sources of its formation. But this monopoly of the carrying trade disintegrates, and with it this trade itself, in proportion as the economic development of peoples advances, whom it exploits at each end of its course, and whose backward development formed the basis of this trade. In the carrying trade, this appears not only as the disintegration of a special line of commerce, but also as the disintegration of the supremacy of purely commercial nations and of their commercial wealth in general, which rested upon this carrying trade. This is but one of the special forms, which expresses the subordination of the commercial capital to the industrial capital with the advance of capitalist production. The manner in which merchants' capital behaves wherever it rules over production is drastically illustrated, not only by the colonial economy (the colonial system) in general, but particularly by the methods of the old Dutch East India Company.

Since the movement of merchants' capital is M–C–M', the profit of the merchant is made, in the first place, only within the process of circulation, by the two transactions of buying and selling; and in the second place, it is realised in the last transactions, the sale. It is a profit upon alienation. At first sight, a pure and independent commercial profit seems impossible, so long as products are sold at their value. To buy cheap in order to sell dear is the rule of trade. It is not supposed to be an exchange of equivalents. The conception of value is included in it only to the extent that the individual commodities all have a value and are to that extent money. In quality, they are all expressions of social labour. But they are not values of equal magnitude. The quantitative ratio, in which products are exchanged, is at first quite arbitrary."

This arbitrariness could prevail because the market was not developed, and the producers were not able to effect an exchange of their products on any more than a parochial scale. This was to the best advantage of merchant capital, and so the traders were determined to preserve it, as an authority on this subject has remarked:[34]

"It was the separation of the raw material from the craftsman and the craftsman from the consumer at this period, and the fact that the resources in the hands of the producer were so meagre and their meagreness so straitly bounded his horizon in space and time which formed the source of commercial profit. It was the very co-existence of local gluts and local famines on which merchant capital thrived. Moreover, in conditions of primitive communications the existence of narrow local markets, each separate from others, meant that any small change in the volume of purchases or in the quantities offered for sale tended to exert a disproportionately large effect on the market price, so that the temptation to enforce regulations in the interest of those trading between these markets was very great. So long as these primitive conditions continued, so did the chances of exceptional gain for those who had the means to exploit them; and it was only natural that the perpetuation of such conditions, and not their removal, should become the conscious policy of merchant capital. For this reason monopoly was of the essence of economic life in this epoch."

Also Marx, while discussing, as quoted above, the arbitrariness of the "quantitative ratio, in which products are exchanged," noted.[95]

"They assume the form of commodities inasmuch as they are exchangeable, that is, inasmuch as they may be expressed in terms of the same third thing. The continued exchange and the more regular reproduction for exchange reduces this arbitrariness more and more. But this applies not at once to the producer and consumer, but only to the mediator between them, the merchant, who compares the money-prices and pockets their difference. By his own movements he establishes the equivalence of commodities."

Hence, in order to retard this levelling tendency, the merchant bourgeoisie depended on monopolistic trade. As their main concern was for the maintenance of a profit-margin between the price in the market of purchase and the price in the market for sale, (so that the principle of "Buying in order to sell, or more accurately, buying in order to sell dearer"[96] could be best maintained), the merchant bourgeoisie could not do otherwise. For, if they were subjected to unrestrained competition, what source could there be for the immense profits they reaped? Therefore, monopoly was the watch-word of the merchant bourgeoisie, resulting in the formation of commercial monopolies as soon as they were able to form corporate bodies.

This, as a distinct feature in the development of the early bourgeoisie and in the formation of the merchant gilds, has been mentioned before. What is of further importance to note is that, because foreign commerce was the most important source of accumulation of the merchant bourgeoisie, this development was most marked among the companies dealing with foreign trade. There one can see most clearly the characteristics of the merchant bourgeoisie, to whom monopoly rights, exclusive organizations, special concessions in the trading countries as well as regarding the trade-routes, etc., became the key-points in their prosperous career.

In the sphere of foreign trade, these key-demands had to be enforced in two separate areas; one in relation to the country where the trade-goods were to be sold dear (usually, and in the vigorous phase of merchant capital at least, the Home country), and the other in relation to the country where the goods were to be purchased cheap. To consider the former first, the Royal Charter for monopolistic trade was the basic foundation for these merchant companies, on the basis of which they wanted to fulfill their key-demands. As mentioned before, the careers of the Company of Merchant Adventurers, the Russia Company, Africa Company, Eastland Company, Spanish Company, Turkey Company, Levant Company, East India Company, etc., were all based on royal charters or patents, giving them the right to monopolistic trade in different spheres of the world with which the English merchant bourgeoisie had come in contact.

Owing their unique position to the sanctions incorporated in the Royal Charters, these foreign trading companies were highly exclusive bodies. Not everybody could secure admission to these privileged companies, and this was particularly enforced in the case of craftsmen and retailers. The members of the Company of Merchant Adventurers, for instance, "were forbidden to exercise a manual occupation or even to be retail shopkeepers;"[97] and the "one common feature which characterizes the whole of the charters" of the foreign trading companies was the desire to exclude the craftsmen and retailers from their organisations.[98] Also, some of these companies were so exclusive that, for example, "in the case of the Levant Company no one residing within twenty miles of London other than 'noblemen and gentlemen of quality' were admitted unless they were freemen of the city;"[99] and for the Merchant Adventurers there was the rule that: "No freeman of the Company of Merchant Adventurers was even allowed to marry a woman born out of the realm of England."[100]

Moreover, even for those cases where admission was allowed, it was restricted by a limitation of apprenticeship and by entrance fees which generally grew heavier in course of time. In the case of the Levant Company, for instance, "the entrance fee was £ 25 to £ 50; and high premiums had to be paid for apprenticeship,

Dudley North paying £ 50, and at the end of the seventeenth century a sum of £ 1,000 sometimes being demanded."[101] Likewise, during the reign of James I, "the entrance fee to the Merchant Adventurers rose to £ 200 (although in face of opposition it was subsequently lowered), and apprentices paid £ 50 for admission or more."[102] For the East India Company, which was the first important joint-stock company in England, the entrance fee was £ 50 for a merchant, £ 66 for a shopkeeper, and for a gentleman "such terms as they thought fit."[103]

Also, it "often happened in practice, at any rate in the provinces, that leading members in a locality had a power of veto on the admission of new members from the district."[104] Thus, patrimony was the main channel of getting a place in such companies, just like inheriting a vast property.

No doubt, this was a feature already known in the gild organization. As for example, in 1926, "it was ordered by the stewards and brethren of Andover that no one in the future shall sell or give away his gild except within the third degree, and those thus admitted shall pay a half of a mark to the Gild; but if the father gives it to his son, the payment shall be only two shillings."[105] However, it appears that when merchant capital was dominating the English society such exclusiveness of the chartered companies was vigorously enforced. Indeed, it became a characteristic feature of the merchant companies.

Within these organizations, again, even when the total membership was fairly large, the essential operations were controlled by a very narrow circle, thus giving it the most exclusive character. The *modus operandi* of the East India Company in this respect will be discussed in the course of the present study. Here it may be of interest to note what a seventeenth-century writer stated in regard to the Company of Merchant Adventurers:[106]

> "All the Trade of the Merchants of the Staple, of the merchant Strangers, and of all other English Merchants, concerning th' exportation of all the Commodities of Wooll into those Countries where the same are especially to bee vented, is in the Power of the Merchant Adventurours only; and it is come to be managed by 40 or 50 persons of that Company, consisting of three or foure thousand."

Thus basking under the favours granted by the Royal Charters for monopoly trading, these companies were allowed to function not merely as trading bodies. To a considerable extent they were military and political authorities in their spheres of trade, so that their exclusive rights over the spoils from the "trading areas" might not be challenged. It has been noted before that in its sphere of trade the Eastland Company received powers "to make bye-laws and to impose fines, imprisonment, etc., on all non-freemen trading to these parts." Similarly, the Merchant Adventurers "conducted a vigorous struggle against any interloping in its trade, so that this profitable intercourse might be preserved for the few and prices be fenced against the influence of competition;" the Russia Company "made strenuous (if far from successful) efforts to exclude interlopers trading through Narva; and both the Eastlanders and the Spanish Company used their powers to control the trade."[107] As regards the East India Company much will be said later in this regard; but here it may be of interest to note that it went so far that even before the Company captured power in India, in the last decade of the seventeenth century,

> "Sir Josiah Child, as Chairman of the Court of Directors, wrote to the Governor of Bombay, to spare no severity to crush their countrymen who invaded the ground of the Company's pretensions in India. The Governor replied, by professing his readiness to omit nothing which lay within the sphere of his power, to satisfy the wishes of the Company; but the laws of England, unhappily, would not let him proceed so far as might otherwise be desirable. Sir Josiah wrote back with anger: 'That he expected his orders were to be his rules, and not the laws of England, which were a heap of nonsense, compiled by a few ignorant country gentlemen, who hardly knew how to make laws for the good of their own private families, much less for the regulating of companies, and foreign commerce' (Hamilton's New Account of India, i., 232)."[108]

It is also worthy of note that besides restricting the fortunes of their enterprise to narrow circles, the quantities traded by these companies were carefully regulated, presumably in the interests of price-maintenance, by the control of shipping that the company exercised. Also, minimum selling-prices and maximum buying-prices were sometimes enforced on members. Thus, in the reign of James I, "the Levant Company not only controlled the supply but fixed buying prices for produce purchased in the Near East."[109]

This attempt to control the members of the trading companies on the maximum buying-prices gives an inkling as to the *aim* of the merchant bourgeoisie in the "purchasing" countries, where they had to satisfy the second component of monopolistic trade. Since they were not only interested in selling commodities dear by means of their monopoly rights but also buying these commodities cheap, eventually it meant not only controlling their members on the maximum buying-prices in the purchasing countries but also controlling the buying-prices of these countries as a whole. Obviously, this necessitated substantial control over the buying countries, so that goods could be bought at a very low price, or practically for nothing, when they were obtained by means of virtual robbery.

In those places, where the governments were weak or where in some way or other these foreign merchants could dominate over the local area, robbery became a distinct feature of their enormous gains. In 1580, Captain Drake returned to England from his first world-tour "with half a million pounds worth of loot, as much as the whole revenue of the Crown for a year."[110] Except the voyage of 1607, the other seven of the first eight expeditions of the English East India Company in the Eastern Seas during 1603–1613 fetched clear profits at the rate "in general more than 200 on the capital of the voyage,"[111] for, "independently of the fact that whole fleets were sometimes laden with captured goods, trade was often carried on by compulsory means, calculated to ensure a profitable return only to the stronger party."[112] And, when the European merchant bourgeoisie were engaged in the "commercial hunting of black skins," the slave-trade from the African coasts was virtually based on kidnapping or using force in all possible ways on the weaker governments of the "trading" areas. How profitable this mercantile venture was is evident from the fact that although in the British-run Jamaica trade, slave losses were "12½ per cent in harbour, 4½ per cent before sale, and 33 per cent in 'seasoning,'"[113] yet the trade was very lucrative indeed.

"By 1680 wealthy and respectable merchants of Bristol, Liverpool and London were exporting 15,000 Africans yearly. Later, the total increased. Britain alone seized, transported and sold over two million slaves between 1680 and 1786. At the height of the trade there were 192 British ships engaged, carrying 47,000 Africans between them on each trip. By 1791 there were forty slaving stations, euphemistically called 'factories,' on the West Coast alone."[114]

Such an open practice of kidnapping, piracy or robbery could not, of course, be enforced on those governments which were strong enough to resist these methods and with which the merchant companies had to have long-term settlements for their commercial enterprise. But that in every purchasing country the merchant companies wanted special favour from the established governments in regard to their "terms of trade," and that for this purpose they used various means, honourable or not, with a view to influencing and, if possible, controlling the social forces in these countries to their advantage, is evident from the history of the merchant companies. Adam Smith referred to such practices of the English as well as of other European merchant companies in his writings;[115] Marx noted the same and further explained why such practices were necessary to the augmentation of merchant capital;[116] and in course of the present study also several instances of this nature will be given for the Portuguese, Dutch, French and English merchants in India, noting particularly how the English East India Company (which was the most powerful organization of British merchant capital) persevered to control the buying-prices of goods in India and how after attaining political power in this land it carried on an indiscriminate extraction of the country's wealth behind the thin veil of commerce. What is of particular importance to stress here is that for the purpose of buying goods at the cheapest price possible an *ultimate* political control over the countries they traded with was a *sine qua non* of the policy of the merchant companies.

The need for controlling the buying-country was also implicit in the mercantile conception of an *inelastic* foreign demand. Thus, while commenting on the mercantile theories, Dobb noted:[117]

"If, as a result of attracting money, wages as well as prices in the home country had risen, then to this extent, of course, the advantage to the merchant or manufacturer would have been partly nullified by the consequent rise in cost of exported goods. But Mercantilist writers seem to have presumed that State regulation could and would ensure that this did not occur. Little attention, again, was paid to the possible effects of such a policy in depressing the demand-price that the foreign buyer was able or willing to pay for the goods exported to his markets, and thereby provoking an inevitable reaction in the direction of an import surplus. There is, however, a hint of recognition of this point in a passage in Mun's *England's Treasure by Forraign Trade*. Here he remarks that 'all men do consent that plenty of money in a Kingdom doth make the natife commodities dearer, as plenty, which as it is to the profit of some private men in their revenues, so is it directly against the benefit of the Publique in the quantity of the trade; for as plenty of money makes wares dearer, so dear wares decline their use and consumption.' Hales, in the course of his dialogue, makes his 'Doctor' reply to his 'Knight' on the subject of retaliation that English exports are indispensable to foreigners; which suggests that among writers of the time a highly inelastic foreign demand for English products was taken for granted. Mun elsewhere speaks of selling exports at a high price 'so far forth as the high price cause not a less vent in the quantity'.

The reason why an inelastic foreign demand should have been so easily assumed is not at first glance clear. A principal reason why they imagined that exports could be forced on other countries at an enhanced price without diminution of quantity was probably because they were thinking, not in terms of nineteenth-century conditions where alternative markets were generally available to a country, but of a situation where considerable pressure, if not actual coercion, could be applied to the countries with whom one did the bulk of one's trade. Their policy chiefly depended for its success on its application to a system of *colonial* trade, where political influence could be brought to bear to ensure to the parent country some element of monopoly; and it is essentially as applied to the exploitation of a dependent colonial system that Mercantilist trade–theories acquire a meaning."

Strictly speaking, such a situation began to be evident when merchant capital "was already acquiring a direct interest in production," and was fully revealed in the next era of industrial capital when any "favourable turn in the terms of trade would, therefore, tend to lower industrial costs relatively to the price of finished industrial goods and consequently augment industrial profit."[118] Therefore, in India for instance, this feature of British rule was clearly noticed from the time her exploitation by British industrial capital gained an upper hand. But it should be borne in mind that germs of this situation were laid down much earlier, of which evidence is obtained from the time the East India Company usurped political power in India.

Furthermore, it may be worth noting that "part of Mun's defence of the East India trade and its licence to export bullion was that this trade brought in raw materials for manufacture;"[119] a process which history has shown could be best organized when the raw material supplying country was turned into a colony. Also Colbert, who was the spirit behind the formation of the *Compagnie des Indes Orientales* (the final version of the French East India Company) and who was characterized by Adam Smith as having been "imposed upon by the sophistry of merchants and manufacturers,"[120] "defined 'the whole business of commerce' as consisting in 'facilitating the import of those goods which serve the country's manufacture and playing embargo on those which enter in a manufactured state'."[121] Obviously, Colbert was also of the same meaning as Mun with regard to the purpose of foreign trade, which could come to the most satisfactory conclusion after turning the trading country into a colony, as India exemplified during the British rule from the last quarter of the eighteenth century.

Thus, both for buying cheap and selling dear, the conquest of the countries they traded with was the most satisfactory solution to the mercantile demand for the augmentation of their capital and profit. No doubt, this could not be accomplished in each and every territory where the merchant companies established their marts; but there is also hardly any doubt that, keeping in view the relative strength of the local governments and the historical situation, from securing special privileges to dominating the local rulers almost as vassals and, lastly, transforming the countries into colonies, remained the essential steps in the manoeuvres of the merchant companies in the lands they traded with. For this reason, as it will be illustrated in this study by the role of the English East India Company from the beginning of its penetration into India, contrary to a current viewpoint, the conquest of this land by the Company was not an accidental phenomenon but the consummation of the governing desire of merchant capital.

Evidently, this is a point on which there are divergent views. But has not History proved conclusively that the "spirit of conquest" and the "astonishing expansion of British power overseas" were implicit in the growth of merchant capital in England, just as it was in other nation states of Europe where the merchant bourgeoisie had come to maturity and which had developed into maritime powers?

The fifteenth century found Europe in a melting pot; in "an age of economic, not less than political, sensations."[122]

> "Europe as a whole, however lacerated by political and religious struggles, seemed to have solved the most pressing of the economic problems which had haunted her in the later Middle Ages. During a thousand years of unresting struggle with marsh and forest and moor, she had colonized her own waste places. That tremendous achievement almost accomplished, she now turned to the task of colonizing the world. No longer on the defensive, she entered on a phase of economic expansion which was to grow for the next four hundred years, and which only in the twentieth century was to show signs of drawing towards its close."[123]

There, the "economic power, long at home in Italy, was lacking through a thousand creeks and inlets into Western Europe for a century before," and now "with the climax of the great Discoveries, the flood came on breast-high."[124] Nation States had then emerged with strong central governments, including "Spain and Portugal, created out of the struggle to expel the Moors, France, created out of the struggle with England, and, a little later, the Habsburg monarchy which arose from the defence of Eastern Europe against the Turks."[125] In these and other nation states, like England, the growing merchant bourgeoisie were coming to maturity, striving impatiently with their pervading desire to break through the trade monopoly of Venice and Genoa in the Eastern trade by which they wanted to strengthen themselves. Simultaneously, while, on the one hand, maritime powers were developing on the Atlantic sea-board (such as Portugal and Spain, Holland and England) in order to undertake transoceanic voyage, the old routes to the Eastern trade via the Mediterranean region and

Western Asia were disintegrating with the onslaught of the Turks in Asia Minor and of the Mongols in large parts of Russia. The commercial centre of gravity of Europe, therefore, moved away from the Mediterranean region to the Atlantic; and from there the organized bodies of merchant capital endeavoured to reach the East, which the European merchant bourgeoisie then considered to be the Eldorado of incredible richness, as a land yielding immeasurable quantities of spices and precious stones, of silks and other goods. The expansion of the European powers overseas began.

In this momentous venture of the European merchant bourgeoisie, first "Portugal and Spain held the keys of the treasure-house of East and West."[126] In his search for a transoceanic route to India, Columbus discovered America in 1492; and his voyage "was the signal for the commencement of the first, the greatest and, in its effects, the most far-reaching of the world's gold rushes."[127] Vasco da Gama cast anchor at an Indian port in 1498; and his return cargo, valued at sixtyfold the cost of his voyage to India, startled Europe and filled the merchant bourgeoisie of other nations with envy and longing to expand their powers overseas. Shortly, the "phenomenon which dazzled contemporaries was the swift start into apparent opulence, first of Portugal and then of Spain;"[128] but neither of the two could hold on to the economic energies of this "new civilization" for long. Next, the "economic capital of the new civilization was Antwerp;" and, lastly, it was England, where the main institutions of this civilisation, viz. "international money-market and produce-exchange," and its "typical figure, the paymaster of princes, . . . the international financier," finally established themselves.[129]

"Compared with the currents which raced in Italy, or Germany, or the Low Countries, English life was an economic backwater. But even its stagnant shallows were stirred by the eddy and rush of the continental whirpool. When Henry VII came to the throne, the economic organization of the country differed little from that of the age of Wyclif. When Henry VIII died, full of years and sin, some of the main characteristics which were to distinguish it till the advent of steam-power and machinery could already, though faintly, be descried. The door that remained to be unlocked was colonial expansion, and forty years later the first experiment in colonial expansion had begun."[130]

Henry VII came to the throne in 1485; and from the last decades of the fifteenth century, along with Spain and Portugal, England began to search for a route to India and the East. During the reign of Henry VII (1485–1509) and before Columbus' discovery, the merchants of Bristol sent several vessels in search of "the island of Brazil or that of the Seven Cities, placed on medieval maps to the west of Ireland," for "these should form the first halting-places on the route to Asia by the west."[131] When in the summer of 1493 the news spread that Columbus "had reached the Indies," Cabot and his English "friends at once determined to forgo further search for the islands and to push straight on to Asia."[132] Accordingly, Cabot sailed from Bristol in 1497 and reached Cape Breton Island, which he considered as the "north-eastern coast of Asia, whence came the silks and precious stones he had seen at Mecca."[133] In his next voyage westwards, in 1498, Cabot was "to follow the coast southward as far as Cipangu or Japan, then placed near the equator," for "once Cipangu had been reached London would become a greater centre for spices than Alexandria."[134] Cabot could not find the route to India, but from his two voyages originated Britain's claim to the mainland of America by right of discovery. In 1501 the Bristol merchants obtained a patent from the English monarch to settle colonies in the newly discovered territories.

Henry VIII died in 1547; and, in 1553, from the efforts of the English merchant bourgeoisie to reach India by the north-east passage, the Russia Company originated when one of the ships of the expedition arrived in the harbour of Archangel and "so well did Chancellour, its captain, improve the incident, that he opened a commercial intercourse with the natives, visited the monarch in his capital, stipulated important privileges for his countrymen, and laid the foundation of a trade which was immediately persecuted to no inconsiderable extent."[135] Afterwards, as described before, new merchant companies were formed and British power was extended in west Africa and elsewhere. Also, in 1578, Sir Humphrey Gilbert annexed the Bahamas, and in 1583 he proclaimed the sovereignty and jurisdiction of England on Newfoundland, on the basis of which Newfoundland is usually claimed as the first English colony. Then, in 1585, the first

English colony in Virginia was established by Sir Walter Raleigh; and, after the battle of the Armada in 1588, an association, styling itself as "The Governor and Company of Merchant Adventurers trading with the East Indies," was formed in London in 1599. The next year this primary version of the English East India Company received its first royal charter, and in 1612 the first English settlement in India was established at Surat. Half a century later the President of the English settlement at Surat wrote to the Court of Directors of the Company in London that "the time new require to manage your general commerce with the sword in your hands:" and, in December 1687, the Court of Directors wrote from London to the English Chief of Madras "to establish such a politie of civil and military power, and create and secure such a large revenue to secure both . . . as may be the foundation of a large, well grounded, secure English domain in India for a long time to come."[136] Another half century elapsed; and then, with the conquest of Bengal in 1757, the first edifice of the Indian Empire was erected under the auspices of the English East India Company.

Thus, it was not merely "private enterprise, courage and audacity" of the Britons which led to the "extraordinary expansion" of British power overseas. Neither was the "spirit of conquest" an innate trait of the British nation nor was it an accidental upsurge of the merchants in a trading country. These were *sui generis* of merchant capital; and it was the "new civilization," governed at first by the power of merchant capital and heralded by the merchant bourgeoisie, which shattered the integuments of the old society, roused the "spirit of conquest" of the nation, and led to the "astonishing expansion of British power overseas." In this dynamic and overpowering role of merchant capital in the English society in those days lay the life-force of the East India Company, the typical and the most powerful monopolist company of the English merchant bourgeoisie.

4. Fall of the First Architects

Merchant capital, however, could not have an undisputed career in England for a long time. The reason for this was mainly the peculiar character of the role of merchant capital in a country and that of the *class* of merchant bourgeoisie. As is evident from the preceeding pages, instead of taking interest in production itself, the merchants were only, or mainly, interested in making their money as intermediaries between producers and consumers. Moreover, a rapid increase in the rate and volume of production as well as an extension of the market was an anathema to this class, for they would lower the price of the goods with more extensive supply. Therefore, a serious obstruction to the growth of the market, and in a measure to the development of the productive forces of society, was inherent in the flourishing of merchant capital. In consequence, the role of merchant capital in society soon became reactionary.

These features of merchant capital were already visible when trade-gilds had come into existence in England and monopoly in commerce was usurped by a class of merchants. As a nineteenth-century scholar, with faith in the policy of *laissez faire-laissez aller* in trade, wrote in 1890:[137]

> "Such were the fetters with which the English Gild Merchant of the middle ages, under the guise of a so-called 'freedom', completely shackled free commercial intercourse. Whatever may be said in extenuation of its shortcomings owing to the exigencies of the times, it must be condemned as an institution that blindly aimed to reduce free competition to a minimum, regarded what we now consider legitimate speculation as a crime, deflected from the town every powerful current of trade, mercillessly obliterated the spirit of mercantile enterprise, and crushed out every stimulus to extensive production."

Later, when the power of merchant capital had reached its zenith and several commercial monopolies were exploiting different spheres of world-trade, the basic weakness in the role of merchant capital as inhibiting progress in society became more manifest. Monopolistic trade did not only keep the market restricted to the limit desired by these companies in order to obtain the maximum return for the goods they traded with, but, as they were mainly interested in pocketing the difference between the buying and selling prices of goods and using their capital mainly for such gains only, merchant capital by itself did not give encouragement to extensive production even in its country of origin. As an authority on the subject has remarked:[138]

"The degree to which merchant capital flourished in a country at this period affords us no measure of the ease and speed with which capitalist production was destined to develop; in many cases quite the contrary. Having previously existed, as Marx aptly remarked, 'like the gods of Epicurus in the intermediate worlds of the universe,' merchant capital in its efflorescence between the fourteenth and the sixteenth centuries exercised a profoundly disintegrating effect. But in an important sense it continued to exist 'in the pores of society.' It flourished as an intermediary, whose fortune depended on its insinuating cunning, its facility for adaptation, and the political favours it could win. The needs that merchants and usurers served were largely those of lords and princes and kings. These new men had to be ingratiating as well as crafty; they had to temper extortion with fawning, combine avarice with flattery, and clothe a usurer's hardness in the vestments of chivalry. In the producer they had little interest save in his continuing submissiveness and for the system of production they had little regard save as a cheap and ready source of supply. They had as much concern for the terms of trade (on which their profit-margin depended) as for its volume; and they minded nothing whether what they bartered was slaves or ivory, wool or woollens, tin or gold as long as it was lucrative."

Because of this fundamental weakness in the career of merchant capital, after playing a progressive role for a short while by breaking through the feudal order of society, as a specific social stratum the merchant bourgeoisie began to ally themselves with the feudal elements whose days in society were already gone but who still held the political power. This compromise or adjustment was called for in order to maintain the interests of merchant capital in society. For, to the merchant bourgeoisie, "to acquire political privilege was their first ambition: their second that as few as possible should enjoy it;" and, therefore, "since they were essentially parasites on the old economic order, while they might bleed and weaken it, their fortune was in the last analysis associated with that of their hosts."[139] Hence it is seen that–

"... while the influence of commerce as a dissolvent of feudal relationships was considerable, merchant capital remained nevertheless in large measure a parasite on the old order, and its conscious role, when it had passed its adolescence, was conservative and not revolutionary. Moreover, once capital had begun to accumulate, whether from commercial profits or from urban land-values, a further vista of prosperous increase opened before it. This capital could now be fattened on the fruits of usury: usury practised on the one hand against the petty producers and on the other against decadent feudal society—against needy feudal knights and barons and the even less satiable needs of the Crown."[140]

No doubt, in the circle of feudals, "the influence of the *rentier* and of the financier" was not viewed with equanimity, and it caused "apprehension and jealousy, both for political and economic reasons."[141] There was indeed more than a grain of truth in the retort the merchant of Defoe's story gave to the squire when he was told that he was no gentleman: "No Sir, but I can buy a gentleman."[142] Also Tawney quotes what wrote "an indignant pamphleteer of the Puritan capitalists who specialised in money-lending" as follows:[143]

"By this single stratagem they avoyd all contributions of tithes and taxes to the King, Church, Poor (a soverain cordial to tender consciences); they decline all services and offices of burthen of publick allegiance or private fealty. ...They enjoy both the secular applause of prudent conduct, and withal the spiritual comfort of thriving easily and devoutly.. leaving their adversaries the censures of improvidence, together with the misery of decay. They keep many of the nobility and gentry in perfect vassalage (as their poor copy-holders), which eclipses honour, enervates justice, and oftimes protects them in their boldest conceptions. By engrossing cash and credit, they in effect give the price to land and law to markets. By commanding ready money, they likewise command such offices as they widely affect. ... they feather and enlarge their own nest, the corporations."

But, while such "lamentations, the protests of senatorial dignity against equestrian upstarts or of the *noblesse* against the *roturier,* were natural in a conservative aristocracy, which for a century had felt authority and prestige slipping from its grasp," and while in answer to their reviling the merchant bourgeoisie as "*parvenus,* usurers and blood-suckers" the latter retorted: "how would merchants thrive if gentlemen would not be unthriftes," the feudal stratum in society could not but realise that the only way to maintain its hold on authority and prestige was "by resigning itself, as ultimately it did, to sharing them with its rival."[144] It is, therefore, not surprising to find that "the upper strata of these bourgeois *nouveaux-riches* took to country mansions and to falconing and cut capers like a gentleman without great embarrassment, and what remained of the baronical families took these upstarts into partnership with a fairly cheerful grace."[145]

The evolution of this new aristocracy was based on a three-fold compromise between the feudals and the merchant bourgeoisie. In the economic sphere, the latter "purchased land, entered into business partnerships with the aristocracy, and welcomed local gentry and their sons to membership of its leading gilds"; in its social aspect there was the desire of the commercial *parvenu* to raise their status by inter-marriage and by the acquisition of titles to gentility; and in the political sphere, there was the "readiness to accept a political coalition (as often happened in the government of Italian and other continental towns between the wealthy burghers and the older noble families) or to accept ministerial offices and a place at Court on the basis of the old State-form (as occurred with the Tudor régime in England)."[146] The upshot was that—

> "By the latter part of the seventeenth century, partly as a result of the common struggles which made the Revolution, still more perhaps through the redistribution of wealth by commerce and finance, the former rivals were on the way to be compounded in the gilded clay of a plutocracy embracing both. The landed gentry were increasingly sending their sons into business; 'the tradesman meek and much a liar' looked forward, as a matter of course, to buying an estate from a bankrupt noble. Georgian England was to astonish foreign observers, like Voltaire and Montesquieu, as the Paradise of the *bourgeoisie,* in which the prosperous merchant shouldered easily aside the impoverished bearers of aristocratic names."[147]

One should not, however, fail to realise that the new nobility came into being in the period of the final decline of feudalism and therefore the role of the merchant bourgeoisie, because of "the readiness with which this class compromised with feudal society once its privileges had been won"[148], also became decadent.

"As they shed their social functions the new nobility developed a fantastic if superficial refinement of manners, an elaborate mask of pseudo-feudal behaviour hiding the reality of decay. Clothing and armour became increasingly ostentatious, gold and silver were made into plate and ornaments as the lords vied with each other to produce the most magnificent effect at court. Heraldry, the tournament, the elaboration of the code of chivalry reached their highest pitch just at the time when they were losing all relation to the business of war. This extravagance was at bottom the result of the gradual displacement of land by money as the prevailing form of property. While tenacious of their land and as eager as ever to add to their estates, the nobility were mere children where money was concerned as compared with the great merchants. The extravagance of the age enabled many of these merchants to secure a financial hold upon the nobility through usury, and some were able themselves to enter the ranks of the nobles. The de la Pole family, for example, were originally Hull merchants."[149]

In this way, already by the end of the sixteenth century, the new aristocracy of the merchant bourgeoisie, "jealous of its new-found prerogatives, had become a conservative rather than a revolutionary force; and its influence and the influence of the institution it fostered, such as the chartered companies, was to retard rather than to accelerate the development of capitalism as a mode of production."[150] As years went by, this decadent role of the merchant bourgeoisie became more and more pronounced, and in later years it could be best noticed in the role of the East India Company which was the most solid basis of English merchant capital in the seventeenth and the eighteenth centuries.

Appearing at the zenith of merchant capital's influence in England, the East India Company was not only the most powerful of all chartered companies but it revealed to the full the essential characteristics of the merchant bourgeoisie as outlined above. Thus it will be seen while perusing the subsequent chapters how by plying every tool of trade the East India Company consolidated its position in England and India. To obtain and maintain the exclusive economic and political privileges in England, it combined bribery with protestations of honesty, intrigues with outward submission, plunder of foreign lands for the small clique with declarations of serving the British interest of promoting trade; and, later, rapine of India with the martyrdom of bearing the "White Man's Burden" in the colony. To obtain the mastery of the Eastern waters (and particularly of India) vis-a-vis its European rivals, it alternated between truce and treachery, peace and war, as the occasion demanded. And with the same governing objective of acquiring fortunes irrespective of scruple or any such accepted virtue, in India, so long as the Indian powers were strong, it used flattery, bribery and court-intrigues, played with guile and ostentation of friendship and alliance, alternated acquiescence to the Indian rulers and sudden attacks, and after it became *the* political power in India, it let itself loose on this proverbially rich land to "make hay while the sun shines." But there was another essential background to the career of the East India Company, which was that it was a late product of the time. The Company saw the light of the day with the opening of the seventeenth century, while already by the end of the sixteenth century decadence had set in within the class of English merchant bourgeoisie. Therefore, while on the one hand it could employ the pooled experience of the merchant bourgeoisie over the earlier period in order to become the most powerful representative of British merchant capital, on the other hand very soon it came against the opposition of the British industrial bourgeoisie.

Even when merchant capital was dominating the English society, however hampered in its progress, industries developed in England and eventually a class of industrial bourgeoisie came into existence, to which also belonged a section of the merchant bourgeoisie who had interested themselves in production. In order to have India as their market without the intermediacy of a monopolist company of merchant capital, the British industrialists launched a series of struggles against the privileges and power of the East India Company as will be described in the last chapter. And while these struggles gathered momentum in course of time, this newly-evolving class of industrial bourgeoisie reached its maturity with the industrial revolution of England in the second half of the eighteenth century, which owed to a considerable extent to the drain of India's wealth and resources since the conquest of Bengal in 1757.[151] Henceforth their struggle became more and more insistent and increasingly successful,[152] while the merchant bourgeoisie who were constantly coming in conflict with the rising force of the industrial capitalists had no more place in the developing society. They were already giving away to the interests of industrial capital; and now, after England became the "workshop of the world," the onslaught of industrial capital saw an end to the chartered companies—the medium of wealth and power of the merchant bourgeoisie. In this process of liquidating the decadent organizations, the East India Company was to be the most important victim as being the most powerful of all chartered companies of merchant capital. Therefore, when the force of the industrial bourgeoisie was ruling England, they won complete victory in 1858 with the transfer of India from the hands of the East India Company to the British Crown.

Thus, born in the wake of reaction, the East India Company, after bitter struggles to retain power, had to liquidate itself when British industrial capital finally decided not to tolerate any more any vestige of this obstruction towards its full play in the colony of India. Now industrial capital had the day, and so with the end of the East India Company's career British merchant capital withered away. The first architects of the "new civilization" in England disappeared completely from the social arena.

Notes and References

1 Collis, Maurice—*British Merchant Adventurers*, William Collins, London, 1942, p. 7.
2 Torrens, W. M.—*Empire in Asia—How we came by it: A Book of Confessions*, Trübner & Co., London, 1872, p. 6.
3 See, for instance, Max Webers *Die protestantische Ethik und der Geist des Kapitalismus*, Verlag von J. C. B. Mohr (Paul Siebeck), Tübingen, 1934; R. H. Tawney's *Religion and the Rise of Capitalism*, Pelican Books, England, 1948; etc.
4 Tawney, R. H.—*Religion and the Rise of Capitalism*, Pelican Books, England, 1948, p. 79.
5 *ibid.*, pp. 76–77
6 Morton, A. L.—*A People's History of England*, Lawrence & Wishart Ltd., London, 1951, p. 206.

7 Marx, Karl—*Capital: A Critique of Political Economy*, Charles H. Kerr & Company, Chicago, 1909, Vol. III, p. 930.
8 *loc. cit.* 4, p. 103
9 *ibid.*, p. 92
10 *ibid.*, pp. 111, 222, 249
11 *ibid.*, p. 183.
12 *ibid.*, p. 245
13 Marx, Karl—*Capital: A Critical Analysis of Capitalist Production*, George Allen & Unwin Ltd., London, 1949, Vol. I, p. 775.
14 Quoted in *loc. cit.* 6, p. 160
15 Quoted in *loc. cit.* 4, p. 113
16 *loc. cit.* 4, p. 113
17 *ibid.*, p. 114
18 *ibid.*, p. 114.
19 *ibid.*, pp. 121, 238
20 *ibid.*, p. 190.
21 *ibid.*, p. 199.
22 *ibid.*, pp. 250—251.
23 *ibid.*, p. 222.
24 *ibid.*, pp. 180, 234.
25 See, for instance, W. W. Stoklizkaja-Tereschkowitschs *Der Ursprung der feudalen Stadt in Westeuropa, Sowjetwissenschaft*: Gesellschaftswissenschaftliche Abteilung Berlin, 1955, Heft 5, pp. 714—715, etc.; Maurice Dobb's *Studies in the Development of Capitalism*, George Routledge & Sons Ltd., London, 1946, p. 83 ff., etc.
26 *loc. cit.* 4, p. 39
27 Dobb, Maurice—*Studies in the Development of Capitalism*, George Routledge & Sons Ltd., London, 1946, p. 84.
28 *loc. cit.* 6, pp. 91—92
29 Gross, Charles—*The Gild Merchant*, Oxford at the Clarendon Press, 1890, Vol. I, p. 74.
30 *ibid.*, p. 74, n. 3
31 *loc. cit.* 27, p. 86
32 *loc. cit.* 4, pp. 38—39
33 *ibid.*, pp. 95—96
34 *loc. cit.* 29, p. 107
35 *loc. cit.* 6, p. 92
36 *ibid.*, p. 93
37 *loc. cit.* 27, p. 98
38 *ibid.*, p. 100
39 *ibid.*, p. 102
40 *loc. cit.* 29, pp. 41—42
41 *ibid.*, pp. 36, 36—n 1
42 *ibid.*, p. 157
43 *ibid.*, pp. 43—44, 45, 46, 47—48, 49
44 *loc. cit.* 27, p. 102

45 *loc. cit.* 29, pp. 123–126
46 *loc. cit.* 27, p. 104
47 Colby, C. W.—*Growth of Oligarchy in English Towns*, English Historical Review, Vol. V, 1890, pp. 643, 648; also quoted in *loc. cit.* 27, p. 105.
48 *loc. cit.* 29, p. 29
49 *loc. cit.* 27, p. 108
50 *ibid.*, p. 109
51 *loc. cit.* 6, pp. 93–96
52 *ibid.*, p. 93
53 *ibid.*, p. 94
54 *loc. cit.* 27, p. 109
55 *ibid.*, pp. 109–110
56 *loc. cit.* 6, p. 96
57 *loc. cit.* 27, p. 110
58 *ibid.*, p. 110
59 *loc. cit.* 29, pp. 140–141, 143, 144
60 *Statutes of the Realm, Rec. Com.*, London, 1810–1828, Vol. I, p. 333; also quoted in *loc. cit.* 29, p. 144.
61 *loc. cit.* 6, p. 96
62 *loc. cit.* 27, p. 110
63 *ibid.*, p. 110
64 *ibid.*, pp. 111–112
65 *ibid.*, p. 112
66 *ibid.*, p. 112
67 *ibid.*, p. 112
68 *loc. cit.* 29, p. 149
69 *ibid.*, p. 148
70 *ibid.*, p. 148
71 *loc. cit.* 27, 27, p. 112
72 *loc. cit.* 29, p. 147
73 *loc. cit.* 27, p. 109
74 *loc. cit.* 4, p. 79
75 *loc. cit.* 27, pp. 113–114
76 *ibid.*, p. 114
77 *ibid.*, p. 114
78 Senior, Nassau—*Slavery in the U. S.*, p. 4; quoted in *loc. cit.* 27, p. 114.
79 *loc. cit.* 13, p. 775
80 *loc. cit.* 78, p. 4
81 *loc. cit.* 27, p. 114
82 *ibid.*, p. 114
83 *ibid.*, p. 115
84 *ibid.*, p. 115
85 *loc. cit.* 29, p. 115
86 *ibid.*, p. 155
87 *ibid.*, p. 156
88 *loc. cit.* 4, p. 248

89 *loc. cit.* 27, p. 213 n
90 *loc. cit.* 13, p. 133
91 *loc. cit.* 27, p. 88
92 *ibid.*, p. 88
93 *loc. cit.* 7, pp. 387–388
94 *loc. cit.* 27, p. 89
95 *loc. cit.* 7, p. 388
96 *loc. cit.* 13, p. 133
97 *loc. cit.* 29, p. 155
98 Unwin, G.—*Studies in Economic History*, pp. 173, 181; quoted in *loc. cit.* 27, p. 116.
99 *loc. cit.* 27, p. 192, n 2
100 *loc. cit.* 29, p. 148, n 5
101 *loc. cit.* 27, p. 192, n 2
102 *ibid.*, p. 192, n 2
103 Scott, W. R.—*Joint Stock Companies*, Vol. I, p. 152; quoted in *loc. cit.* 27, p. 192, n 2.
104 *loc. cit.* 27, p. 192, n 2
105 *loc. cit.* 29, pp. 31–32
106 Malynes, Gerard de—*The Maintenance of Free Trade*, London, 1622; quoted in *loc. cit.* 29, p. 151.
107 *loc. cit.* 27, p. 115
108 Mill, James—*The History of British India*, James Madden, London, 1858, Vol. I, p. 91 ff.
109 *loc. cit.* 27, p. 116
110 *loc. cit.* 1, p. 8
111 *loc. cit.* 108, i, p. 20
112 Murray, Hugh—*History of British India*, T. Nelson and Sons, London, 1860, p. 147.
113 Kartun, Derek—*Africa, Africa!*, Lawrence & Wishart, London, 1954, p. 9.
114 *ibid.*, p. 9
115 See, for instance, *An Inquiry into the Nature and Causes of the Wealth of Nations* by Adam Smith.
116 See, for instance, *Capital* (4 volumes) by Karl Marx.
117 *loc. cit.* 27, pp. 203–204
118 *ibid.*, p. 204
119 *ibid.*, p. 205
120 Smith, Adam—*An Inquiry into the Nature and Causes of the Wealth of Nations*, Everyman's Library, London, 1911, Vol. I, p. 411.
121 *loc. cit.* 27, p. 205
122 *loc. cit.* 4, p. 79
123 *ibid.*, p. 81
124 *ibid.*, p. 77
125 *loc. cit.* 6, p. 162
126 *loc. cit.* 4, p. 81
127 *loc. cit.* 6, p. 160

128 *loc. cit.* 4, p. 81
129 *ibid.*, p. 82
130 *ibid.*, p. 80
131 Bigger, H. P.—*Cabot, John*, Encyclopaedia Britannica, 11th Edition, Cambridge, 1911, Vol. 4, p. 922.
132 *ibid.*, p. 922
133 *ibid.*, p. 922
134 *ibid.*, p. 922
135 *loc. cit.* 108, i, p. 5
136 Majumdar, R. C.; Raychaudhuri, H. C.; Datta, Kalikinkar—*An Advanced History of India*, Macmillan, London, 1953, p. 638.
137 *loc. cit.* 29, pp. 50—51
138 *loc. cit.* 27. p. 121
139 *ibid.*, p. 121
140 *ibid.*, pp. 89–90
141 *loc. cit.* 4, p. 209
142 Quoted in *loc. cit.* 27, p. 121.
143 *loc. cit.* 4, p. 209
144 *ibid.*, p. 209
145 *loc. cit.* 27, p. 121
146 *ibid.*, pp. 120—121
147 *loc. cit.* 4. p. 208
148 *loc. cit.* 27, p. 120
149 *loc. cit.* 6, p. 138
150 *loc. cit.* 27, pp. 121—122
151 See, for instance, Brooks, Adams—*The Law of Civilisation and Decay*, pp. 263—264; etc.
152 Examine, for instance, Lord North's Regulating Act of 1773, Pitt's India Bill of 1784, the decisions of the British Parliament in 1813 regarding the subsequent role of the East India Company in India, etc., which will be discussed in some details in Chapter 6.

CHAPTER 2

COMPANY AND THE ENGLISH MERCHANTS

1. Birth of the Company

The wealth and splendour of India were not unknown to Europe long before the advent of the European merchant companies in the subcontinent. The Greeks and Romans were well acquainted with Indian merchandise, and this might have been one of the principal reasons "enabling the ancients to obtain a great accession to their knowledge respecting India."[1] In those times, direct commerce developed between Europe and the western seaports of India; but "the weakness and distractions of the Roman Empire, and subsequently the rise of the Mohammedan power, cut off the nations of Europe from all direct communication with India."[2]

"During the Middle Ages trade between Europe and Asia was carried on along several routes. The most easterly was by way of Trebizond, up the Don and Volga and into the Baltic, with the Hanse towns at its northern extremities. A second was by way of the Persian Gulf, Bagdad and Aleppo and thence by sea to Constantinople, Venice and Genoa. A third was up the Red Sea and overland to the Nile, where Italian galleys awaited their cargoes at Alexandria. All these routes had one thing in common: they involved the transhipment of goods and their carriage overland on horse or camel back, in most cases for considerable distances. The sea voyages were purely coastal, and, in their Asiatic part, were carried out by Arab sailors and shipping. All goods were passed on from merchant to merchant along the route, each taking a substantial profit.

The high cost of land transport made it unprofitable to carry any but the least bulky merchandise. So for Europe the East became 'gorgeous,' a land yielding silks, spices and precious stones, an Eldorado of incredible richness. And, in the main, the trade was a one way trade, since Europe had no commodities small enough in bulk to export and was compelled to pay for goods in gold and silver, diminishing her already inadequate store of bullion. The Eastern trade was frowned upon by the statesmen as immoral, wasting treasure in return for luxuries, but the merchants of Italy and the Hanse, who received goods by a continuation up the Rhine of the Mediterranean routes as well as through Russia, found it exceedingly profitable. Each route was the jealously guarded monopoly of a city or group, which kept out all competitors, if necessary by armed force."[3]

As far as India was particularly concerned, her external trade with Europe was mainly by the sea-route—by the Arabian Sea and the Persian Gulf or the Red Sea. Some goods also trickled to places like Bokhara by the overland route, but this was never a very successful trade-route in India, mainly because it was rather inaccessible. The subcontinent has a land-frontier of about 4,000 miles, but as it is studded with insurmountable peaks of the Himalayas and with impassable regions it could not allow a brisk external trade by the overland route. Hence, the Arab traders, who had taken over the commerce between India and Europe in the Middle Ages, collected their wares from Indian border towns and ports and handed them over to the European traders in the Mediterranean ports and trade-centres in Western Asia. But, significantly enough, although the "Eastern trade" was "exceedingly profitable" in Europe, the Arab merchants do not appear to have ever risen above their position as intermediaries between the Indian and the European traders.

"The rich productions of that country were, during a considerable period, conveyed by Arabian navigators or by inland caravans, and sold to the Venetians and Genoese on the shores of the Mediterranean or of the Black Sea; but these traders themselves, so distinguished in the Middle Ages by their maritime enterprise, made no attempt to open a direct commerce with the distant regions whence those precious commodities were imported."[4]

The situation began to change with the rise of the *class* of merchants in Europe and the emergence of some European nation states as the foremost maritime powers in the world.

"The Europe of the earlier Middle Ages, like the world of the twentieth century, had been a closed circle. But it had been closed, not by the growth of knowledge, but by the continuance of ignorance; and, while the latter, having drawn the whole globe into a single economic system, has no space left for fresh expansion, for the former, with the Mediterranean as its immemorial pivot, expansion had hardly begun. Tapping the wealth of the East by way of the narrow apertures in the Levant, it resembled, in the rigidity of the limits imposed on its commercial strategy, a giant fed through the chinks of a wall. ... This narrow framework had been a home. In the fifteenth century it was felt to be a prison. Expanding energies pressed against the walls; restless appetites gnawed and fretted wherever a crack in the surface offered room for erosion."[5]

Obviously, this restlessness was caused by the growing merchant bourgeoisie of different European nations under formation, to whom foreign trade had become the chief medium for acquiring wealth.

"Long before the southward march of the Turks cut the last of the great routes from the East, the Venetian monopoly was felt to be intolerable. Long before the plunder of Mexico and the silver of Potosi flooded Europe with treasure, the mines of Germany and the Tyrol were yielding increasing, if still slender, streams of bullion, which stimulated rather than allayed its thirst. It was not the lords of great estates, but eager and prosperous peasants, who in England first nibbled at commons and undermined the manorial custom, behind which, as behind a dyke, their small savings had been accumulated. It was not great capitalists, but enterprising gildsmen, who began to make the control of the fraternity the basis of a system of plutocratic exploitation, or who fled, precocious individualists, from the fellowship of borough and craft, that they might grow to what stature they pleased in rural isolation. It was not even the Discoveries which first began the enormous tilt of economic power from south and east to north and west. The records of German and English trade suggest that the powers of northern Europe had for a century before the Discoveries been growing in wealth and civilization, and for a century after them English economic development was to be closely wedded to its continental connections, as though Diaz had never rounded the Cape, nor Columbus praised Heaven for leading him to the shores of Zayton and Guinsay. First attempted as a counterpoise to the Italian monopolist, then pressed home with ever greater eagerness to turn the flank of the Turk, as his stranglehold on the eastern commerce tightened, the Discoveries were neither a happy accident nor the fruit of the disinterested curiosity of science. They were the climax of almost a century of patient economic effort. They were as practical in their motive as the steam-engine."[6]

It is seen, therefore, that the fifteenth century in Europe saw "a great advance in the technique of ship building and of navigation"[7] as well as in seaworthiness.

"The typical merchant ship of the Middle Ages was a basin-shaped affair with a single mast in the middle. It was quite incapable of sailing against the wind, and, in rough weather, was almost unmanageable. In England, at any rate, ships larger than 100 tons were seldom built before 1400. After this rapid progress was made. A list of ships used by the Government in 1439 for the transport of troops included eleven between 200 and 360 tons. Another similar list made in 1451 contains twenty-three ships of 200 to 400 tons. A little later William Canynge, a famous Bristol merchant, owned 2,853 tons of shipping, including one vessel of 900 tons.

Corresponding advances were made in seaworthiness. The Spanish and Portuguese developed the caravel for coastal trade in the Atlantic. It was a longer, narrower craft, with a high forecastle and three or four masts. The compass, known since the Twelfth Century, was perfected and came into general use, the astrolabe was adapted for the calculation of latitude and map makers were beginning to replace mythical cities and dragons with a certain measure of accurate information. It was at last technically possible to leave the coasts and to undertake transoceanic voyages."[8]

And, just about this time, while the riches of India "violently attracted the attention of Europe,"[9] and while the merchant bourgeoisie of several European states were striving to destroy the monopoly of Venice and Genoa in Eastern trade, the old routes for conducting this trade was seriously threatened.

"During the Fifteenth Century these routes were threatened by invading Mongols who overran much of Russia and by Turks who drove the Arabs out of Asia Minor and in 1453 captured Constantinople. The Egyptian route, though not cut, was threatened. The overland routes were not rendered impossible but the risk was much greater, freigths rose and profits declined."[10]

But such a situation only further whetted the appetite of the European merchant bourgeoisie, all of whom from the different nation states wanted to enrich themselves by means of this trade. For:

"The commerce of India, even when confined to those narrow limits which a carriage by land had prescribed, was supposed to have elevated feeble states into great ones; and to have constituted an enviable part in the fortune even of the most opulent and powerful: to have contributed largely to support the Grecian monarchies both in Syria and Egypt; to have retarded the downfall of Constantinople; and to have raised the small and obscure republic of Venice to the rank and influence of the most potent kingdoms."[11]

Under the circumstances, when the Mediterranean routes were practically cut off, the seat of the Eastern trade moved away to Western Europe, where the new maritime powers were developing and which could undertake transoceanic voyages. In 1492 Columbus discovered America in his attempt to reach India by the long sea-route. In 1497 Cabot sailed from Bristol in order to reach Asia across the ocean, and reaching Cape Breton Island which he thought to be the north-eastern coast of Asia, hoisted the English flag and took possession of the country in the name of King Henry VII. In 1498 Vasco da Gama reached India passing by the Cape of Good Hope, and with this startling voyage the centre of India trade in Europe definitely shifted from the Mediterranean region to the Atlantic sea-board.

"When Vasco da Gama returned to Lisbon from India, with a cargo that is said to have repaid sixtyfold the cost of his voyage, the effect was shattering. Even under the most favourable circumstances imaginable the old routes with their high freigths and the score of merchants who handled the goods in transit could never compete. The power of the Italian merchant towns was destroyed and the whole centre of gravity of Europe shifted towards the Atlantic coast."[12]

Henceforth, true to the position that foreign trade occupied in the flowering of merchant capital, the cupidity of all maritime nations in Europe was roused, and all of them set about establishing direct "trade relations" with India.

With the great discovery that Vasco da Gama made, naturally the Portuguese were the first to take the field. A Russian merchant, Afanassi Nikitin, had visited India prior to the Portuguese (1469–1472), and spent most of his time in South India. But, if he had any commercial mission other than as merely an individual trader, it does not appear to have been very successful;[13] at any rate, so far very little is known about it. The Portuguese, on the other hand, began splendidly. It is said that Vasco da Gama and his crew came in search of "Christians and spices." Christians they did not find many, but spices in plenty; and especially in the islands of Sumatra, Java, etc., in what were then known as "Indian Waters." They began to import to Europe spices, then one of the most coveted commodities from the Orient. By the beginning of the sixteenth century, the Portuguese merchants had established themselves as a trading body in India. A number of Portuguese settlements grew up near the sea, namely, Goa, Diu, Daman, Salsette, Bassein, Chaul and Bombay at the west coast; San Thomé near Madras at the south-east; and in eastern India, at Hugli in Bengal. Their authority also extended over the major part of Ceylon.

Next to the Portuguese, came the Dutch to India. Since the discovery of the India-route via the Cape of Good Hope, the Portuguese were very keen on preserving their exclusive rights to this route, and fought with any other nation which might attempt to jeopardise their monopoly by voyaging to Indian waters by this only available sea-path and thus supplant them in their lucrative pursuit. They had therefore fortified ports on this route where vessels might call in for supplies, and cruised the water with armed ships. Even so, the Dutch in 1595 were bold enough to send four ships to trade with India by this route.

Furthermore, in 1595–96, a great work on India was published by one Jan Huyghen van Linschoten, a Hollander, who had lived six years at Goa. In this book he revealed to the world how insecure was the Portuguese grip upon the East. This book was speedily translated into English, Latin, German, and French, and obviously had a significant bearing on the formation of both the Dutch and the English East India Companies.

The United East India Company of the Netherlands was incorporated for trading in the East with a capital of over £ 500,000, and in 1602, it was furnished with a Charter by the Dutch States General which empowered the company to make war, conclude treaties, acquire territories and build fortresses. It was thus made "a great instrument of war and conquest,"[14] like the other Chartered Companies of Merchant Capital in Europe in those days.

Although the Dutch paid more attention to the Far Eastern areas, such as Sumatra, Java and Borneo, they also established *factories*, as the trading depots of all these merchant companies were called, in Gujarat in West India, on the Coromandel Coast in south-eastern India, and in Bengal, Bihar and Orissa, that is, in eastern India. They entered deep into the interior of the lower Ganges valley; and in 1658 they also got possession of the last Portuguese settlement in Ceylon.

By supplanting the Portuguese, the Dutch practically maintained a monopoly of the spice trade in the East throughout the seventeenth century. They also became the carriers of trade between India and the islands of the Far East, "thus reviving a very old connection maintained in the palmy days of the Vijayanagar Empire."[15] At Surat, where they established themselves in 1616, the Dutch were supplied with large quantities of indigo, manufactured in central India and the Jumna valley. From Bengal, Bihar, Gujarat and Coromandel, they exported raw silk, textiles, saltpetre, rice and Gangetic opium.

The English did not lag far behind. Since the penetration of the Portuguese merchants into India, they had their eye on the subcontinent, and were devising ways and means to accomplish the task. Their first known attempt was probably in 1527, when an English merchant by the name of Robert Thorne, who, having spent a number of years at Seville in Spain, had acquired very definite knowledge about the Portuguese trade relations with India, submitted a project to Henry VIII by which the English merchant bourgeoisie could gain a passage to India and attain the same enviable position as that of the Portuguese at that time. Since the Portuguese defended by force their exclusive right to the passage to India via the Cape of Good Hope, the suggestion of Thorne was to reach India "by sailing to the north-west, and thus obtain a passage at once expeditious and undisputed."[16] Two voyages were thus made during the reign of Henry VIII, one about 1527 and the other ten years later; but both of them ended in failure. Several more voyages to explore the north-west passage to India were undertaken before the close of the century, but, as before, nothing came out of such ventures.

The English merchant bourgeoisie also "anticipated a happier issue from a voyage to the north-east."[17] Accordingly, during the reign of Edward VI a squadron went sailing along the coast of Norway, doubled the North Cape, and one of the two principal ships "found shelter in the harbour of Archangel, and was the first foreign ship by which it was entered."[18] This ultimately resulted in the birth of the Russia Company, which although not dealing with India, brought rich profit to the English merchant bourgeoisie. In 1580, another attempt was made to explore the north-east passage, but it ended in failure.

The English then made up their mind to defy the Portuguese, and sent two expeditions to China via the Cape of Good Hope. The first one was in 1582, and the second in 1596; the latter carrying Queen Elizabeth's letters to the Emperor of China. But both the expeditions ended in fiasco.

Meanwhile, in 1580, Captain Drake completed his round the world voyage by sailing via the New Hemisphere and returning via the Cape of Good Hope, "with half a million pounds worth of loot, as much as the whole revenue of the Crown for a year."[19] His assertion that the voyage to India by the Cape was also possible for the English raised once again the high hopes of the English merchant bourgeoisie. A second round the world expedition left England in 1586 and returned in 1588, carrying nautical data on sailing via the Cape of Good Hope.

By then, trade with India had become irresistible to the English merchant bourgeoisie.

> "They sailed to the eastern shores of the Mediterranean Sea, where they found cargoes of Indian goods conveyed over land; and a mercantile company, denominated the Levant Company, was instituted, according to the policy of the age, to secure to the nation the advantages of so important a commerce."[20]

The Russia Company also had sent a representative to open trade relations with Persia, who in the city of Bokhara "found merchants not only from various parts of the Persian Empire, but from Russia and China, and India;" and having performed seven times his voyage to Persia, he "opened a considerable trade for raw and wrought silk, carpets, spices, precious stones, and other Asiatic productions."[21] By 1563, the business had reached such a dimension that it required "the presence of three agents at Casbin, the seat of Persian Court; and the traffic flourished for several years."[22] Then, by 1593, two Portuguese ships carrying merchandise from India were captured by the English. The cargoes of the first ship "inflamed the imaginations of the merchants; and the papers which she carried afforded information respecting the traffic in which she was engaged;" and the second vessel was the largest "which had ever been seen in England, laden with spices, calicoes, silks, gold, pearls, drugs, porcelain, ebony, etc.; and stimulated the impatience of the English to be engaged in so opulent a commerce."[23]

Further preparations had also been made during such expeditions and piratical actions. The English merchants who had long before been organized for trade under the name of Merchant Adventurers decided in 1581 to send out men to report on what could be bought and sold in Asia. These traders were to go via Syria and the Persian Gulf, for they apprehended that the Portuguese would try to sink intruders who went via the Cape of Good Hope. So, in February 1583, a party of merchant-travellers, set out on their mission, carrying letters from the Queen Elizabeth addressed to Akbar, the Great Mughal Emperor of India. The party was financed by the Turkey or the Levant Company.

Having arrived at Basra, via Aleppo, the party was divided. Ralph Fitch, Newberry, Leeds and Storey were deputed to proceed to India, and the rest remained there. Fitch and his friends intended to slip across the Arabian Sea from Ormuz, an island at the mouth of the Persian Gulf. But they were arrested by the Portuguese who had a fortress there. This gives an idea of how the mercantilist states of the Atlantic seaboard guarded their exclusive interests.

Imprisonment was not the only fate awaiting Fitch and his party. Religion was called in aid of the rival merchants, and the charge of heresy was levelled by the Portuguese against Fitch and his colleagues. So, as heretics, they were sent prisoners to Goa, the capital of the Portuguese Indies. An inquisition existed in Goa, and a Grand Inquisitor was waiting for them. However, with the help of an English Jesuit who was then at Goa, Fitch and his colleagues, except Storey, managed to escape from the Inquisition. Storey became a monk at Goa. The other three secretly entered the Indian subcontinent, and travelled to Fatehpur Sikri, the wonderful red sandstone city which Akbar had just built. They saw the splendour of the Mughal Court at its greatest moment. But they were not given formal audience by the Emperor, evidently because, to a grand monarch like Akbar, England and her Queen were not matters of great concern, and as mere merchant-travellers without any presents to offer the party of Fitch was not qualified for that honour. The party was therefore unable to deliver the Queen's letter, but Leeds, who was a jeweller, was given employment at Court on a good salary.

Fitch decided to travel farther eastwards, and taking a boat on the Ganges in September 1584 he floated down to Hugli in Bengal. From Hugli he passed into Chittagong, and thence by boat to Pegu in Burma. He stayed in Burma for some time, visiting Rangoon and other places, and then went to Chiengmai in northern Siam. After investigating the trade at Chiengmai he returned to Pegu and went to Malacca near Singapura. Thence, "having noted the vital importance of the Straits of Malacca for a maritime power trading to the Far East,"[24] (or, to be more exact, for holding the Far East for *colonial trade* on account of which the British later built the town of Singapore), Fitch returned to Pegu. And then he set out for home, travelling by sea to Ceylon, thence up the west coast of India to Cochin, then to Goa, and so on to Basra, Babylon, Mosul, Aleppo, and finally to London. Newberry died on his way home by the Punjab.

Fitch was away for eight years. In this period he had noted the tremendous prosperity of the eastern countries compared to which his own country appeared to him very insignificant. He found even Pegu much bigger than London.[25] In four years of British occupation from 1852 Pegu was reduced to such a state and was considered so well suited for transportation for life that after the Santhal Insurrection of 1855–56 the mouth-piece of the British in India, the journal entitled "Friends of India" wrote editorially:[26]

> "It is to Pegu that we would convey the Santhals, not one or two of the ring-leaders, but the entire population of the infected districts."

During his voyage in the East, Fitch had also collected a mass of information of the greatest importance to the English merchants. As a shrewd observer he had also noted about Nanda Bayin, the King of all-Burma, who had conquered Siam, that "This king hath little force by sea, because he hath but very few ships."[27] Such comments emphasize the importance of a strong naval power on which the prosperity and final supremacy of these merchant companies ultimately depended. Indeed, for this reason, the merchant bourgeoisie of different European nations were continuously striving to make their navy the strongest, so that only one of them would have the undisputed sway over the sea-borne trade, and, consequently, over the colonies. It appears that to a significant extent herein lay the maximum success of the English as the greatest coloniser of the world, for eventually they became the unrivalled sea-faring nation in Europe and in the world; and, as will be seen later, because of the lack of a strong Indian navy, the growing mercantile interests in India could not but make alliance with the European merchant companies, which, in the end, brought their doom.

To go back to Fitch, the information collected by him, along with the details about trade in India, Burma and Siam, was found very useful by the merchants in London. They went through his information for a number of years; and, it is said that this information finally "led to the founding nine years later of the East India Company, the great organization which in the course of two hundred and fifty years was to acquire for England almost all the towns he had visited."[28]

Meanwhile, in 1591, Sir James Lancaster doubled the Cape and traversed the Indian Ocean. He and a few survivors struggled home after much sufferings, but he had proved once more the voyage to be a possibility. This, no doubt, further influenced the London merchants to float the East India Company, who had by then more intelligence about India from another Englishman by the name of Stevens who had "sailed with the Portuguese from Lisbon to Goa, by the Cape of Good Hope, and wrote an account of his voyage, which was read with avidity, and contributed to swell the general current of enterprise which now ran so vehemently toward India."[29] And, added to these was the publication by the Hollander Linschoten which further speeded the formation of the English East India Company, as has been mentioned before. Finally, the successful expedition of the Dutch to India via the Cape route in 1595 was more than the outrivalled English merchant bourgeoisie could bear. So, in 1599, under the direct auspices of the Merchant Adventurers, "an association was formed, and a fund subscribed, which amounted to 30,133 *l.* 6s. 8d., and consisted of 101 shares: the subscriptions of individuals varying from 100 *l.* to 3,000 *l.*"[30]

The association petitioned the Queen "for a warrant to fit out three ships, and export bullion, and also for a charter of privileges,"[31] but the ruling circles hesitated to break peace with Spain and Portugal on this account. The Queen was, however, persuaded to send a merchant by the name of John Mildenhall on an embassy to the Great Mughal by the overland route via Constantinople, while the official acknowledgement of the Company was under discussion. Carrying a letter from the Queen to the Emporer Akbar, Mildenhall could not reach Agra before 1603, but having stayed in India for three years he successfully returned to England in 1607, carrying a *firman* or Royal Order from Jahangir, the successor of Akbar, in favour of English trade in India.

In the meantime, in England, the Merchant Adventurers had by the end of 1600 succeeded in winning the consent of the government to prepare their voyage to India. For this, they obtained a Royal Charter on the 31st December 1600. The raising of the price of pepper by the Dutch in 1600, "at one sweep from 3s. a pound to 6s. and 8s.," by taking advantage of their monopoly in spice-trade, was an immediate cause for the official recognition of the Company and the granting of its charter.[32]

The Company was entitled, "the Governor and Company of Merchants of London, trading to the East Indies." Of the many exclusive privileges obtained by the Company according to the Royal Charter, the most important ones were:

1) "prohibiting the rest of the community from trading within limits assigned to the Company, but granting to them the power, whenever they please, of bestowing licenses for that purpose;"

2) power "to export in each voyage 30,000 *l.* in gold and silver; also English goods for the first four voyages exempt from duties, and to re-export Indian goods in English ships under the same privilege to the end of the charter;"

3) validity of the charter for fifteen years, "but under condition that, if not found to be advantageous to the country, it might be annulled at any time under a notice of two years: if advantageous, it might, if desired by the Company, be renewed for fifteen years."[33]

In other words, the charter contained similar rights and privileges to those obtained by other monopolist companies of merchant capital in those days.

It is interesting to note further, how the merchant bourgeoisie strove to maintain from the beginning their exclusive hold in this venture. When the East India Company was organizing its first voyage to India, the government suggested the employment of Sir Edward Michelbourne in the expedition. But the leaders of the venture, although they waited upon favours from the Queen and the Lords, made known their desire quite categorically:—"not to employ any *gentleman* in any place of charge," and to be allowed "to sort theire business with men of their own qualitye, lest the suspicion of employm[t] of *gentlemen* being taken hold uppon by the generalitie, do dryve a great number of the adventurers to withdraw their contributions."[34] The Company, however, in all essentials, remained closely linked with the monarchy from the start; Queen Elizabeth being one of its shareholders.

Thus began the career of the English East India Company, the first ship of which sailed from England on the 2nd of May, 1601, "carrying letters of recommendation from the Queen to the sovereigns of the different ports to which it might resort."[35]

2. Struggle of the *Have-not* English Merchants

Since the birth of the Company, it was motivated by three guiding principles:

1) Preservation of its monopoly rights and privileges with regard to Eastern trade vis-a-vis other English merchants;

2) Execution of plans to oust rival mercantile interests from the eastern theatre;

3) Securing special and exclusive privileges for itself from the Oriental governments in order to receive goods from the buying-countries at the least possible expense.

Of these three principles, the last two will be discussed in subsequent chapters. In the following it will be examined how the Company fared in England.

While from 1601 the East India Company embarked upon a prosperous career in eastern trade, basking in the favour of the monarchy in the form of a royal charter, opinions were getting stronger in England against royal monopolies. Those merchant-manufacturers who could not secure admission to the privileged ranks of the export companies (which, incidentally, always remained their ruling ambition) came into acute conflict with the trading monopolies which limited their market and depressed the price at which they could effect a sale.

In this situation, the East India Company soon became the greatest eye-sore to them, for it was the most important foreign-trading company in England. At the beginning, all those merchants who had joined together to promote trade with India were not sure of its outcome. So, until 1612, the Company did not function as a joint-stock company. Only those "subscribers who had paid were invited to take upon themselves the expense of the voyage, and, as they sustained the whole of the risk, to reap the whole of the profit."[36] For a company in its infancy and facing formidable opposition from the Portuguese and the Dutch in Eastern Waters, the initial ventures did not pay badly. A summary of the results of the separate voyages which came to an end with the first terminable joint-stock of 1613–16 shows that from 1601 to 1612 twenty-six large ships sailed for the East, representing a total investment of £ 466,179, of which £ 138,127 was exported in money and £ 62,413 in goods; the remainder being consumed by working expenses. The average profit for the period, allowing for losses by delay in winding up, was about 20 per cent per annum.[37] How big this profit was per voyage undertaken would be evident from the fact that during 1603 and 1613 eight voyages were carried out, of which that in 1607 fetched nothing as the vessels were lost; but the remaining seven voyages were so prosperous that the clear profits were "hardly ever below 100 per cent, being in general more than 200 on the capital of the voyage."[38]

And how were such immense profits made? Here one gets a glimpse of the essential basis of foreign trade of these merchant bourgeoisie, in which there was but a very small gap between legitimate commerce and piracy. Commenting on these eight expeditions of the Company, Murray, who, like others, did not show any less admiration for the integrity of British character in relation to the Company's European rivals in eastern trade, or in its dealings with the Indian rulers, noted[39]:

"The Company had now sent eight expeditions, the result of which was judged on the whole to be extremely advantageous. Leaving out of the account the unfortunate voyage of Sharpey, they had derived an average profit of not less than 171 per cent. Mr. Mill hence draws the natural inference, that these had been conducted in a manner decidedly more judicious than subsequent adventures that yielded a very different return. Yet we cannot forbear observing, that many of the cargoes were made up on such very easy terms as their successors could not expect to command. Independently of the fact that whole fleets were sometimes laden with captured goods, trade was often carried on by compulsory means, calculated to ensure a profitable return only to the stronger party. These first voyages, in short, exhibit the profits of trade combined with the produce the piracy."

Thus, in the first ventures of the Company piracy played a considerable part. In subsequent years its role had to diminish in importance because of the sharp contest between European Powers over the eastern trade, and because of the growing resistance of the Asian peoples to such vandalism, who could obtain some redress until political power over them was fully usurped by the Colonial Powers. As it will be seen in Chapter 5, after the East India Company became the ruler of India, the mask of honourable trade was torn off and there remained no difference between commerce and open plunder.

However, to go back to the first phase of the Company's trade, from the beginning the East India Company was coming out as the most important of all chartered companies in England. It was the only one among many concerns which was exploiting the capital and manufactures of the country. So the other subscribers of the company who had so far held back from its ventures came together to form the first joint-stock company for the period 1613–16. The total amount put forward was £ 429,000, which made a total profit of 87½ per cent.[40] The second joint-stock of 1617–32 raised a capital of £ 1,629,000, and promised a satisfactory return.[41] In 1617, the Company made a profit of £ 1,000,000 on a capital of £ 200,000.[42] Evidently, the East India Company had become the most important joint-stock company in England. In the seventeenth century, it "averaged a rate of profit of about 100 per cent."[43]

And while thus reaping great fortunes, the small clique of the Company's shareholders endeavoured to maintain their privileged position by proclaiming how the Company was serving the interests of the British nation. Mill wrote:[44]

"Of the sort of views held out at this period to excite the favour of the nation towards the East India Company, a specimen has come down to us of considerable value. Sir Josiah Child, an eminent member of the body of Directors, in his celebrated Discourses on Trade, written in 1665, and published in 1667, represents the trade to India as the most beneficial branch of English commerce; and in proof of this opinion he asserts, that it employs from twenty-five to thirty sail of the most warlike mercantile ships of the kingdom, manned with mariners from 60 to 100 each; that it supplies the kingdom with saltpetre, which would otherwise cost the nation an immense sum to the Dutch; with pepper, indigo, calicoes, and drugs, to the value of 150,000 *l.* or 180,000 *l.* yearly, for which it would otherwise pay to the same people an exorbitant price; with materials for export to Turkey, France, Spain, Italy, and Guinea, to the amount of 200,000 *l.* or 300,000 *l.* yearly, countries with which, if the nation were deprived of these commodities, a profitable trade could not be carried on."

Naturally, the *have-not* merchant-manufacturers of England were not particularly pleased with such "services" rendered by the East India Company to the nation. They, therefore, conducted a vigorous campaign against the monopolist companies. But the influence of the monarchy was on the side of the "great whale," or the big chartered companies; for, with them the monarchy was closely affiliated. Consequently, little was done immediately to give the little fishes greater freedom of movement.

This, however, did not mean smooth sailing for the big companies. The practice of the Stuarts of selling monopolies was increasing on a large scale. The practice had originated with the last Tudor monarch, Queen Elizabeth, who bestowed valuable patents even upon servants of the Queen's household and upon clerks in lieu of salaries. But, "what his predecessor had started as an occasional expedient James I developed into a regular system," in order to "replenish a treasury depleted by the rising expenditures due to the price-revolution."[45] And this system, while furthering royal prerogatives in foreign trade and thus in principle supporting the aims of the merchant-monopolies, led to temporary but quite serious inconvenience to the big monopolist companies.

With their characteristic policy of appeasing royalty and proclaiming the nation how they served the interests of England, the big trading bodies of course maintained their privileges, and the East India Company even further fortified its position in this period, but they had also to suffer temporary set-backs.

Thus, at the very beginning of the reign of James I,

"In 1604, the Company were alarmed by a license, in violation of their charter, granted to Sir Edward Michelborne and others, to trade to 'Cathaia, China, Japan, Corea, and Cambaya, etc.' The injury was compensated in 1609, when the facility and indiscretion of King James encouraged the Company to aim at a removal of those restrictions which the more cautious policy of Elizabeth had imposed. They obtained a renewal of their charter, confirming all their preceding privileges, and constituting them a body corporate, not for fifteen years, or any other limited time, but for ever; still, however, providing that, on experience of injury to the nation, their exclusive privileges should, after three years' notice, cease and expire."[46]

And, at the close of the reign of the same monarch,

"In 1624, the Company applied by petition, to the King, for authority to punish his servants abroad, by martial as well as municipal laws. It appears not that any difficulty was experienced in obtaining their request; or that any parliamentary proceeding for transferring unlimited power over the lives and fortunes of the citizens, was deemed even a necessary ceremony. This ought to be regarded as an era in the history of the Company."[47]

Another set-back to the Company, however, came during the rule of the next monarch, when "Charles I was even so foolish as to annoy the East India Company by sanctioning a rival company from which he was to receive a share of the profits; while persons so anciently privileged as the Merchant Adventurers remembered that they had recently had to distribute some £70,000 in bribes in order to win a new charter."[48] This time also the Company, like the Merchant Adventurers, was able to regain its position; the King giving his consent in 1639 "to withdraw the license granted to those rivals"[49] in 1635, which however was not put into effect before 1650.

In these manoeuvres of the East India Company and other such foremost trading bodies of England to resolve the difficulties created by royalty and for further fortification of their positions by the favour of the same agency, bribery evidently remained one of their chief weapons. As will be shown later in greater detail, up to the reign of Charles I, the yearly expenditure of the East India Company on this account, in order to appease the King and other "great men" of England, went up to £ 1,200. Moreover, how the Company had to pay in other ways for royal favours was illustrated during the reign of Charles I, whose grant of license to the Courten's Association for trading in the East created such difficulties to the Company.

> "The King having resolved to draw the sword for terminating the disputes between him and his people; and finding himself destitute of money; fixed his eyes, as the most convenient mass of property within his reach, on the magazines of the East India Company. A price being named, which was probably a high one, he bought upon credit the whole of their pepper (for a total sum of £ 63,283–11 s.–1 d.–RKM), and sold it again at a lower price (for a total sum of £ 50,626–17 s.–1 d.–RKM) for ready money. Bonds, four in number, one of which was promised to be paid every six months, were given by the farmers of the customs and Lord Cottington for the amount; of which only a small portion seems ever to have been paid. On a pressing application, about the beginning of the year 1642, it was stated, that 13,000 *l.* had been allowed them out of the duties they owed; the remainder the farmers declared it to be out of their power to advance. A prayer was presented that the customs, now due by them, amounting to 12,000 *l.*, might be applied in liquidation of the debt; but for this they were afterwards pressed by the parliament. The King exerted himself to protect the parties who stood responsible for him; and what the Company were obliged to pay to the parliament, or what they succeeded in getting from the King or his sureties, nowhere appears."[50]

While, like other big trading bodies of England, the East India Company was thus sheltering behind royalty, and by paying substantial sums was further fortifying its position, the attack of the *have-not* merchant-manufacturers came from another direction. The power in England was then shifting from absolute monarchy to Parliament, which was run in an increasing measure by the upper classes in the towns and the landowners. In this situation the fight of the deprived section of the English merchant bourgeoisie took the parliamentary form of dissolution of all royal monopolies. The fight developed with mounting virulence, for the "antipathy to particular restrictions, damaging to a sectional interest, became transformed into a general movement against monopoly."[51]

The opposition to monopolies waged its first Parliamentary battle in 1601, and the fight was resumed in 1604, when a Bill was introduced to abolish all privileges in foreign trade. It was suggested that foreign trading companies should be open to all persons on payment of a moderate entrance fee. In supporting this Bill, Sir Edwin Sandys declared that "merchandise being the chiefest and richest of all other and of greater extent and importance than all the rest, it is against the natural right and liberty of the subjects of England to restrain it into the hands of some few."[52] The brunt of the attack was against the privileged "200 families" which were already an entity in Stuart times, for, the speaker added, "governors of these companies by their monopolizing orders have so handled the matter as that the mass of the whole trade of the realm is in the hands of some 200 persons at the most, the rest serving for a show and reaping small benefit."[53] Since foreign trade was virtually monopolized by the London merchants, their provincial colleagues were very vocal in their complaints. The Newcastle traders, for instance, "fought a long and partly successful battle with the Merchant Adventurers, claiming prior rights granted to their own Merchant Gild in the Middle Ages, and the merchants of Bristol and the West Country ports strongly opposed the attempt of London to monopolise the Spanish and French trade, which, in 1604, was declared open to all Englishmen."[54]

Later also, after some intermittent skirmishing, the opposition returned to the attack with a general anti-monopoly Act in 1624. And, then, "together with its denial of the right of arbitrary taxation and imprisonment, the challenge by Parliament to royal grants of economic privilege and monopoly can be said to have formed the central issue in the outbreak of the seventeenth century revolution."[55]

A few years afterwards, in the sphere of foreign trade, not only did the Navigation Act of 1651 give a powerful stimulus to English commerce and English shipping, but the privileges of the monopolist companies were somewhat reduced. According to this Act, it was prohibited to import into England, Ireland, and the colonies goods from Asia, Africa and America unless in ships owned by Englishmen, Irishmen or colonists, and manned by crews of whom more than half were English, Irish or colonial. Also, by the Navigation Act of 1650, it was earlier declared that none but English ships could lawfully be found in any colonial port. Even Williamson, who appears to be strongly on the side of monarchy, noted: "This was the first step in establishing a parliamentary code in supersession of the royal prerogative and its regulations."[56]

Naturally, the monopolist companies faced grave difficulties under the circumstances. As the complaints of the chartered companies, fattening on the Royal Charters, to the Crown after 1660 witness, it was a period when interlopers thrived and obtained important concessions. How this affected the East India Company will be discussed later, but it is worthy of note here that when at the conclusion of the Dutch War (1654) all concerned looked to Cromwell to reorganize the East Indian trade, for a period of three years during the Protectorate the East Indies trade was actually free and open, to the delight of the enemies of the chartered companies. Even when, under the threats from the East India Company to sell all its forts and stations in India, the charter of the Company was renewed in 1657, this renewal was on the basis of a compromise between competing interests. And, "There is some evidence that the net result of such relaxation of monopoly was that trade expanded and export-prices and the profits of the foreign trading companies fell."[57]

Some of these social and political changes of course disappeared with the Commonwealth, but surely not all of them; and there cannot be any doubt that the Restoration was not at all a simple return to the *status quo ante*, as some historians would like the world to believe. As it has been remarked:[58]

"... the Restoration of 1660 was in effect a re-combination of class forces to establish a government more in harmony with the real distribution of strength. It was less a restoration of the monarchy than a new compromise between the landowners and the upper classes in the towns."

Politically, the royal prerogative had suffered a mortal blow. The control of trade and finance, of judiciary and the army were henceforth in the hands of Parliament. "The field of industry was no longer encumbered by royal grants of monopoly; and, except for the East India Company, the exclusive privileges of the foreign-trading companies had been too much undermined for these bodies to regain their former position."[59] Shortly afterwards, by an Act of 1688, trade was thrown open and former monopoly-rights abolished, "except in the spheres of the Levant, Russia, Africa and Eastland Companies."[60] One of the effects of this was a big expansion of the trade of other English ports relatively to London.

The East India Company is thus seen to have maintained its privileges during this turbulent period, and was probably on the most secure ground of all such big monopolies. But it had to pay a heavier price for its existence and privileges. For instance, just after the Restoration, the Directors of the Company "greeted Charles II with an address of loyalty and a present of plate," and the king, in return, "granted them a favourable charter and availed himself of their practical goodwill by accepting loans amounting to £ 170,000 in the space of sixteen years."[61]

Although the East India Company had thus to pay an immense price, it enjoyed some amount of stability during the reign of Charles II and his brother. The charter of 1661 confirmed to the Company "the privileges accorded by previous grants, and gave additional rights of jurisdiction over all Englishmen in the east and power to maintain fortifications and to raise troops for their defence."[62] In short, the Company was now equipped with political and military powers to have its way much more smoothly for profit-hunting than before.

The paid-up capital "with which the Company began the new era totalled £ 370,000."[63] This "became a permanent joint-stock upon which the Directors could operate with greater confidence than in the old days of terminable joint-stocks," and they "increased their resources by limitation of dividends in the first years and also by acting as bankers, accepting deposits repayable at short notice and on low rates of interest."[64] How rapidly the Company prospered at this time when they were extending their influence in India and were also enjoying some amount of tranquillity at home was revealed in 1683 when a test case was brought to determine whether the king could grant royal monopolies outside the realm, with special reference to the East India Company's monopoly in Asia. This case has a little history.

While after the Restoration the shareholders of the Company as a body leaned to the Court and their Royal patrons, under the leadership of Sir Josiah Child who was made the Governor of the Company, the Deputy-Governor, Thomas Papillon, was against such arrangement. It has been said that Child was a monarchist, while Papillon was almost a republican.[65] Whether that is true or not, it appears that while "the former saw that the charter was as safe as the throne, the latter envisaged the overthrow of both"[66] or the aligning of the Company more towards the favour of Parliament than that of the King. Therefore, the minority of shareholders in the Company, under the leadership of Papillon, asked for the inclusion of the unprivileged merchants into the Company. The majority however stood firm for the maintenance of the vested interest. The minority in the end sold their stock, and withdrew from the Company. Papillon, since he was the ring-leader of the rebels, was not allowed to retire unscathed. His enemies prosecuted him as an "exclusionist,"[67] which incidentally reveals the real character of these chartered companies of merchant capital in the seventeenth century. The case came before the Lord Chief Justice Jeffreys who was an ardent monarchist. He naturally found in favour of the Crown, and the Company's exclusive rights. Papillon was fined £ 10,000 for sedition, and he fled overseas.[68]

The verdict was very pleasing to the Company's present shareholders;—"a small clique of about forty persons closely connected with the Court."[69] As compared with the capital of £ 30,133–6 s.–8 d. of the first association formed in 1599, or that of £ 68,373 as the sum advanced in 1600 when the Company was properly founded and received its first royal charter,[70] a few years previously the stock of the Company "was valued at £ 1,700,000, on which the dividends averaged 22 per cent."[71] Now, Jeffrey's verdict guaranteed their further future profits. Indeed, everything came up to expectations. During the whole period of 1657–1691, "the average annual dividend was about 25 per cent."[72] The stock reached the highest price in 1683, "when a £ 100 share fetched £ 500 in the market."[73]

The conflict between the privileged and deprived merchants at home, however, was not yet resolved. Although the Company's monopoly was re-established, it was not as comfortable as could be desired by the narrow interest of its shareholders. England was then flourishing from her foreign trade. As Mill wrote:[74]

> "Sir William Petty, who wrote his celebrated work, entitled 'Political Arithmetic', in 1676, says: '1. The streets of London showed that city to be double what it was forty years before; great increase was also manifested at Newcastle, Yarmouth, Norwich, Exeter, Portsmouth, and Cowes; and in Ireland, at Dublin, Kingsale, Coleraine, and Londonderry. 2. With respect to shipping, the navy was triple or quadruple what it was at that time; the shipping of Newcastle was 80,000 tons, and could not then have exceeded a quarter of that amount. 3. The number and splendour of coaches, equipages, and furniture, had much increased since that period. 4. The postage of letters had increased from one to twenty. 5. The king's revenue had tripled itself.'"

Hence, the English merchants who were deprived of holding shares in the Company continued to trade in Asia on their own. These people from earlier times called themselves "Free Merchants," while the shareholders of the Company dubbed them as Interlopers.

It would be of interest here to discuss briefly how the Interlopers acted in the trading countries and vis-a-vis the East India Company, in particular; and how they created conditions whereby the Company was ultimately forced to come to a compromise with them.

3. Interlopers

In fact, from the start of the East India Company, those merchants who wanted but could not get into the "favoured ring" took the field as "Free Merchants." At first, they made attempts to obtain sanctions from the English monarchs for trading in eastern seas, for in the pre-Reformation days Royal prerogative was a factor which could hardly be ignored directly. The monarchs, however, as stated before, in return for suitable presents or in lieu of some service rendered to them by these merchants, were not ill-disposed to grant the desired favour, provided by that they did not make the chartered companies too angry. Also it is not improbable to think that this might have been another method the monarchs sometimes adopted to extort more money, in forms of "loans," etc., from the chartered companies by promising them to withdraw the "undue" favour bestowed on the "Interlopers." Thus, as mentioned earlier, James I licensed at least one English, and one Scotch courtier, to make independent voyages of their own in the eastern seas, which obviously went against the interests of the East India Company, and so it had to make "efforts" to get rid of such nuisances.

It has been said that the behaviour of the English Interlopers in the eastern seas was so atrocious that James thus imperilled the whole credit of his countrymen in the eyes of the Asiatics. For instance, the first interloper Sir Edward Michaelbourne, a member of James' Court, was also one of the original members of the East India Company, but he was expelled from it for non-payment of his venture in the first expedition. In 1604, as stated before, Michaelborne obtained from James a license to make an independent voyage in violation of the royal charter, and for two years he cruised in the eastern archipelago, doing very little trade but robbing any ship which came in his way. His victims included Dutch and Chinese merchants, and he thoroughly compromised the position of his fellow-countrymen in the islands. He returned in 1606, and died not long afterwards, the Company never obtaining any redress for the damages he had done to their interests, except that it made its position much stronger in 1609, as noted before. Whether Michaelborne acted with prudence or not, it will be evident from the following chapters that the Company itself was also not unskilled in resorting to every possible trick, the very meanest in many cases, to uphold or to further spread its influence in Eastern Waters. So the argument of the peculiar behaviour of the Interlopers does not appear to hold much water. And, in any case, James' example was followed by Charles I. He, being in constant need of money, instigated the formation of the rival association of Sir William Courten, whereby the East India Company fell into a state of disorganization wherefrom it was fully restored as late as in 1657.

Moreover, when the "Free Merchants" did not, or could not, secure a sanction from the monarch, they took direct initiative in interloping trade, for which conditions were being created with the gradual weakening of royal prerogatives, and which became particularly manifest with the establishment of the Commonwealth. Since the time of Charles II, this was not at all a risky undertaking, for, as a result of constant pressure from the *have-not* merchants of England, the East India Company was forced to admit the "Free Merchants" into port to port trade in the eastern seas as well as in the inland trade in India. In no case, however, did they allow the Interlopers to indulge in trading between the Orient and Europe. This remained their exclusive source of profit-hunting.

Such was the background when Samuel White came into the picture as perhaps the most remarkable of these Interlopers. A short account of White's activities in the eastern seas would not be out of place here to indicate how the East India Company fared both at home and in the East at the hands of its own compatriots.[75] As it will be seen from the following, all of them—the Company, its officials and their compatriots, the "Free Merchants"—were guided only by the lust for loot from the East.

Samuel White began his life as an employee of the East India Company. The trade at that time consisted mainly in the buying of cotton-goods in India, for cash or in exchange for English manufactures, but there also existed another trade, known as the country trade. This comprised of exchanging commodities between the various countries inside Asia. The East India Company was not directly interested in that trade, which was carried on by the local inhabitants and the Interlopers. But, "the employees of the Company were allowed to engage in it for their private profit in a half-open partnership with the Interlopers."[76] The Company connived at it (in fact, was indirectly interested in it as it will be seen in Chapter 5, when dealing with the internal trade of Bengal after the Company came to power), for the salary it offered to its employees was much too meagre to lure them to go abroad without the possibilities of making fortunes by means of internal trade. The internal trade was thus an indirect source of income to the Company, and thus "there existed a good deal of give and take between the East India Company and the Free Merchants,"[77] which the former could not help in the declining phase of monopoly privileges granted by royalty. The *de facto* arrangement was that as long as the Interlopers confined themselves to the local trade and made no attempt to compete in the London market, or "embarrass" the regular trade of the Company by agreements with Asian rulers contrary to the interests of the Company, or with rival European merchants, the activities of the "Free Merchants," though not officially recognised, were winked at.

This was the world, and these were the possibilities, to which Samuel White had arrived in Madras in 1676. His salary was "£ 10 a year, with the prospect later of promotion and private trade,"[78] provided White kept to the easy way. But, instead of keeping his safe job, White joined his brother George who was established as a Free Merchant at Ayudhya, the capital of Siam. In 1677 White was appointed by the King of Siam as Captain of one of the king's ships plying between Mergui and Masulipatam on the Indian border; and henceforth for six years he sailed back and forth across the Bay of Bengal, delivering the royal cargo—elephants—, and trading on his own account.

Meanwhile, the King of Siam looked more favourably to the French to fortify his position against other Asiatic kingdoms as well as the Europeans (particularly Dutch encroachments which were then a serious matter in this area), and decided to take the first step with the help of the English Interlopers in the Siamese service. Accordingly,

"White was sent for in 1683, created Mandarin and made Shabandar of Mergui, an appointment which combined the duties of a Superintendent of Trade and a Commissioner of Maritime Affairs."[79] He was instructed "to fortify Mergui and get together a fleet of armed merchantmen so that when the French arrived Mergui would already be a port of the first importance on the Canton-Masulipatam trade-route, a base where the French ships could anchor and from which with their assistance Siam could dominate the Bay of Bengal."[80]

The Siamese plan was, no doubt, a direct threat to the English East India Company, for it was the English Company's ships which commanded the Bay of Bengal and its approaches. But, just as the governing desire of the merchant bourgeoisie as a social category was to amass wealth from cleverly-secured trading privileges, the attitude of White was to make a quick fortune by hook or crook. Likewise, just as the patriotism of the merchant bourgeoisie did not go far enough to help in rapidly industrialising their own country, so the Englishman White did not care the very least whether the French or the English were going to be the supreme power in the East so long as his personal loot was assured. All of them belonged to the same category of decadent merchant bourgeoisie which had already spent its force, and their actions were motivated mainly, or only, by self-interest. Hence, White's behaviour in working for the King of Siam against the interest of the East India Company may not be regarded either as exceptional or unnatural. It was in the nature of things outlined in the previous chapter.

Following his line of conduct, "as soon as some of the armed ships which he was authorised to build or purchase were available," White "placed them under the command of English interloper captains and, declaring an unprovoked war on Burma and Golconda, an Indian kingdom independent of the Mughal, without the knowledge or sanction of the Siamese Government, proceeded to seize all ships belonging to those states which were encountered in the Bay of Bengal."[81] Afterwards, "manning the prizes with his own crews, he sent them to ports in Sumatra or the Persian Gulf, where their cargoes were sold as his private property!"[82]

In this way, White preyed on Asian shipping for two years; and this "enabled him to remit home £ 15,740 and to keep by him a trading capital in cash and jewels of a like amount, a total of which nowadays would be equivalent to at least £ 150,000."[83] Moreover, "besides this commerce with other people's property, he made very free with the money granted to him by the Siamese treasury, for he embezzled the entire sum allotted for the fortification of Mergui and, by maintaining a garrison which only existed on paper, was able on pay-day to credit himself with their wages."[84]

Such a happy state of affairs, however, did not last very long. The East India Company finally decided to remove White from the scene, for he was now associated with the French policy of the Siamese Government and thus the interest of the English Company, as opposed to the interests of the Asian traders, was at stake. If the French established themselves at Mergui, which was placed immediately opposite Madras and on the route to the Far East, the whole position of the Company would be in danger. Hence the Directors of the Company procured from King James II, who was incidentally a large share-holder of the Company,[85] an order recalling White from service with the Siamese king.

White was now in a difficult situation. The people of Mergui were very much against him, being incensed by his high-handed policy which never looked after their interest; in the capital of Siam, Ayudhya, also White would not feel secure because the whole administration was in disintegration, as a result of corruption and intrigues, and there were strong currents against him; and to go to Madras with the person who had come on behalf of the Company to escort him back would be certain ruin and possibly death on a charge of piracy or treason. On the other hand, to fight the representative of the Company would be a capital offence, for which, if he escaped afterwards to England, he could be arrested and tried. So, taking all these points into consideration, White sailed in 1687 in his own ship towards Madras, escorted by the ship of the Company which came to fetch him; but one day managed to slip away from the escort and sail for England with all his treasures. He arrived in England long before any news of his recent doings at Mergui had reached the Directors of the Company. At Mergui in order to remove the Company's escort, his last escapade was to tell the Siamese Council that the escort Weldon "had come to seize their town," which so incensed the Siamese that they attacked the entire community of English Interlopers (White managed to escape with Weldon as escort) and "some eighty Englishmen were killed."[86]

When White arrived in England, James II had just fled the realm, and William had come to the throne. The time was very favourable to White and all other Interlopers, for the Revolution of 1688–89 was the precursor of misfortune for the shareholders of the East India Company who were previously established in a stable position by the notorious Judge Jeffreys as described earlier. The Bill of Rights, under which William and Mary took the throne, "although effecting little theoretical curtailment of the royal prerogative, practically made parliament the arbiter in all questions of national importance;" and, consequently, "monopolies based solely on royal grants, whilst not absolutely more illegal than before, were thus rendered subject to reversal by legislation."[87] In this mood of Parliament against royal monopolies, White saw his chance. He decided to anticipate "any charges which the Company might subsequently bring by himself sueing them for damages to the extent of £ 40,000."[88] But before the case came up, he died suddenly in 1689.

4. Company Re-constituted

White might have died, but the other "Free Merchants" did not wish to miss this chance. Like White, they were quick to perceive that their time had come. So, with Thomas Papillon, who had in the meantime returned from abroad, at their head, they subscribed a fund, formed themselves into a society, and petitioned the Parliament in 1690 to throw open the Indian trade. A general election and the pressing business of the French war delayed their success. Sir Josiah Child, the Governor of the East India Company, also fought stiffly to the last. The Company spent nearly £ 90,000 in bribes in a single year to maintain its exclusive rights in the eastern seas. Bribing royalty and the "great men" of England was an usual practice with the Company, and it had by now increased to a colossal dimension. This was noted by Mill as follows[89]:

> "The Company meanwhile did not neglect the usual corrupt methods of obtaining favours at home. It appeared that they had distributed large sums of money to men in power, before obtaining their charter. The House of Commons were, at the present period, disposed to inquire into such transactions. They ordered the books of the Company to be examined; where it appeared that it had been the practice, and even habit of the Company, to give bribes to great men; that, previous to the revolution, their annual expense, under that head, had scarcely ever exceeded 1,200 *l.*; that since the revolution it had gradually increased; and that in the year 1693, it had amounted to nearly 90,000 *l.* The Duke of Leeds, who was charged with having received a bribe of 5000 *l.*, was impeached by the Commons. But the principal witness against him was sent out of the way, and it was not till nine days after it was demanded by the Lords that a proclamation was issued to stop his flight. Great men were concerned in smothering the inquiry; parliament was prorogued; and the scene was here permitted to close."

The virtuous king also had his share in the spoils; probably the highest individual share,—"10,000 *l.* is said to have been traced to the king."[90]

But the trend of events was now against the small clique of shareholders of the Company depending on royal prerogative rather than on statutory law. The upshot was that the agitation against the Company, of which White's petition to the Parliament was a part, culminated in a resolution of the House of Commons in 1694 that "it was the right of all Englishmen to trade to the East Indies, or any part of the world, unless prohibited by act of parliament."[91] Thus, the rule of Parliament was established over that of royalty.

The trade now being thrown open, the Interlopers founded a rival company. The Old Company again resorted to its cardinal policy of bribing, but here also it was superseded by the rivals!

> "In the year 1698, both parties were urging their pretensions with the greatest possible zeal, when the necessities of the government pointed out to both the project of bribing it by the accommodation of money. The Company offered to lend to government 700,000 *l.* at 4 per cent. interest, provided their charter should be confirmed, and the monopoly of India secured to them by

act of parliament. Their rivals, knowing on how effectual an expedient they had fallen, resolved to augment the temptation. They offered to advance 2,000,000 *l* at 8 per cent., provided they should be invested with the monopoly, free from obligation of trading on a joint-stock, except as they themselves should afterwards desire."[92]

Needless to say, the Interlopers' much bigger offer was readily accepted by the parliament, and in July 1698 Papillon and his followers obtained an Act of Parliament recognizing them as the New or English East India Company in contradistinction to the Old or London Corporation. The grant was contingent upon the New Company lending £ 2,000,000 to the government at 8 per cent. All subscribers to the loan were to enjoy a proportionate share in the Indian trade, with liberty to organize themselves for that purpose in any way they thought fit. William confirmed the Act and gave three years' formal notice to the Old Company of the termination of its privileges.[93]

Still, the Old Company did not accept defeat. If the New Company was strong at home, it was none the less firmly entrenched in the East. It had many factories, a loyal staff—fattening on inland trade and other legal or semi-legal and even illegal operations, and nearly a century's experience. Moreover, by a clever manipulation, the Old Company made inroads into the New Company. Shortly after the publication of the Act of Parliament stated above:

"The subscription books for the two million loan were opened and in three days the great amount was underwritten. Among the entries appeared the name of John du Bois, for the sum of £ 315,000, nearly one-sixth of the whole. John du Bois was the secretary of the Old Company."[94]

Thus, even under the New Act, the Old Company stood to gain almost as much as they were losing by the dissolution of its charter. For it could henceforth trade in whichever way it wished up to the extent of its new holding. The Directors of the Old Company, therefore, decided to outrival the New Company in the latter's ability to establish factories, to "attract" trade, to "negotiate" with Eastern Courts, and to accumulate the necessary "prestige" in a new land. How utterly incredible it appeared to the masters of the Old Company that merchant capital can prosper without monopoly privileges would be evident from what the Directors of the Old Company wrote to the Company's representatives abroad when the New Company had begun to function.

"In the instructions to their servants abroad they represented the late measures of parliament as rather the result of the power of a particular party than the fruit of legislative wisdom: 'The Interlopers,' so they called the New Company, 'had prevailed by their offer of having the trade free, and not on a joint-stock;' but they were resolved by large equipments (if their servants would only second their endeavours) to frustrate the speculations of those opponents: 'Two East India Companies in England,' these are their own words, 'could no more subsist without destroying one the other, than two kings, at the same time regnant in the same kingdom: that now a civil battle was to be fought between the Old and the New Company; and that two or three years must end this war, as the Old or the New must give way; that, being veterans, if their servants abroad would do their duty, they did not doubt of the victory; that if the world laughed at the pains the two Companies took to ruin each other, they could not help it, as they were on good ground and had a charter.'"[95]

The New Company also realized its shortcomings, and came to the conclusion that a fusion of interests with the Old Company was the best solution for the English merchant bourgeoisie as a whole. It, therefore, proposed a fusion, but did not receive a warm response. Having no other course left to it, the New Company "sent out presidents, factors and clerks to India with orders to open business at all places where the Old Company was already established;" but "its untrained servants had little success in face of their rivals' long-standing hold upon the country."[96] Moreover, in "diplomacy" the New Company met with its heaviest defeat. Williamson noted: "Sir William Norris, whom it sent as ambassador to Aurangzeb, made himself ridiculous by his pretensions and his ignorance of the Mogul court, and narrowly escaped being murdered whilst making a retirement which resembled a flight!"[97]

No doubt, on all sides the Old Company was foiling the New, but at ruinous cost to both. Thus, internal tension within the English merchant bourgeoisie was in no way serving the interests of the group as a whole. Evidently, amalgamation was the only remedy, and this both the companies realized. But now the terms of the union became the struggle between the Old and the New. The upshot was:

"Both sides looked to parliamentary influence to carry the day, and in the general election of 1700—01 the din of the rival arguments eclipsed all questions of general politics. Bribes flowed like water, and the eighteenth-century system of borough-mongering was said to have taken shape from the electioneering methods of the East India Companies."[98]

Finally, in 1702, "by the Instrument of Union of that year the financial issues were adjusted, the Old Company received seven years' grace in which to wind up its affairs, and thereafter the two bodies were to merge into The United Company of Merchants of England trading to the East Indies."[99]

The tension between the *have* and the most vocal *have-not* merchants of England thus came to a satisfactory end, and the newly organized East India Company began to represent more broadly the interests of British Merchant Capital. This is why Marx wrote about the East India Company:[100]

"The true commencement of the East India Company cannot be dated from a more remote epoch than the year 1702, when the different societies, claiming the monopoly of the East India Trade, united together in one single company. Till then, the very existence of the original East India Company was repeatedly endangered, once suspended for years under the protectorate of Cromwell, and once threatened with utter dissolution by Parliamentary interference under the reign of William III. It was under the ascendency of that Dutch Prince when the Whigs became the farmers of the revenues of the British Empire, when the Bank of England sprung into life, when the protective system was formally established in England, and the Balance of Power in Europe was definitely settled, that the existence of an East India Company was recognised by Parliament. That era of apparent liberty was in reality the era of monopolies, not created by Royal Grants, as in the times of Elizabeth and Charles I, but authorized by the sanction of Parliament. This epoch in the history of England bears, in fact, an extreme likeness to the epoch of Louis Phillippe in France, the old landed aristocracy having been defeated, and the bourgeoisie not being able to take its place except under the banner of *moneyocracy* or the '*haute finance*.' The East India Company excluded them from parliamentary representation. In this. as well as other instances, we find the first decisive victory of the *bourgeoisie* over the feudal aristocracy, coinciding with the most pronounced reaction against the people, a phenomenon which has driven more than one popular writer, like Cobbett, to look for popular liberty rather in the past than in the future."

The East India Company of Britain is thus seen to have been born at the beginning of the seventeenth century, by which time merchant capital in England and in Europe had already passed beyond its initial progressive stage; and it is also seen that the final consolidation of the Company, effected by the amalgamation of its old and new variants at the beginning of the eighteenth century, coincided "with the most pronounced reaction against the people." Such was the character of the East India Company from the very beginning.

Notes and References

1 Murray, Hugh—*History of British India*, T. Nelson and Sons, London, 1860, p. 42.
2 *ibid.*, p. 46
3 Morton, A. L.—*A People's History of England*, Lawrence & Wishart, London, 1951, pp. 161—162.
4 *loc. cit.* 1, pp. 46—47
5 Tawney, R. H.—*Religion and the Rise of Capitalism*, Pelican Books, England, 1948, pp. 77—78.
6 *ibid.*, pp. 78—79
7 *loc cit.* 3, p. 162
8 *ibid.*, pp. 162—163
9 Mill, James—*The History of British India*, James Madden, London, 1858, Vol. I, p. 3.
10 *loc. cit.* 3, p. 162
11 loc. cit. 9, i, p. 3
12 *loc. cit.* 3, p. 163
13 See, for instance, Konstantin Iljitsch Kumins *Hinter drei Meeren*, Verlag Neues Leben, Berlin, 1952.
14 Quoted by R. C. Majumdar, H. C. Raychaudhuri and Kalikinkar Datta in *An Advanced History of India*, Macmillan and Co., London, 1953, p. 633.
15 Majumdar, R. C.; Raychaudhuri, H. C.: Datta, Kalikinkar—*An Advanced History of India*, Macmillan, London, 1953, p. 634.
16 loc. cit. 9, i, p. 4
17 *ibid.*, i, p. 5
18 *ibid.*, i, p. 5
19 Collis, Maurice—*British Merchant Adventurers*, William Collins of London, 1942, p. 8.
20 *loc. cit.* 9, i, p. 12

21 *ibid.*, i, p. 13
22 *ibid.*, i, p. 13
23 *ibid.*, i, p. 13
24 *loc. cit.* 19, p. 15
25 *ibid.*, p. 12
26 Datta, Kalikinkar—*The Santhal Insurrection of 1855—57*, Calcutta, 1940, pp. 67—68; quoted by L. Natarajan *Peasant Uprisings in India: 1850—1900*, People's Publishing House, Bombay, 1953, p. 30.
27 *loc. cit.* 19, p. 15
28 *ibid.*, p. 15
29 *loc. cit.* 9, i, p. 14
30 *ibid.*, p. 15
31 *ibid.*, p. 15
32 *loc. cit.* 3, p. 211
33 *loc. cit.* 9, i, pp. 17—18
34 Quoted in *loc. cit.* 9, i, p. 16 from the *Minutes of a General Court of Adventurers*, preserved in the Indian Register Office: Bruce's *Annals of the East India Company*, i, p. 128.
36 *ibid.*, i, p. 18
37 Hunter, W. W.—*History of British India*, London, 1899—1900, Vol. I, p. 291.
38 *loc. cit.* 9, i, p. 20
39 *loc. cit.* 1, pp. 146—147
40 *loc. cit.* 9, i, pp. 22—23
41 Williamson, James A.—*A Short History of British Expansion: The Old Colonial Empire*, Macmillan and Co, Limited, London, 1951, p. 228.
42 Dobb, Maurice—*Studi.. in the Development of Capitalism*, George Routledge & Sons, Ltd., London, 1946, p. 192, n 1.
43 *ibid.*, p. 192
44 *loc. cit.* 9, i, pp. 76—77
45 *loc. cit.* 42, p. 165
46 *loc. cit.* 9, i, p. 20
47 *ibid.*, i, p. 41
48 *loc. cit.* 42, p. 167
49 *loc. cit.* 9, i, p. 53
50 *ibid.*, i, p. 51
51 *loc. cit.* 42, p. 165
52 *ibid.*, p. 168
53 *ibid.*, p. 168
54 *loc. cit.* 3, p. 209
55 *loc. cit.* 42, p. 168
56 *loc. cit.* 41, p. 246
57 *loc. cit.* 42, p. 175
58 *loc. cit.* 3, p. 274
59 *loc. cit.* 42, p. 176
60 *ibid.*, p. 176, n 1
61 *loc. cit.* 41, p. 304

62 *ibid.*, p. 304
63 *ibid.*, p. 304
64 *ibid.*, p. 304
65 *ibid.*, p. 310
66 *ibid.*, p. 310
67 *ibid.*, p. 310
68 *ibid.*, p. 310
69 *loc. cit.* 19, p. 23
70 *loc. cit.* 9, i, pp. 15, 18
71 *loc. cit.* 19, pp. 23—24
72 *loc. cit.* 41, p. 308
73 *ibid.*, p. 308
74 *loc. cit.* 9, i, p. 74, n 2
75 For details regarding Samuel White's career in the East, see, for instance, *loc. cit.* 19, pp. 23—29.
76 *loc. cit.* 19, p. 24
77 *ibid.*, p. 24
78 *ibid.*, p. 25
79 *ibid.*, p. 26
80 *ibid.*, p. 26
81 *ibid.*, p. 26
82 *ibid.*, p. 26
83 *ibid.*, p. 26
84 *ibid.*, p. 26
85 In the List of Adventurers in the East India Company for April, 1689, the following principalities were entered as shareholders: The King—£ 7,000; Sir Josiah Child—£ 51,000; Sir Thomas Cooke—£ 120,000; Sir Nathaniel Herne—£ 108,000. (cf. *The East India Trade in the XVIIth Century* by Shafaat Ahmad Khan, Oxford University Press, London, 1923, p. 173).
86 *loc. cit.* 18, p. 28
87 *loc. cit.* 41, p. 310
88 *loc. cit.* 19, p. 29
89 *loc. cit.* 9, i, p. 93
90 *ibid.*, i, p. 93, n 1
91 Quoted in *loc. cit.* 9, i, p. 92.
92 *loc. cit.* 9, i, pp. 94—95
93 *ibid.*, i, pp. 97—98
94 *loc. cit.* 41, p. 311
95 *loc. cit.* 9, i, p. 100
96 *loc. cit.* 41, p. 311
97 *ibid.*, p. 311
98 *ibid.*, p. 311
99 *ibid.*, p. 311
100 Marx, Karl—*The East India Company*, New York Daily Tribune, June 11, 1853.

CHAPTER 3

COMPANY AND ITS EUROPEAN RIVALS

Besides monopoly in the Home country, one of the other basic demands of merchant capital was that it must have full sway in the country with which trade was conducted. Although the renowned British historian James Mill accounted for this feature of merchant capital by professing ignorance of the science of political economy in those days, he noted[1]:

> "During that age, the principles of public wealth were very imperfectly understood, and hardly any trade was regarded as profitable but that which was exclusive. The different nations which traded to India, all traded by way of monopoly; and the several exclusive companies treated every proposal for a participation in their traffic, as a proposal for their ruin. In the same spirit, every nation which obtained admittance into any newly explored channel of commerce endeavoured to exclude from it all participators, and considered its own profits as depending on the absence of all competition."

India thus became the theatre of conflict between four European Powers, viz. Portuguese, Dutch, English and French. Public Power in their respective countries could serve the interest of the class in power, and so in their mother countries the exclusive position of the respective companies was assured by their monopoly rights. But over them there was no *supra-national power*. Hence, they had to fight among themselves in order to decide who would gain supreme control of the India Trade. Jungle Law prevailed; the stronger in a contest between any two of them could dictate its own terms, or, if possible, eat up the other.

Thus triangular contests developed in the seventeenth century over the eastern trade; contests between the Portuguese and the Dutch, the

Portuguese and the English, and the Dutch and the English, for they were the three main European Powers in the East in that century. Although the French had ventured into the East in the same century, in the beginning they could not make much headway. Therefore, the conflict between the English and the French, which outrivalled all other rivalries of the European Powers in the East, could not fully emerge before the middle of the eighteenth century.

A few other European nations were also interested in the Eastern trade; but they were interested only in small-scale and often "clandestine" trade, or they were not interested in India in particular, or they worked for British capital and thus did not represent any particular "national" interest other than that of the English Interlopers. Thus, the Danes came to India in 1616. But, not only "British capital played a large part in their operations," but "the Danes never had any pretensions to empire on a grand scale," and they were more engaged clandestinely in the private inland trade or otherwise.[2] A Swedish East India Company was also formed in 1731, but its trade was confined almost exclusively to China. Then there was the Ostend Company, organized by the merchants of Flanders and formally chartered in 1722; but it had a brief career in India. Moreover, as has been reported[3]:

> "In the 1770's and 1780's, Copenhagen, Ostend, and Lisbon became the centres of an Indian trade which was for the most part British in all but name."

Thus, besides the Portuguese and the Dutch, who had gained access to the Eastern trade prior to the English, the other mercantile force that the English East India Company had to reckon with in its designs over India was the French Company. In the following, therefore, the activities of the English East India Company in relation to these three European rivals will be discussed in the order of Portuguese first, the Dutch next, and lastly the French.

1. English-Portuguese Rivalry

Although the Portuguese arrived in India at the end of the fifteenth century, their commercial "mission" did not begin before the beginning of the sixteenth century. The real foundation of Portuguese Power in India was laid by Alfonso de Albuquerque, who "was the first European since Alexander the Great who dreamed of establishing an empire in India, or rather in Asia, governed from Europe."[4] Arriving in India in 1503, as commander of a squadron, he was appointed the Governor of Portuguese Affairs in India in 1509 because of his satisfactory naval activities. In 1510, he captured the port of Goa from the Bijapur Sultanate, and this port still remains the most important possession of the Portuguese in India. Some other ports also came into their hands, as noted in the previous chapter, and in the Mughal Court also they consolidated their position. So the Dutch and the English companies, in order to gain "concessions" from the Great Mughals for their trading activities in India, had to face this opposition.

The Portuguese influence however did not last long in India. From the beginning, the Indian rulers were not favourably disposed to them, although when Vasco da Gama had first anchored at Calicut in 1498 he received a warm reception from the local king and obtained permission to open trade relations, even though his presents to the king were so insignificant that the courtiers laughed when he presented them to the king.[5] The rapid deterioration of the position of the Portuguese merchants in the eyes of the Indian rulers was for several reasons. Firstly, in order to establish their supremacy in the Eastern Seas, they from the beginning started forcibly to stop the merchants of other nations (Arabs, for example) from carrying on trade in India, using their strong naval force for this purpose. Secondly, their zeal to make Christian converts was too strong for the Moslem rulers and even for the rather more tolerant Hindu monarchs in the southern part of the subcontinent. Thus it appears that while they had the same aim as the other European representatives of merchant capital as regards exclusive privileges, they were too hasty in executing their designs. And added to their piratical actions on the coast of India was their proselytising vigour which became a nuisance in India, as in this respect also they did not proceed craftily like the English.* The upshot was that the other European merchant companies which arrived in India in the wake of the Portuguese, namely the Dutch and the English, could muster support from the Indian rulers and drive the Portuguese out of the subcontinent. It is also true that the discovery of Brazil drew their colonizing activities in the West.

However, at the initial stage of the English Company's adventures in the Eastern Waters, the Portuguese were still a force to be reckoned with. They had fortified positions on the west coast of India, and could draw support from a fairly strong clique in the Mughal Court. Also, as noted before, they professedly held mastery over the Cape route to India, as an alternative to which in the previous century the English had to try in vain to find the north-west and the north-east passages to India. Although the Portuguese could not withhold this privilege any more from either the Dutch or the English, they were not willing to surrender their other exclusive privileges without serious opposition and stiff fights.

Besides their fortifications on the coasts of India—east and west—and Ceylon, the Portuguese were in control of the port of Aden at the entrance to the Red Sea, of Ormus in the Persian Gulf, parts of Bengal where they possessed "factories", and several places in the Eastern Islands. In the areas east of India, the Portuguese were tackled mainly by the Dutch Company, but on the western coast of India the English Company had to encounter them, for the latter decided to open a "factory" at Surat as "in 1608, the factors at Bantam and in the Moluccas reported that the cloths and calicoes imported from the continent of India were in great request in the islands; and recommended the opening of a trade at Surat and Cambaya, to

* Why the English merchant bourgeoisie took a non-proselytising or a "neutral" attitude vis-a-vis the non-Christian religions of India will be briefly discussed in Chapter 5.

supply them with those commodities, which might be exchanged, with extra-ordinary profit, for the spices and other productions of the islands."[6] So, for the first time in its life-history the East India Company attempted in 1608 to develop trade relations with India.

The English Company sent William Hawkins, who bringing his ship to Surat, which was then the main western port of the Mughal Empire, went to Agra—the Imperial Capital—to obtain permission from the Mughal Emperor Jahangir to open trade with the sub-continent. Patiently pursuing his plan for three years, Hawkins could persuade the Emperor to grant leave to trade at Surat, but as "the Portuguese, who were strongly represented at Court by Jesuits, succeeded in obtaining the cancellation of this grant and the virtual expulsion of Hawkins in 1611,"[7] the Company's first bid for penetration into India ended in failure. There was also the point that "the unruly behaviour of British ship-wrecked sailors produced a bad impression and trade facilities were denied."[8]

The Company's next attempt was more successful. This time its representative, Captain Best, came with full preparations, and in the clash between his fleet of two vessels and the Portuguese squadron in 1612 at Swally, a place not at a great distance from Surat, the Portuguese were defeated. The prestige of the English rose in the eyes of the Indian rulers; as a result, in January 1613, Best managed to receive an Imperial Firman (Royal Order) from the Emperor granting the English Company the permission to open trade at Surat, Ahmedabad, Cambaya and Goga. This was the beginning of the Company's relations with India.

For reasons explained before, the Company was of course not satisfied only with the permission to open trade.

> "The Company wanted a charter of rights from the Emperor himself which would place English commerce on a firm and enduring basis."[9]

So, in London, the brains behind the Company came to the conclusion: "To effect this the Jesuit diplomats at the Court of Agra must be confronted by an English diplomat as clever as themselves."[10] The man chosen for the purpose was Sir Thomas Roe who arrived in January 1616 at the Mughal Court carrying a letter from the King of England to the Mughal Emperor.

Meanwhile, a Portuguese fleet had burnt "the towns of Baroach and Goga: and a powerful armament arrived at Swally with the Portuguese Viceroy, in January 1614; which attacked the English; but was defeated, with a loss of 350 men."[11] Roe knew that the position of the Portuguese in the East was not as good as before and that they were also facing serious opposition from the Dutch. So, "if it came to a fight, he knew the British could beat her armadas;" but "Roe did not want it to come to a fight," as "that would annoy the Mughul and, moreover, cause such expenditure that the trade would pay no dividends for years."[12]

Roe was just the right type of diplomat that merchant capital could select for England at a time when the Company was only making in-roads into India. With his cunning he put the English in a better light in the Mughal Court than the Portuguese, secured a treaty from the Emperor stating the right of trading and establishing factories by the English Company in any part of the Mughal Empire, in which Surat, Bengal and Sind were particularly named, and also did his best to undermine the growing influence of the Dutch. The following extracts from Mill's "History of British India" gives an insight as to how Roe worked to oust the rivals from the field.[13]

"Besides his other services, Sir Thomas bestowed advice upon the Company. 'At my first arrival,' says he, 'I understood a fort was very necessary; but experience teaches me we are refused it to our own advantage.* If the Emperor would offer me ten, I would not accept one.' He then states his reasons: first, he adduces evidence that it would be of no service to their trade: 'secondly, the charge,' he says, 'is greater than the trade can bear; for to maintain a garrison will eat out your profit; a war and traffic are incompatible. By my consent you shall never engage yourselves but at sea, where you are like to gain as often as to lose.** The Portugueses, notwithstanding

* This, of course, did not remain the consistent principle of the Company when it had consolidated its position in India.

** One should note the clever tactic suggested by Roe which was diligently followed by the Company until it had come into a position to launch a direct their many rich residences, are beggared by keeping of soldiers; and yet their garrisons are but mean. They never made advantage of the Indies since they defended them: observe this well. It has also been the error of the Dutch, who seek plantations here by the sword. They turn a wonderful stock; they prole in all places; they possess some of the best: yet their dead pays consume all the gain. Let this be received as a rule, that if you will profit, seek it at sea, and in quiet trade; for, without controversies, it is an error to affect garrisons and land wars in India.

'It is not a number of ports, residences, and factories that will profit you. They will increase charge, but not recompense it. The conveniency of one, with respect to your sails, and to the commodity of investments, and the well employing of your servants, is all you need.' ...

'The settling your traffic here will not need so much help at court as you suppose. A little countenance and the discretion of your factors will, with easy charge, return you most profit; but you must alter your stock. Let not your servants deceive you; cloth, lead, teeth, quicksilver, are dead commodities, and will never drive this trade; you must succour it by change.' ...

Sir Thomas tells the Company that he was very industrious to injure the Dutch. 'The Dutch,' he says, 'are arrived at Surat from the Red Sea, with some money and southern commodities. I have done my best to disgrace them; but could not turn them out without further danger. Your comfort is, here are goods enough for both.... The 10th, 11th, and 12th, I spent in giving the prince* advice that a Dutch ship lay before Surat, and would not declare upon what design it came, till a fleet arrived; which was expected with the first fit of season. This I improved to fill their heads with jealousies of the designs of the Dutch, and the dangers that might arise from them; which was well taken: and, being demanded, I gave my advice to prevent coming to a rupture with them, and yet exclude them the trade of India.'"

Such was the role the British Ambassador Roe played in the Mughal Court vis-a-vis the European rivals of the English Company. Roe was highly praised by well-known British writers as late as in 1953.**

---

onslaught. The next chapter will show how this policy was useful while conquering Bengal, and later in this chapter also it will be seen how skilfully this stratagem was applied by the English in their fight with the French over India.

* The prince referred to was probably Khurram, who later became the Emperor Shah Jahan, and who at that time supported the Portuguese faction in the Mughal Court.

** See, for instance, Chapter II in Part I of Philip Woodruff's *The Men Who Ruled India: The Founders*, Jonathan Cape, London, 1954.

His role with regard to the Mughals themselves will be discussed in the next chapter.

In a sense however Roe's embassy was a failure, for he came not merely to open trade in various parts of India, but to obtain a "treaty between Jehangir and King James," so that the English Company could eventually ask for support from the Mughals to drive their European rivals out of the subcontinent, and un-rivalled it could pursue its designs over India. Yet, "it was a satisfying compromise."[14] India was so rich in her commodities that the English Company could comfort itself that "here are goods enough for both"–the English and the Dutch. Mill commented on this assertion of Roe–"If so, why seek to turn them (the Dutch) out?"[15] Evidently, here lay one of the essential characteristics of merchant capital. However, as the best executors of the aims of merchant capital, the English Company knew when to come to a compromise and when to take up arms. It was therefore willing to mark time.

The Portuguese, on the other hand, were exasperated. With their declining influence in India, they continued their offensive against the English who had in a short time established themselves securely at Surat and spread their influence in other parts of the subcontinent. In 1620, a Portuguese fleet blockaded two of the Company's ships which were sailing from Surat to Persia. The English ships returned to Surat for reinforcement, and then attacked the Portuguese. The battle, however, ended without a decision, and the Portuguese returned to Ormus, their stronghold in the Persian Gulf. Then followed a tough struggle between the English and the Portuguese, in which the English were ultimately victorious. With its usual consumate skill, the English Company did not rest content with that victory; it made the best use of the vantage point it had gained to crush Portuguese might in the Orient. The victory had enhanced the prestige of the English in Persian eyes; the Persians also were not favourably disposed to the Portuguese for their overbearing activities on the Persian coast and their seizure of Ormus in their days of greatest prosperity in Eastern Seas. So, upon mutual agreement, the English and the Persians jointly attacked the Portuguese on the island of Ormus, the Persians supplying the land force and the English the navy. On the 22nd of April, 1622, the Portuguese surrendered their possession, and, "For this service the English received part of the plunder of Ormus, and a grant of half the customs at the port of Gombroon; which became their principal station in the Persian Gulf."[16]

Since then the Portuguese could not hold for long to their previous power over the Eastern Seas. In rapid succession they lost all their possessions in India, with the exception of Goa, Diu and Daman which they still retain. Notable parts of the Portuguese possessions in this region, their property and fortifications on the eastern coast of India and in Ceylon were, from the beginning of the seventeenth century, taken away by the Dutch; now, in 1662, Bombay went to King Charles II of England as dowry for marrying a Portuguese princess, Salsette and Bassein were captured by the Maratha Power of India in 1793, and Hugli was taken over during the rule of the Mughals much earlier, and all of them finally came in the hands of the British along with the Dutch possessions in India.

Officially, the capitulation of the Portuguese in India began from 1630, when by the Madrid Treaty, hostilities between the English and the Portuguese came to an end. Four years later, "Methold, the President of the English factory at Surat, and the Portuguese Viceroy of Goa signed a convention, which 'actually guaranteed commercial inter-relations' between the two nations in India."[17] Finally, by the treaty of July 1654, Portugal fully accepted the rights of the English to the Eastern trade, and the treaty of 1661 enjoined the English to support the Portuguese in their actions against the Dutch in India. Thus, having beaten down the previous foe, the crafty English could now use him to crush the other formidable European rival in India in the seventeenth century.

Because the Portuguese could not play the game well, by the middle of the seventeenth century "the English were no longer faced with bitter commercial rivalry from the Portuguese in India, who came to be too degenerate to pursue any consistent policy, though individual Portuguese traders occasionally obstructed the collection of investments by the English in their factories in the eighteenth century."[18]

It should, however, be stated in conclusion that in their class character the Portuguese mercantile bourgeoisie were no better and no worse than their English or Dutch colleagues, although from both the latter quarters consistent attempts were made to paint them as the villain of the piece. To quote Mill who could maintain some sober judgement in this matter[19]:

"The Portuguese followed their merchandise as their chief occupation, but like the English and Dutch of the same period, had no objection to plunder, when it fell in their way."

Also, the following extracts from the speech imputed to Alfonso de Albuquerque before capturing Malacca (which, even if it was not a verbatim report, was "thoroughly consonant with Albuquerque's character, and exhibits the aims of his policy so clearly"[20]) are revealing.

"The first is the great service which we shall perform to Our Lord in casting the Moors out of this country, and quenching the fire of this sect of Muhammad so that it may never burst out again hereafter; and I am so sanguine as to hope for this from our undertaking, that if we can only achieve the task before us, it will result in the Moors resigning India altogether to our rule, for the greater part of them—or perhaps all of them—live upon the trade of this country, and are become great and rich, and lords of extensive treasures.... And the other reason is the additional service which we shall render to the King Dom Manoel in taking this city, because it is the headquarters of all the spices and drugs which the Moors carry every year hence to the Straits, without our being able to prevent them from so doing; but if we deprive them of this, their ancient market, there does not remain for them a single port nor a single situation as commodious in the whole of these parts, where they can carry on their trade in these things. For after we were in possession of the pepper of Malabar, never more did any reach Cairo, except that which the Moors carried thither from these parts, and the forty or fifty ships, which sail hence every year laden with all sorts of spices bound to Mecca, cannot be stopped without great expense and large fleets, which must necessarily cruise about continually in the offing of Cape Comorin; and the pepper of Malabar, of which they may hope to get some portion, because they have the King of Calicut on their side, is in our hands, under the eyes of the Governor of India, from whom the Moors cannot carry off so much with impunity as they hope to do; and I hold it as very certain that, if we take this trade of Malacca away out of their hands, Cairo and Mecca will be entirely ruined, and to Venice will no spices be conveyed, except what her merchants go and buy in Portugal."[21]

Indeed, from the very beginning of Portuguese influence in India and the conquest of Goa, while Albuquerque posed himself "as the destroyer of Muhammadanism and the liberator of the natives," his governing aim was that "Portugal was to control the commerce of India with Europe."[22] Albuquerque's biographer Stephens stated in the nineteenth century that this attitude was "not very different from that adopted by the English 300 years later, and it is a remarkable conception for a statesman at the very beginning of the sixteenth century."[23] There is, no doubt, some truth in the above statement, and especially in recognising the genius of Albuquerque. But one should not fail to realize at the same time that this attitude of Albuquerque was neither unique for the sixteenth century, as the earlier chapters have pointed out, nor was this aim suddenly adopted by the English three centuries later. The following pages will bear out that from the time they appeared on the scene, all the European mercantile Powers, incl. the Dutch, the English and the French, were governed by the single motive of controlling "the commerce of India with Europe." Evidently, the leading representative of the Portuguese merchant bourgeoisie nurtured the same plan as that launched by his other European colleagues on their arrival in India. Only the Portuguese merchant bourgeoisie (like their Dutch and French colleagues) could not successfully steer the plan through, and, therefore, had to retire from the arena at an early date.

2. English-Dutch Rivalry

It will be remembered that one of the immediate reasons which facilitated the receipt of the Royal Charter by the English Company was that by monopolizing the pepper-trade from the East the Dutch had sharply increased its price in 1600. Following the dictates of their principles, the English Company therefore first ventured into the Spice Islands in the Eastern Seas. Probably in the beginning the Company also apprehended more serious resistance to its "trade mission" from the Portuguese, who were longer established in the Eastern trade and had their headquarters at Goa on the west coast of India, than from the newcomer Dutch who were making in-roads into the Spice Islands by ousting the Portuguese from their possession there. In this process the Dutch were helped by the local inhabitants, for, like in India, in the Far East also the Portuguese had made themselves very disagreeable to the people by their too hasty actions. And now the English wanted to take a share in the spoils which the Dutch were going to monopolize.

Although newly-arrived in the field, the Dutch were a much stronger rival to the English than the Portuguese. In those days:

> "The augmentation of capital was rapid, in Holland, beyond what has often been witnessed in any other part of the globe. A proportional share of this capital naturally found its way into the channel of the India trade, and gave both extent and vigour to the enterprises of the nation in the East; while the English, whose country, oppressed by misgovernment, or scourged with civil war, afforded little capital to extend its trade, or means to afford it protection, found themselves unequal competitors with a people so favourably situated as the Dutch."[24]

The English, however, had made their position sufficiently felt by their connection with Sumatra and Java, to have "their full share in the article of pepper; but were excluded from cinnamon, cloves, nutmegs, and all the finer spices."[25] Naturally, the Company could not remain satisfied with only that much of a share! Pepper was produced in so great quantities in the East that it could not be a subject of monopoly. Hence, it was the finer spices that the English Company was after. But, the Dutch "who were governed by the same prejudices (!) as their contemporaries,... beheld, with great impatience, the attempts of the English to share with them in the spice trade."[26] According to the English version, the agents of the English Company who were despatched from Bantam to Amboyna, Banda, and other islands, "fired the jealously and cupidity of the Dutch."[27] This endeavour of the English could not therefore produce any tangible result; the Company was driven out from all places in the Spice Islands where the Dutch had solidly established themselves after first throwing out the Portuguese. Evidently, the Dutch at that time had the upper hand. Their naval supremacy, and "the negotiation of twenty-one years' truce between Spain and Holland in 1609, by freeing them from the danger of war in Europe and some restrictions in the Spice Islands, encouraged the Dutch to oppose English trade in the East Indies more vigorously than before."[28]

Yet, the English Company could not give up its guiding principle. Characteristic of merchant capital's demand for "trade" without rivals and for trading in whatever goods they could acquire as long as the profit-margin was high, the agents of the English Company reported to London in 1617:[29]

> "That Surat was the place at which the cloths of India could best be obtained, though nothing could there be disposed of in return, except China goods, spices, and money: That large quantities of Indian wove goods might be sold, and gold, camphor, and benjamin obtained, at the two factories of Acheen and Tekoo, on the island of Sumatra: That Bantam afforded a still larger demand for the wove goods of India, and supplied pepper for the European market: That Jacatra, Jambee, and Polania, agreed with the two former places in the articles both of demand and supply though both on a smaller scale: That Siam might afford a large vent for similar commodities, and would yield gold, silver, and deer-skins for the Japan market: That English cloth, lead, deer-skins, silks, and other goods, might be disposed of at Japan for silver, copper, and iron, though hitherto want of skill had rendered the adventures to that kingdom unprofitable: That, on the island of Borneo, diamonds, bezoar stones, and gold, might be obtained at Succadania, notwithstanding the mischief occasioned by the ignorance of the first factors: but from Banjarmassin, where the same articles were found, it would be expedient, on account of the treacherous character (!) of the natives, to withdraw the factory: That the best rice in India could be bought, and the wove goods of India sold, at Macassar: And that at Banda the same goods could be sold, and nutmegs and mace procured, even to a large amount, if the obstruction of European rivals were removed."

Thus, while the Company had by then established its principal stations at Surat and Bantam, its immediate occupation was to remove the "obstruction of European rivals," namely of the Portuguese in the west coast of India (which they did successfully as described above) and of the Dutch in the Eastern Seas.

The latter was not an easy task. Having been unable to establish themselves anywhere in the Spice Islands where the Dutch had already moved in, the English Company chose Macassar, "of which the produce was only rice, but which might serve as a magazine for spices collected from the neighbouring islands."[30] But the British fortresses in the small islands of Pularoon and Rosengin, although they contained no Dutch settlements, were not viewed amicably by the Dutch. So the Dutch, "after having in vain endeavoured to expel their rivals from these strongholds, seized two of their vessels, announcing their determination not to release them till England should have withdrawn her pretensions to the trade of the Spice Islands."[31] This led to the outbreak of hostilities between the English and the Dutch, which, though it affected both, was "particularly disastrous to our countrymen (the English)."[32] Moreover, since as representatives of merchant capital both the companies had the same governing principles, the English Company could not make out a good case in its favour; the Dutch, on the other hand, could demand "justice" from the King of England himself! Mill noted:[33]

"The proceedings of the Dutch, though regarded by the English as in the highest degree unjust and rapacious, were founded on pretensions, not inferior to those on which the English Company endeavoured to convert claims into rights; and on pretensions which it is clear, at any rate, that the Dutch themselves regarded as valid and equitable; since they presented them to the English monarch, as the ground of complaint against his subjects, and of a demand for his interference to prevent the recurrence of similar injuries. In a memorial to James, in 1618, the Dutch Company set forth, that, at their own cost and hazard, they had expelled the Portuguese from the Spice Islands, and had established a treaty with the natives, on the express condition of affording the natives protection against the Portuguese, and enjoying the exclusive advantage of their trade; that the agents of the English Company, however, had interfered with those well-established rights, and had not only endeavoured to trade with the natives, but to incite them against the Dutch."

Inter-change of hostilities between the English and the Dutch Companies, spiced with intrigues, went on for some time, in which the English faced the worse situation. The Dutch began to buy up pepper at a price which the English Company could not afford, and in 1619 by means of their superior naval force the former intercepted four English ships near the Isles of Tekoo. As the balance of forces were at that time, the English had to come to terms with the Dutch, and so a treaty was concluded in London on the 17th July 1619, according to which the English Company was allowed half the trade in pepper and one-third of the finer spices. The English were also allowed to trade freely "at Pullicate, on the Coromandel coast, on paying half the expense of the garrison," and the treaty included "arrangements for mutual profit and defence," and "mutual amnesty, and a mutual restitution of ships and property."[34] Thus, the English and the Dutch "agreed to become, as it were, copartners in the Indian traffic."[35]

Naturally, such co-partnership could not run for long, as it affected the very basis of the role of merchant capital. Ousting of one from the field of "business" evidently remained the historical course for the other. And, in this case, the Dutch being superior in strength, they took the offensive. In 1623, along with nine Japanese and one Portuguese sailor, they put ten Englishmen to the rack and later executed them on the plea of conspiracy against their possessions in the East Indies. In virtuous indignation the English Company stirred up the people of England against such a barbarous act, although as Mill commented, such actions were also not unknown either in England or in the Company's possessions in the East where until "they were entrusted with the powers of martial law, having no power to punish capitally any but pirates, they made it a rule to whip to death, or starve to death, those of whom they wished to get rid."[36] In other words, both were equally representatives of merchant capital, and neither the English Company nor the Dutch Company were better or worse than each other. But now the English Company wanted to make the best of the situation and utilise the English people for its own end. So, the Directors of the Company even went to the length of ordering the painting of a picture "in which their countrymen were represented expiring upon the rack, with the most shocking expressions of horror and agony in their countenance and attitudes, and the most frightful instruments of torture applied to their bodies."[37] Their propaganda had some effect; the people pressed on the British Government to retaliate; and, fearing severe retaliation, the Dutch Government and the Dutch Company retreated a little from their uncompromising position, although the Dutch Company did not surrender its principle of remaining superior in the Eastern Seas. The Dutch agreed "to permit the English to retire from the Dutch settlements without paying any duties,"[38] which, in lieu of any better solution, the English Company was forced to accept.

While the English could only hope to retaliate at a later date, the Dutch, remaining the superior of the two, took the offensive again. In 1653–54, the English Company suspended its trade at Surat, when a large fleet of Dutch ships appeared near Swally. Three of the English Company's ships were taken by the Dutch in the Gulf of Persia, and one was destroyed, and "the whole of the coasting trade of the English, consisting of the interchange of goods from one of their stations to another, became, under the naval superiority of the Dutch, so hazardous, as to be nearly suspended; and at Bantam, traffic seems to have been rendered wholly impracticable."[39] The Dutch had by then thrown out the Portuguese from Malacca (1640), and had become "complete masters of the Eastern Islands."[40]

Moreover, after having totally removed the Portuguese from East Indies, in 1644, "the Dutch followed the example of the English in forming a convention with the Portuguese at Goa," and "though it is not pretended that in this any partiality was shown to the Dutch, or any privilege granted to them which was withheld from the English, the Company found themselves, as usual, unable to sustain competition, and complained of this convention as an additional source of misfortune."[41]

While the role of merchant capital was thus again illustrated from one aspect, its another aspect was brought to light as an apparent paradox, when, although the Dutch East India Company was fighting tooth and nail with the English East India Company for permanent supremacy over Eastern trade, "the merchants of Amsterdam, having heard that the Lord Protector would dissolve the East India Company at London, and declare the navigation and commerce to the Indies to be free and open, were greatly alarmed; considering such a measure as ruinous to their own East India Company."[42] Here one hears the voice of Merchant Capital, in contradistinction to the internal quarrels, against the curtailment of its basic demand for monopoly rights. The Dutch merchant bourgeoisie knew that abolition of monopoly rights for their English contemporaries would not only intensify competition between the two, as the previously *have-not* merchants of England would also take to Eastern trade, but the social and political atmosphere which would be produced by such a measure in England would not be favourable to their own position in Holland.

The English Company, however, soon resumed its monopoly rights, as described before; and from about this time the English began to supersede the Dutch. Gradually the situation improved for the British. In 1665, after the Dutch War of 1654, the English Company obtained from the Dutch £ 3,615 as compensation for the massacre of Amboyna in 1623, as well as the island of Polaroon. The latter the English ceded back to the Dutch by the treaty of Breda. It is worthy of note that while it is true that the amount received as compensation was much less than what the English Company had demanded from the Dutch Company, as Mill commented:[43]

> "The English Company, who have never found themselves at a loss to make out heavy claims for compensation, whether it was their own government, or of a foreign, with which they had to deal, stated their damages, ascertained by a series of accounts, from the year 1611 to the year 1652, at the vast amount of 2,695,999 *l.* 15s."

This was but only one of the many instances of the Company's honesty in dealing with others.

Hostilities, however, still went on between the English and the Dutch companies, but now the power of the latter was broken. During the years 1672–74, the Dutch frequently obstructed the communications of the English Company between Surat and the new

English settlement of Bombay. They also captured three English vessels in the Bay of Bengal. But Anglo-Dutch rivalry did not produce any profound effect on India, because, while the Dutch had the power to retain their rights over the Eastern Islands (where they developed their colonial empire), they were no longer in a position to make an attempt to drive the English from the Indian subcontinent.

The English Company, on the other hand, while it could do little in the Dutch possessions in the Eastern Seas, now took the offensive to drive the Dutch from Indian soil. It will be remembered that to deal finally with the Dutch, the English Company had entered into a treaty with its former rivals—the Portuguese—for action against the Dutch in India. This was necessary, for, as noted before, although the Dutch had always paid more attention in the Far Eastern areas, their position in India was also not of little importance. Notable among their factories in India were those at Pulicat (1610), Surat (1616), Chinsura (1653), Cassimbazar, Baranagore, Patna, Balasore, Negapatam (1659) and Cochin (1663). Now it was the turn of the English Company to drive the Dutch from these possessions and from their trade. This, in course of time, the English brought to a successful conclusion, so that with the defeat of the Dutch in the battle of Bedara (Biderra) in 1759, Dutch opposition to the growth of English influence in India collapsed completely.

After this date the Dutch Company in India began to limit itself more to the "country trade" only, and the officers of the company interested themselves in making private fortunes in collaboration with officers of the English Company.[44] Whatever conflict remained between the two companies in India were henceforth resolved in favour of the English. Thus, in 1759, although "the Dutch were not then at war with England," they, "being excited to cupidity by the lofty reports of the rich harvest lately reaped by the English in Bengal, possibly aimed at no more than a share of the same advantages, or to balance before its irresistible ascendency the increasing power of their rivals," and fitted out a fleet at Batavia destined for Bengal.[45] But now the English had no more scruple than the Dutch previously had when they attacked the latter's fleet although they were not at war, and after reducing them to submission Clive was quick to close "the irregularity of his interference" by accepting compensation from the Dutch factors at Chinsurah (near Calcutta).[46]

In the same way, the English Company did not wish that the Dutch "should enjoy the advantage of retaining" their possessions of the seaport town of Nagore and its dependencies which they had received "in assignment for the money which they had lent to the Raja of Tanjore;" so, a war was declared, and since the Dutch "were not in a condition to make effectual resistance," they "made a solemn protest against the injustice" and "prudently retired" in 1773.[47] The Dutch settlement of Negapatam, which was their principal settlement on the Coromandel coast, along with the whole of the Dutch possessions on the coast, and Trincomalle—"a celebrated Dutch settlement on the island of Ceylon"—were occupied by the English in 1782.[48] Finally, in 1795, the English expelled Dutch Power from India, as well as removing it from its strategic hold on the Cape of Good Hope. Mill wrote on the occasion:[49]

> "Though, by the compound opposition of the Supreme Government, and of the powerful class of individuals whose profit depended upon the misgovernment of the country, no reform could be introduced, the war, which the progress of the French revolution brought on with the Dutch, provided for the Governor a sort of triumph, to which the enemies of reform, that is, of mankind, have seldom any objection. In 1795, an armament was fitted out at Madras, which, aided by a squadron of his Majesty's fleet under Admiral Ranier, completely reduced the settlements of the Dutch, on Ceylon, Malacca, Banda, and Amboyna, without any incident of sufficient importance to require a particular description. Their possessions on the Peninsula were likewise subdued; Cochin, after a great resistance. And their grand settlement at the Cape of Good Hope fell into the hands of the English, the same year."

3. English-French Rivalry

While the English found a tougher rival in the Dutch than in the Portuguese, the French outrivalled both. Both the Powers, the English and the French, fought their utmost in the eighteenth century to obtain, in the end, India—"the jewel of the East" as booty.

Why was the Anglo-French rivalry so many times more virulent than the Anglo-Portuguese or the Anglo-Dutch rivalries? The reason appears to lie in the fact that in the first half of the seventeenth century, when the Portuguese and the English fought most seriously over India, the Mughal Power was strong and so it could resist any aggressive move of a foreign power. Hence, the rival merchant powers could only snipe at each other's trading advantages, while maintaining the facade of remaining "peaceful traders" to the Mughal Emperor and his vassals and pleasing them with flattery and presents. In later years also, even though the Mughal Power had begun to disintegrate from the beginning of the eighteenth century, it was yet strong enough to punish any impudence on the part of foreign merchants; so the Anglo-Dutch rivalry, reaching its climax in the second half of the seventeenth century, could also not come completely out in the open, although it was more virulent than the Anglo-Portuguese rivalry. The Anglo-French rivalry, however, took place mainly after the fourth decade of the eighteenth century, when after the death of the Mughal Emperor Aurangzeb in 1707 the disintegration of the Mughal Empire could not pass unnoticed even by a superficial observer. So, a serious contest with a view to control India for the supreme "trading" advantages of one company at the expense of others, by means of subdueing the power of the Indian rulers and using this power to the favour of one company only, a contest which could not unfold itself in the previous phase of "commercial enterprises" of the European merchant bourgeoisie in India, now came out very openly.

Neither the Portuguese nor the Dutch could avail themselves of this wonderful situation, as their powers were already broken. The English Company, therefore, found itself without any serious rival in India except the French. And the fight which ensued between them after the fourth decade of the eighteenth century was quite naked as regards the ultimate objective of merchant capital. Since this rivalry not only manifested itself with the utmost virulence, but also unfolded quite openly the pervading ambition of the representatives of merchant capital to usurp political power over India for their total exploitation, and simultaneously exhibited the shrewd policy of utilising, not always honestly or in a "gentlemanly way," the local conflicts and disunity between the Indian Powers to further their own ends, this phase in the life of the Company should be treated in a little greater detail.

Although "the desire for eastern traffic displayed itself at a very early date among the French," they were "the last of the European powers to compete for commercial gains in the East with the other European Companies."[50] It is said that during the reign of Francis I (1515–1547) the first French expedition to India took place, when some merchants of Rouen fitted out two ships for trading in Eastern Seas and sailed from Havre; but they remained untraced.[51] Then, in 1604, the first East India Company was floated in France, with letters patent granted by Henry IV on the first of June of that year. The project did not mature, and a second company was organized with letters patent from Louis XIII on the 2nd of March, 1611. This Company was also still-born. Afterwards, in 1615, new letters patent were issued, two ships sailed for India, and one returned. Twenty-seven years later, under the auspices of Richelieu, "en qualité de Sur-Intendant du Commerce et de la Navigation de France," another East India Company, styling itself as *La Compagnie des Indes* was formed in 1642, with the exclusive privilege "d'envoier dans ce Isles pour y établir des Colonies et en prendre possession au nom du Roi Louis XIII."[52] After the death of the king in the month of May, 1642, the privileges granted to the Company were confirmed under the Regency of Louis XIV on the 20th of September, 1643; but apparently this company also failed to make head-way. Finally, on the initiative of Colbert, the finance-minister of France, *La Compagnie des Indes Orientales* came into existence in 1664, as a part of "his projects for rendering his country commercial and opulent."[53] Adam Smith characterized Colbert as "a man of probity, of great industry and knowledge of detail, of great experience and acuteness in the examination of public accounts, and of abilities, in short, every way fitted for introducing method and good order into the collection and expenditure of the public revenue;" but as having "unfortunately embraced all the prejudices of the mercantile system, in its nature and essence a system of restraint and regulation, and such as could scarce fail to be agreeable to a laborious and plodding man of business, who had been accustomed to regulate the different departments of public offices, and to establish the necessary checks and controls for confining each to its proper sphere."[54] Smith's strong words give an indication of the fact that it was the desire of the French mercantile bourgeoisie which was fulfilled by the floating of this company at last.

The French East India Company, however, was a state-controlled organization, and in this respect it differed from the chartered companies of merchant capital in England and Holland in those days. W. B. Duffield wrote in relation to the chartered companies formed under the "old commercial system:"[55]

> "In England historic protests were made against such monopolies, but the chartered companies were less exclusive in England than in either France or Holland... French commercial companies were more privileged, exclusive and artificial than those in Holland and England. Those of Holland may be said to have been national enterprise. French companies rested more than did their rivals on false principles; they were more fettered by the royal power, and had less initiative of their own, and therefore had less chance of surviving. As an example of the kind of rules which prevented the growth of the French companies, it may be pointed out that no Protestants were allowed to take part in them. State subventions, rather than commerce or colonization, were often their object; but that has been a characteristic of French colonial enterprise at all times."

This important variation in the organization of the French East India Company from that of the Dutch and the English had a significant effect on its eventual career in India. As it will be seen from the following pages, the over-all policy of the French Government in politics and other aspects sometimes adversely affected the French Company in spreading its influence in India, and contributed in no small measure to its final liquidation in spite of the great genius of Dupleix and the military skill of Lally. But it should not be overlooked at the same time that this chartered company also reflected the interests of merchant capital of a specific national state, just as it was with the English or the Dutch Companies. Henceforth, the French merchant bourgeoisie could have a direct hand in India trade. Therefore, after an expedition to Madagascar, the *Compagnie des Indes Orientales* sent another to India in 1667. This expedition reached Surat in 1668, and thus began the eventful tension between the English and the French mercantile bourgeoisie, which was finally resolved by the Carnatic Wars.

From the time the French East India Company came to life, the Directors of the English Company naturally did not view this new rival amicably. But, "the subservience of the English government to that of France was already so apparent, as to make them afraid of disputes in which they were likely to have their own rulers against them."[56] So, the English Company had to be content for the time being to describe the French merchants in India as "Dutch pirates," and by instructing their agents in India "to afford these rivals no aid or protection, but to behave towards them with circumspection and delicacy."[57] In India, the agents of the English Company abided by the wishes and instructions of their masters in London, while the first French factory was established at Surat in 1668, the place where the principal station of the English Company in India was situated.

In the beginning, however, the English Company had not much to fear from its French contemporary, for, although the arrival "of a French fleet of twelve ships, and a stock computed at 130,000 *l*." had embarrased the Company officials at Surat, and "the inconsiderate purchases and sales of the French reduced the price of European goods, and raised that of India," yet, "these adventurers exhibited so little of the spirit and knowledge of commerce, as convinced the Company's agents that they would not prove formidable rivals."[58] In short, in the beginning, the French mercantile bourgeoisie failed in one of the basic principles of merchant capital, namely, to buy cheap and sell dear, so that their fundamental mistake, the English Company concluded, would remove them from the field.

But, because of a mistake committed by the English Company at about this time, the French Company could spread its influence in India at this initial stage, in spite of the serious error it had committed. Prematurely the English Company took up arms to usurp political power, and thus fully to establish the control of English merchant capital over India. But, as will be described in the next chapter, although the Mughal Empire had by then begun to disintegrate, it still had power enough to retaliate strongly and bring the English Company to submission. The Mughal Emperor Aurangzeb issued orders "to expel the English from his dominions," and this "exposed the Company's establishments to ruin in every part of India."[59] By the attack of the Mughal Power on the English Company, "the factory at Surat was seized; the island of Bombay was attacked by the fleet of the Siddees; the greater part of it was taken, and the governor besieged in the town and castle. ... the factory at Masulipatam was seized; as was also that at Vizagapatam, where the Company's agent and several of their servants were slain."[60] The Company was reduced to abject submission, and appealed for restoration of its properties in India. Since the stoppage of English trade also meant a serious reduction in income to the Mughal Treasury,[61] the Emperor after putting a stop to the Company's ambition for political power was not averse to coming to a settlement. The properties of the English Company were therefore restored, "but the interruption and delay sustained by the Company made them pay dearly for their premature ambition, and for the unreasonable insolence, or the imprudence of their servants."[62] The situation was of course favourable to the French Company, and so "during these contests, the French found an interval in which they improved their footing."[63] They had already penetrated into India to a far extent, having established a factory at Masulipatam in 1669, building on a modest scale the town of Pondicherry, near the British settlement at Madras, in 1673, and receiving a site near Calcutta in 1674 from the Nawab of Bengal, where now, during 1690–92, they built the town of Chandernagore, and at Pondicherry they erected fortifications.

In the seventeenth century, however, the French were more or less in the background. Their rivalry with the Dutch over India (the latter discretely supported by the English)[64] affected their position adversely. Pondicherry was captured by the Dutch in 1693, and although it was handed back to the French by the treaty of Ryswick and the latter then fortified it as noted above, in other places the influence of the French Company was on the decline. The upshot was that by the beginning of the eighteenth century the factories of the French Company at Bantam, Surat and Masulipatam were abandoned, and its resources were practically exhausted, Till 1720, "it passed through very bad days, even selling its licences to other."[65]

In 1720 the French mercantile bourgeoisie revived their interest in India and reconstituted themselves in a new Company, entitled *La Compagnie perpétuelle des Indes*. In 1721, they occupied Mauritius, which was a very distinct gain to the French as enhancing their naval power in the East and thus making them a formidable enemy to English designs over India. For supremacy over the sea had a very significant bearing on the fulfilment of the cherished wish of the merchant capitalists of all European nations finally to bring the governments and the peoples of the Asian countries they "traded" with into submission. It will be remembered that the Portuguese influence in the East was mainly because of their naval power; the Dutch supremacy in the Eastern Waters for a time can also be traced to the same to a large extent; and it will be seen in the course of this chapter that in their bid for the exclusive control of "the commerce of India with Europe" supremacy over the sea counted a good deal with the English and the French Powers in the later decades of the eighteenth century. For this reason, the French occupation of Mauritius in the first half of the eighteenth century had a significant bearing on the successive development of the tension between the English and the French over India.

Moreover, apart from Mauritius, the Frech Company very soon also established itself firmly on Indian soil. In 1725, it settled at Mahe on the Malabar coast, and in 1739 at Karikal. Anglo-French rivalry was thus resumed, and it was not finally resolved until in all essentials the French were eliminated from India as a result of the cleverer moves of the English Company and because of the Seven Years' War in which, along with North America, India was the stake between the contending bourgeoisie of England and France, and in which again the English bourgeoisie played a cleverer role.

The Anglo-French rivalry, now revived in India, emerged in full-scale armed conflict when the wars of Frederick II "found the English and the French opposed to each other in the battlefields of Europe, Asia and America for well-nigh twenty years, from 1744 to 1763."[66] Henceforth, the French and the English companies made open alliance with the Indian princes and their underlings, "besieged each other's commercial settlements, and evinced in the East those bitter jealousies which divided them in the West."[67] The upshot was that the English mercantile bourgeoisie were able to get rid of their last European rival in India, for, of the two, only the English could grasp the situation better both in India and elsewhere.

When in 1744 the English and the French Governments came to mutual declarations of war, technically it placed the English and the French companies in a state of war in India. The French Company, however, wanted to avoid the spread of Anglo-French tension on Indian soil, and so requested the English Company to maintain strict neutrality. But the English Company, while professing to avoid hostilities, declined to accept the proposal, evidently because it was encouraged to take up the contest in India to further its own ends. Hostilities therefore soon began with the capture of French ships by the English off the south-eastern coast of India. The French at that time had no fleet in Indian waters, but they were in possession of Mauritius on the Indian Ocean. So, a squadron soon arrived from the French colony of Mauritius, and the First Carnatic War began.

The French besieged Madras both by land and sea, and within a week the English surrendered Madras to the French. The English appealed to the Nawab of the Carnatic, and the Nawab Anwar-ud-din, true to his role of protector, asked the French Governor of Pondicherry, Dupleix, to raise the siege of Madras. The French did not pay any heed to his orders, just as previously the English did not respect the Nawab's authority when it suited them and had attacked the French ships contrary to his wishes. As noted above, this was the reason for the outbreak of hostilities in India between the two Powers, but there was no reason why the English should recall that.

With the Nawab the situation was now different. Since he hardly possessed any navy, like all other kings and Nawabs of India at that time (including the Mughals), he could not have interfered previously when the English started fighting in his territory. But it was a different matter in the case of warfare on land, and he was determined to establish his sovereignty before the foreign merchants. So, he sent an army against the French troops besieging Madras in order to stop fights between the foreign merchant companies in his kingdom. But, although the Nawab's army was much bigger than that of the French, the latter was much better equipped. The French "astonished them beyond measure by the rapidity of their artillery; with a numerical force which bore no proportion to the enemy, gained over them a decisive victory."[68]

The English, however, managed to retake Madras by means of a large squadron sent from England in 1748, and now they in their turn sieged the French settlement of Pondicherry. But before the final outcome of this warfare between the two companies in India, the war in Europe was concluded by the Treaty of Aix-la-Chapelle (1748), and under the terms of the treaty, Madras was restored to the English.

The First Carnatic War revealed two important features of the Indian situation in those days. Firstly, supremacy in naval power was a deciding factor in the Anglo-French hostilities in which the Indian Powers could not have any say at all, for all of them lacked navies. Secondly, while in small numbers, the European troops could possibly out-class larger Indian armies at this time, because of the up-to-date military equipment of the former and possibly also their better discipline, since with the disintegration of the Mughal Empire discipline and the fighting quality of the local troops under minor vassals could not be enhanced, as previously, by the arrival of superior military leaders and their troops from the centre when occasion demanded.

These two lessons could now be made use of by the English and the French companies, for, as will be described in the next chapter, in those days of political unrest in India when the Mughal Power was crumbling to pieces, the time had become ripe for either of the two companies to ask for all possible "concessions" from the Indian rulers and, failing them, to usurp political power in order to ensure that only their wishes and demands were honoured.

It is generally said that the French, under the leadership of Dupleix who in 1742 was vested with supreme command over the French settlements in India, took the first initiative in territorial acquisition, while the "peaceful" English were forced to take up arms in the end—only to defend their "trading interests," and thus by a series of accidents and good luck they became the masters of India. But there can be no room for doubt that, whoever might have taken the first initiative in the matter, the policy itself, that is, political control over India, was inseparably linked with the full flowering of merchant capital in this "trading" country.

At the latest in the 1680's, if not earlier, the activities of the English Company had left no shadow of doubt that they had come to the logical conclusion that ultimately "concessions" for their commercial pursuits in India would have to be obtained at the point of sword. It is not necessary to elaborate the point any further that this was in the *nature* of merchant capital, as opposed to its being the product of brain-wave of an individual person, however talented he might have been. If the fundamental motto is to buy cheap and sell dear, "concessions" are indispensable; and such "concessions" can be obtained to the fullest extent only when the commercial body has also got political power over the country with which commerce is undertaken, and can thus uncompromisingly dictate its terms to the local inhabitants. Indeed, that it had become the cardinal policy of the English Company in the seventeenth century when the officials of the Company were witnessing the break-up of the Mughal Empire and reporting the same to their Directors in London, became completely clear in 1689 when the Directors in their instructions to the agents of the Company in India wrote as follows:[69]

"The increase of our revenue is the subject of our care, as much as our trade:—'tis that must maintain our force, when twenty accidents may interrupt our trade; 'tis that must make us a nation in India;—without that we are but as a great number of interlopers, united by his Majesty's royal charter, fit only to trade where nobody of power thinks it their interest to prevent us;—and upon this account it is that the wise Dutch, in all their general advices which we have seen, write ten paragraphs concerning their government, their civil and military policy, warfare, and the increase of their revenue, for one paragraph they write concerning trade."*

Mill commented on this as follows:[70]

"It thus appears at how early a period, when trade and sovereignty were blended, the trade, as was abundantly natural, became an object of contempt, and by necessary consequence, a subject of neglect. A trade, the subject of neglect, is of course a trade without profit."

Wilson further commented on it:[71]

"The anxiety of the Directors to maintain a trade 'without profit,' would be somewhat inexplicable, if it was true, but the injuries to which that trade had been exposed from European competition and native exactions, had sufficiently proved that it could not be carried on without the means of maintaining an independent position in India."

In short, not only the monopoly in the Home country, but also that in the country with which trade is carried on was the *sine qua non* of merchant capital, and for this the merchant capitalists of the two countries were striving for political power to fulfil all their demands as well as to stop the local inhabitants and their rulers from receiving their dues in the commercial transactions. While this point will be better investigated in the next chapter while examining the relations between the English Company and the Indian rulers, it would be of interest to describe in the following how both the English and the French companies put this policy in operation.

* One should note that just as in their Home country they dubbed the Free Merchants who did not enjoy monopoly privileges as Interlopers, so they considered themselves in India until they could usurp political power. One should further note their very material interest in studies of Indian societies, which some decades later became the quest for "pure" scientific knowledge.

Although the policy of territorial acquisition was decided by the role of merchant capital itself, how it could be put into practice lay evidently in the hands of the two companies. Here, it appears, Dupleix's initiative, talent and organizing abilities were brought into full play; while the English soon learnt the game, and in a short time out-played the French. A characteristic feature of the manoeuvres of the two companies was to uphold the interests of rival political adventurers, *rajas, nawabs,* etc., all of whom in those unsettled days were striving to improve their position. This led to the resumption of armed hostilities between the English and the French in the Second Carnatic War.

Before the First Carnatic War, the Marathas (who had become a formidable power in India with the disintegration of the Mughal Empire) had invaded the Carnatic, killed its governor, Nawab Dost Ali, and taken his son-in-law, Chand Sahib, prisoner. The son of Dost Ali, who was allowed to save his life and kingdom by promising to pay the Marathas ten million rupees, was soon murdered by a cousin, and his young son was proclaimed the Nawab. Since these incidents had created a feeling of panic and uncertainty in the Carnatic, the Nizam of Hyderabad, under whom the Nawab of Carnatic was placed, came in person in 1743 to restore order. He appointed one of his favourite servants, Anwar-ud-din, the Nawab of the Carnatic.

This appointment made the situation worse, and particularly so after 1748 when Chand Sahib was set free by the Marathas after seven years of captivity. Chand Sahib now began to form a conspiracy in order to become the Nawab, for Asaf Jah Nizam-ul-Mulk of Hyderabad died in 1748, and was succeeded by his son, Nasir Jang, but his grandson, Muzaffar Jang laid claim to the throne on the ground that the Mughal Emperor had appointed him as the Subhadar (Governor) of the Deccan. Now Chand Sahib and Muzaffar Jang came to an agreement to fight together to gain the respective seats at Carnatic and Hyderabad.

This was a wonderful situation for the foreign merchant companies to pursue their own ends. The French immediately took the initiative and made up their mind to utilize the discord in Hyderabad and the Deccan in their favour. Dupleix concluded a secret treaty with Chand Sahib and Muzaffar Jang with a view to placing them on the thrones of the Carnatic and the Deccan, respectively. In 1749, the three allies defeated and killed Anwar-ud-din in a battle, and Muhammad Ali, the son of Anwar-ud-din, fled to Trichinopoly. A French army was sent to reduce that town.

The English understood the situation very well: Indeed, "from the beginning of 1747, the English had been intriguing, both with Nizam al Mulk and with Nazir Jung, against the French."[72] A letter from Commodore Griffin to the Nizam-ul-Mulk, dated March 6, 1747, which is quoted below gives some idea of how the English Company was then playing the game.

> "I shall not enter into a particular detail of the robberies, cruelties, and depredations, committed on shore upon the King my Master's subjects, by that insolent, perfidious nation the French; connived at, and abetted by those under your Excellency, (the Nabob of Arcot,) whose duty it was to have preserved the peace of your country, instead of selling the interest of a nation, with whom you have had the strictest friendship time out of mind; a nation that has been the means not only of enriching this part of the country, but the whole dominions of the grand Mogul; and that to a people who are remarkable all over the world for encroaching upon, and giving disturbances and disquiet to all near them; a people who are strangers in your country, in comparison of those who have been robbed by them of that most important fortress and factory, Madras; and now they are possessed of it, have neither money nor credit, to carry on the trade.... And now, excellent Sir, we have laid this before you, for your information and consideration; and must entreat you, in the name of the King of Great Britain, my Royal Master, to call the Nabob to an account for his past transactions, and interpose your power to restore as near as possible in its original state, what has been so unjustly taken from us."[73]

This was during the First Carnatic War, when the English had also established friendship with Nasir Jang, who in return had persuaded the Nizam-ul-Mulk to write to Anwar-ud-din to drive out the French from the Carnatic, so that "the English nation may be restored to their right, establish themselves in their former place, as before, and carry on their trade and commerce for the flourishment of the place."[74] But the Nawab Anwar-ud-din, as the English Company was informed by their Indian Agent at Arcot, "is but a *Renter*, he does not much regard the distress of the people of this province, but in all shapes has respect to his own interest and benefit; therefore there is no trusting to his promises."[75] Hence, to make the request of the English Company effective, the agent instructed the Company that just as "the French are very generous in making presents of other people's goods, both to the old and young," so the English should also be "equally liberal with their gifts."[76] Thus, whether the Nawab of Arcot fought against the French solely to maintain his sovereignty or not, the English are seen to have been securing their position in the Deccan and the Carnatic by means of intrigues and possibly also bribes. But, Dupleix's quick moves outmanoeuvred them for a time. Finding however that the initiative was slipping out of their hands, the English now persuaded Nasir Jang to come and crush his enemies in the Carnatic, and sent some help to Muhammad Ali at Trichinopoly. But Nasir Jang was killed in 1750, and Muzaffar Jang was proclaimed Subhadar of the Deccan.

The grateful Subhadar suitably rewarded the service of his French ally. He appointed Dupleix as Governor of the Mughal Dominions on the coast of Coromandel from the river Krishna to Cape Comorin, and ceded territories to the French near Pondicherry as well as on the Orissa coast, including the famous market-town of Masulipatam. In return, at the request of Muzaffar Jang, Dupleix placed at his disposal the service of his best officer, Bussy, with a French army. The shrewd General knew that this was the surest means to guarantee French influence at the court of the Nizam, and thus guarantee the French hold over the Deccan.

In this way, within less than two years, an insignificant body of foreign merchants was raised to the position of supreme political authority in the Deccan and the Carnatic. The merchants however were the French, and not the British. The rising tide of the French thus only sharpened the antagonism between these two contending sections of European merchant bourgeoisie. Mill wrote:[77]

"The Europeans in India, who hitherto had crouched at the feet of the meanest of the petty governors of a district, were astonished at the progress of the French, who now seemed to preside over the whole region of the Deccan. A letter to Dupleix, from a friend in the camp of Salabat Jung, affirmed that in a little time the Mogul on his throne would tremble at the name of Dupleix; and however presumptuous this prophecy might appear, little was wanting to secure its fulfilment."

Although "sunk in apathy or despair," the English did not give up completely. Very soon they turned the scale in their favour, and the French were routed from India for all practical purposes.

To follow the developments chronologically, in order to complete its success, it was necessary for the French Company to come to a settlement with Muhammad Ali who had taken refuge at the strong fort of Trichinopoly. The French forces sent to reduce that city did not prove up to the task. Overjoyed with their initial success, they had only wasted their energy in a fruitless effort to reduce Tanjore. The French now tried to make up for their mistake, and so Dupleix tried to conciliate Muhammad Ali through diplomatic moves. Muhammad Ali was also very much scared by the recent development, and "now offered to resign his pretensions to the Nabobship of the Carnatic, provided Dupleix, who listened to the overture, would obtain from the new Subhadar a command for him, in any other part of his dominions."[78] But the English were better masters in diplomacy, and now they had decided to come out in full force to oust the French. So they earnestly took up the cause of Muhammad Ali, and advised him to gain time by prolonging the negotiation between him and the French during which the English would prepare for a full-scale offensive. The French were fooled in this game. In May 1751, the English Company sent a detachment towards Trichinopoly to help Ali against the French. Moreover, by the end of the year, the English also persuaded Morari Rao, the Maratha chief, as well as the rulers of Mysore and Tanjore, to join them and Muhammad Ali. The English Company also sent an expedition to Arcot, the capital of the Carnatic, and occupied it without any serious opposition. The upshot was that Chand Sahib surrendered and was beheaded on the orders of the Tanjorean Generals.

The French were now in a bad situation. Yet, Dupleix was not despondent: "As it was the character of this man to form schemes, which from their magnitude appears romantic, so was it his practice to adhere to them with constancy, even when the disasters which he encountered in their execution seemed to counsel nothing but despair."[79] By counter-moves he won over Morari Rao and the ruler of Mysore to the side of the French and secured the neutrality of the Raja of Tanjore. Thus he effected a balance of strength with the English Company, in order to "oppose a nearly equal, in a little time a more than equal, force to his opponents."[80] Then, on 31st December 1752, the French renewed the siege of Trichinopoly.

Dupleix, however, was no longer ably assisted by his compatriots.

> "The French East India Company were much poorer than even the English; the resources which they furnished from Europe were proportionally feeble; and though perfectly willing to share with Dupleix in the hopes of conquest, when enjoyment was speedily promised, their impatience for gain made them soon tired of the war; and they were now importunately urging Dupleix to find the means of concluding a peace."[81]

Dupleix staked his own fortune and his own credit for pursuing the war, and persuaded Mortiz Ali, the Governor of Vellore, to contribute to the war expenses with "the prospect of even the Nabobship itself."[82] Mortiz Ali, however, soon realized that Dupleix was only making use of him, and so broke off the negotiation. The troops that Dupleix commanded were also far worse than those of the English; especially the French recruits he received from France, whom he described in his letter to the French Minister, dated 16th October 1753, as "enfans, décroteurs, et bandits."[83] Yet, the siege of Trichinopoly was ably continued by the French for more than a year, and "neither of the contending parties seemed nearer their object."[84]

Meanwhile, in Europe, the leaders of both the companies were exasperated; and "to them the burden of the war had become exceedingly hateful."[85] Realizing that the stalemate was due to an equal balance of forces between the French and the English, both the companies instructed their representatives in India to come to an amicable settlement. Negotiations were started in January 1754, but as neither of the two parties was willing to concede the victory to the other, the proceedings broke up in mutual recriminations.

After this the tide went against Dupleix, and thus against the French Company. Unlike the English East India Company which was a private body, the French East India Company was directly controlled by the French Government and thus it was more vulnerable to the larger political issues confronting the State. So, when in fear of serious complications in America, the Government of France decided not to fight the English in India, the French Company and its representatives had to accept the decision unequivocally. The English Company further scored a point by removing Dupleix from the scene. It fanned the sentiments growing against him in France for "wasting the resources of the Company in ambitious wars" by further accusing him "of embroiling the two nations in India."[86] Moreover, as "the English ministry prudently despatched a considerable fleet to India, while the negotiation was still proceeding;" and as "the French ministry had no fleet to spare; and dreaded the superiority which such a force might bestow;" and as "the French Company were, at the same time, extremely eager to taste the gains of commerce, which they promised themselves in peace; and, from all these causes, were disposed to make ample concessions;" it was not difficult for the English to get rid of Dupleix by asserting against "any negotiation which was to be conducted by Dupleix, the object of which, they affirmed, his ambition and artifice would be sure to defeat."[87] This was a decisive victory for the English Company over its French rival. Mill wrote:[88]

> "A point was thus gained in favour of the English, on which their fortune in India very probably hinged; for when, after the short interval of two years, war was renewed between the English and French; when the English were expelled from Bengal; and the influence of Bussy was paramount at the court of the Subahdar; had Dupleix remained at the head of French

affairs in India, the scheme of that enterprising governor, to render himself master of the Carnatic, and the Subahdar master of Bengal, would have stood a fair chance of complete accomplishment."

Henceforth, the fate of the French Company was sealed in India. The treaty of 1754 between the two companies, the provisions of which were readily conceded by the French representative Godheu who replaced Dupleix in India and the English representative Saunders who remained in command of the English Company as he was before at the time of Dupleix, dealt a mortal blow to the French Power in India. According to this treaty, "everything for which they had been contending was gained by the English; every advantage of which they had come into possession was given up by the French."[89] Ostensibly, the treaty concluded peace between the two rivals and outwardly acknowledged the balance of forces between the two companies, by agreeing to leave each company in possession of the territories which they had actually occupied at the time of the treaty, and enjoining them not to interfere in the quarrels of the Indian rulers. But the English Company had now gained the upper hand, and the initiative was decisively taken away from the French.

In the Deccan the French retained some influence. Bussy, the French officer with the Nizam-ul-Mulk, induced the latter to grant him the Northern Sarkars for the payment of his troops kept in Hyderabad. These consisted of the four districts of Mustafanagar, Ellore, Rajahmundry, and Chicacole, which altogether yielded an annual revenue of more than three million rupees.[90] But the political power of the French in India was a lost thing.

As the events following on the signing of the treaty of 1754 showed, the English in their ascendency were in no mood to abide by its provisions.

"In a short time after the conclusion of this treaty, both Saunders and Godheu took their departure for Europe; pleasing themselves with the consideration that, by means of their exertions, the blessings of peace between the two nations in India were now permanently bestowed. Never was expectation more completely deceived. Their treaty procured not so much as a moment's repose. The English proceeded to reduce to the obedience of their Nabob the districts of Madura and Tinivelly. The French exclaimed against these transactions, as an infringement of the treaty with Godheu; but finding their remonstrances without avail, they followed the English example, and sent a body of troops to reduce to their obedience the petty sovereignty of Terriore."[91]

Moreover, in 1755, the English Company decided to subjugate Mortiz Ali, the Governor of Vellore, for his "reputed riches," but as "M. Deleyrit, who was Governor of Pondicherry, informed the English Presidency, that he regarded their proceedings at Vellore as a violation of the treaty, and that he should commence hostilities, if their troops were not immediately withdrawn," "the English rulers, soon aware that Vellore could not be easily taken, and unwilling to put to proof the threat of Deleyrit, who had made 700 Europeans and 2000 Sepoys take the field, recalled the army of Madras."[92]

On the whole, however, the English Company was doing well, while its French counterpart was not only crippled by lack of assistance and encouragement from the Home Government, but "during these transactions of the English, not very consistent with their agreement not to interfere in the disputes of the native princes, or add to their territory in India, the French were restrained from that active opposition which, otherwise, it is probable, they would have raised, by the dangerous situation of their affairs under the government of the Subahdar [of the Deccan]."[93] This relates to the difficulties Bussy was experiencing in the court of Nizam-ul-Mulk to retain the French influence there against the powerful opposition of the nobilities of the court led by the Prime Minister and two brothers of the Nizam who were probably more favourably disposed to the English, and who in 1756 succeeded in securing the Nizam's order to expel the French troops from the Nizam's territory. Bussy, however, managed to regain his position by the "brilliant exploit of 1756, when he defended himself at Hyderabad against the whole power of the Subahdar, and imposed his own terms upon his enemies;"[94] and by 1758 he had virtually got rid of his enemies at Hyderabad. But, in the meantime, taking advantage of their respite from French attacks, and by following their usual course of bribery, intrigues and treachery among the Indian rulers and adventurous aspirants for power, the English had managed to conquer the *subah* of Bengal (the States of Bengal, Bihar and Orissa of today, that is, practically the whole of eastern India) in the well-known battle of Plassey. More will be said in the next chapter about the conquest of Bengal in 1757 and what followed in India thereafter, but it should be noted here that after Plassey there remained no trace of hope for the accession of French Power in India. With their most precious gain of one of the richest portions of India, it was no more a difficult task for the English to crush completely their French rival. It has therefore been said that the battle of Plassey finally decided the fate of the French in India, and that this is quite true became only too evident from the outcome of the Third Carnatic War.

With the outbreak of the Seven Years' War in 1756 between the English and the French in Europe, an immediate action of the English Company was to capture Chandernagore, the important French settlement in Bengal near Calcutta. Siraj-ud-Daula, the Nawab of Bengal, was enraged at this behaviour of the Company, for when this proposal was previously made to him by the English he had argued "that he could never allow one section of his subjects to be molested by another;" and so, after the capture of the town by the English, "the Nawab, gallantly enough, afforded shelter to the French fugitives at his court, and refused to drive them away even when the English offered in exchange military help against a threatened invasion of Bengal by the heir-apparent to the Mughul Empire."[95] As will be seen in the next chapter, this refusal of the Nawab to hand over the French was one of the immediate causes of war between him and the English Company. Meanwhile, the Nawab had also written to Bussy, "inviting him, by the largest offers, to assist him in expelling the English from Bengal;" but while Bussy was waiting in the Northern Sarkars to hear from him again, he learnt of the capture of Chandernagore and changing his mind "proceeded to the attack of the English establishments within the Circars."[96] The Nawab of Bengal thus could not avail himself of the very useful service of Bussy at this crucial moment; and although the French fugitives in the court of

Siraj-ud-Daula fought bravely with the Nawab's army, the conspiracy launched by the English Company had so devitalized the Nawab's government and his army that he lost his throne and his head without a single serious battle. The French in Bengal were completely at the mercy of the English.

While in eastern India the French fared badly from the time news were received of the outbreak of the war in 1756, in South India both the English and the French were not in a position to start hostilities at once. The English at that time were fully occupied in Bengal, and the French resources were similarly crippled as the Governor of Pondicherry had to send assistance to Bussy at Hyderabad. However, this time, with the outbreak of the war, the French Government had "resolved to strike an important blow in India," and so had sent reinforcements to the French Company headed by Count de Lally. But encountering several difficulties on the way, the reinforcements could not reach India before the second quarter of 1758. By then the English fleet also returned from Bengal bringing reinforcements in men and money, and the war in the Carnatic began in full scale.

The French began splendidly. They took Fort St. David from the English, after besieging it for just a month, on the 2nd June 1758. Also, by the 24th June, Bussy had taken over all the English settlements in Northern Sarkars, including the fort at Visakhapatnam (Vizagapatam). As in the previous wars between the English and the French in India, the former were now greatly alarmed by the successes of their rivals. Mill wrote:[97]

> "The English were thrown into the greatest alarm. So much was the power of the enemy now superior to their own, that they scarcely anticipated any other result, than their expulsion from the country; and had Dupleix been still the guide and conductor of the enemy's affairs, it is more than probable that their most gloomy apprehensions would have been realized."

The English of course had not by then fully realized that the relative position of the two companies had undergone a fundamental change in India with their subjugation of the *subah* of Bengal; but while that became clearer to them as the Third Carnatic War proceeded on its course, they could not overlook the immediate fact that the ever-present worry of the French Company as regards finance had now come up as a serious bar to the next offensive of Lally. Clive declared in 1772:[98]

> "Mr. Lally arrived with a force as threatened not only the destruction of all the settlements there, but of all the East India Company's possessions, and nothing saved Madras from sharing the fate of Fort St. David, at that time, but their want of money, which gave time for strengthening and reinforcing the place."

And, added to this financial trouble of the French Company was the rude and haughty conduct of its General, Lally, by which he alienated almost all his colleagues in India. Furthermore, by refusing to listen to them, Lally made serious political and diplomatic blunders, although as a military leader he was excellent, according to all accounts.

After the capture of Fort St. David, Lally had "wisely decided to strike at the root of the British power in the Carnatic by reducing Madras," but, because while he was in supreme command over civil and military affairs of the French he had no control over the naval forces commanded by d'Ache, he had to put his decision in abeyance, for "d'Ache, who had already been defeated by the English fleet on the 28th April, refused to sail."[99] Such lack of coordination between the army and the navy seriously hampered successful operations on the part of the French, and further speeded the victory of the English.

Next, Lally wanted to solve the financial trouble of the French Company "by forcing the Raja of Tanjore to pay 70 lacs (700,000) rupees," which the king was declared to have owed the company from the time of Dupleix, but although he laid a siege on Tanjore on the 18th July and the military power of the Raja was not anything formidable, he could not bring his scheme to a successful conclusion due to "lack of ammunition" and because "there was no spirit of mutual trust and concord between Lally and his men."[100] Meanwhile, the English fleet inflicted heavy losses on d'Ache's squadron on the 3rd of August, and the French fleet left the Indian seas. On hearing this news, Lally left Tanjore with his army on the 10th August, "thereby inflicting a heavy blow not only to his own reputation but also to the prestige of the French army."[101]

Then, until the English fleet left the harbourless Madras coast with the onset of monsoon, Lally went on conquering minor English settlements, so that the English were left only with Madras, Trichinopoly and Chingleput in the Carnatic; and when the English fleet had left the Madras coast and he required no help from the navy, Lally laid siege on Madras on the 14th of December. But the siege of Madras, "marked by defects of the same kind as were noticed in the case of Tanjore,"[102] went on for three months, until with the appearance of the English fleet it was immediately lifted on the 16th February 1759.

Lally could no more retrieve the French position: "The next twelve months completed the debacle."[103] He had also made the mistake of recalling Bussy from Hyderabad, and in spite of repeated requests from the latter to send him back left the French troop there "under incompetent commanders."[104] Taking advantage of the situation, the English had sent an army from Bengal to the Northern Sarkars, which "successively occupied Rajahmundry (7th December) and Masulipatam (6th March) and concluded a favourable treaty with the Nizam Salabat Jang."[105] The French thus lost all their influence in the Deccan, while by playing the same old game of utilizing the Indian rulers the English established their influence in the court of Hyderabad.

The English had also taken the offensive in the Carnatic. At first, they were defeated near Conjeevaram, "but the French could not follow up their success on account of discontent among their troops for lack of pay, which ultimately led to an open mutiny."[106] Moreover, the French fleet was again severely beaten by the English, and "after this third defeat at the hands of Pocock, d'Ache left India for good, leaving the English the undisputed masters of the sea."[107] Then, after a number of minor engagements a decisive battle took place on the 22nd of January 1760 near the fort of Wandiwash which the French were besieging. Here the French lost decisively, and in the next three months they had nothing left in the Carnatic except Jinje and Pondicherry. In May 1760, the English laid siege to Pondicherry.

The French hoped to retrieve the situation by an alliance with Hyder Ali who was then at the helm of affairs in Mysore. But they could not decide on a concerted plan of action, and Hyder's contingent which was sent to help the French returned to Mysore without a single battle. On the 16th of January, 1761, Pondicherry made an unconditional surrender. The victors "ruthlessly destroyed not merely the fortifications, but also the city itself;" and as Ormy described, "in a few months more not a roof was left standing in this once fair and flourishing city."[106]

Shortly after Pondicherry, Jinji and Mahe, the two French settlements on the Malabar coast, fell into the hands of the English. Nothing was left to the French in India.

This final failure of the French power in India is sometimes ascribed, besides the chronic financial difficulties of the French Company and its direct control by the French Government, to the personality of Lally as opposed to that of Dupleix. While there is some amount of truth in this, it should be borne in mind that the governing feature of the Third Carnatic War was the previous possession of the *subah* of Bengal by the English Company. As three Indian historians have written:[109]

> "... the possession of the military and financial resources of Bengal gave the English a decisive advantage over Lally. From this secure base they could send a constant supply of men and money to Madras, and create a diversion in its favour by attacking the French in the Northern Sarkars. Although it was not fully recognised at the time, the position of the English in Bengal made the struggle of the French a hopeless one from the very beginning of the Third Carnatic War. The battle of Plassey may be truly said to have decided the fate of the French in India. ... In spite of Lally's undoubted failings and short-comings, it is only fair to remember that the difficulties confronting him were really insurmountable, and that the French had no real chance of success against the English even under the best of leaders. There is a large element of truth in the remark of a historian, that 'neither Alexander the Great nor Napoleon could have won the empire of India by starting from Pondicherry as a base and contending with the power which held Bengal and command of the sea.'"

The sun of the British thus shone forth as the brightest in India.

4. Company without Rivals

On the world-scale also British supremacy was established in these days. William Pitt accepted the leadership of the British ruling class with the declaration: "I am sure that I can save the country, and that no one else can;"[110] and, singularly enough, 1757 to 1761, the period of his administration, marked the rise of the British Empire. England's ally, Frederick II, "won the battle of Rossbach in 1757, made Prussia and humbled France;" Wolfe took Quebec in 1759, "and the whole of Canada was conquered from the French in 1760;" Clive got rid of the last independent Nawab of Bengal in 1757, and "Eyre Coote crushed the French Power in India in 1761."[111] Within five years, the place of Britain as a World Power was assured; "France was humbled in Europe, and effaced in Asia and America;"[112] and the Portuguese and Dutch rivals of the English in India had already ceased to be of any importance.

Henceforth, Britain ruled the waves, and the English Company had no European rival in India. By the Peace of Paris, the French "factories" in India were restored to the French Company; but the French East India Company ended its career in 1769, and "the French Crown feebly kept up for the benefit of French private traders the 'factories' which the French Company, founded under Richelieu in 1642 and strengthened by Colbert in 1664, had gradually established in order to compete with the English."[113] Like the few Portuguese and Dutch settlements in India, the French also concentrated on the "country trade," and both in Europe and in India their business transactions were in collaboration either with the English Company directly or with its officials and private English traders living in India under the protection of the English Company.[114] In short, none of these European Powers could any more pose as rivals to the English Company. Referring to the last quarter of the eighteenth century, it has been reported:[115]

"Hastings could thus look back over the greater part of the era of conquest and turmoil which had given the British such mastery in India as to make it appear that other European nations existed there merely on sufferance, to be tolerated as long as they proved useful and to be thrust out when they did not."

Indeed, how helpless and abjectly dependent had become the position of the French Company, the strongest of the British rivals in India, was revealed from the series of events which followed the Third Carnatic War. Thus, on receipt of intelligence in Bengal at the beginning of July 1778 that Anglo-French hostilities were resumed in Europe, all the French possessions in India were again taken by the English, and on the conclusion of peace between the two nations the French "factories" were again returned to them in 1783.[116] Once more, when in 1793 "the change of government in France precipitated the people of England into a war with that country," with so little resistance "the whole of the French settlements in India were added to the English possessions" that within such a short time Lord Cornwallis could not manage to arrive from Bengal "to obtain the honour of extirpating the republicans."[117]

The French, however, again got back their "factories," and, along with the Portuguese in their settlements of Goa, Diu and Daman, the French held Pondicherry, Karikal, Mahe and Yanam throughout the British Period of India's history. But the French settlements (with a latest population of 313,000) and the Portuguese settlement (with 620,000) were pygmies in comparison with the British mastery over four hundred millions. Moreover, as noted before, they had to remain always subservient to the British. For a period in later years after the Third Carnatic War the French repeatedly endeavoured to gain some political power by intriguing with the Indian rulers; for example at the court of Hyderabad and with Tipu Sultan of Mysore. But, as the Portuguese, Dutch, Danes and other European merchant bourgeoisie had fully realized by then, it was now a futile dream for any European Power to oust the English from India. Referring to the French, Furber noted:[118]

"From many points of view it was a misfortune for France ever to have striven for political power and prestige in India after the days of Dupleix. This story of Anglo-French relations in India affairs after 1783 reveals the existence of 'rivets' of British power unappreciated and largely unknown to the great majority of Englishmen and Frenchmen. Utterly unable to carry on an East India trade without British assistance, completely powerless to reassert political dominance and military prestige with the resources she could then muster, France's only opportunity in India lay in turning Britain's increasing responsibilities in India to her own advantage. Bourdieu, with his advice to make 'golden' voyages during Britain's war with Tipu, had a truer grasp of realities than Vergennes. War and revolution intervened to make any fulfillment of Bourdieu's plans impossible. When the 'domestic situation' in France once more enabled French statesmen to think of India, they never thought of the commercial advantages that could be obtained in India without conquest. Napoleonic France thought only of Vergennes' old dream of re-creating by force of arms a French Indian empire which really never had existed and was destined never to exist."

Having thus eliminated its European rivals from the Indian field, the English Company, together with the process of subjugating the Indian rulers (of which more in the next chapter), went on fortifying the frontiers of India. The sea-frontier was not a problem, for Britain had by then emerged as the greatest sea-faring nation in the world. As regards the land-frontier, in order to stop possibilities of Afgan invasions or the imputed designs of the Russian Tsar to become interested in India, the Company joined with the Nawab of Oudh to launch the Ruhela War in 1774. This war, commanded by the British army, completely annihilated the peaceful Ruhelas and fortified the Company's position. Then, by the middle of the nineteenth century, the British had established themselves securely in the north-western provinces of India and had also obtained full control over its eastern frontier. Any possibility of invasions into India was thus ruled out, and un-rivalled the Company ruled in India until 1858. In the words of Marx:[119]

"No longer conquering, it had become *the* conqueror. The armies at its disposition no longer had to extend its dominion, but only to maintain it. From soldiers they were converted into policemen."

Notes and References

1 Mill, James—*The History of British India*, James Madden, London, 1858, i, p. 29.

2 Furber, Holden—*John Company at Work*, Harvard University Press, U.S.A., 1951, pp. 110—159.
3 *ibid.*, p. 110
4 Stephens, H. Morse—*Rulers of India: Albuquerque*, Oxford, Clarendon Press, 1892, p. 7.
5 Murray, Hugh—*History of British India*, T. Nelson and Sons, London, 1860, p. 66.
6 *loc. cit.* 1, i, p. 20
7 Collis, Maurice—*British Merchant Adventurers*, William Collins of London, 1942, p. 16.
8 Burn, Sir Richard—*Jahangir* in "The Cambridge History of India: The Mughul Period," Cambridge University Press, Great Britain, 1937, Vol. IV, p. 162.
9 *loc. cit.* 7, p. 16
10 *ibid.*, p. 16
11 *loc. cit.* 1, i, p. 23
12 *loc. cit.* 7, pp. 19—20
13 *loc. cit.* 1, i, pp. 23—25
14 *loc. cit.* 7, p. 22
15 *loc. cit.* 1, i, p. 25
16 *ibid.*, i, p. 35
17 Majumdar, R. C.; Raychaudhuri, H. C.; Datta, Kalikinkar—*An Advanced History of India*, Macmillan and Co., Limited, London, 1953, p. 634.
18 *ibid.*, p. 634
19 *loc. cit.* 1, ii, p. 264 n
20 *loc. cit.* 4, p. 102
21 Quoted in *loc. cit.* 4, pp. 103—104.
22 *loc. cit.* 4, p. 67
23 *ibid.*, p. 67
24 *loc. cit.* 1, i, p. 29
25 *ibid.*, i, p. 25
26 *ibid.*, i, p. 29
27 *ibid.*, i, p. 26
28 *loc. cit.* 17, p. 635
29 *loc. cit.* 1, i, p. 26
30 *ibid.*, i, p. 26
31 *loc. cit.* 5, pp. 148—149
32 *ibid.*, p. 149
33 *loc. cit.* 1, i, p. 31
34 *ibid.*, i, p. 32
35 *loc. cit.* 5, p. 149
36 *loc. cit.* 1, i, p. 38, n 1
37 *ibid.*, i, p. 40
38 *ibid.*, i, p. 40
39 *ibid.*, i, p. 56
40 *loc. cit.* 5, p. 118
41 *loc. cit.* 1, i, pp. 52—53

42 Quoted from Anderson's *History of Commerce* in *loc. cit.* 1, i, p. 61, n 1.
43 *loc. cit.* 1, i, p. 56
44 *loc. cit.* 2, pp. 78—109
45 *loc. cit.* 1, iii, p. 204
46 *ibid.*, iii, pp. 204—205
47 *ibid.*, iv, p. 82
48 *ibid.*, iv, p. 159
49 *ibid.*, vi, p. 49
50 *loc. cit.* 17, pp. 642—643
51 For details regarding the initial aspirations of the French merchant bourgeoisie to open direct trade-relations with India and the subsequent career of the French East India Company in its earlier stages, one may consult Mr. l'Abbé Guyon's *Histoire des Indes Orientales: Anciennes et Modernes*, Paris, 1744, Vol. III, Part III, Chapter II.
52 *loc. cit.* 51, Vol. III, p. 86
53 *loc. cit.* 1, i, p. 72
54 Smith, Adam—*An Inquiry into the Nature and Causes of the Wealth of Nations*, Everyman's Library, London, Vol. 2, p. 157.
55 Duffield, W. B.—*Chartered Companies* in "The Encyclopaedia Britannica," Eleventh Edition, Cambridge, England, 1911, Vol. V, p. 951.
56 *loc. cit.* 1, i, p. 72
57 *ibid.*, i, p. 72
58 *ibid.*, i, p. 76
59 *ibid.*, i, p. 86
60 *ibid.*, i, p. 86
61 Sarkar, Sir Jadunath—*Aurangzib* in "The Cambridge History of India: The Mughul Period," Vol. IV, Cambridge at the University Press, England, 1937, p. 308.
62 *loc. cit.* 1, i, p. 87
63 *ibid.*, i, p. 87
64 *ibid.*, i, p. 72 ff.
65 *loc. cit.* 17, p. 643
66 Dutt, Romesh—*The Economic History of India under Early British Rule*, Routledge & Kegan Paul Ltd., London, 1950, p. 3.
67 *ibid.*, p. 3
68 *loc. cit.* 1, iii, p. 52
69 *ibid.*, i, pp. 87—88
70 *ibid.*, i, p. 88
71 *ibid.*, i, p. 88, n 2
72 *ibid.*, iii, p. 73
73 *ibid.*, iii, pp. 73—74
74 *ibid.*, iii, p. 74
75 *ibid.*, iii, p. 74
76 *ibid.*, iii, pp. 74—75
77 *ibid.*, iii, pp. 79—80
78 *ibid.*, iii, p. 79

79 *ibid.*, iii, p. 89
80 *ibid.*, iii, p. 89
81 *ibid.*, iii, p. 91
82 *ibid.*, iii, p. 91
83 Quoted in *loc. cit.* 1, iii, p. 92, n 1.
84 *loc. cit.* 1, iii, p. 94
85 *ibid.*, iii, p. 95
86 *ibid.*, iii, p. 97
87 *ibid.*, iii, p. 97
88 *ibid.*, iii, pp. 97—98
89 *ibid.*, iii, p. 98
90 *loc. cit.* 17, p. 653
91 *loc. cit.* 1, iii, p. 103
92 *ibid.*, iii, p. 105
93 *ibid.*, iii, p. 106
94 *ibid.*, iii, p. 148
95 *loc. cit.* 17, p. 661
96 *loc. cit.* 1, iii, p. 149
97 *ibid.*, iii, p. 148
98 *ibid.*, iii, p. 148, n 2
99 *loc. cit.* 17, pp. 666—667
100 *ibid.*, p. 667
101 *ibid.*, p. 667
102 *ibid.*, p. 667
103 *ibid.*, p. 667
104 *ibid.*, p. 667
105 *ibid.*, p. 667
106 *ibid.*, p. 667
107 *ibid.*, p. 668
108 *ibid.*, p. 668
109 *ibid.*, pp. 668—669
110 Quoted in *loc. cit.* 66, p. 1.
111 *loc. cit.* 66, p. 1
112 *ibid.*, p. 1
113 *loc. cit.* 2, p. 10
114 *ibid.*, Chapter II, etc.
115 *ibid.*, p. 11
116 *loc. cit.* 1, iv, p. 113 ff.
117 *ibid.*, v, pp. 330—331
118 *loc. cit.* 2, pp. 76—77
119 Marx, Karl—*Indian Mutiny*, New York Daily Tribune, July 15, 1857.

CHAPTER 4

THE COMPANY AND INDIAN RULERS

For a proper understanding of the role of the East India Company vis-a-vis the Indian rulers, it is necessary to examine the following points:

1) Why the European merchant companies were welcomed into India.

2) Why up to the first decades of the eighteenth century these companies had to remain as "peaceful" traders, while snipeing at one another whenever a suitable opportunity offered, and simultaneously striving consistently to obtain exclusive "concessions" from the Indian rulers for their commercial pursuits (that is, at the expense of other merchants–Indians or foreigners), in which operations the English Company excelled others and thus consolidated its position best in India during this period.

3) How, after the close of the seventeenth century, with the disintegration of the Mughal Empire and the confusion prevailing throughout India while the Indian Powers were bidding for supreme power, the situation was maturing in India for the two merchant companies –the English and the French–to aspire for the kingdom of India.

4) And how, when this state of affairs became quite apparent to all towards the middle of the eighteenth century, the English Company finally emerged as the ruler of the subcontinent.

To appreciate the above points, it is first necessary to inquire into the social background of India at that time. Such inquiry reveals that while the merchant bourgeoisie of England were consolidating their position in society, in India also far-reaching changes had taken place during the fourteenth to the sixteenth centuries of the present era.

1. The Social Organism

Just as in Europe conditions were created from about the fourteenth century for the emergence of the merchant bourgeoisie and the ultimate formation of the East India Company in England in 1600, so during the same period a situation was developing in India which led to a demand for foreign traders to buy Indian goods. This created the basis for the European mercantile powers to penetrate into India, and secure bases in the subcontinent. Of such changes, however, only a few pregnant glimpses are available, for the traditional chroniclers have dealt almost entirely with the change of dynasties, details of battles between rival kings, and such "spectacular" events. Yet, such scattered information as is available today suggests that towards the end of the sixteenth and the beginning of the seventeenth centuries while the feudal grandeur of the Mughals had gained its supreme height, the centralized administration of the Mughals had begun to intervene directly in the village community system—the backbone of India's economy—and thus undermined the basic principles of the system. At the same time, the Bhakti movement, probably led by the artisans and traders, was spreading over India. This movement, with its opposition to the caste system, was affecting the social and ideological stability of the village community system. And this was also the time when the Indian mercantile class was making itself felt in Indian society, and Royalty had also become interested in commercial pursuits, especially in foreign trade.

That India was then basking in the glory of the Mughal's splendour was noticed by every foreign visitor. Ralph Fitch, the first envoy of the English merchant bourgeoisie, who arrived in India during the last days of Akbar's reign, was very greatly impressed by the big towns and lavish wealth of the Mughal Empire, compared to which his own country appeared to him as poor and undeveloped. Very truly Marx noted that Akbar "Macht *Delhi* zur größten und schönsten Stadt damals existing in the world."[1] Sir Thomas Roe the first "Merchant-Ambassador" of England to the Mughal Court during the reign of Jahangir (successor of Akbar), felt himself very small in the society of Mughal nobles.

"His salary was fixed at £ 600 a year, a sum equal to at least £ 5,000 nowadays, but the incomes of the big people at Jahangir's Court ran into tens or even hundreds of thousands. Moreover, his staff was not very brilliant. A chaplain and a doctor on £ 50 and £ 24 per annum were supplied, Roe himself having to pay the wages of the rest of his retinue from the annual grant of £ 100. Later he records in his diary how ashamed he was of his clothes. The Mughals were dressed in the most dazzling manner. 'Five years allowance would not have furnished me with one indifferent suit sortable to theirs,' he writes."[2]

Such magnificence of the Royal Court was of course based, as previously, on the village economy in the main, and therefore all sources of central revenue taken together "were quite small when compared with the land-revenue."[3] But there is some evidence to suggest that (i) the essential characteristics of Indian village life had begun to undergo changes from about the fourteenth century, (ii) a new economy was making in-roads into the society, and (iii) the social organization was in the process of being eventually altered. However, before discussing these changes, it is first necessary to examine the specific features of Indian social organization in the pre-British period of India's history. For it was the *social system,* as reflected by the character of social organization in those days, which was undergoing changes, and these changes had a vital bearing on the points raised at the beginning of this chapter.

That up to the advent of the British in India her social organization was predominantly characterized by the village community system has been noted by several authorities. It is true that this system was found to be absent or rudimentary in the south-western extreme of the subcontinent (such as in the present-day state of Kerala), but that in all other parts of India it was or had been the dominant institution in society is borne out from the findings of the officials of the East India Company at the early stage of expansion of the Company's power in India. Already in the last decades of the eighteenth century, the officers of the East India Company were struck by the presence of village communities in India, and their reports formed the basis for the exhaustive description of this institution in British *Parliamentary Papers.*[4] This description was essentially based on the findings of the Company's officials in the Madras Presidency, wherefrom further details emanated in later years.[5] Also, in 1819, Holt Mackenzie reported the existence of village communities in northern India while in service there as the Secretary to the Board of Commissioners in the Conquered and Ceded Provinces; and further details came in 1830 from Sir Charles Metcalfe, a member of the Governor-General's Council.[6] Likewise, Elphinstone noted the presence of village communities in the Deccan in his report, written in 1819, on the territories conquered from the Peswa; and it was further confirmed from Poona in the administrative report of Captain Robertson in 1821; etc.[7] Similarly, the First Punjab Administrative Report, published in 1852 after the consolidation of British power in that territory, recorded that "the corporate capacities of Village Communities" used to be recognized there also.[8] And even for eastern India (that is, Bengal, Bihar and Orissa), which Baden-Powell stated to have given the impression "that all land must have some *landlord,* with tenants under him,"[9] the British *Parliamentary Papers* recorded quite categorically that previously the *zemindars* (that is, revenue farmers, who were turned into landlords during British rule, as explained in Chapters 5 and 6) were essentially "accountable managers and collectors [of revenue], and not lords and proprietors of the lands;" that "the sale of land by auction, or in any other way, for realizing arrears of land revenue, appears to have been unusual, if not unknown in all parts of India, before its introduction by the British government into the Company's dominions;" and that traces still remained to show that the village community system existed also in this part of India.[10]

In short, except in the south-western tip of the subcontinent, the village community system flourished practically all over India. Therefore, in order to understand the social organization of India in the pre-British period of her history, one should first examine what was this village community system, why it came into existence, and how it attained its stability in Indian society.

While the working of the village community system in different parts of India was described by several East India Company officers, and on the basis of some of these notes a general account was published in British *Parliamentary Papers* in 1812, it may not be an exaggaration to state that one can get the best idea of how these village communities functioned from the classic description given by Marx on the basis of the literature available to him. What he wrote in this respect while discussing "Division of Labour and Manufacture" in pre-capitalist societies is of inestimable value as a brilliant piece of scientific generalization.[11]

"Those small and extremely ancient Indian communities, some of which have continued down to this day, are based on possession in common of the land, on the blending of agriculture and handicrafts, and on an unalterable division of labour, which serves, whenever a new community is started, as a plan and scheme ready cut and dried. Occupying areas from 100 up to several thousand acres, each forms a compact whole producing all it requires. The chief part of the products is destined for direct use by the community itself, and does not take the form of a commodity. Hence, production here is independent of that division of labour brought about, in Indian society as a whole, by means of the exchange of commodities. It is the surplus alone that becomes a commodity, and a portion of even that, not until it has reached the hands of the State, into whose hands from time immemorial a certain quantity of these products has found its way in the shape of rent in kind. The constitution of these communities varies in different parts of India. In those of the simplest form, the land is tilled in common, and the produce divided among the members. At the same time, spinning and weaving are carried on in each family as subsidiary industries. Side by side with the masses thus occupied with one and the same work, we find the 'chief inhabitant,' who is judge, police, and tax-gatherer in one; the book-keeper who keeps the accounts of the tillage and registers everything relating thereto; another official, who prosecutes criminals, protects strangers travelling through, and escorts them to the next village; the boundary man, who guards the boundaries against neighbouring communities; the water-overseer, who distributes the water from the common tanks for irrigation; the Brahmin, who conducts the religious services; the schoolmaster, who on the sand teaches the children reading and writing; the calender-Brahmin, or astrologer, who makes known the lucky or unlucky days for seed-time and harvest, and for every other kind of agricultural work; a smith and a carpenter, who make and repair all the agricultural implements; the potter, who makes all the pottery of the village; the barber, the washerman, who washes clothes, the silversmith, here and there the poet, who in some communities replaces the silversmith, in others the schoolmaster. This dozen of individuals is maintained at the expense of the whole community. If the population increases, a new community is founded, on the pattern of the old one, on unoccupied land. The whole mechanism discloses a systematic division of labour; but a division like that in manufactures is impossible, since the smith and the carpenter, etc., find an unchanging market, and at the most there occur, according to the sizes of the villages, two or three of each, instead of one. The law that regulates the division of labour in the community acts with the irresistible authority of a law of Nature, at the same time that each individual artificer, the smith, the carpenter, and so on, conducts in his workshop all the operations of his handicraft in the traditional way, but independently, and without recognizing any authority over him. The simplicity of the organisation for production in these self-sufficing communities that constantly reproduce themselves in the same form, and when accidentally destroyed, spring up again on the spot and with the same name—this simplicity supplies the key to the secret of the unchangeableness of Asiatic societies, an unchangeableness in such striking contrast with the constant dissolution and refounding of Asiatic States, and the never-ceasing changes of dynasty. The structure of the economical elements of society remains untouched by the storm-clouds of the political sky."

Possibly, within a village the peasant-householders were keen to maintain their respective rights over the plots under use and sometimes transfer or alienation of land also took place. Such features of land relations within a village have been noted by several research scholars in recent times; and they have prompted some social scientists to denounce the view that the Indian social organization was based on the village community system. But the descriptions given of the administrative organization and the socio-economic life in India by reputed Indologists and historians suggest that from about the fourth or fifth centuries of the Christian era the village community system had become the dominant note of Indian society.[12]

From these descriptions one sees that in those days "agriculture was the main occupation of the villages, but each of them had usually its own compliment of weavers, potters, carpenters, oil-pressers and goldsmiths."[13] Thus forming a self-sufficient economic unit, the villagers were organized into a community which had a headman who, "designated as *Grāmeyaka* in some place and *Grāmādhyaksha* in others, was at the head of the village administration."[14] There was also a "non-official local council" composed of all or the representatives of the *Great Men of the Village* (viz. *mahattamas* in the Uttar Pradesh area of today, *mahattaras* in Maharashtra, *mahājanas* in Karnatak, and *perumakkāl* in the Tamil country), who were either the "leading householders of the village"[15] or the village-elders, that is, the "senior persons of different classes [castes?], who had acquired a pre-eminent status by their age, experience and character."[16] In addition, in some parts of India at least, such as in Maharashtra, Karnatak and the Tamil country, there used to be a Primary Assembly of all villagers, (viz. *ur* and *sabha* in the Tamil country), which was entrusted among other duties with the most important task "to elect the village executive."[17]

The autonomous character of these village communities is evident from the facts elicited by the scholars that the "jurisdiction of the village authorities extended over houses, streets, *bazars* [markets], burning grounds, temples, wells, tanks, waste lands, forests and cultivable lands;"[18] that the village council "looked after village defence, settled village disputes, organized works of public utility, acted as a trustee for minors, and collected the government revenues and paid them into the central treasury;"[19] and that the central state governments "could eventually reach the people and discharge their functions mainly through these bodies."[20] On the other hand, it has been stated that "the representatives of the people had a decisive voice in them" (that is, in the village councils), for the "local executive officers were usually hereditary servants and not members of the central bureaucracy; they, therefore, usually sided with the local bodies in their tussle with the central government."[21] Thus, while, on one side, "almost all functions of the government, except that of organizing the army, determining foreign policy, and declaring and conducting a war, were discharged through the agency of the local bodies, where the representatives of the locality had a powerful voice,"[22] on the other, the village communities were such independent and powerful societal units that: "Kings may impose any number of taxes; eventually those only could be realised which the village councils could agree to collect."[23]

Indeed, the relevance of the village community system to the Indian society is further stressed by the fact that while it has sometimes been said that peasant-proprietorship and direct access of the sovereign to the peasants were the predominant features of social organization in the south, during the period from the middle of the sixth to the middle of the ninth century of the Christian era in this part of India—

> "The organization which made for the continuity of life and tradition, held society together, and carried it safe through the storms and turmoils of political revolution was the autonomous, self-sufficient village. It was the primary cell of the body politic, and the vitality of its institutions is well-attested by hundreds of inscriptions from all parts of the country. Usually, it comprised a number of families, each occupying a house of its own in the residential quarter of the village, owning its own share of the arable land, and enjoying privileges like the right to graze cattle and gather firewood in the waste land and forest lying round about and held in common by the villagers as a body. ... The villagers met periodically to consider matters of common concern and for the settlement of disputes and the administration of justice. ... The village had a headman, variously called *mutuḍa, kilān, grāmabhōjaka* and so on, who was its leader and mediator with the royal government. How he was appointed and whether the office was hereditary cannot be determined. The village elders are also particularly mentioned besides the headmen and the assembly."[24]

On the strength of the above facts it seems that whether or not land transfer and alienation took place within a village, village communities did exist in India in those days. But could they be properly characterized as "based on possession in common of the land?" There is more than one piece of evidence to suggest that this characterization is not based on wrong or incomplete information.

Firstly, one cannot fail to note that even for south India (and there also during the sixth to the seventeenth century of the Christian era), on the one side, it was stated that "great prestige attached to ownership of land, and everyone, whatever his occupation, aimed at having a small plot he could call his own," and, on the other, it was noted that a "periodical redistribution of the arable land of a village among its inhabitants prevailed in many parts of the country till comparatively recent times."[25] It appears probable, therefore, that what is meant by "ownership of land" in the above and several such studies was essentially a usufructuary right vested on the "arable land" at least, if not on the homesteads (*vāstu*).

Secondly, the cases of land alienation recorded in those days show that they were overwhelmingly, if not entirely, as religious gifts and endowments to Brahmins and religious organizations.[26] Moreover, as has been shown particularly for Bengal, in that period the individual *possessors* could make a gift of their land for religious purposes to Brahmins or to religious organizations after first "buying" the land from the sovereign authority for a sum considered to meet the commuted tax-dues of the state, for the donated land would not henceforth bear any tax payable to the king.[27] Thus, in the case of Bengal at least, the "purchase" of land meant really the purchase of the exemption from the king's tax-demand, and the "sale" of land, accordingly, the transfer of the right to collect taxes from the area sold.[28] Whether or not the *sale* and *purchase* of land in other parts of India meant the same as cited for Bengal, it appears from the following extract quoted from the studies of an authority on ancient India that during the period c. 200–550 A. D. land alienation essentially meant the transfer of the right to collect the land-tax previously received by the state; it did not imply the sense of private ownership of land as it is understood today, that is, land as a property for gain and use as well as a commodity to be bought and sold.

"It does not seem that anything like the modern *zamindari* system of Bengal or the Uttar Pradesh existed in the country. It is referred to neither in the inscriptions nor in the Smṛtis. Occasionally, Brāhmaṇas, temples and monasteries were assigned entire villages, but the donees acquired only the right to receive the royal revenues and could not dispossess any tenants. The donees were often required to stay in the villages alienated to them, which discouraged absentee landlordism."[29]

Thirdly, besides as religious gifts, those lands underwent transfer which had fallen vacant on account of "want of heirs or failure to pay the land-tax," and therefore the sovereign authority was interested to see that some individuals possess them as otherwise no land-tax would be forthcoming from these lands. Here, again, the cases of land transfer do not refer to an inherent right vested with the private "ownership" to buy and sale land freely. On the contrary, these land-holdings were usually given "in charity" by the king, that is, without payment, probably signifying thereby that land had not become a coveted *commodity*. And it is also worthy of note in this connection that such holdings were for no other purposes than *possession* and *use*, and therefore were with the stipulation that like other landholders the new possessors will also have to pay a land-tax.

"In several villages, the State owned small fields of cultivable land, which are expressly described as *rājyavastu* i. e., Crownlands or the property of the state, in some of our records. These fields used to come under the state ownership usually on account of want of heirs or failure to pay the land-tax. Kings are often seen granting them in charity. Donees in such cases acquired full ownership of land, and not a right to its land-tax, in fact they were often not exempted from it."[30]

It may not, therefore, be wrong to interpret the cases of land alienation and transfer in those days more in terms of *possession* than, strictly speaking, of *ownership* of land by individual villagers. But what was the role of the village community in such transactions wherefrom one may argue for or against its characterization as "based on possession in common of the lands?" On this point it is seen that such was the authority of the village community that all cases of transfer and alienation of land, as noted above, had to be sanctioned by it or its council. It has been stated:[31]

"Land was regarded as a very valuable piece of property and its transfer could be effected only through the consent of the fellow villagers or the permission of the village or town council. The actual transfer of ownership (?) was effected in the presence of the village elders, who formally demarcated the piece."

And the same power was held by the village community in regard to the disposal of other lands in the village. For instance:

"The fallow and waste lands belonged to the state, but their actual disposal was made with the consent and through the agency of the local village *Panchāyat* or town council."[32]

Thus it appears that the village communities were indeed "based on possession in common of the land," and that even the sovereign authority did not have the right to interfere therein. Hence—

"When however entire villages were given away in charity, what was donated was the right to receive the royal dues. The inhabitants of these villages were never exhorted to quit their private lands in favour of the donee, but to pay him the different taxes and to show him proper courtesy; future kings were besought to desist not from evicting private owners but from collecting the royal dues. Cases are also on record where an entire village was granted to a donee along with specific fields or plots in it. It is clear that in such cases the state was the owner of only some small plots of land in the villages concerned, which it could easily transfer to the donee. As far as the rest of the cultivable land was concerned, it was owned by private individuals; the state could not dispossess them, but could only direct them to pay the usual taxes to the donee. The available evidence thus makes it clear that the ownership (?) of the cultivable land vested in private individuals or families, and not in the state."[33]

It need not be discussed further whether the land was *owned* by "private individuals or families" in the sense ownership of land is understood today or whether they had essentially an usufructuary right over the land held in common by the village community. No doubt, further researches are needed in order to substantiate the respective viewpoints and finally to arrive at a definite conclusion, for one cannot ignore the fact that in an old treaty like Kautilyá's *Aribaśāstra* also there was the provision in Book III, Chapter 9, for selling the *vāstu* to certain categories of people. But, in any case, it is evident from the above that, in a broad sense at least, land was held in common by the village community, so that all transactions in land *within* a village could be undertaken by the villagers with the permission and direct supervision of the village assembly or council. The sovereign authority, on the other hand, ruled over the whole territory, that is, *over* the villages, while what went on *within* them was a matter for the village communities to look after and not *directly* of the ruler.

In such an independent existence of the village communities the essential basis of contact between them and the ruler was in connection with the payment of land-tax, which, as later researches have brought to light, could have been paid partly in cash instead of only "in the shape of rent in kind." But, as has been asserted, up to the ninth century of the Christian era at least, "the evidence to show that the land tax was usually paid in kind is overwhelming."[34] Moreover, even if cash payment also existed side by side, the payment in kind was not of an insignificant measure. This is evident from the fact that "the government had to make elaborate arrangements for the proper administration of its granaries,"[35] and that also in "mediaeval" south India "there were local granaries in the villages and small townships where the share of the state collected in kind was stored."[36]

In any case, even though a part of the rent was sometimes paid in cash and this would have led to the circulation of currency in the villages to a certain extent, by itself the land-tax could have but little effect in transforming the rural produces into commodities. In the villages the market in commodities was poorly developed. The circulation of currency was so much restricted that in south India during the sixth to the seventeenth century of the Christian era the "day labourer was usually paid for in grain;" and, even though it has been asserted that "there was a fairly large class of landless labourers," they "shared the proceeds of agriculture."[37] Similarly, there was "a staff of menial servants from the outcastes who were likewise rewarded by shares in the common land," and the "artisans of the village had shares from the common land of the village, which were of the nature of retainers or inducements to them to stay in the village."[38] In addition, although there were some peasants who have been described as tenant-cultivators, "especially on lands belonging to temples and other corporate institutions," their terms of tenancy were "fixed either by the terms of original endowment or by separate negotiation in each case," and "very often such tenants had rights which made them more or less part-owners (?) of the land they cultivated."[39] Also, for India during the third to the sixth century of the Christian era, it has been noted that those (mainly the royal donees, Brahmins, etc., as stated before) who did not till "their own lands, used to lease them to tenants; the latter used to receive as the return for their labours a share which varied from 33 to 50 per cent of the gross produce."[40]

Evidently, production in the villages had only (or predominantly) a use-value. A part of the rural production would be consumed directly by the producing households and another would be bartered between the peasants and artisans and other members in the village community in exchange of products and services; an arrangement which had become so traditional that it was noted by Dr. Francis Buchanan as late as in the early years of the nineteenth century while conducting socio-economic surveys in different parts of the East India Company's territory in India.[41] This direct relation between production and consumption was further assured by the artisans' and the so-called menial servants' shares in the common land of the village, as stated before. And, finally, it should be borne in mind that the village was "primarily a settlement of peasants;"[42] that the so-called tenant-cultivators could not be very many, as tenancy-cultivation depended on how much land was donated to temples or other corporate organizations or to the Brahmins and the total area thus bestowed as gifts could obviously account for only a small share of the territory of any sovereign authority; that because of "an unchanging market" in the villages, craft production could function only as an ancillary to cultivation; and that within a subsistence economy of the rural areas the scope for the growth of wage labourers (even though paid in kind) had to be limited. The village community system of India may, therefore, be rightly characterized as "based on possession in common of the land, on the blending of agriculture and handicrafts, and on the unalterable division of labour;" as depending on a subsistence economy, for "the chief part of the products is destined for direct use by the community itself, and does not take the form of commodity," and, therefore, "production here is independent of that division of labour brought about, in Indian society as a whole, by means of the exchange of commodities;" and as revealing by "the simplicity of the organisation for production in these self-sufficing communities that constantly reproduce themselves in the same form, and when accidentally destroyed, spring up again on the spot and with the same name," the key to "the secret of the unchangeableness of Asiatic societies, an unchangeableness in such striking contrast with the constant dissolution and refounding of Asiatic States, and the never-ceasing changes of dynasty."

The question that follows is why did the village community system come into existence in India? Here one should bear in mind the distinctive features of her geography which influenced the early stages of India's social development, and especially her agrarian economy. No doubt, there were several factors which worked conjointly and led to the formation of the village community system in India. But, curiously enough, among them the role of geography seems to have been constantly present, explicitly or implicitly.

There was, for instance, the characteristic isolation of the Indian subcontinent. Guarded by mountain ranges from the North-West Frontier area and Kashmir to Assam and Chittagong Hill Tracts in north, north-east and east, by the arid regions of Baluchistan and Sind in north-west, and by the not-easily navigable seas in south-west, south and south-east, India was a veritable *cul de sac* for human migrants in the times when transport and communication were poorly developed.[43] Therefore, when attracted by her richness or for other reasons people of different racial composition and ethnic varieties and at different stages of social development arrived in India in waves of migration (in dribbles or in hordes), most of them settled down permanently in the subcontinent, except some trickles of emigrants farther east and southwards in early years.[44]

There was also the point that India in her vastness and in her extensive topographical variation could accomodate all the migrants. Hence, although following successive immigrations the weaker groups were pushed away by the newly-arrived powerful ones to regions other than the focal points of migration, and the weakest groups were driven to comparatively inaccessible hills and forests and rocky plateus,[45] yet India being a world in itself could provide for them all. Thus from early times India presented a mosaic of various races and ethnic groups residing in the subcontinent as friendly neighbours or distant foes and undergoing their course of social development.[46]

Later, when on the basis of plough cultivation agriculture developed as the predominant form of production in India and agrarian village settlements were on the sway, a new civilization began to emerge in the subcontinent, for the propagation of which the establishment of a stable relation between different groups of people coming together in a village settlement or residing in close juxtaposition was an indispensable necessity. It will be explained further on that such a stable relation between peoples at different stages of social development or exhibiting different ethnic characteristics was founded on the village community system and its socio-spiritual super-structure of the caste system; a point which has been stressed by some distinguished sociologists in order to indicate the function of the village community system in India in the pre-British days.[47] One should not, however, forget at the same time that primarily it was the climate and territorial conditions which had a dominant say in the matter of India's agricultural development in the early days and thus led to the formation of the village communities.

Because of India's peculiar climatic and territorial conditions, artificial irrigation by canals and waterworks had to be the basis of a flourishing agrarian economy. But, owing to her territorial vastness and diversity of her people, her decentralized and dispersed social configurations, and foremost of all, owing to the technical resources at the disposal of the individual peasant-householders, this imperative demand could not be met by them individually, although field cultivation had by then come into vogue and with the extensive use of the plough peasant-farming on specific plots of land had become the unit of cultivation. Under the circumstances the village community system was the solution that was worked out. As Marx wrote:[48]

> "Climate and territorial conditions, especially the vast tracts of desert, extending from the Sahara, through Arabia, Persia, India and Tartary, to the most elevated Asiatic highlands, constituted artificial irrigation by canals and waterworks, the basis of Oriental agriculture. As in Egypt and India, inundations are used for fertilising the soil in Mesopotamia, Persia, etc.; advantage is taken of a high level for feeding irrigative canals. This prime necessity of an economical and common use of water, which in the Occident drove private enterprise to voluntary association, as in Flanders and Italy, necessitated in the Orient, where civilisation was too low and the territorial extent too vast to call into life voluntary association, the interference of the centralising power of government. Hence an economical function devolved upon all Asiatic governments, the function of providing public works....
>
> However changing the political aspect of India's past must appear, its social condition has remained unaltered since its remote antiquity, until the first decennium of the nineteenth century. The handloom and the spinning wheel, producing their regular myriads of spinners and weavers were the pivots of the structure of that society....
>
> These two circumstances—the Hindu, on the one hand, leaving, like all Oriental peoples, to the central government the care of the great public works, the prime condition of his agriculture and commerce, dispersed, on the other hand, over the surface of the country, and agglomerated in small centres by the domestic union of agricultural and manufacturing pursuits —these two circumstances had brought about, since the remotest times, a social system of particular features—the so-called *village system* which gave to each of these small unions their independent organisation and distinct life."

Indeed, that geography played a vital role in the economic organization of India when plough cultivation had come into use but with respect to a major demand of nature the state of productive forces was at a low stage of development is confirmed by the fact that in the south-western tip of the Indian subcontinent the village community system did not emerge as a dominant institution in society. Unlike the rest of India, this part is blessed with two monsoons instead of one. Here the south-west monsoon covers the months of June to

September, and the north-east monsoon extends the rainy period over October and November. Thus covering two main crop periods (viz. *kharif* and *rabi* of north India) the monsoons lead to a rainfall of over one hundred inches per year; and therefore in this area there is no great need for artificial irrigation for the agrarian economy. On the other hand, for practically the whole of north India and the remaining regions of south India this remains as an indispensable necessity.[49] Hence, when village settlement was under way with the spread of plough cultivation, the village community system established itself on the Indo-Gangetic plain of northern and eastern India, in the Narbada-Tapti region of the Deccan, and the Mahanadi-Godavari to the Kistna-Cauvery region of south India.

From the rivers (like Indus, Ganges, Jumna, Mahanadi and others in northern and eastern India as well as Narbada, Tapti, Godavari, Kistna, Cauvery and others in the Deccan and south India) water-reservoirs were built and canals were constructed by the ruling authorities;[50] and their remains were seen by the East India Company officers as late as in the early part of the nineteenth century.[51] And while these public works were under the control and supervision of the ruling authorities, in order to make full use of the facilities for artificial irrigation, in the villages which were strewn over the vast areas of a kingdom "voluntary associations" sprang up empowered with the responsibility to look after the feeding canals, the culverts and bridges over these canals, the protection and maintenance of the villages, etc., as brought to light by the research scholars on ancient India with respect to the working of the village communities in those days.

Some of these scholars have noted the connection between the spread of the agrarian village economy and the formation or assumption of autonomous power by the village communities from about the fourth century of the Christian era;[52] some others, on the other hand, have put forward suggestions or have furnished materials from which such a connection can be established;[53] while some others, again, have only noted that a specific feature of Indian social organization in the "Gupta and post-Gupta period (c. 300 to 1200 A. D.)" was—

"...the remarkable development it recorded in the powers and functions of the village and town councils. These institutions existed in the earlier period also, but the available evidence does not show that they were then so much non-official in character, and were wielding such extensive powers as they did from the 4th century onwards both in northern and southern India."[54]

From these evidences furnished by the Indologists and historians one is inclined to agree with the observations made by one of them that: "The advance of agrarian village economy over tribal country is the first great social revolution in India: the change from an aggregate of gentes to a society;" and that: "If the village seems to exist from 'Time Immemorial,' it is only because the memory of time served no useful function in the village economy that dominated the country."[55]

How did the village community system attain such a stability that it came to be regarded as existing from "time immemorial?" This question should be examined from two aspects,–(i) economic and (ii) social and ideological; viz. one in relation to a village community and its outer world, and the other in relation to its internal mechanism. Regarding the former, which is essentially economic in character, one should not forget that the autonomous and self-sufficient character of the village community system as well as the simplicity of its organization (as noted by Marx) maintained the villages as independent units of society and contributed greatly to the stability of the system over hundreds of years. As Charles Metcalfe noted so forcefully as late as in the nineteenth century:[56]

"The Village Communities are little Republics, having nearly everything they can want within themselves, and almost independent of any foreign relations. They seem to last where nothing else lasts. Dynasty after dynasty tumbles down; revolution succeeds to revolution; Hindoo, Patan, Mogul, Mahratta, Sikh, English, are all masters in turn; but the Village Communities remain the same. In times of trouble they arm and fortify themselves; an hostile army passes through the country; the Village Communities collect their cattle within their walls, and let the enemy pass unprovoked. If plunder and devastation be directed against themselves, and the force employed be irresistible, they flee to friendly villages at a distance; but, when the storm has passed over, they return and resume their occupations. If a country remain for a series of years the scene of continued pillage and massacre, so that the villages cannot be inhabited, the scattered villagers nevertheless return whenever the power of peaceable possession revives. A generation may pass away, but the succeeding generation will return. The sons will take the places of their fathers, the same site for the village, the same position for the houses, the same lands, will be re-occupied by the descendants of those who were driven out when the village was depopulated; and it is not a trifling matter that will drive them out, for they will often maintain their post through times of disturbance and convulsion, and acquire strength sufficient to resist pillage and oppression with success.

The union of the Village Communities, each one forming a separate little State in itself, has, I conceive, contributed more than any other cause to the preservation of the people of India through all revolutions and changes which they have suffered, and it is in a high degree conductive to their happiness and to the enjoyment of a great portion of freedom and independence."

But what supplied the *social force* to this kind of vegetative existence and reproduction of the villages, and thus upheld the village community system of India for centuries as unaffected by the political clouds over the Indian sky? This question leads one to the second aspect of stabilization of the village community system, for it was the peculiar development of the Indian social structure on the basis of the *jati*-division of society which provided the internal mechanism of the village community system and stabilized it socially and ideologically.[57]

The *jati*-division of Indian society (strictly speaking, of the Hindu society at first) is represented by the immutable social units, demarcated from one another by the three main attributes of (i) hereditarily-fixed occupations, (ii) endogamy, and (iii) commensality, and arranged in hierarchical orders in particular societies in different parts of India, such as in Bengal, Maharashtra, Tamilnad, the Punjab, etc.[58] These *jatis* truly represented the Indian caste system and showed the unique character of Indian social organization (along with the village community system). For the previous division of the Aryan society into four *varnas* of Brahmins, Kshatriyas, Vaishyas and Sudras could only present a social ranking based on birth qualification, and this, as Senart stated quite precisely, is not unknown in other parts of the world.

"La répartition hiérarchique de la population en classes est un fait presque universal; le régime des castes est un phénomène unique."[59]

Some of these *jatis* came into existence with increasing social division of labour in the Aryan society, whereby several *jatis* were formed with their specific avocations and privileges and obligations in society.[60] But the *jati*-division of the Indian society was not limited only to the Aryans; it took place in the *total* social complex and embraced all the people who took part in building the Indian civilization. When the Aryan civilization began to spread over the plains of India, and when, as stated by some scholars, the Dravidians, imbued with the socio-economic and spiritual developments of the Aryans,[61] undertook the same process of development in south India, what emerged in Indian society has been aptly characterized as "the advance of agrarian village economy." In this process of development the social structure that evolved incorporated various peoples. There were the autochthones of an area who might have still remained as tribes or among some of whom rudimentary class divisions might have begun to take place,[62] and there were the invaders. The latter, again, might have appeared *en bloc* (such as the Aryans in large parts of north India and the Dravidians influenced by the Aryan ideology spreading the agrarian village economy in south India by bringing together other peoples)[63] or only some of them might have carried a new socio-economic and spiritual outlook to outlying areas (such as the Brahmin groups to Bengal in the Gupta and post-Gupta periods).[64] In any case, in whichever way various ethnic and social groups were thus brought together to build the Indian civilization, the upshot of such a conglomeration of several peoples at different stages of social development was that the new society could not be based on a *gentile organization*; it had to be founded on a different social structure which subscribed to the key demand of the society to establish agrarian village communities as representing a higher stage in socio-economic organization. Maine remarked:[65]

"Although, in the North of India, the archives, as I am informed, almost invariably show that the Community was founded by a single assemblage of blood-relations, they also supply information that men of alien extraction have always, from time to time, been engrafted on it. ... In the South of the Peninsula there are often Communities which appear to have sprung not from one but from two or more families; and there are some whose composition is known to be entirely artificial; indeed, the occasional aggregation of men of different castes in the same society is fatal to the hypothesis of a common descent. Yet in all these brotherhoods either the tradition is preserved, or the assumption made, of an original common parentage. ... The Village Community then is not necessarily an assemblage of blood-relations, but it is *either* such an assemblage *or* a body of co-proprietors formed on the model of an association of kinsmen."

In the society thus built on the initiative of the Aryans or Dravidians with a better knowledge of the natural forces in the area, if the autochthonous people were at an undifferentiated stage in their previous societies, they were usually incorporated *en bloc* as specific *jatis* within the developing social structure; and if socio-economic differentiations had already taken place within the engulfed societies, their members were sometimes grouped to form different *jatis* in accordance with their position in the previous society and the division of labour crystallized in the society that emerged.[66] In this way, rooted in the social division of labour within the evolved society, the *jatis* came into existence when stable relations were established between various peoples in different regions of India and the village communities were established.[67]

The *jatis*, however, were located as immutable social units within the broad framework of the *varna*-stratification of society, evidently because the Aryans dominated these societies either directly (as in north India) or ideologically (as it is stated by some authorities to have been the case in south India). Also, for the same reason as above and because the *varna*-stratification of society was upheld on the basis of nobility of birth and "purity" of maintaining one's obligations and privileges in the three levels of the *dvijas*, some "jatis" probably came into being from *varnasaṁkara* (mixture of *varnas*) and from other ways of failing to maintain one's standard in society.[68] But that the emergence of "jatis" in this way was not fundamental to the evolution of the caste system, and that contrary to some views the *varna* classification was *not* the corner-stone on which the caste structure was built,[69] are particularly illustrated from Bengal.

The aryanization of this part of India and the introduction of the caste structure in her society began with the establishment of the rule of the Guptas in north Bengal and neighbouring areas; and in this process the previous tribes of Paundrika, Avira, and Bhilla (according to *Brahmabaibarta Purana*) were turned into castes and located as *asat-sudra* in the *varna* classification of the society; the Koncha, Mallo, Kol, and Bhilla (according to Bhabadeva) were described as *antyaja*; Pukkas, Khas, Khar and Kamboga were characterized as *mléchha*; and the two oldest tribes in Bengal, viz. Sumba and Savara, as well as Pulinda were equated with the *yabana.*[70] Furthermore, while before the spread of the Aryan civilization social division of labour had taken place to such an extent in the plains of Bengal that there the people were following different vocations (such as trade, various forms of craft-production, tillage, etc.), now as the Aryan civilization went deeper into the society these people were classified into different *jatis* in accordance with the specific occupations they were performing before. Henceforth these specific occupations of the *jatis* were fixed hereditarily, and all the *jatis* were arranged in a social hierarchy whereby the hereditarily transmitted detailed occupational groups were segregated from one another by the rules of inter-marriage and inter-dining and they occupied permanently fixed position in the societal hierarchy in accordance with the prescribed rights and duties, privileges and obligations, of each *jati* vis-a-vis others.[71] In this way, the caste structure of Bengal was made up of imported Brahmins from west, south and north India;[72] the autochthonous artisans, traders, tillers, and such people in the society of Bengal at that time who had not previously followed the *varnāśbramadbarma* but all of whom now became Sudras; and the tribal peoples who in course of time were detribalized and came within the pale of the Aryan civilization.[73] Here the *varnas* of Kshatriya and Vaishya were distinctly lacking;[74] yet the caste system with all its rigidity developed in Bengal on the basis of the *jatidbarma,* proving thereby that it was the *jati*-division of society which represented the caste system and not the four *varnas* which need not even be fully represented in order to develop the caste structure!

Evidently, the caste system of India is represented by the *jati*-division of society, and, significantly enough, it came into existence practically wherever the agrarian village economy penetrated. This point has already been noted, but it is worth mentioning that this is further substantiated from Bengal. On the basis of epigraphic and other evidences, Ray concluded in regard to the land settlement and the evolution of the caste structure in Bengal that: (1) "the first undisputed proof of settlement of the people and extension of agriculture is from the fifth century; prior to that there is no evidence available in regard to land" and (2) "it is possible to surmise that although the caste structure of the twelfth-thirteen centuries had not emerged very clearly in the fifth-eighth centuries, its general framework was built up in this period."[75]

The reason behind such a simultaneous development of the caste system and the village community system is that while the latter fulfilled a vital demand of the Indian society concerning its material needs, the former supplied the *social* foundation to the latter. For the village community system it was a *social* need that the village-units should not burst asunder by the tension generated *within* them by contradictory aspirations of the people in social and material life; and this need was fulfilled by the *jati*-division of society, whereby everybody (however humbly or loftily placed in the societal hierarchy) had a definite socio-spiritual position and *specific* work to do.[76] Indeed, more than that; such positions of the respective individuals and families in the village communities remained stationary through generations. Thus, a Brahmin priest's son became a Brahmin priest, and so also his son; and it was the same in the family of a calender Brahmin or of other Brahmins living on distinct professions within the community. Likewise, a blacksmith's son and grandson and their later descendants, all remained blacksmiths; and so it was with all other *jatis* (castes) of artisans, traders, peasants, fishermen, hunters, the so-called "menial servants," etc. Therefore, from one village, when it was over-saturated, households belonging to various castes (which could bring about an autonomous and self-sufficient existence in another site) would separate and form another village in the exact image of the parent one without creating discord either between different castes and occupational groups or within the village as a whole. In the same way, new villages would be formed when with the spread of civilization the people in outlying areas were brought under a stable economic life of plough cultivation and craft production; and along with it the detailed occupational groups among them as well as any ethnic or cultural differences in the assimilated communities of the local area would be located in the caste structure. A similar pattern of societal mosaic would thus appear in the village community established in a new settlement.

It was in this way that the *jati*-division of society supplied the social foundation to the village community system in India by providing "an unalterable division of labour" in society, whereby "the whole mechanism discloses a systematic division of labour" which is regulated "with the irresistible authority of a law of Nature."

Moreover, the village community system was further stabilized by the spiritual sanctions accompanying the *jati*-division of society as contained in the doctrine of *Karma* and the theory of Reincarnation. The doctrine of *Karma* and the theory of Reincarnation taught the people that their position in society was the consequence of their work in the previous birth and that their obedience to the ethics of the society (viz. to obey the caste rules and regulations and to accept the privileges and obligations of the respective castes in which they were born) would improve or deteriorate their caste position in the next life or might even lead to their deliverance from any future worldly existence.[77] Following this ideology not enough force could generate within the society to disrupt the standardized harmony, and if any one was fool enough to challenge this doctrine and seek his improvement in the existing rather than in the next life, he could be effectively silenced by the sanction of law.[78] And if his crime was so great that he became an outcaste, then he was lost to the society and practically dead for all purposes. It is not difficult to imagine what a fate awaited an individual who was thrown out of the village community system and received no quarter from anywhere in the society with respect to his economic, social and spiritual needs.

Thus fulfilling the social and economic needs of the society at a certain stage of its development, the caste system played the most significant role in Indian social organization so long as the village community system dominated Indian life. And simultaneously these two institutions (namely, the caste and the village community systems) transformed a self-developing social state into a never-changing natural destiny, as it appeared to the people and still appears so to a very large number of Indians and others.[79]

Indeed, such was the decentralized strength of the village community system and its accompanying caste-structure that they did not remain confined to the Hindu society alone. Although it is sometimes declared that the caste system is purely the ideological and ethical basis of the Hindu society (that is, the society which produced the *varna* division and which is regarded as comprising those in India who profess to follow the Brahminical system of religion and philosophy), it remains a fact that both the caste and the village community systems engulfed the Buddhists as well as the immigrants to India in ancient times, as for example, the Sakas, Hunas, etc.[80] Moreover, when the Moslem invaders began to settle down in India from about the tenth century of the Christian era and substantially increased their number by converting large masses of people to Islam, they also did not forsake the village community system and at the same time were not immune to the caste system. As a community they were segregated from the Hindus and others by the taboos of inter-marriage and inter-dining; and, furthermore, although Islam strictly prohibits any distinction between the "true believers," such was the socio-economic and ideological force of the institution of castes as providing the *social basis* for the village community system (under which the Moslems–immigrants or converts–settled down in Indian society) that caste-differentiation began to make inroads into this community as well. As later evidence has brought to light, like the Hindus, the Moslems also began to prohibit inter-marriage and in some places also inter-dining between their different categories (such as Mughals, Pathans, Shias, Sunnis, Khojāhs, etc.); and various occupational groups of weavers, oilpressers, etc., which were hardly in any way different from the previously-formed Hindu *jatis*, also eventually emerged in this community or were introduced by the local converts to Islam who had forsaken the *varnāśhramadharma* of the Hindus but not the *jatidharma*, evidently because it was an Indian rather than only a Hindu institution.[81]

In short, the village community system and its accompanying caste structure engulfed practically all those who settled down in India in those days, for these two institutions were found peculiarly suitable to the demands of India's economic and social life in that period.

What was, then, the character of the Indian society high-lighted by the village community and the caste systems? In order to understand this, it should, firstly, be borne in mind that although the village community system has been characterized as the prolongation of "primitive democracy" in India in later times,[82] the village communities were established permanently not by the gentile organization of a tribal society but by the conglomeration of different occupational groups, which reflected the stabilized system of division of labour at a higher stage of development of the society, and by the emergence of stable relations between different cultural and ethnic groups residing in an area.[83] Secondly, although features of "primitive democracy" were visible in the village communities in the common possession of land and in the function of the village assemblies, class exploitation was established not only by the control of the sovereign and his representatives *over* the villages, but also by the control exercised by the priests, headmen, accountants, and such other elements *within* the village communities, who, living on the surplus labour of the peasantry and the rural artisans, and belonging to several castes in the *varna*-levels of Brahmins and Kshatriyas,[84] represented the interests of the ruling class in these smallest units of the Indian society in those days.

Such an emergence of class relations in Indian society on the basis of the village community system and the elaboration of the social structure by the *jati*-division of society should be examined in greater detail, for this indicates the stage of social development India had reached in those days. Previously, class relations in society were represented only by the *varna*-stratification of society;[85] but in this epoch of India's social development the *jatis* built up the economic structure of society, and the *varna* system, while losing its previous usefulness, went on broadly representing the class relations in society by grouping the *jatis* in the previously-mentioned four levels. Thus, it is true that the Brahmins and Kshatriyas went on living on the surplus labour of the remaining *varnabindus*, viz. the Vaishyas and Sudras; but this particular stage of social development had some special features.

Firstly, the forms of production and usurpation had become manifold, and they were reflected—

(a) in the multitude of *usurping* castes of Brahmins (religious priests of various denominations, calender Brahmins, bard Brahmins, teachers, astrologers, etc.) and of Kshatriyas (kings, nobles, state and revenue officials, village headmen, etc.);[86]

(b) in the large number of *producing* and distributing castes of artisans, agriculturists, traders, etc., in the levels of Vaishyas and Sudras, which specialized in particular forms of production and exchange;[87] and

(c) in the presence of *serving* castes, which were formed mainly of those who were described as Antyaja, Mlechha, etc., and who were probably in a tribal stage before.[88]

Secondly, while the usurping castes also could not easily change their position, the producing and serving castes were rigidly fixed to their place in production and service. The renowned law-giver Manu ordained that "a Brâhmaṉa, unable to subsist by his peculiar occupations ... may live according to the law applicable to Kshatriyas; for the latter is next to him in rank;" and if he fails to make a living thereby, "he may adopt a Vaiṣya's mode of life, employing himself in agriculture and rearing cattle."[89] Similarly, a Kshatriya, "who has fallen into distress," may subsist by taking up the Vaishya's mode of life; while "he must never arrogantly adopt the mode of life (prescribed for his) betters."[90] But, even though it appears that the Brahmins and the Kshatriyas could thus take up the occupations of the producing castes in dire circumstances, in fact their participation in actual production was strongly discouraged. Along with the above recommendations, Manu gave the injunctions that "a Bráhmaṉa, or a Kshatriya, living by a Vaiṣya's mode of subsistence, shall carefully avoid (the pursuit of) agriculture, (which causes) injury to many beings and depends on others;" and that "he who, through a want of means of subsistence, gives up the strictness with respect to his duties, may sell, in order to increase his wealth, the commodities sold by Vaiṣyas," making, however, certain exceptions.[91] The Brahmins and the Kshatriyas could thus become only, or mainly, traders under unusual circumstances.

Regarding the Vaishyas and the Sudras, on the other hand, Manu's dictates were that a "Vaiṣya who is unable to subsist by his own duties, may even maintain himself by a Ṣûdra's mode of life, avoiding (however) acts forbidden to him;" and "a Ṣûdra, being unable to find service with the twice-born and threatened with the loss of his sons and wife (through hunger), may maintain himself by handicrafts," but he should follow "those mechanical occupations and those various practical arts by following which the twice-born are (best) served."[92] In other words, what have been described here as the usurping professions were strictly forbidden to the Vaishyas and Sudras, and the latter had to be particularly subservient to the needs of the *dvija* and especially of the Brahmins and the Kshatriyas. Manu noted further that: "The service of Brâhmaṉas alone is declared (to be) an excellent occupation for a Ṣûdra; for whatever else besides this he may perform will bear him no fruit;" but: "If a Ṣûdra, (unable to subsist by serving Brâhmaṉas,) seeks a livelihood, he may serve Kshatriyas, or he may also seek to maintain himself by attending on a wealthy Vaiṣya."[93]

Such respective positions accorded by Manu to the usurping and the producing and serving castes hardly altered in their main characteristics in the hands of subsequent law-givers.[94] Hence, while the son of a Brahmin priest or of a Kshatriya warrior could become a trader (and even a farmer under exceptional circumstances), the son of a Vaishya farmer or a Sudra oilpresser or fisherman could not rise along the societal ladder from his fixed position in society as a primary producer. And such a strict obedience to the regulations in society was particularly enforced for the Sudras and the *untouchables,* who had to perform the heaviest and the most unwholesome tasks in society.[95] As Altekar stated quite precisely, the State in those days "gave a general support to the *varnāśhramadharma,* which was undoubtedly iniquitous, especially to the Sudras and Untouchables."[96] The producing and the serving castes had, therefore, to remain tied to their respective occupations, and it was only by accepting such a position as depended on the societal hierarchy and allegiance to the ideological, social, political and economic life propounded and upheld by the ruling class comprising the Brahmins and the Kshatriyas that these producing and serving castes could exist in society. Otherwise, the members of these castes could be physically punished or thrown out of society, which meant, if not physical extermination, social death.[97]

Thirdly, the share of their labour, which these producing and serving castes (as well as the trading castes) had to give to the ruling class, was determined and enforced by the authority of the State functioning on the basis of *Dharma,* as enunciated and expounded by the Brahmins (from the highest authority at the centre of the State power to the petty village priest) and as upheld and executed by the Kshatriyas (from the king at the centre down to the village headmen in the smallest units in society, and through the medium of the hierarchical representatives of the king, viz. the state and revenue officials).[98] Manu prescribed for a Brahmin three occupations as "his means of subsistence, (viz.) sacrificing for others, teaching, and accepting gifts from pure men;" for a Kshatriya "to carry arms for striking and for throwing," evidently to maintain law and order in society; for a Vaishya "to trade, (to rear) cattle, and agriculture;" and for a Sudra only one occupation, viz. "to serve meekly even these (other) three castes," [the translator meaning thereby the three *dvija varnas* of Brahmin, Kshatriya and Vaishya].[99] In addition, Manu noted that: (i) "Whatever exists in the world is the property of the Brâhmaṉa; on account of the excellence of his origin the Brâhmaṉa is, indeed, entitled to it all;" (ii) "(The king) should carefully compel Vaiṣyas and Ṣûdras to perform the work (prescribed) for them; for if these two (castes) swerved from their duties, they would throw this (whole) world into confusion;" and (iii) "No collection of wealth must be made by a Sûdra, even though he be able (to do it); for a Sûdra who had acquired wealth, gives pain to Brâhmaṇas."[100] Furthermore he fixed the share of the contributions from the agriculturists, artisans, traders, etc., which will be enjoyed by the ruling class; enjoined the forms of services the so-called "menial servants" were to perform in society; and enforced that the king as the sovereign of all lands was to maintain this *dharma* or law and order, and "as the leech, the calf, and the bee take their food little by little, even so much the king draw from his realm moderate annual taxes" through a hierarchy of officials responsible for one, ten, twenty, hundred, and thousand villages, with a minister placed on top of all of them.[101] It was, primarily, on the basis of this law or *dharma*, further expounded and elaborated by subsequent law-givers[102], that the Indian society was ruled wherever the new civilization established itself in this country.

Evidently, the above features in Indian society tend to indicate that the village communities were based on a form of hereditary serfdom; in which as the serving castes (most of them *untouchables*) had the worst lot they have often been clearly characterized as serfs by several indologists and historians.[103] On the other hand, the ideological, political, and economic power in society was held by the Brahmin and Kshatriya castes, which in a hierarchical order from the capital down to the village-units ran the State and as non-producing castes lived on the surplus surrendered to them by the producing castes and enjoyed the services performed by the serving castes. It is true that some Vaishya merchants did acquire considerable wealth in those days and thereby they could influence the ruling class of the Brahmins and Kshatriyas; but, firstly, such Vaishya merchants were not very many in comparison with the Vaishya farmers, petty traders, etc. in the villages, secondly, the law-givers did not give them a position other than as subservient to the Brahmins and the Kshatriyas, and, thirdly, they could not assume any other role than as intermediaries between the usurping and the producing castes. It may, therefore, be justified to conclude that in this epoch of India's history while the producing and serving castes, belonging to the ranks of Vaishya and Sudra and to the groups of detribalized autochthones (*untouchables*—the Antyajas, etc.), had a serf-like existence in society, the usurping castes of Brahmins and Kshatriyas lived as feudal rent-receivers *from* and *within* the villages.

In other words, India in those days was in the feudal epoch of social development. There, while the *varnadharma* represented the previously-evolved class relations in society, in conformity with the extensive social division of labour and the *social* demands for production in the new civilization which flourished with the formation of the village communities, the *jatidharma* built the socio-economic structure of the feudal society of India. Probably this was the reason why Marx recorded in his draft on *Grundrisse der Kritik der politischen Ökonomie*:[104]

"... wo die besondre Art der Arbeit — die Meisterschaft in derselben, und dementsprechend das Eigentum am Arbeitsinstrument = Eigentum an den Produktionsbedingungen —, so schließt es zwar Sklaverei und Leibeigenschaft aus; kann aber in der Form des Kastenwesens eine analoge negative Entwicklung erhalten."

It should further be noted that because the village communities maintained a vegetative but a very stable economic organization of society on the basis of its autonomy, self-sufficiency, and the "simplicity of the organisation for production," and because these communities were socially and ideologically stabilized in society by the caste system of *jatidharma*, the feudal epoch of India' history was of a long duration. Indeed, the village community system, with its accompanying caste-structure and caste-ideology, gave a special imprint on Indian feudalism, because of which Shelvanker stated that "Indian feudalism remained fiscal and military in character, it was not manorial." To quote Shelvanker in full, as it is relevant to the present discussion:[105]

"The king under European feudalism combined in himself authority over all persons and things in his kingdom. When the king's dominium was delegated under vows of allegiance to a number of barons and fief-holders of different degrees, and a hierarchy of authority was created, the power and the rights that were passed on from superior to inferior were power and rights over things (i. e., over the land of a given area) as well as over the persons connected with it.

In India there was nothing analogous to the *Roman* conception of dominium, and the sovereign's power was not, until a late period, regarded as absolute and unlimited over the agricultural land of the kingdom. The king did not, in theory, create subordinate owners of land because he himself was not in theory the supreme owner of the land. What he delegated to the intermediaries was not even his sovereignty understood in this restricted sense, but only the specific and individual rights of *zamin,* the revenue-collecting power.

Hence there did not occur, as in England, a conflict between the king and his baronage, with the baronage endeavouring to delimit and circumscribe the claims which the king could make upon them in virtue of his exercise of the supreme dominium. The king was not *primus inter pares*; and the baronage were not co-sharer with him of sovereignty. From the beginning they held no more than a fairly well-defined title to the collection of taxes, or rents, and they could escape this condition not by fighting with the king for the clarification and settlement of their mutual relationship—which was precise enough—but by taking up arms against the insignia of royalty. The conflict between the king and his feudatories did not therefore lead to political and constitutional developments within the frame-work of the State, but merely to the creation of a new State in no way dissimilar to that from which its ruler had torn himself apart.

In order to resist, when necessary, the overlord's terms or conditions made even on the narrow ground of the *zamin* power, a principle of cohesion was necessary, and that was lacking among the intermediate baronage. They were intermediaries of different grades, different powers, different environments and languages, whose allegiance was never centralised and focused on a single person or institution, and who were, moreover, scattered widely over an immense territory. They could never as an organised and coherent body, resist a common overlord and impose checks on him, partly because there was no common overlord to whom all of them had sworn allegiance, and partly because they themselves were rent asunder, were scattered and had each a different historical antecedent.

Save in some exceptional cases the intermediary in his relations with the peasantry and the village had no occasion to convert his *zamin* rights into one of *de facto* dominium in the European sense by any attempt directly to influence the course of rural operations. Indian feudalism remained fiscal and military in character, it was not manorial. There was in general none of the intermingling of peasant land with demesne land in a common village, nor interdependence for labour services such as marked the manorial system. The peasant was not the lord's serf, nor was the lord directly interested in cultivation. There was therefore nothing similar to the direct conflict between the manorial lord and the peasantry over the disposal and cultivation of the land and of labour services which agitated Europe from the twelfth to the eighteenth centuries.

When there was a conflict, it was over the share of the agricultural produce to be retained by the peasant or surrendered to the lord. The foundations of agriculture themselves were not affected. Nor was there any such widespread and general rise in prices or the temptation of greater income by turning arable into pasture, to lead the baronage to assert their power in a manner capable of introducing fundamental changes in the rural economy. Even as late as the eighteenth century there was an abundance of land, and the hard-pressed peasant could always abscond on the open plains of the Ganges. The lord therefore was in general satisfied to exact his utmost from the peasant in the shape of produce, without concerning himself with economic and technical questions of increasing production.

At the base of the Indian agrarian system, as at the basis of all ancient agrarian systems, there was the more or less collective or co-operative village, in which individual family claims and obligations are determined on customary lines. On top of this grows up, with monarchy and feudalism, a system variously and unevenly hierarchical of rights belonging to individuals who are themselves not cultivators, but who, by the direct or indirect exercise of force, establish the practice of receiving a more or less big fraction of the final produce of the soil. In broad outline, this superimposition of a military hierarchy over groups of cultivators organised in villages is characteristic of Indian and European feudalism in general.

Owing to the special features of Indian feudalism, which we have pointed out, this agrarian system did not develop any farther. The two sets of conflicts: (a) between the baronage and the king, and (b) between the baronage and the peasantry, which were so settled that proprietary rights over independent and seperate tracts of lands, farms, came to be lodged in separate and independent individuals, the conflicts which shattered the pre-capitalist agrarian systems of the West, never took place in India. The rights based on custom and the rights based on political and military power continued to run side by side, without leading by their interaction, as in England, to any important changes in rural organisation.

There was no security or safeguard for a right against the State, as critics sometimes observe, for the simple reason that the right was in fact and manifestly a concession of the State, a delegation of its political revenue-collecting power. But this applies only to the non-cultivating classes. As for the village and the peasantry, they had strictly neither rights nor safeguards—except such as were grounded in custom. They tilled the land not because it was a right or a duty, but because it was the *métier* of their fathers. And no one was foolish enough to try to evict them, because there was plenty of other land to which they could go. What their masters wanted was not the peasant's land, but his surplus value.

None of the major conflicts in Indian history had for its object the exercise of rights within the village, but the exercise of rights over the village. They were conflicts between overlords of various grades for the right or power to get a payment from the peasant, not to seize his land. European history, on the contrary, reveals a conflict between the peasantry and the manorial lords because the latter not only demanded a share of the produce, but desired to retain a particular method of cultivation—by forced labour—or to introduce new methods of cultivation (enclosures, large-scale farming). The Indian conflict was one between lords who were concerned not at all with methods of cultivation, but only to draw an income from the peasantry. If all ownership of land rests ultimately either on the claim of the sword or the claim of the plough, the issue in India was never fought out between the claimants of the plough and the claimants of the sword. The issue was always between different claimants of the sword, the village and the peasantry remaining throughout the passive subject of conflict, the booty over which the rival powers fought each other."

It thus appears from the above discussion that the village community system and the *jati*-division of society provided the basic characteristics of Indian feudalism, whereby feudalism in India was more stable than, for instance, in western Europe. As Takahashi also remarked:[106]

"The decisive factor in checking the autonomous growth of modern capitalist society in Eastern Europe and Asia was precisely the stability of the internal structure of feudal land property in those countries."

Indeed, as mentioned before, the internal structure of feudal land property in India was so stable that when the Moslems settled down in India they were also engulfed by the village community system like the previous immigrants. As it was under the former Hindu kings, during the rule of the Turko-Afghans from the twelfth century, the "village communities continued unaffected by the establishment of a new government in the country;"[107] and during the Mughal rule from the sixteenth century, although Baden-Powell observed that "the Mughal revenue-system is the direct cause of the (unforeseen) growth of the zamíndár landlord of Bengal," he also noted that their ideas of collecting taxes and tributes "fell in with the system of the land-revenue payment already in force."[108]

It is true that the Turko-Afghan and the Mughal monarchs created nobles out of their associates and settled territories on them, whereby they have often been described by historians as *fief-holders*. It is also known that the might of some fief-holders led them to revolt against the monarch's power and declare their sovereignty over the territories placed under their management. Similarly, on the basis of an alliance with some fief-holders, conspiracies to overthrow a reigning monarch by some rebellious princes and other powerful usurpers were practically a regular phenomenon throughout the Moslem period of India's history. But such features hardly at all affected the basic institution in the society, viz. the village community system. For these fief-holders, like the monarch himself, did not have a direct control within the villages and of the peasants. They were essentially the collectors of king's revenue from the territories conferred on them, with the stipulation that a part of the collection they made directly or through their intermediaries was to be retained for their own maintenance and of their army, etc. Therefore, while on the one hand, because of the nature of relation between the monarch and the fief-holders (as pointed out by Shelvanker) the political super-structure of India was unstable and hence, as Metcalfe noted, "dynasty after dynasty tumbles down; revolution succeeds to revolution," on the other hand, because "Indian feudalism remained fiscal and military in character, it was not manorial," the village community system remained in force "in such striking contrast with the constant dissolution and reforming of Asiatic States, and the never-ceasing changes of dynasty."

Moreover, as stated before, because the village community system remained in force and it was so stable an institution because of its accompanying caste-structure and caste-ideology, even though the Moslems were not fully absorbed within the caste system of the previous society like their fore-runners (viz. the Sakas, Hunas, etc.), not only they formed a part of the social structure as a distinct community segregated by the rules of inter-marriage and inter-dining but, living within the village communities, among them also the *jati*-division began to make in-roads while they remained unaffected by the *varna*-stratification of Hindu society. The converts to Islam forsook the ethics of *varnāśhramadharma*, but generally did not give up the *jati*-division of society; and among the immigrants eventually the *jati*-like segregation began to take place. The upshot was that because at that particular stage of social development the social forces were so well-balanced by the village community system and the *jatidharma* that to many the life in pre-British India, as based on these two predominant institutions in Indian society, appeared as static and unchanging from immemorial times.

Such was the social organism that prevailed in pre-British India. The village community system provided the basis of the structure of Indian feudalism, and the socio-spiritual structure of the latter was built and sustained on the caste-ideology of *jatidharma*.

2. Emergence of New Forces

While in general the village community system, accompanied by its caste-structure and caste-ideology, continued to exist, there are reasons to believe that because of forces attacking the institution from outside and within, feudalism in India had begun to weaken from about the fourteenth century onwards. The external forces working against the essential characteristics of the system in India came from the ruling powers. It is true that, in general, the village communities maintained their autonomous character; but it appears that from about the ninth century onwards the State had begun to intervene into them, although in the beginning such interference might have been occasional in nature and might not have extended over all the villages. As it has been stated referring particularly to south India:[100]

"When the Central Government became more organised and developed, it often sought to control and curtail the powers of the Village Councils. Sometimes king's officers are seen to be present, when the Primary Assemblies met to change their constitution; sometimes the rules are stated to have received the approval of the king himself. These, however, were rather exceptional cases; it is not unlikely that king's officers may have been occasionally present because they happened to be in the village; and that the king may have accorded approval to proposals formally submitted to him by the Primary Assembly. A perusal of the evidence, however, clearly suggests that usually the village Primary Assemblies themselves determined the constitution of their committees and not the Central Government. The same probably was the case in northern India as well."

Further changes were noticed in farming out the revenue of a territory to some individuals. Instead of the revenue being directly collected from the village communities by the revenue ministers through royal officers, in some places at least the State farmed out its revenue to the highest bidder. Simultaneously, the State granted portions of its territory to some individuals in return for military service and the regular payment of a fixed tribute. These features in revenue administration, known to have been in vogue in north India during the rule of the Turko-Afghan and the Mughal monarchs, have also been noted for south India in this period.

"It is a noteworthy fact that in the seventeenth century the agrarian system of the Vijayanagar territory was practically identical with that of the Moslem kingdom of Golkonda, and it is most unlikely that the former should have borrowed a new system from the latter; the more probable inference is that farming had become established as the mainstay of the Hindu agrarian system in the South by the end of the thirteenth century."[110]

The farming out of the State's revenue and the grant of estates for military service might not have directly affected the economic stability of the village community system, for these intermediaries also generally collected the land-tax through the medium of the village councils.[111] But the extraction of the surplus labour of the villagers by the revenue farmers was probably raised to a higher pitch, as has been remarked by some authorities,[112] and this might have in some extent devitalized the village communities.

More important, however, in its effect on the village community system than the revenue-farming was the State's direct interference in the collection of the land-revenue without the medium of village councils. In order to curtail the growing power of his nobles, Alauddin Khilji (1296–1316) confiscated the previous grants and endowments[113], and ordered that–

"... one half of the produce, by actual measurement, should be taken by the state without any deduction; and the headmen and chowdhris [the headmen of various castes and trades] and all other rayyats were placed on the same footing; so that the burden of the strong was not thrown on the weak. He also ordered that what used to be the perquisites of the chowdhris should be collected and paid into the treasury, and that grazing fees for each head of buffalo and sheep should also be realized. The scrutiny into the conduct of the ministerial officers and scribes was carried to such an extreme, that they were not able to misappropriate even one *jital*. If any of them took anything in addition to his fixed salary, this at once appeared against him in the papers of the patwari (the village accountant); and was immediately exacted from him with the greatest rigour and contumely. Men gave up all ministerial offices, and all appointments as scribes, as something blameworthy. The condition of headmen and chowdhris, who had always gone about on horseback, and had carried arms, and worn beautiful clothes, became so wretched, that their wives had to do menial work in the houses of others, and had to buy their food with what they got as wages."[114]

Alauddin's successors to the Delhi Sultanate reverted back to the grant of estate and revenue-farming, but it was not a complete reversal to the *status quo ante*. During the reign of his son Mubarak (1316–1320), "some of the lands and endowments confiscated by the late Sultān were restored to their original grantees," and in the year 1320 Nasiruddin Khusrav "distributed honours and rewards among his relatives and tribesmen, who had helped him in the accomplishment of his design" to overthrow and murder Mubarak[115]; but thereafter the Tughluqs generally endeavoured to curb the practice of estate and revenue-farming. Ghiyasuddin Tughluq (1320–1325) "ordered a strict enquiry to be made into all claims and *jāgīrs*," and, in consequence, "unlawful grants were confiscated to the State."[116] His successor Muhammad bin Tughluq (1325–1351) "first ordered the compilation of a register of the land revenue on the model of the register already kept, and the revenue department then worked smoothly."[117] Only Firuz Shah (1351–1388), successor to Muhammad bin Tughluq, "revived the *jāgīr* system, which had been abolished by 'Alā-ud-dīn, and farmed out the whole kingdom among them [the nobles and the officials] besides granting them increased salaries and allowances."[118]

But probably because the revival of the *jagir* system "produced a tendency towards decentralization to the prejudice of the integrity of the State," when the Lodis ascended the Delhi throne, Buhlul Khan (1451–1489) "frustrated an attempt on the part of Mahmūd Shāh Sharqī of Jaunpur to get possession of Delhi, and reduced to submission some provincial fief-holders and chieftains, who had enjoyed independence for several years."[119] Also his successor Sikandar Shah (1489–1517) "made earnest efforts to increase the strength of the kingdom by removing the disorders and confusion into which it had been thrown during the preceding reigns, due largely to the refractoriness of the provincial governors, chieftains, and zamindārs," and also took care "to check the accounts of the leading Afghān *jāgīrdārs*, much against their will."[120]

The Lodis, however, could not rule for long, and the years between A. D. 1526–1556 saw India in the throes of "the Mughul-Afghān contest for supremacy in this land."[121] But that did not mean that the thread of social changes which had begun in the Indian society was snapped by the political and military struggles in its super-structure. In the midst of this contest, Sher Shah came fully into the picture in 1539 with his assumption of sovereignty, and during his reign (1539–1545) the changes incipient before were distinctly marked; and afterwards they were noticeable to everyone during the reign of the Mughal Emperor Akbar (1556–1605). It has been said that Sher Shah "displayed an aptitude for civil government and instituted reforms, which were based to some extent on the institutions of Alāu-d dīn Khiljī and were developed by Akbar,"[122] indicating thereby the continued process of change in the Indian society in those days. Moreover, as it will be seen from the following pages, a similar course of change was no less apparent also in south India in this period. These facts thus lead one to conclude that changes in the internal structure of society was of far greater importance than the changes of dynasties and successive rules of the Turko-Afghan and the Mughal and other monarchs in different parts of India.

Hence to examine the changes in Indian society from the time of Sher Shah, perhaps the most notable of his administrative measures was in regard to the collection of land revenue. Moreland remarked that Sher Shah "distrusted the village headmen" and that he "regarded equitable assessment and strict collection as the two essentials of revenue administration."[123] But whether Sher Shah really distrusted the village headmen or not, and whether or not it is entirely true, as Moreland noted, that "the practice of farming the revenue of a village, or larger area, is of long standing in India" and therefore "it was a common practice for the revenue assessors to come to terms with the headmen year by year for the revenue to be paid by the village as a whole," (for "the sum to be paid was fixed on a consideration of the productive resources of the village, but was not assessed directly on the separate portions of cultivated land, or on the individual peasants,")[124] there is no doubt that the distinctive change made by the centralized authority of the State.

"Above all he established direct relations with the cultivator and deprived the headmen of the village of all rights in assessing the revenue. This could not but have curtailed the autonomy of the village communities."[125]

In addition, instead of recognizing the presence of the village headman as a representative of the village community, or instead of neglecting his presence altogether, Sher Shah endeavoured to turn him into a civil servant answerable not to the village council but to the centralized authority of the State.

"Sher Shah threw upon the village headman the responsibility of collecting the land revenue. He was expected to execute a bond and furnish securities for the due discharge of his duties. The muqaddam gave a receipt to the cultivator. The revenue demand was to be rigorously enforced. If a cultivator failed to pay, probably the usual methods of extorting the money from his were resorted to. He was imprisoned and tortured till he managed to pay the requisite amount in kind or cash."[126]

And what Sher Shah had started, Akbar brought to a fuller conclusion. It has been said that "the basis of Akbar's distinctive system is to be found in the reorganisation effected by Sher Shah."[127] This distinctive system consisted of "the direct relationship which it established between the collector and the individual peasant, who was to be treated as an independent unit, encouraged to increase production, and assisted with loans for that purpose, but held firmly to the engagements into which he had ventured."[128] As Marx remarked on Akbar's revenue system:[129]

> "1582–85. ... *Acher's Revenue system* (autore *Rajah Toder Mull*, the finance minister); um *revenue to collect von den cultivators*:
>
> 1) first established an uniform standard of measurement und dann a *regular survey system* set on foot.
>
> 2) to *ascertain* the *produce of each separate 'bigha,'* and hence *the amount it ought to pay to government*: The land divided *into 3 different classes, according to their varying degrees of fertility*. Dann, for each *bigah*, the *average yield of its class taken* und *the king's share made* = 1/3 *of this amount in kind.*
>
> 3) *to settle the equivalent of this amount in money* regular *statements of prices over all the country for 19.*
>
> Der *Machtmißbrauch der petty officers put down*; *the amount of revenue* nahm ab, aber die *expenses of collection lessened*, so blieb *net revenue dieselbe. Akber schafft ab the custom of farming the revenues*, which had been *source of so much cruelty und exhortion.*"

Changes in south India also were in the same direction. In the Vijayanagar Empire (1336–1650 A. D.), where four methods of land-revenue collection had prevailed, viz. direct collection by the State, revenue-farming, estate-farming in return for military service, and indirect collection through village councils,–

> "... as the village assembly slowly lost its vitality and hold on the villages in which it existed, the principle of farming out the taxes from villages was extended to such villages, and later taken over by the government itself which appointed its own village officers for purposes of collection. But the system of farming out the revenues of the state, and the granting of *jagir inãms*,

which carried with them certain financial obligations, continued to be in vogue right up the period of permanent establishment of the British power in South India."[130]

And in Bijapur, during the reign of Ibrahim Adil Shah II (1580–1626):[131]

"Without the distraction of war, he applied himself to civil affairs with much care; and the land settlements of the provinces of his kingdom, many of which are still extant among district records, show an admirable and efficient system of registration of property and its valuation. In this respect the system of Todar Mull introduced by the Emperor Akbar seems to have been followed with the necessary local modifications."

Simultaneously with thus making attempts to penetrate *within* the village economy, money rents were diligently collected by the monarchs. In Sher Shah's time, "the peasants were now required to pay in cash;"[132] during Akbar's time, "from the outset the demand was made in cash, the produce due under the schedule being valued at prices fixed by order of the emperor;"[133] and in the south also Harihara Rāya of Vijayanagar Empire (1336–56?) "wanted to convert the payment in kind into payment in cash."[134] In fact, from the reign of Akbar money rent became a fairly established feature in the Mughal administration, and it was generally followed by Akbar's successors; while in south India, "after the weakening of Vijayanagar, under the Nāyaks, the ryots were generally compelled to purchase the state's share of the grain at prices arbitrarily fixed by the tax-gatherer."[135]

Another interesting feature of this time was that, as in the time of Sher Shah, during Akbar's reign, the government "encouraged the sowing of the crops yielding a better cash value ... by granting advances to the cultivators which were repayable within a year."[136] Significantly enough, in this and later periods, production of non-food crops, other than those of direct interest to the village communities leading a self-supporting life, was gaining ground; and even those crops, like cotton, spices, dye crops, etc., which were also demanded by the villagers, were now produced in great quantities as exportable surplus or for manufacture. It is true that previously also some non-food as well as food crops were grown as commodities for manufacture or for export,[137] but henceforth the production of commercial crops was definitely market both in north and south India.[138] Moreover, it has been reported:[139]

> "Pelsaert definitely tells us of the large-scale production and manufacture of indigo in the Jumna valley and Central India. To meet the demands of widespread manufactures of cotton and silk goods, both cotton and silk were cultivated extensively in certain parts of India."

As will be mentioned later, indigo-trade became a royal monopoly, and silk and textiles—the chief articles of export from India. The village economy had until now maintained an independent existence of its own, irrespective of how the urban economy went its way; and this dualism which gave a peculiar imprint on the characteristics of Indian feudalism, was now being gradually drawn into the needs of manufacture and commerce.

At the same time, the insistence on the payment of money-rent appears to have reflected the penetration of commodity circulation in the villages on a large scale; a feature which, if true, indicated how the subsistence character of the village communities was undergoing changes in this period. In any case, it meant the rise of new forces in society, namely, that of money-changers and usurers, who while present before would have now an important say in rural economics.[140] For "money forces the commodity form even on the objects which have hitherto been produced for the producer's own use; it drags them into exchange."[141] Furthermore, even though "under Asiatic forms usury may last for a long time," it "works revolutionary effects in all pre-capitalist modes of production;" and, therefore, it cannot but produce eventually "economic disintegration and political rottenness."[142]

All such intrusions into the internal arrangement of the village community system could not but have weakened the institution itself, and thus affected one of the basic props of Indian feudalism. Indeed, in south India, where the village community system was very well developed and where the task of the Vijayanagar Empire was "to conserve Hindu society and save it from the dissolution which threatened it from several directions,"[143] even though the village community system was first evolved by the Hindu society, the new forces in society saw to it that this institution received a severe battering. Referring to the Vijayanagar Empire, and particularly its later days, it has been noted:[144]

> "The admirable system of autonomous village rule that had been established under the Cholas, and that survived intact for several generations after them, now fell into neglect and all but disappeared in this period, thanks to the pressure of military needs on the emperors and the feudatory *nāyakas*."

Evidently, the days of the village community system were over, although it still remained in force for some time longer. Feudalism in India was, obviously, on the decline.

Moreover, along with the attack on the economic basis of the village communities, movements had developed against its ideological basis, namely, the caste system. These movements, emerging in different parts of the subcontinent in this period, were high-lighted by what is generally described as the Bhakti Movement, "which swept over India from the twelfth century A. D.," and preached "its essential doctrine that salvation may be attained, independently of priests, ritual and caste, by devotion to the Divine Name."[145] As it has been said by a well-known Indian historian on this movement:[146]

> "Like the Protestant Reformation in Europe in the 16th century, there was a religious, social, and literary revival and Reformation in India, but notably in the Deccan in the 15th and 16th centuries. This religious revival was not Brahmanical in its orthodoxy; it was heterodox in its spirit of protest against forms and ceremonies and class distinctions based on birth, and ethical in its preference of a pure heart, and of the law of love, to all other acquired merits and good works. This religious revival was the work also of the people, of the masses, and not of the classes. At its head were saints and prophets, poets and philosophers, who sprang chiefly from the lower orders of society,—tailors, carpenters, potters, gardeners, shop-keepers, barbers, and even *mahars* (scavengers)—more often than from Brahmans."

Although it is stated in the above extract that the Bhakti movement emerged "notably in the Deccan in the 15th and 16th centuries," in fact the movement was no less vigorous in other parts of India, and it did not confine itself to the fifteenth and the sixteenth centuries only but continued till later years. Indeed, it is well to remember how extensive was this movement and how it sprang up simultaneously in various parts of the subcontinent, suggesting thereby that it was the *social system* which gave rise to this movement.

In the south, there were Ramanuja, Madhva, Vallabhacharya, and others, who led the movement. Ramanuja, who died in the twelfth century of the Christian era, "combated the absolute monism of Saṅkara and laid emphasis on *Bhakti* as a means of salvation;"[147] but he did not oppose the caste system. Madhva, who was born near Udipi in 1199 A. D., however, came out directly against the institution of castes. He insisted "on a social reconstruction in which no body should go without philosophy;" preferred merit to birth "in characterizing the disposition favourable for philosophy;" held that "even the lowest caste (*śudras*) may study the philosophy of Brahman;" and recognized that "even the untouchable (*antyajas*) are devoted to Viṣṇu."[148] And Vallabhacharya (A. D. 1473–1531), who preached mainly in the kingdom of Vijayanagar, disregarded all distinctions of castes. His "teaching elevated the life of all the sections of society and proved to be completely democratic."[149]

In northern India, Ramananda was one of the pioneers of the Bhakti movement. Either born in A. D. 1299 or preaching in the fourteenth century (as his date is uncertain), he put forward the maxim: "*Jati pati puchai nahiloi, Hari-ku bhajai so Hari-kau hoi*;" that is,

> "Let no one ask a man's caste or sect.
> Whoever adores God, he is God's own."[150]

Kabir, one of his disciples, preached his ideas in north and central India in the fifteenth century and came to be known as the founder of the sect of *Kabir-panthis*. He propagated the message:[151]

> "O Servant, where dost thou seek Me? Lo! I am beside thee. I am neither in temple nor in mosque; I am neither in Kaaba nor in Kailash:

Neither am I in rites and ceremonies, nor in Yoga and renunciation. If thou art a true seeker, thou shalt at once see Me:

. . . .

It is needless to ask of a saint the caste to which be belongs; For the priest, the warrior, the tradesman, and all the thirty-six castes, alike are seeking for God. . . .

Hindus and Moslems alike have achieved that End, where remains no mark of distinction.

. . . .

The Purana and the Koran are mere words; lifting up the curtain, I have seen.

Kabir gives utterance to the words of experience; and he knows very well that all other things are untrue."

And then there were many others, like the great poet Dadu (1544–1603) who "had frequent interviews with Akbar in the cause of cementing Islam and Hinduism."[152]

In Maharashtra, Namdev propagated his views in the latter half of the fourteenth or in the first half of the fifteenth century. Like other leaders of the Bhakti movement, he was against caste distinction and put his faith in the unity of Godhead. He declared:[153]

> "Love for him who filleth my heart shall never be sundered;
> Nāma has applied his heart to the true Name.
> As the love between a child and his mother,
> So is my soul imbued in the God."

This part of India also saw other important figures in Bhakti movement, such as Eknath of Paithan who died in 1608, Tukaram (1607–1649), and Ramdas who is said to have been the *guru* (religious master) of Sivaji in the seventeenth century.

In the Punjab, Nanak founded Sikhism in the latter half of the fifteenth century, and preached his gospel of universal toleration on the basis of what is good in Hinduism and Islam and abolition of caste distinction. He was also of the opinion:

"Religion consisteth not in mere words;

He who looketh on all men as equal is religious.

Religion consisteth not in wandering to tombs or places of cremation, or sitting in attitudes of contemplation.

Religion consisteth not in wandering in foreign countries, or in bathing at places of pilgrimage.
Abide pure amidst the impurities of the world;
Thus shalt thou find the way to religion."[154]

A late successor to Nanak, the Sikh leader Guru Govind in the seventeenth century, "waged no war against polytheism but wished to found a religious commonwealth equally independent of Hindu castes and Mohammedan sultans."[155]

And in eastern India, the powerful movement organized by Chaitanya (1485–1533) spread from Bengal to Orissa and Assam, and went beyond to other parts of northern India and the Deccan. Chaitanya also was against priestly ritualism and caste segregation, and "is said to have admitted many Moslims to membership and to have regarded all worshippers of Krishna as equal."[156] His views found an echoe in the preachings of Sankar Deb in Assam in the sixteenth century and of the latter's successor, Madhab Deb.

The message of these and other leaders of the Bhakti movement and of their disciples could not but have an adverse effect on the fundamental basis of Indian feudalism, as the caste structure provided the basic social organization of India in those days. It is true that these reformers brought a religious rather than a secular inspiration to the people; but was it not a common feature also in Europe in that period? There, as early as in the tenth century of the Christian era, the Bogomil movement developed in Bulgaria, and later it penetrated the Byzantine Empire, Serbia and Bosnia as well as northern Italy, southern France, Hungary, Bohemia, Germany, Flanders and other areas in Europe (including Russia), with or without minor variations.[157] This movement, which was religious in form but *social* in character with a strongly pronounced anti-feudal stamp, led to great cultural activities and education of the masses along with bringing a new consciousness to the people. Bogomil and the associated leaders of the movement are regarded as distant forerunners of such reformers as Jan Huss, John Wycliffee, Zwingli, Luther and Calvin; and Calvin (1509–1564) has been characterized by a reputed English historian to have done "for the bourgeoisie of the sixteenth century what Marx did for the proletariat of the nineteenth."[158] Indeed, there is a good deal of truth in the statement that:

"In der Feudalgesellschaft stand das gesamte geistige Leben unter der Kontrolle der Geistlichkeit und entwickelte sich in religiös-scholastischer Form. Daher bildeten die Abhandlungen über das wirtschaftliche Leben jener Zeit besondere Abschnitte in den theologischen Traktaten ... Der Klassenkampf der unterdrückten und ausgebeuteten Massen gegen die herrschenden Klassen der Feudalgesellschaft wurde jahrhundertelang in religiöser Form geführt ... Mit der weiteren Entwicklung des Klassenkampfes trat die religiöse Form der Bewegung der unterdrückten Massen in den Hintergrund, und der revolutionäre Charakter dieser Bewegung trat immer klarer zutage."[159]

Hence the Bhakti movement should not be considered only from its religious and philosophical aspects; it had, indeed, a great rôle to play in the *social* transfiguration of the Indian society which had earlier been founded on the caste system.

Moreover, it is worthy of note that the leaders of the Bhakti movement encouraged the development of local languages and literature, and thus brought the new consciousness emerging in society within the reach of the common people. Previously, religious doctrines developed mainly through the medium of Sanskrit, and also Pali. Even in the south, "Sanskrit was the language of higher culture throughout South India," and because "in the sphere of religion, as generally in all matters of spiritual culture, South India began by being heavily indebted to the north," Sanskrit became the chief medium for ethical and ideological discussions, although, unlike in the north, the local languages (Tamil, for instance) played some role in this matter.[160] The upshot was that the masses were hardly at all brought within the compass of the ideas contained in the socio-religious doctrines, for the language conveying the ideological aspect of society was no more the vernacular of the masses. Such a situation, however, now became different.

"The psalms of the Buddhists and even the hymns of the Rig Veda were vernacular literature in their dav, and in the south the songs of the Devaram and Nâlâyiram are of some antiquity. But in the north, though some Prâkrit literature has been preserved, Sanskrit was long considered the only proper language for religion. We can hardly doubt that vernacular hymns existed, but they did not receive the imprimatur of any teacher, and have not survived. But about 1400 all this changes. Though Râmânand was not much of a writer he gave his authority to the use of the vernacular: he did not, like Râmânuja, either employ or enjoin Sanskrit and the meagre details which we have of his circle lead us to imagine him surrounded by men of homely speech."[161]

Similarly, from "Vallabhacarya sprang the group of poets who adorned Braj or the Muttra district;"[162] and it is said that "painting, music and literature in Sanskrit, Hindi and Gujarati have richly flourished under the inspiration obtained from the system of Vallabha."[163] Likewise, based on the Bhakti movement, great strides were made in the development of languages and literature in south India,[164] in the Punjab, in Maharashtra, etc. And in eastern India, the Bengali language is said to have been raised to the status of a literary language from the time of Chaitanya.[165]

The sum-total result of such an inspiration emanating from the leaders of the Bhakti movement was a tremendous flourish of national languages and literature, and a new awakening of the people. Kabir's *dohas* and *sakhis*, which spoke against caste and other social distinctions and for the unity of Godhead, are considered as fine specimens of Hindi literature. Tulsi Das's Ramayana reached practically every home where Hindi was spoken. Sur Das became so famous for his sweet lyrics that it was said that "Krishna himself came down and acted as his amanuensis."[166] Nabha Das's *Bhakta Mala* became "one of the most popular religious works of northern India."[167] Mira Bai's songs composed in *Brajbhasa* echoed over large parts of India. Tiruvalluvar rose as a great Tamilian poet, and Vemana as a popular Telegu writer in the south. Nanak and his disciples "encouraged Punjabi and Gurumukhi;"[168] and Namdev "greatly helped the development of Marathi literature,"[169] while Tukaram came to be "better known than Namdev and his poetry which was part of the intellectual awakening that accompanied the rise of the Maratha power is still a living force wherever Marathi is spoken."[170] And in Bengal there were no less than 159 *padakartas* inspired by the Vaishnava movement. Among the celebrated literary figures in Bengal in those days, there was Chandidas at the end of the fourteenth century; Vidyapati who was a native of Mithila but is considered as a poet of Bengal; and there was Krittivas who being born in 1346 A. D. was roughly contemporary with Ramanand and whose translation of Ramayana in Bengali came to be known as "the Bible of the people of the Gangetic Valley and it is for the most part the peasants who read it."[171] In addition, there was the poetess Lalla of Kashmir in the fourteenth century, and similar figures in all parts of India, including Gujarat, Kanara, Malabar, Orissa, Assam, etc.[172]

These messengers of love and devotion spoke, in general, against caste and other social segregations, and their message spoken in local languages and literatures went straight to the people. Vemana wrote, for instance,[173]

"If we look through all the earth,
Men, we see, have equal birth,
Made in one great brotherhood,
Equal in the sight of God.

Food or caste or place of birth
Cannot alter human worth.
Why let caste be supreme?
'Tis but folly's passing stream....

Empty is a caste-dispute:
All the castes have but one root.
Who on earth can e'er decide
Whom to praise and whom deride?

Why should we the Pariah scorn,
When his flesh and blood were born
Like to ours? What caste is he
Who doth dwell in all we see?"

The Bhakti movement, therefore, could not but lead to a popular upheaval directed against India's feudal structure. The question, however, arises as to the class force that led this movement. In this connection it is of interest to note that most of the progenitors and proponents of the Bhakti movement belonged to the castes of traders and artisans. Thus, of the twelve disciples of Ramananda, Kabir was a weaver, Raidas a cobbler, Sena a barber; Rishi Swapacha was "a tanner by caste;"[174] Tukaram was a Sudra and a poor trader by profession; Kabir's successor, Dharmadas, was a trader by caste; Namdev and Nanak were by caste tailor or calico-printer and trader, respectively; Dadu is said to have been a cobbler, and his disciple Sundardas was a trader; Malukdas was a *khatri* (trader); Vemana was an "uncultured peasant;" and Tiruvalluver was a *pariah*. Also worthy of note, several distinguished disciples of Chaitanya were traders by caste; and when Vallabha's son Vithalnath assumed the former's authority, his "converts came chiefly from the mercantile classes but also included some Brahmans and Mussulmans."[175] From this as well as from other evidence it appears that the Bhakti movement was the expression of the rising force of artisans and traders as well as of the oppressed peasantry. As it has been remarked:[176]

"... the Bhakti movement among all the larger peoples of India started everywhere as a movement of artisans and traders in towns and later, in the XVII century, in certain regions it was joined by the peasants. It happened, for instance, in the Agra-Mathura region, where a great peasant rebellion took place in which Jat peasants played a leading role. The same happened in Punjab, where the peasants of the central districts rose under the leadership of the Sikhs. The dissatisfaction of oppressed artisans and traders with the feudal system turned into an armed struggle against the rule of the great feudal lords.

Everywhere the Bhakti movement went hand in hand with the development of national literature in the vernaculars and it became an important stimulus in the development of national culture of India's peoples. The literature, mostly poetry, which was called to life by this movement was more or less of an anti-feudal character. It expressed a protest against the caste system, against the rites of official Hinduism and Islam. The movement was especially wide-spread among the Hindu population of India, and therefore took the form of Vaishnava sectarianism; but the lower strata of Moslem society also took part in the movement. This is evidenced by the fact that there were Moslems among its leaders (Malik Muhammad Baba Farid). The strong growth of genuinely national literature, which left an indelible trace in the literature of nearly all the peoples of India, testifies to the fact that beginning from the XV century, in certain regions of India inhabited by its most numerous peoples, local markets were emerging and the role of the town handicrafts and trade was increasing in economic life. This process was bound to create the need in literatures in various national languages for these languages alone could serve as a means of intercourse between sellers and buyers."

Indeed, there is additional evidence to indicate that, along with the growth of national languages and literature stimulated by the role of artisans and traders in different parts of India, this stratum was going beyond its traditional regulations in society and some of the artisans and traders were important enough to be mentioned in historical studies as violating their caste-rules and taking up professions in contradistinction to their *jatidharma*. It has been mentioned in a brief review of the state of affairs in India at that time:[177]

"Tilak, who is said to have been well-versed in both Hindi and Persian and served Abdul Hasan and Mahmud Ghazanavi, was the son of a barber. Mandawar had been held by Rahup, an 'Agarwal Baniya' against Iltumish and he had taken this fort from a prince of the Parihar dynasty (*Cambridge History of India*, Vol. III, p. 53). The fact that a *baniya* (trader) should seize a fort from a prince is a very strong indication of the changes taking place in the relations of the various *varnas* in Indian society. In Gujerat, a rebellion against the Delhi Emperor had been led by Taghi, a cobbler (ibid., p. 169). Sidharan and Sidhupal, involved in the court intrigues and the murder of a Delhi king, were Khatris. The famous Hemu, who took the field against young Akbar, was a baniya. He has been described as an able general who had won twenty-two victories for his Pathan king. The leading painter of Akbar's time, Daswanth, was a kahar (a palanquin bearer)."

Many such cases may be cited to indicate that, besides among those who professed or sympathized with the Bhakti cult, among others also the previous social structure was undergoing transformation in those times. What is, however, of particular importance to stress here is that a large number of such noted persons who are mentioned in standard historical literature came from various trading and artisan castes, just as was the case with many leaders and prominent supporters of the Bhakti movement. Thus it appears that while changes were taking place not merely "in the relations of the various *varnas* in

Indian society" but *within* the caste structure as a whole, the social stratum composed of artisans and traders was gaining in importance.

Moreover, even without violating their caste-rules, the trading castes grew in importance in this period. The Khatris, for instance, migrated to the upper Gangetic plain from the Punjab and "took a leading part in the formation of the new bureaucracy and the growth of trade;"[178] and in regard to south India it has been noted:[179]

"In most of the common industries the rule was production for the local market; but the movements of individual merchants from one part of the country to another, and the highly developed organization of mercantile corporations in different parts of it, provide adequate evidence of a brisk internal trade in certain sorts of goods. ... Merchants were generally organized in powerful guilds and corporations which often transcended political divisions and were therefore not much affected by the wars and revolutions going on about them."

Such a situation, obviously, suggests that trade was flourishing in India in those days, and, in fact, this was the case. For it was not only the trading castes and communities which were interested in the spread of commerce and thereby to increase their wealth and influence in society, but the ruling powers also were more and more subscribing to such a policy. It has been noted referring to the Turko-Afghan rulers of Delhi:[180]

"The system of posts through horsemen or runners, the use of tokens by foreign merchants, the abolition of octroi duties 'which had weighed heavily upon merchants and tradesmen,' etc., under various Delhi kings, before Shershah, contributed to the strengthening of trade and commerce in the country. Firuz Tughlak in particular paid greater attention to irrigation and built up a number of canal systems which not only helped agriculture but also linked the countryside with the towns. The growth of new towns at this time cannot be ascribed solely to the magnanimity of a monarch. They are an indication of new forces within the womb of the feudal system. On the site of old Indraprastha, there arose Firuzabad. Hissar, Fathabad, Firuzpur, Budaun, Jaunpur, etc., testify to the further growth of exchange centres in Northern India.

The men employed for finance and revenue by the Delhi Sultans were mostly from the indigenous population. The existence of a ministry for dealing with markets, the rules for regulating weights and measures, etc., testify to the same fact."

Sher Shah, during his reign, further accelerated commercial activities in his domains. According to some, he "realised the importance of Agra both for his authority and for the growth of commerce, (so that) Agra became an important centre of communications."[181] Sher Shah was "also a builder and a road-maker."

"Of his four great roads one ran form Sonargaon in Bengal through Agra, Delhi and Lahore to the Indus, one from Agra to Mandu, one from Agra to Jodhpur and Chitor, and one from Lahore to Multan. On either side of all were planted fruit trees, and beside them were erected 1700 caravanserais with separate lodgings for Muslims and Hindus and servants to supply food to those of each religion. Grain and fodder were supplied for horses and cattle, and each caravanserai contained a well and a mosque of burnt brick, with a *mu'azzin* and an *inam* in attendance. A police official kept the peace and prevented crime, and two post-horses were stabled in each building for the use of riders conveying the royal mail."[182]

Such measures could not but have given help to commercial pursuits. Sher Shah also built new towns as important trade-centres. One of them was the town of Patna, built on the ruins of the famous old town of Pataliputra, about which Sher Shah was reported to have remarked:[183] "One day Patna will become one of the leading cities of the country." It has also been reported:[184]

"According to V. A. Smith, Patna had extensive trade in raw cotton, cotton cloths, sugar, opium and other commodities. Ralph Fitch found Patna a flourishing trade centre in 1586. Both politically and commercially, Patna was linked with Banaras and Agra. It also became a connecting link between Bengal and Northern Hindustan though essentially it formed a part of the Hindustani market."

Furthermore, an efficient execution of law and order made Sher Shah's kingdom safe for travellers.

"Crime was rigorously suppressed and the headmen of villages were held responsible for the surrender of those who committed crimes in their villages or of criminals who took refuge in them. Even the historians of the Timurids admit that in the Afgan's reign an old woman with a basket of gold could safely sleep in the open plain at night without a guard, and the historian Badauni, born in 1540, imitates the founder of his faith by thanking God that he was born the subject of so just a king."[185]

Under such protection the merchants could travel to distant regions without any anxiety, and thus facilitate the spread of commerce in bulk and extent. It has been noted:[186]

"Sher Shah assured a prosperous trade in the country by the measures he took for the purpose of maintaining law and order in the country. His improved means of communication further made transport cheaper and less inconvenient. The serais assured the merchants safe places for the deposit of their valuable goods. To encourage commerce still further he abolished the vexatious transit duties charged as commerce passed from city to city. Custom dues were to be paid at the frontiers, taxes on sales were collected when an article had been actually sold. To help trade and industry and encourage sales he reformed the coinage. A standard weight and uniform fineness were adopted for all coins issued so that these could be easily accepted without any fear of any discount being charged later on. Gold, silver and copper coins were issued from various mint towns."

After Sher Shah, during the reign of Akbar, further measures were taken to facilitate trade and commerce. Akbar, "like Sher Shah, tried to regulate the currency of the State;" as a result, the "mercantile affairs of the Empire during the reigns of Akbar and his successors were transacted in round gold *mohars*, rupees and *dams*."[187] A uniform currency throughout the empire was certainly beneficial to the traders, and especially so when a brisk trade was conducted over large parts of India in the big and prosperous cities, ancient or lately established and new ones being constantly built.

"Writing in A.D. 1585, Fitch observed: 'Agra and Fatehpore are two very great cities, either of them much greater than London and very populous. Between Agra and Fatehpore are twelve miles, and all the way is a market of victual and other things, as full as though a man were still in a town, and so many people, as if a man were in a market.' Terry refers to the Punjab as 'a large province, and most fruitful. Lahore is the chief city thereof, built very large, and abounds both in people and riches, one of the principal cities for trade in all India.' Monserrate asserted that in 1581 Lahore was 'not second to any city in Europe or Asia.' Burhanpur in Khandesh was 'very great, rich and full of people.' Ahmadabad in Gujarat has been described by Abul Fazl as 'a noble city in a high state of prosperity,' which 'for the pleasantness of its climate and display of the choicest productions of the whole globe is almost unrivalled.' In Eastern India there was much opulence in cities like Benares, Patna, Rajmahal, Burdwan, Hugli, Dacca and Chittagong."[188]

Also, in order to reach distant trade-centres, the system of transport and communication was kept in a fairly good order.

"There was no want of communications, along roads and rivers, for the purpose of the vast mercantile traffic, though they compare unfavourably with those of the present day improved under scientific conditions. Of course, with the exception of certain highways, the roads were generally unmetalled, but the 'main routes of land travel were clearly defined, in some cases by avenues of tress, and more generally by walled enclosures, known as *sarāis*, in which travellers and merchants could pass the night in comparative security.' The rivers, some of which were navigable throughout the year and some through a part of it, afforded excellent means for the carriage of heavy traffic."[189]

The hey-day of the Mughals passed away with Akbar, for his successors had neither his genius nor his ability. Yet, if not with such a vigour as during the reign of Akbar, his successors also diligently promoted commerce in their domains. Manouchi, for instance, noted about Akbar's grandson, the Emperor Shah Jahan:[190]

"His Laws for purging his Dominions of Highway Men are commendable above all the rest. The Roads before his Reign had been infested with 'em, and Commerce very much interrupted. The Emperor was so severe a Prosecutor of these Offenders, that they were at last intirely suppress'd. The means he made use of for clearing his Country of 'em, was to render the Civil Magistrates accountable for all the Robberies committed within their Districts. Thus the *Hollanders* Storehouse at *Surate*, being plunder'd in the Night, *Cha-Jaham* made the Governor pay the Sum, which their Effects amounted to."

In the south also the situation was not different. Powerful merchant guilds had developed there, and they received support and encouragement from the reigning monarchs. For instance, referring to the merchants belonging to one such guild, it has been reported that:

"In the Chola country they had their own settlements called *vira-pattanas* where with the sanction of the local powers and the central government, they enjoyed special privileges in matters of trade."[191]

It is also worthy of note that with reference to the Vijayanagar Empire it has been remarked: "The most remarkable feature in the economic condition of the kingdom was commerce, inland, coasting and overseas."[192]

Evidently, helped by the state powers, India was then bustling with trading activities, and this means that production was also on the increase. For south India it has been noted:[193]

"Spinning and weaving formed a major industry which occupied considerable numbers, and guilds of weavers were generally in a flourishing condition and took an active part in many local concerns. ... Warangal specialized in the manufacture of carpets which were much sought after, and other places had other specialities. The metal industries and the jeweller's art had reached a high state of perfection. ... Iron was used for making arms, and some places like Palnad attained celebrity for the excellence of their output. The manufacture and sale of salt was generally the concern of government which derived a considerable revenue from it."

And as for north India, referring to the conditions during the rule of the Turko-Afghans and the Mughals, respectively, it has been stated that "the royal *kārkhānās* or manufactories at Delhi sometimes employed 4,000 weavers of silk besides manufactures of other stuffs to satisfy royal demands;" and that "one of the most important factors in the economic history of India during the period under review [the Mughal Period] was the extensive and varied industrial activity of the people, which besides supplying the needs of the local aristocracy and merchants could meet the demands of traders coming from Europe and other parts of Asia."[194]

It thus appears that the new forces which were emerging in Indian society in this period were helping in many ways to break through the socio-economic and spiritual basis of the feudal society, by means of undermining the roots of the village community system and the caste structure, and to bring in a new social order in which the system of production of commodities and trading in them was constantly gaining ground.

In this situation, there was another significant feature of the period which is worthy of note. This concerns the attempts made by several monarchs to separate their secular rule of the subjects from religious injunctions, which, again, could not but help the new forces to gain a stronger foothold in society. For, as it will be evident from a following discussion, in a state which was not governed purely by the orthodox doctrines of Islam or Brahmanism and where either there was only one religion or the state power tolerated all religions, the people holding various faiths could develop as homogeneous communities without or irrespective of religious differences and this could have given the artisans and traders belonging to diverse religions an additional filip to their pursuits by bringing them under a unified system and control.

First to give some indications of this form of change taking place in the Indian states, as regards the Vijayanagar Empire, which has sometimes been characterized as the last representative of a typical Hindu kingdom in later periods of Indian history, it has been asserted by reputed Indian historians: "The only law of the land was not 'the law of the Brāhmaṇas which is that of the priests,' as Nuniz would ask us to believe, but was based on traditional regulations and customs, strengthened by the constitutional usage of the country, and its observance was strictly enforced."[195] Moreover,

> "The King was assisted in the task of administration by a council of ministers, appointed by him. Though the Brāhmaṇas held high offices in the administration and had considerable influence, the ministers were recruited not only from their ranks but also from those of the Kshatriyas and the Vaiśyas.... the Vijayanagar Emperors employed Muslims in their military service from the time of Deva Rāya II, and patronised 'the cause of Islam in and outside their great capital.' A famous Muslim general, Asad Khān of Bijāpur, was once invited to Vijayanagar to witness the Mahānavamī festival."[196]

In the Punjab also the Sikh Gurus began to assume secular powers. The fifth Guru of the Sikhs, Arjun, "was treated as a temporal king and girt round by a body of courtiers and ministers called *masands*, which is the Hindi corruption of the title *masnad-i-ala* borne by nobles under the Pathan sultans of Delhi."[197]

During these days, some of the Moslem monarchs also were seen to diverge or to indicate their inclination to diverge from the previously ordained government of their territories according to the codes of Islam as prescribed and interpreted by the orthodox Moslem religious dignitaries. Among the Sultans at Delhi, Alauddin Khilji "repeatedly said, that the orders and rules of government depended solely on the judgement of the Sovereign, and that the law (of the Prophet) had no concern with them."[198] Accordingly, "he carried into effect whatever he judged, in his mind, to be for the better government of the country; and paid no heed to the question as to whether what he did was or was not authorized by the law."[199] Similarly, it has been said that one of his successors to the Delhi Sultanate, namely "Muhammad bin Tuglaq's chief offence was that, probably inspired by the example of the Khaljis, 'he ignored the canon law' as expounded by learned Doctors and based his political conduct on his own experience of the world."[200]

Likewise, in Kashmir, Sultan Zain-'ul-'Ābidīn is said to have "anticipated Akbar in his pro-Hindu and liberal policy," for he "recalled the Brāhmaṇas who had left the kingdom during his father's reign, admitted learned Hindus to his society, abolished the *jizya* and granted perfect religious freedom to all."[201] Under his initiative, "the *Mahābhārata* and the *Rājataranginī* were translated from Sanskrit into Persian, and several Arabic and Persian books were translated into the Hindi language."[202]

In Bengal, Husain Shah employed many Hindus as high officials of the State, such as Purandar Khan, Rup and Sanatan; the last two later becoming devout followers of Chaitanya. Moreover, "frequent references are found in old Bengali literature indicating the esteem and trust in which the Emperor Husen Saha was held by the Hindus;" and, in fact, "the patronage and favour of the Muhammadan emperors and chiefs gave the first start towards the recognition of Bengali in the courts of the Hindu Rajas," who previously used to encourage Sanskrit more strongly.[203]

In the south, several Hindus held positions as ministers in the Moslem kingdom of Golconda. In Malwa also, which was another State ruled by Moslems, "Medinī Rāi of Chanderī and his friends held high positions."[204] And in Bijapur, Yusuf Adil Shah "entrusted the Hindus with offices of responsibility and the records of his State were ordinarily kept in the Marāthī language."[205] During the rule of his fifth successor to the head of the kingdom, "the Muslim subjects of Ibrāhīm 'Ādil Shāh of Bijapur described him as 'Jagadguru' for his patronage of the Hindus in his state."[206] Meadows Taylor stated with regard to this king:[207]

"Although he changed the profession of the State religion immediately upon assuming the direction of State affairs from Shia to Sunni, Ibrahim was yet extremely tolerant of all creeds and faiths. Hindus not only suffered no persecution at his hands, but many of his chief civil and military officers were Brahmans and Marathas. With the Portuguese of Goa he seems to have kept up a friendly intercourse. Portuguese painters decorated his palaces, and their merchants traded freely in his dominions. To their missionaries also he extended his protection; and there are many anecdotes current in the country that his tolerance of Christians equalled, if it did not exceed, that of his contemporary Akbar."

Indeed, those were the days when in India attempts were definitely made to secularize political life, and to establish a permanent harmony between the Hindus and Moslems. The latter was also a dominant note in the life of the Rajput heroes of that period. For instance, Rana Sanga respected the independence of his conquered enemy, Mahmud II of Malwa; Rana Ban Pal of Santur protected Qutlugh Khan after the latter was defeated by Sultan Nasiruddin; Hamir Deva of Ranthambhor gave shelter to a rebel chief of Alauddin Khilji; etc. From all accounts, therefore, there was no exaggaration in Sir John Marshall's remark:[208]

"... seldom in the history of mankind has the spectacle been witnessed of two civilisations, so vast and so strongly developed, yet so radically dissimilar as the Muhammadan and Hindu, meeting and mingling together. The very contrasts which existed between them, the wide divergences in their culture and their religions, make the history of their impact peculiarly instructive."

The above features pervading in Indian society received support from Sher Shah, and Akbar encouraged them further. He initiated many socially progressive measures, which showed that during his reign new values were entering into society. Marx noted:[209]

"1582–85: Ruhe; *Acber settles the Empire.* War selbst gleichgültig in religious matters, daher tolerant; seine Haupt religious und literacy advisers Feizi and *Abul Fazl.* Feizi übersetzt old Sanscrit poems, u. a.: '*Ramayana*' und '*Mahabaratta*' (später auch, nachdem Akber röm/isch/kathol/ischen/ portugies/ischen/ Priest *von Goa* mitgebracht, übersetzt Feizi die evangelists. '*Indulgenz gegen die Hindus*); Akber bestand nur auf *abolition* of *Suttee* (burning of widows on the husband's funeral pyre) etc. *Er schaft ab 'Jezia,' i. e., capitation tax,* which every Hindu had been *compelled to pay to the Mussulman* government."

Not only by the abolition of the *jezia* tax in 1563 did Akbar endeavour to bring amity between the Hindus and Moslems, which was certainly necessary for an all-round development of the new forces in society, but at the same time he also abolished the pilgrimage tax which "was levied on the Hindus not only when they visited their famous places of pilgrimage but for their local religious fairs and festivities."[210] Furthermore, "Akber reformed the *Code of punishments*, founding them partly on *Mahommedan custom, partly on the laws of Menu*;"[211] and he "discontinued making prisoners of war first slaves and then Muslims."[212] In addition,

"Akbar tried to prevent child marriages even though both the Hindu and the Muslim orthodoxy backed this evil custom. He permitted Hindu widows to remarry. He declared himself against marriages between near relatives. He tried to stop the circumcision of children though with what success we do not know.

Many Muslim rulers before him had left the evil of drink alone. Akbar decided that it was not possible to prohibit it altogether and that it would be better to control its use. Wine was allowed to be sold ostensibly for medical purposes, but every purchaser had to give his name. Being drunk in public became an offence, disorderly conduct in public was punished. To control the evil of prostitution, all women of ill fame were assigned separate quarters, names of those visiting them or sending for them were taken down. He allowed women to come out of their seclusion to the Mina Bazar (a step directly against the social standard set up by the Hindu and Moslem feudal nobility—RKM). In education and literature he was not content with the study or spread of the Muslim theology alone. He patronized astronomy, mathematics, history, *belles lettres,* medicine and many other subjects. His patronage of painting, including portrait painting, led to the foundation of a new school of art in India."[213]

Finally, in later years, propounding his "Divine Faith," Akbar definitely claimed the spiritual leadership of the State besides his secular reign over the subjects.

There are divergent views on why Akbar took such a step. To some, like Vincent Smith, it was due mainly to his personal idiosyncracies and conceit.[214] Some others, again, thought that his interest in Christian religion was primarily a cover for commercial relations with the Portuguese at Goa rather than expressing a sincere desire towards conversion to Christianity. Manouchi, for instance, wrote: "'Twas easily seen that the Prince in sending for *Jesuits* to *Goa*, had no other Design than that of settling a Trade with the *Portuguese*, and satisfying his Passion for the *European* Sciences."[215] However, whether or not there is some truth in all such remarks, it is of interest to note what is imputed to have been said by Akbar as the motive behind his propagation of "Divine Faith."

"My People, says he, are a strange Medley of Mahometans, Idolaters and Christians. I'm resolved to bring them all to one Opinion. I'll joyn the Baptism of the one, and the Circumcision of the other to the Worship of *Brama*. I'll retain the *Metempsichosis*, plurality of Wives, and the Worship *of Jesus Christ*. Thus compounding my Religion of those Points, which are most agreeable to the Professors of the respective Sects, I shall be able to form 'em into one intire Flock, of which I my self shall be the Leader and Head."[216]

It is also of interest to note that although Akbar's son Jahangir did not propound a new religion, he held liberal views regarding the non-Islam faiths.[217] Sir Thomas Roe characterized him as an atheist, and Vincent Smith wrote in connection with Jahangir's relations with the

Jesuit priests of Goa: "Probably his favour to the priests was accorded chiefly from political motives, in order to secure Portuguese support and trade."[218] But, like Akbar, Jahangir also probably had the desire to establish harmony among the peoples following different religions. As Manouchi remarked with regard to Akbar's "Divine Faith" and Jahangir's tolerance of all religious beliefs:[219]

"The diversity of Religion is another Source of hatred, and consequently of Dissentions in the State. 'Twas doubtless from this Consideration, that *Akebar* and *Jehan-Guir* had form'd a Design of composing one Religion out of all those, profess'd in Indoustan; ..."

Jahangir's successor, Shah Jahan, carried on warfare with the Portuguese after his accession to the throne, but this was probably due more to political reasons than his aversion towards Christianity, as it is said sometimes. Although Manouchi also attributed the Emperor's and the Empress Taigé-Mahal's hatred of Christianity as one of the reasons for this warfare, he noted at the same time that Shah Jahan "thought he might make War advantageously against the *Portuguese*, and by his Arms Exterminate those Merchants once so Formidable in the *Indies*, but now become contemptible by their great Losses, and by the late Conquests of the *English* and *Dutch*."[220] Moreover, whether Shah Jahan nourished an anti-Christian feeling or not, the fact remains that Christians in India were very few and so they hardly counted in society in those days. On the other hand, as regards the two major religious communities in India, Shah Jahan followed, like his predecessors, the policy of amity between the Hindus and Moslems within his domain and in his court; a policy which was vigorously pursued by Akbar and "afforded the strongest support to the throne in the reigns of Akbar and his son, and continued to bear fruit even in the reigns of his grandson, Shāhjahān, and his great-grandson, Aurangzēb."[221]

It thus appears that, following the earlier trend, Akbar and his successors (excluding Aurangzeb, as will be described later) wanted to establish harmony among their subjects professing various religious faiths. This, because of his genius and administrative zeal, Akbar desired to put through his "Divine Faith," whereby he intended to produce lasting peaceful relations in his domain. His successors, on the other hand, were of much less calibre than himself; yet Jahangir pursued the same policy by his tolerant attitude to all religions, and Shah Jahan also did not foment tension between the Hindus and the Moslems.

The question, however, still remains: why did Akbar and his two successors find it necessary to establish harmony among their subjects who held various religious beliefs? There is no doubt that "the diversity of Religion is another Source of hatred, and consequently of Dissentions in the State;" but diversity of religion existed in India from much earlier times. What, then, was the *specific* necessity on the part of the Mughal rulers from Akbar to Shah Jahan to endeavour either to do away with this diversity and gather all the subjects round one faith or assume a liberal attitude to different faiths, as was also the case with some other Indian rulers in this period?

The answer to this question obviously lies not in a sudden realization on the part of some rulers of the banefulness of diversity of religion in a state. For it is evident from the foregoing account of the attempts to secularise political life and establish amity between the Hindus and the Moslems that neither these were accidental in occurrence and isolated in character nor were they due merely to chance whims of some rulers. On the contrary, firstly, the attempts were consistently made by successive monarchs in one domain (as found during the rule of the Turko-Afghans or the Great Mughals) and, secondly, such attempts are seen to have been made in states widely separated from one another, such as Bengal and Bijapur, Kashmir and Vijayanagar, etc. It is likely, therefore, that instead of being the result of a casual and an *abstract* realization on the part of some rulers to do away with religious dissentions in their states, they were outcome of an essential demand (or several such demands) in the Indian society at that time, which, again, received active support from the rulers for some specific reasons.

In a society where, as described before, the previous set of socio-economic and spiritual values was breaking down and in its place a new order of society high-lighted by the role of artisans and traders was slowly making its appearance, one essential *social* demand could have been to create conditions for further promotion of industry and trade by bringing the artisans and traders belonging to different religions under one system or under equal control irrespective of their diversity of faith, so that there could be no hindrance put before their productive and commercial pursuits in the form of special taxes on the Hindus, etc. And it is of interest to note here that this was a demand which had the possibility of receiving active support from the Mughal rulers, from Akbar to Shah Jahan. For, as facts bear out, trade was a profession in which the Mughal Government, some of its officers, and even the Great Mughals themselves were no less interested than the merchants in the empire.

That both Akbar and Jahangir diligently endeavoured to extend commercial activities in their domains has been referred to earlier in connection with their contact with the Jesuit priests of the Portuguese settlement at Goa; and it has also been mentioned that Shah Jahan took measures to promote commerce in the empire. It is of no less importance to note further that the Mughal State had a direct connection with some branches of commerce in the empire. As has been stated in a study of the Mughal government and its administration:[222]

> "The State was not only a great manufacturer, it was a great trader as well. It took part in the maritime trade of the country; it participated in the foreign trade with Persia and Arabia. The manufacture of salt and saltpetre was a State monopoly. From time to time other articles were also declared State monopoly."

In addition, it is of particular relevance to state here that the monarchs themselves indulged in private and personal trade. Vincent Smith noted that "Akbar himself was a trader, and did not disdain to earn commercial profits;"[223] and, in fact, Akbar's interests in commerce were manifold. It is reported that "some of the fine industries of Gujarat and Agra and Kashmir" were reserved for him and that any one selling a horse (which was one of the most valuable imports into India in those days) had first to notify the Emperor or his agents.[224] As regards Jahangir, whether he busied himself with commercial activities or not, his favourite wife Nurjahan has been reported to have "dabbled in indigo and embroidered cloth trade."[225] Also his son, Prince Khurram, conducted private trade with Mocha and Persia;[226] and, after ascending the throne under the title of Shah Jahan, he made indigo and saltpetre his monopoly. He gave a loan from the royal treasury to Mànohardas in order to conduct the indigo trade on the basis of sharing profits with him, while with regard to his control over the trade in saltpetre an Englishman is reported to have complained: "The king hath made it his owne commodity."[227] And following in the foot-steps of her father, Shah Jahan's favourite daughter, Princess Jahanara, was also keenly interested in this profession, which she carried on on her own account.[228]

Furthermore, besides the Royal Family, the near relatives and close friends of the Emperors were also greatly interested in trade. For instance, in collaboration with Nurjahan and Prince Khurram, Zulfikar Khan, the Mughal Governor of Surat during the reign of Jahangir, carried on trading activities with the help of the Portuguese and obstructed the growth of English influence in the Mughal Court;[229] Shah Jahan's father-in-law, Asaf Khan, was well-known as a trader, and made a "fortune of twenty-five millions of rupees in the reign of Shāh Jahān;"[230] and Mir Jumla, one of the close associates of Aurangzeb, was "made *Dewan* for making presents of about 15 lakhs (1,500,000) rupees to Shahjahan,"[231] and he amassed "a vast fortune, by trading in diamonds and precious stones."[232]

Evidently, such a state of affairs did have an influence on the policy of the Mughal Government and the execution of its directives. For while the Emperor would not be averse to upholding a policy which was favourable to the promotion of commerce in the Empire by bringing together the artisans and traders of different religious beliefs under a unified system and control in order to give them an additional filip in their pursuits, his officers and advisers (belonging to the Royal Family or being related to it or associating themselves as close friends and advisers) would support such a policy and work for its satisfactory execution if they were also interested in commercial transactions. In fact, they would encourage the monarch to adopt such an attitude. Hence it is not improbable that the demands of commerce did have an effect on the liberal attitude to religion, which was shown very markedly by Akbar and was followed by his two successors. As has been remarked with reference to Akbar's "Divine Faith:"[233]

> "Akbar followed a policy of religious toleration, a policy in conformity with the interests of the Hindu and Muslim traders. The theory of his spiritual headship of the state was developed by Abul Fazal, a theory which was directly aimed at weakening the hold of the priests on the people. The most important reason for this was that Akbar's interests lay with the merchant class."

Needless to say, it is a disputable point whether the commercial interest of the rulers was "the most important reason" which led Akbar to announce his "Divine Faith" and prompted Jahangir and Shah Jahan to assume a tolerant attitude to all religions as some other Indian rulers did in this period. It is probable that just as personal factors and the desire to create harmony among his subjects for administrative and other purposes might have influenced such a decision on the part of Akbar, there were similar and possibly other reasons which had a say in the changed attitude of those other rulers who attempted to secularize political life and establish concordance between the Hindus and Moslems in their states. But, obviously, the trend of society to promote production and commerce, which from other aspects also was supported and encouraged by these rulers, should not be lost sight of. Indeed, in the light of the emergence of new forces in society as described before, the consistency of the attempts of the rulers to establish harmony among their subjects and the recurrence of these attempts over several generations in those days and in different parts of India suggest that this particular trend did provide an important reason for the amicable attitude of the rulers to different religions, even if it did not account for "the most important reason."

It should further be noted that whether the rulers' attempts to establish amity among their subjects belonging to different religions was motivated by their direct interest in commerce or not, the personal interest shown by Akbar and his successors in trading activities probably gave an indication of the fact that from another aspect also the feudal relations in India were gradually disappearing. Where the duty of the ruler was to "protect" the people while the duty of the trader was to "provide" for them, the monarch's private interest in trade irrespective of his assumed role of remaining impartial to the life and living of all classes of people residing in his domain appears to have indicated that, dominated by the commercial interests of the time, the new values in society had gone deep enough to affect also the political head of a state and the previously ordained social order. Indeed, there is likely to be a good deal of justification in the following comment on the commercial interests shown by the Mughal Emperors down from Akbar:[234]

> "The monarch's personal interest in trade violated the feudal law that the duty of the prince is to 'protect' the people while the duty of the merchant is to provide for the people."

And, in any case, irrespective of the precise motive of the rulers behind their policy of religious toleration and irrespective of the effect their direct interest in commerce had on the previously established feudal values, the fact remains that this practice of theirs to bring about and maintain amity between various religious communities in their domains as well as their private participation in commercial activities could not but encourage the artisans, and especially the traders, to follow their pursuits more vigorously. For production and trade would certainly receive an additional encouragement among the Hindu artisans and traders if they did not suffer any discrimination in a Moslem state and were, on the contrary, supported by the monarchs to pursue such a profession (as for example, Manohardas receiving a loan from the royal treasury during the reign of Shah Jahan for trading in indigo); and the same would be the effect with the Moslem artisans and traders in a Hindu state. Obviously, in many respects the force of the social stratum composed of artisans and traders was constantly gaining ground in Indian society in those days.

Such a situation, however, presupposes as a basic condition a rapid extension of the sphere of commercial activities, involving a marked increase in the demand for production as commodities on the one hand and in the potentiality of trading in these goods on the other. Moreover, such a suggestion is further strengthened by the fact that conditions were then evidently so ripe in India for commercial activities on a large scale that even the supreme rulers were involved in the process. And this is a suggestion which is verified by the fact that not only production in India had by then substantially increased beyond the confines of local consumption, but, besides a rapid expansion of internal trade, foreign commerce had then developed on an unprecedented scale. As it has been written with particular reference to north India:[235]

"By far the most important industry in India during this period was the manufacture of cotton cloth. The principal centres of cotton manufacture were distributed throughout the country, as, for example, at Patan in Gujarāt, Burhānpur in Khāndesh, Jaunpur, Benares, Patna and some other places in the United Provinces and Bihār, and many cities and villages in Orissa and Bengal. The whole country from Orissa to East Bengal looked like a big cotton factory, and the Dacca district was specially reputed for its delicate muslin fabrics, 'the best and finest cloth made of cotton' that was in all India. Pelsaert notes that at Chābāspur and Sonārgāon in East Bengal 'all live by the weaving industry and the produce has the highest reputation and quality.' Bernier observes: "There is in *Bengale* such a quantity of cotton and silk, that the Kingdom may be called the common storehouse for those two kinds of merchandise, not of Hindoustan or the Empire of the *Great Mogul* only, but of all the neighbouring kingdoms, and even of Europe.' The dyeing industry, too, was in a flourishing condition. Terry tells us that coarser cotton cloths were either dyed or printed with a 'variety of well-shaped and well-coloured flowers or figures, which are so fixed in the cloth that no water can wash them out'. Silk-weaving, limited in scope as compared with cotton manufacture, was also an important industry of a section of the people. Abul Fazl writes that it received a considerable impetus in the reign of Akbar due to the imperial patronage. Bengal was the premier centre of silk production and manufacture and supplied the demands of the Indian and European merchants from other parts of India, though silk-weaving was practised in Lahore, Āgra, Fathpur Sīkrī and Gujarāt. Moreland writes on the authority of Tavernier that, about the middle of the seventeenth century, the total production of silk in Bengal was 'about 2¹/₂ million pounds out of which one million pounds were worked up locally, ³/₄ million were exported raw by the Dutch and ³/₄ million distributed over India, most of it going to Gujarāt, but some being taken by merchants from Central Asia'. Shawl and carpet-weaving industries flourished under the patronage of Akbar; the former woven mainly from hair, having originated from Kāshmir, was manufactured also at Lahore, and the latter at Lahore and Āgra. Woollen goods, chiefly coarse blankets, were also woven. ...Saltpetre, used chiefly as an ingredient for gunpowder in India and also exported outside by the Dutch and English traders, was manufactured in widely distributed parts of India during the seventeenth century, particularly in peninsular India and the Bihār section of the Indo-Gangetic region. Bihār henceforth enjoyed a special reputation for the manufacture of this article till the first half of the nineteenth century, and it was in high demand by the Europeans for use in wars in their countries. Besides these major industries, we have testimony regarding various crafts during the Mughul period. Edward Terry noticed that 'many curious boxes, trunks, standishes (pen-cases), carpets, with other excellent manufactures, may be there had.' Pelsaert also writes that in Sind 'ornamental disks, draught-boards, writing cases, and similar goods are manufactured locally in large quantities; they are pretty, inlaid with ivory and ebony, and used to be exported in large quantities from Goa, and the coast towns.' ..."

In south India also the situation was the same. It was been stated that when "at the end of the tenth century, the political situation in China became normal again, and the Sung government of the day showed great interest in foreign trade," such was the reaction in south India with which trade relations had already developed a century earlier that "eager to take advantage of the new conditions, the Cholas sent 'embassies' to China."[236] Moreover, while establishing trade relations with foreign countries, the Cholas saw to it simultaneously that a proper atmosphere prevailed in their domain for commercial activities and the foreign traders received a fair treatment. The Jewish traveller Benjamin of Tudela (1170) stated with regard to the conditions of trade in Quilon under Chola rule:[237]

"This nation is very trustworthy in matters of trade, and whenever foreign merchants enter their port, three secretaries of the king immediately repair on board their vessels, write down their names and report them to him. The king thereupon grants them security for their property, which they may even leave in the open fields without any guard. One of the king's officers sits in the market, and receives goods that may have been found anywhere, and which he returns to those applicants who can minutely describe them. This custom is observed in the whole empire of this king."

Also other kingdoms in south India were not left behind in promoting trade and commerce in their spheres. For instance,

"The Kakatiya monarch Ganapati gave an impetus to the foreign trade of the Andhra country in the middle of the thirteenth century by his charter of security (*abhayaśāsana*). Under this charter the cargo of shipwrecked merchants would no longer be seized as had been the custom till then; moreover, the duty on all exports and imports would not exceed $^1/_{30}$ of their value. This edict was renewed a century later by Annapota Reddi (1378), and corresponded the general practice that prevailed in all the enlightened and progressive ports of South India, though Colombo still retained the older practice in the fourteenth century."[238]

As time went on, foreign trade increased in bulk. The Vijayanagar Empire, which as stated before was notable for its commercial activities, had about 300 harbours, some of which provided for long-distance commerce. It has been noted:[239]

"Our information on condition of industry, trade and travel becomes more copious and precise after the foundation of Vijayanagar and Bāhmanī kingdoms. . . .

The import of horses to India from Arabia was important at all times, and grew to great proportions after the rise of the Bāhmanī and Vijayanagar kingdoms in the fourteenth century. . . .

Calicut, where Razzak landed on his arrival, was a secure harbour for ships from Africa and Arabia; . . . More than seventy years later, Duarte Barbosa found that the trade of Calicut was very large, and on that account natives of diverse lands—Arabs, Persians, Guzerates, Khorassanians and Daquanis—settled there. . . . Here they loaded goods from every place, and every monsoon ten or fifteen ships sailed for the Red Sea, Aden and Mecca, whence the goods went through intermediaries up to Venice. . . .

The Italian Varthema (1505) noted that an immense quantity of cotton was produced near Cambay so that every year forty or fifty vessels were laden with cotton and silk to be carried to different countries. Carnelians and diamonds also came to Cambay from mountains at six and nine day's journey from there. . . .

Barbosa (1515) noted that wheat, rice, millet and gingelly, besides fine muslins and calicos produced in the Bāhmanī kingdom, were exported from Chaul. A few miles inland from Chaul was a big market where 'they bring their goods laden on great droves of trained oxen with pack-saddles, like those of Castille; a driver drives 20 or 30 oxen before him'. Of Malabar, Barbosa makes the very true remark: 'albeit the country is but small, yet it is so fulfilled of people, that it may well be called one town from Mount Dely to Coulam' (Quilon). Caeser Frederick (1567) found much silk imported into Cochin from China, and sugar from Bengal. . . .

The main exports of Golconda were thus cotton goods, iron and steel. Indigo was transported to the west coast and thence to Persia; cotton yarn went to Burma, and other minor items contributed to what was for the time a large export trade. The volume of imports was smaller; spices, dye-woods, metals other than iron, camphor, porcelain, silk and other goods, mainly luxuries, were brought for sale on the coast, and the excess of exports was paid for in gold and silver. There was also a large coasting trade, northward to Bengal and southward to Ceylon. . . .

Caeser Frederick noted the existence of regular trade from San Thomé to Pegu. . . ."

From all accounts it thus appears that foreign trade was then playing a vital role in Indian society, and that commerce was no longer confined only, or mainly, to luxury goods. Demands were created abroad for Indian textiles, metal objects, spices, dye-crops and other goods, and the supply was also increasing in bulk. Referring to the inter-Asian trade, it has been written:[240]

"From the twelfth to the fifteenth century, Chinese sea-going junks were frequent visitors to the west coast of India. Siraf, on the eastern coast of the Persian Gulf, was the chief emporium in the west and the rich merchants of that city feasted the numerous merchants from China, Java, Malaya, and India who visited their city—every Indian insisting on having a separate plate exclusively reserved for him!"

Also for the Mughal period of India's history it was noted:[241]

"India had an active and considerable foreign trade during the greater part of the Mughul period, with different countries of Asia and Europe. The chief imports of the country were bullion, raw silk, horses, metals, ivory, coral, amber, precious stones, velvets, brocades, broadcloth, perfumes, drugs, Chinese porcelain and African slaves, and her exports were various textiles, pepper, indigo, opium and other drugs, and miscellaneous goods."

Evidently, commerce on such a scale as noted above could not depend only on the surplus products of the Indian village communities. On the contrary, not only new towns developed and flourished as trade-centres both in north and south India, but guilds of artisans and traders began to dominate many areas, as has been mentioned before.

Moreover, under the circumstances in which more and more trade goods (and especially textiles) were demanded for the overseas market, the merchants were no longer interested only to pocket the difference between the selling-price of the artisans' products and the buying-price of the consumers or chiefly the long-distance traders. They also began to intervene directly in production in the form of the "putting-out" system in England or the *verlag* system in Germany in those days. Referring to the Mughal Empire it has been noted that "the weavers were directly financed in most cases by middlemen, who must have exploited them greatly;"[242] and as for south India: "The weavers worked in their own houses, but as they depended on advances of capital from buyers they had to produce the quality and quantity of goods prescribed by their customers."[243] It seems, therefore, that, as in Europe in those days, merchant capital had begun to play a significant role in Indian society as well; and, as in Europe, in the evolution of the new forces in the Indian society foreign trade had an important bearing, for it provided a stimulus to break through the subsistence economy and lead to the production of commodities.

Thus the picture one gets of India in this period is a composition of several features which in a total perspective tend to indicate that although feudal forces still dominated the scene their specific features (namely, the village community system and the caste system) were in the process of disintegration; new socio-economic-ideological forces headed mainly by the mercantile class were coming forward in society; and the ruling powers also were aligning themselves with this class and were subscribing to the new forces.

All told, this was indeed a new situation in India. The socio-economic basis of the village communities was being undermined and the Bhakti movement was cutting across the ideological basis of the village community system. Religion was being separated from political and economic life, especially with a view to producing homogeneous communities of people belonging to different faiths and probably also in order to promote commerce in the states. Commodity production and both inland and foreign trade had attained an unprecedented height; merchant capital was intervening in production; and in alliance with the state powers the mercantile class was gaining an importance in society. National markets were developing in different parts of the sub-continent (such as in the Agra-Muttra-Delhi region, in Behar centering on Patna, in Bengal centering on Dacca and Murishidabad, in Gujarat, in the Punjab, in Andhra, in the Tamil-speaking areas, in Malabar, etc.); and different nations were coming into being in these separate areas impressed by their distinctiveness, as portrayed by rapid development of their specific languages and literatures.

This situation in India, in which new social, economic and ideological forces were emerging, has been characterized by some writers as that: "A bourgeois revolution was thus maturing in Hindustan."[244] Whether such a characterization is entirely true or not, and whether it is not a fact that because of the tremendous tenacity of Indian feudalism (as explained before) as well as because of the inability of the Indian merchants to undertake by themselves long-distance foreign trade on a large scale (as explained in the following pages) the new forces while emerging in Indian society had not yet been able to turn the scale against the previous forces, the available evidence surely indicate that the *nature* of development in India in those days was in all essentials similar to those in Europe in that period of transition, as has been briefly summarized in Chapter 1 of this study. As in the first phase of the penetration of the "new civilization" into the English society, India was then at the cross-road; and it was at this critical phase of India's life that the organized bodies of European merchant capital penetrated into India and in course of time the English Company spread its influence over large parts of the subcontinent.

3. India and England

There were, however, important differences in the social development of India and such countries of Europe as England even in that period. It is true that, as in the home country of the East India Company, the Indian merchants, while accumulating wealth and influence with the employment of merchant capital, were sheltering behind the protection of the kings and nobles; and, like the Queen Elizabeth and her successors in England, the Mughal rulers themselves (as well as some others in various parts of India) were interested in mercantile pursuits. It is also true that, as in England and those European states where merchant capital underwent a quick development, in India also foreign trade was playing an important role in this process; and, in spite of the continued presence of the village community system, the duality in the economic life of India characterized by the subsistence economy of the villages and the economy of commodity production in the towns was breaking down and manufacture for the local market as well as for a wider sphere was developing. But while these and several such characteristics of Indian life (as for example, the secularization of political and economic life, etc.) indicated a general similarity with those of England, probably because in both places the direction of social development was the same, in specific features there were many significant differences between them. Of these one is particularly worthy of note for this study, for it gives some indication as to *why* the European mercantile powers could penetrate into India at this critical period of her transition from feudalism to the next higher stage in social development and *how* after establishing itself in the subcontinent the English Company could eventually become the supreme power in India.

While, in the beginning, the emergence of new forces on the ruins of the feudal structure of the European and Indian societies were similar in character, there was this very great difference between India and the maritime nations of Europe like England that, unlike the European mercantile bourgeoisie, the Indian merchants and the Indian states could not by themselves venture on long-distance foreign trade on a large-scale, even though conditions were then created in India for the merchants to indulge in this lucrative pursuit from which the new forces in society could muster their strength and eventually supersede the previous forces, as briefly portrayed for England in Chapter 1 of this study. This lack of the preconditions for a rapid development of the Indian mercantile class and of the Indian bourgeoisie as a whole was due to two main reasons. Firstly, it should be borne in mind that although the subcontinent of India with a land-frontier of about 4,000 miles as compared with her coastal border of about 5,000 miles is not an island, her foreign trade had to be conducted mainly by the sea-route; for, as the land-frontier is studded with insurmountable peaks of mountains and impassable regions, trade-routes over land were difficult. Secondly, while "the sea and the rivers were more advantageous for commercial purposes,"[245] and in earlier years India did have a sea-borne trade of a fair magnitude considering the extent of commerce in those days[246], even in later years the Indian states did not develop as strong maritime powers as compared with those European nations whose mercantile bourgeoisie appeared in India from the last decade of the fifteenth century onward. Regarding the Mughals it was noted:[247]

> "The Mughals had no large fighting vessels. The ships that they maintained were part of the commercial policy of State trade."

Similarly, with regard to the Vijayanagar Empire, which encouraged large-scale commercial activities–inland, coastal and overseas, it has been stated:[248]

> "Epigraphic evidence proves that the rulers of Vijayanagar maintained fleets and the people there were acquainted with the art of ship-building before the advent of the Portuguese. We have, however, no definite knowledge as to how the Vijayanagar Empire dealt with the important question of ocean transport."

And for south India as a whole, even though the peninsula had commercial relations with the Asian countries (from China to Persia) for a long time, it has been remarked:[249]

"Not much information is forthcoming about the navy, though we hear of naval operations, great and small. The conquest of Revatidvīpa and Purī on the West Coast, by the Chālukyas of Bādāmi, and that of Ceylon and the Maldives by the Pallavas, Pāndyas and Cholas as well as by Vijayanagar, above all the great naval expedition of Rājendra Chola against the maritime empire of Sri Vijaya could not have been executed without an efficient naval organization. Furthermore the maritime trade of the country, which was always considerable, must have required protections from the depredations of pirates and hostile powers. The opinions of Chola mariners expressed in treatise on navigation were quoted with approval by their Arab successors in the fifteenth and sixteenth centuries. There is no doubt that the kingdoms of South India had a fairly continuous maritime tradition which served their immediate purpose; but it failed them altogether against the more adventurous nations of Europe."

Why the Indian states did not develop their naval power to the extent the West European nations did in those days, even though the sea-route was important to them for contact with foreign countries (and especially to those in the peninsula), is still a matter for intensive research. Yet, at least partly it may be accounted for by the fact that although from ancient times India had relations with distant countries and traded with them, there was no indispensable necessity for the Indian states to develop as strong maritime powers. For, while in earlier times too there were difficulties in sea-borne commerce and disorders were not altogether absent on the sea, even the sea-faring states in Asia in those days carried on their commercial activities in a more or less peaceful manner. Hence there was no particular need for the Indian rulers to have a strong navy, although there is evidence to suggest that it was not totally lacking in India.

But this situation underwent a marked transformation after several maritime powers emerged on the Atlantic sea-board of Europe and the organized bodies of European merchant capital invaded the Asian sphere of commerce. Henceforth, governed by their bitter jealousy to usurp the Eastern Trade for only one of them, sea-power became a cardinal factor in sea-borne commerce, which, as described in the previous chapters, began to be felt no less strongly in Indian waters. Things came to such a pass that in order to oust one another from this rich field of commerce the European mercantile powers even resorted to piracy against one another; and this affected the Indian interests as well. For lacking their own sea-power, on the sea the Indian interests had to abide by the demands of the European Powers, and occasionally were also the latter's victim. Thus, in 1613, Middleton of the English East India Company captured four Indian ships in "his action against the trading vessels from Gujarāt to the Red Sea" and he found that "they were provided with a Portuguese pass, and Jahāngīr's mother had an interest in the cargo."[250]

Evidently, a strong navy now became a very essential adjunct for trading by the sea-route; but the Indian powers, including the Great Mughals, had not attended to this new need and could not now rise to the occasion. Hence the upshot was that while production had then increased beyond the demands within the society and a class of merchants was rising in wealth and influence on the basis of transactions in such increased production, for trading with foreign countries the Indian merchants as well as the Indian ruling authorities had to depend on European merchant powers. In England, at a similar stage of development, the English mercantile bourgeoisie resented the intrusion of Hansa merchants; in India, their contemporaries could do nothing but to welcome such intrusions. It is no wonder, therefore, that when the European mercantile powers arrived in India one after another—starting with the Portuguese at the end of the fifteenth century, then the Dutch who, appearing at the beginning of the seventeenth century, revived the ancient commerce of India with the Far Eastern Islands of Sumatra, Java and Borneo, and later the English in 1608 and the French in 1668—all of them found receptiveness in India for the pursuit of their commercial activities.

But this weakness of the Indian powers had a telling effect on the future course of India's social development. Firstly, it deprived the Indian mercantile class of the spectacular profit from foreign trade, wherefrom the European mercantile bourgeoisie made most of their fortunes and from such "primary accumulation" the bourgeois development of their societies proceeded at a rapid rate—the capital being ultimately employed for the industrial progress of the nations. On the other hand, because such an opportunity did not exist in India, even though the Indian mercantile class was developing in that period, its development could not be strong and quick enough to make soon a profound and permanent change in the society. The new forces remained in their primary stage; incipient rather than fully established yet. As has been remarked with reference to the class relations in Indian society during the fifteenth-seventeenth centuries[251]

> "... the character of mass movements and uprisings of this period (XVII century) is indicative of the fact that even if primary forms of capitalist relations did exist at that time, in India (which is probable) they were of a sporadic character and formed isolated islets on the territory of India. It also testifies to the absence of the classes of capitalist society which could lead the struggle against feudalism. Even successful popular uprisings led only to the substitution of one feudal lord by another, and not to the elimination of feudal relations (viz. the Jat states in the Ganges-Jumna region, the Mahratta state)."

Secondly, even if at the time the European mercantile powers appeared on the Indian scene the Indian bourgeoisie had already developed as a class (or the Indian merchants were emerging that way by means of their intrusion into production on the basis of something like the "putting-out" or the *verlag* system), because their scope for "primary accumulation" was low and consequently the scope for replacing the old order of society by the growth of wealth and power of the emergent class was limited, they remained much weaker than their European contemporaries. In fact, they could not rise above the position of subservience to the needs of the European merchants, who really controlled India's foreign trade while the Indian merchants could only be their wholesale suppliers. Therefore, although the European merchant powers could not dominate over the Indian mercantile class in every way, they could utilize them in their favour as the English Company did with the Armenian and the *Dadni* merchants, as it will be described in this chapter. It is also not unlikely, as suggested in the following pages, that this subservience of the Indian merchants to the European merchant powers had to play a significant role in the political moves of the rival European powers and particularly in the English conquest of Bengal in 1757, after which it was easy for them to overpower all other Indian rulers.

Thirdly, while since their advent on the subcontinent the European mercantile powers strove for monopoly or special "concessions" in India's foreign trade, as the Indian powers were anything but maritime powers, even when they found this monopoly or the "concession" disadvantageous to them, they could not by themselves expel these powers from the subcontinent or withhold the "concession" for long. On the other hand, in their own interests, they had to subscribe to the presence of the European merchants in India for the purpose of exporting the Indian commodities to foreign countries and thus earn a part of the profit in the chain of distribution. But this fatal helplessness of the Indian powers did not merely preclude a slow development of the new forces in society; eventually it led to the collapse of the Indian powers before the onslaught of the cleverest of these European powers, viz. the English, who in course of time assumed the supreme position in sea-power and began to rule the waves.

From the very beginning of the advent of the European powers on the Indian scene, this helplessness of the Indian powers began to unfold itself. As described before, the mercantile bourgeoisie of Western Europe could arrive in India because they could undertake transoceanic voyage. Also, because the Indian sea-frontier (unlike her land-frontier, especially in the north-west during the Mughal rule) was never well-guarded by the Indian rulers, this was the most convenient course of approach for the European merchants, as is evident from the fact that practically all the merchant powers arrived in India by way of the sea although the Russia Company and the Levant Company of the English merchant bourgeoisie, for instance, had previously penetrated as far as into the Western Asian market. There was also the point that because with the Great Mughals the sea-power was virtually absent and with the smaller semi-independent or independent kingdoms also it was either at a low stage of development or did not exist at all, in any case of difficulty the European merchant powers could easily leave the shores of India without being molested or receiving the punishment due to them for their misbehaviour to the Indian people and the governments, and could even retaliate from the coastal areas.

Indeed, this was shown repeatedly by the conduct of the European powers in India, and irrespective of the fact whether the power was Portuguese or English or any other. Thus, after they had established themselves at the Indian ports, by means of their superior naval power the Portuguese endeavoured to cow the local ruling authorities and oust the Arab merchants completely from the India Trade. Of this, mention has been made in the previous chapters. Moreover, it is learnt from any standard work on the history of India how in order to strengthen their position in the subcontinent the Portuguese captured Goa and several other coastal areas from the Indian rulers, and for a time became supreme in India's sea-borne trade. Ultimately, it came to such a pass that trading in horses, which as noted before was one of the precious imports into India, became virtually their monopoly. Ralph Fitch, during his visit to India in the last decades of the sixteenth century when the Portuguese were the unrivalled sea-power in India, found that "all merchandise carried to Goa in a ship wherein were horses paid no custom in; the horses paid custom, and the goods paid nothing."[252] It has also been reported that while "if there were no horses, the goods paid 8 per cent," such was the hold of the Portuguese in India Trade that: "The Moores cannot pass except they have a passport from the Portugals."[253]

It is true that the Mughals and other Indian rulers had their own ports where the Portuguese could not have a direct control. Yet it will be remembered that the four Indian vessels captured by Middleton in 1613 "were provided with a Portuguese pass, and Jahangir's mother had an interest in the cargo." Undoubtedly, the overpowering influence of the Portuguese on the Arabs' and the Indian shipping as well as their attempts to secure monopoly in India's foreign trade was irksome to the Indian rulers and merchants. For a free competition between all foreign merchants would have been of some advantage to the latter by fetching a competitive price as well as by increasing the state revenue from customs on the precious commodities like horses which the Portuguese imported duty free. But even the Great Mughals could not oust the Portuguese by means of their own power. And, interestingly enough, the English could establish themselves in India because when they first arrived and were making overtures to the Mughals to allow them to found settlements in India for commercial purposes, in spite of the fact that the "unruly behaviour of British shipwrecked sailors produced a bad impression, and trade facilities were denied"[254] at first by the Mughal Government, and in spite of the irritation caused by the capture of four Indian vessels by Middleton as noted before, eventually they received a warm welcome, for they were considered by the Mughals to be a fitted rival to the Portuguese in Indian waters and thus break the latter's monopoly in foreign trade. As reported:[255]

> "At this period (end of 1614) occurs the first mention of the English in the Mughul records. Hawkins had resided at Āgra as ambassador from the king of England during 1609–11 and had received a welcome, though he had been unable to negotiate a treaty. The unruly behaviour of British shipwrecked sailors produced a bad impression, and trade facilities were denied. Sir Henry Middleton's action against the trading vessels from Gujarāt to the Red Sea (1612), however, created a spirit of respect, and the hope that the newcomers might be of assistance to check the claim of the Portuguese to command of the sea."

Two years later,

> "... when Downton arrived off Surat he was pressed by Muqarrab Khān the governor, a Mughul officer who had been envoy to the Portuguese in 1607 and was in the close confidence of the emperor, to join against the Portuguese, who had been intriguing at court to get the English expelled from India. Though Muqarrab Khān promised concessions, Downton was not prepared to do more than defend himself, and Muqarrab Khān sent messages to the Dutch at Masulipatam. In January, 1615, the viceroy of Goa arrived with his fleet, having sent his smaller vessels ahead. Having no naval force, and no promise of help from the English or Dutch, the Mughul governor made overtures for peace, which were contemptuously rejected. The Portuguese, feeling sure of success in crushing the English, attacked Downton and were beaten off with great loss. They were afraid to land troops and attack Surat and withdrew to Goa. This action is mentioned with approval by Jahāngīr in his memoirs, though he passes over in silence the visit of Hawkins and his successor Sir Thomas Roe who arrived in India in September, 1615."[256]

It will be seen in the course of this chapter how this need of the Indian rulers and merchants to expand their foreign trade helped the English Company to establish itself and to spread its influence in the subcontinent in course of time. Furthermore, in later years also, this dependence of the Indian powers on the English merchants for foreign trade was apparent. Thus, following its governing policy of obtaining special "concessions" in the buying-country, when in 1686–87 the English Company gave a violent exhibition of its insubordination to the trade regulations of the Mughal Government and prematurely took to arms, the Mughal Emperor Aurangzeb "ordered the arrest of all Englishmen and the total stoppage of trade with them throughout his empire;" but very soon "he was compelled to make terms with them, as they were supreme at sea and he was anxious to ensure the safe voyage of Indian pilgrims to Mecca; the loss of his custom revenue was also serious."[257] The result of this compromise was that: "This was the foundation of the British power in northern India."[258]

Indeed, such a helpless position of the Indian rulers (and even of the Great Mughals) vis-a-vis the European merchant powers (and especially the English) came out in full view in the eighteenth century, and contributed in no small measure to their final capitulation before the English. For, as it has been described in the previous chapter, not only in naval battles between the English and the French powers in their desire to oust the other from India Trade the Indian side could not behave in any other way than watching the issue merely as an interested spectator, but, as it will be seen in course of this chapter, when the turn came for the Indian powers to tackle the victor of the two, they could not smash the power of the English Company by pursuing it on the sea, even though at first the Nawab of Bengal made it hot for the Company on the land.

Evidently, India's lack of sea-power was the thin end of the wedge by which the European mercantile powers established themselves in the subcontinent; and, as the sea-frontier was always open to them, even when they had to fly from the land sometimes for their misdeeds, they could always muster their strength and reappear with a stronger force. This tactic was very cleverly employed by the English power, especially when after having ousted the Portuguese and the Dutch from the Indian scene it was emerging as the supreme sea-power while fighting the French on Indian soil. And thus this great difference between India and England had ultimately a far-reaching consequence; it having a significant role to play in the conquest of Bengal by the English Company, wherefrom began its victorious march over the rest of India.

4. Company in India in the 17th Century

To consider now the activities of the English East India Company in India in the light of the social background of the subcontinent as described in the above pages, the first phase of the Company's career in India, which lasted until the disintegration of the Mughal Empire in the early years of the eighteenth century, was dictated primarily by the interests of the Indian rulers themselves and of the Indian merchants who probably claimed first priority in commercial enterprise within the country. After the death of Akbar, his son Jahangir ascended the throne in 1605, and the English East India Company made its first appearance in India in 1608 through its representative, William Hawkins. By then, the Mughal Empire had apread all over north India, and a substantial part of the Deccan; in later years, it covered almost the whole of the subcontinent. So it was mainly with the Mughal rulers and their representatives that the Company had to deal with. The Mughal rulers, their representatives in different parts of the subcontinent, and the Indian merchants were interested in having European merchants in India; and while there were indications of the presence of some cliques in favour of one group of merchants as against others, in general it may be true to say (and at any rate it was almost always true for the sovereign) that they were unwilling to show favourable discrimination to any one of them at the expense of others, unless the bargain was on the side of the Indians. Evidently, as noted above, the sovereign in particular, as well as the general run of Indian traders selling their goods to foreign merchants, wanted to have the best out of all foreign traders in India.

Such a situation was, of course, quite contrary to the governing objectives of the monopolist companies of merchant capital. The Portuguese, therefore, "sought to acquire a monopoly in this [horse] trade when they gained command of the routes in the Indian waters;"[259] and in regard to the Vijayanagar Empire it has been remarked that one of the main causes of its disintegration was that, "in consideration of temporary gains, the Emperors allowed the Portuguese to settle on the west coast and thus 'principles of profit' overrode 'the great question of the stability of their Empire.'"[260] How the English East India Company acted in this situation will now be described briefly.

There is no doubt that the consistent aim of the English Company was to obtain "concessions;" for instance, as regards customs dues to be paid to the Government Treasury, so that they could buy *cheap* from India. Another of its fundamental principles was to secure exclusive opportunities for itself as against its European rivals who as a result of competition might raise the price of goods in the buying country (India) and lower the price in the selling country (Europe). But in those days they could not dictate their terms to the Indian government; "they had maintained the character of mere traders, and, by humility and submission, endeavoured to preserve a footing in that distant country, under the protection or oppression of the native powers."[261] So flattery, presents and guile were their weapons in the presence of Indian rulers to achieve their desired objectives (as it was in the Home country); and behind the backs of the Indian rulers their course of action was sniping at their rivals and fortifying their position and increasing their strength in India. This is the picture one gets from the activities of the East India Company in India in the seventeenth century.

In the beginning, of course, the aim of the Company was to secure a permanent establishment in India wherefrom it could extend its commerce and consolidate its position against its rivals. So, in 1608, William Hawkins, the first representative of the Company arrived in the Mughal Court. He was very well received, and was "the first to have held a Mughul assignment,"[262] that is, the royal grant of a territory from which he was to collect revenue for the state and make his living,–a prosperous one, no doubt. But, although in 1611 Hawkins received the Emperor's permission to open trade at Surat, the strong clique of the Portuguese in the Mughal Court as well as the unruly behaviour of the English sailors at Surat, which have been mentioned earlier, nullified the gain.

However, after the performence of Middleton and Best against the sea-power of the Portuguese, in 1613, the English Company was again given permission to open trade at Surat as well as at Ahmedabad, Cambaya and Goga.

But the Company wanted more secure and extensive arrangements, and that meant going over the strong clique which had already been formed by the Jesuit diplomats on behalf of the Portuguese at the Court at Agra. Hence, with King James's sanction and credentials, Sir Thomas Roe was sent as an ambassador to the Mughal Emperor Jahangir. King James of course obliged, for he was a shareholder of the Company and so directly interested in securing trading privileges in India. Roe's mission was to take up residence in the Indian capital, get the better of the Portuguese Jesuits, and foster and expand the trading concessions in which the first footing had just been made. James gave Roe a letter addressed to Jahangir. Roe was to press for a treaty of "free trade" between the two countries.

Roe did not have a good reception at Surat. The Governor, Zulfikar Khan, who was a nominee of Prince Khurram (Jahangir's favourite son and the future Emperor Shah Jahan), supported the Portuguese clique in the court. He, therefore, made difficulties when Roe announced in Surat that he desired to proceed to the capital. But eventually Roe managed to travel on December 13, 1615, to Ajmere, where the Court was then being held. Roe appeared at a time when Portugal's position in Eastern waters was not so strong as it had been before, and the Dutch had also recently appeared in Indian seas and like the English were bent on breaking the Portuguese monopoly in India's foreign trade. Naturally, Roe took advantage of the situation, and evidently the sovereign himself and the general body of the Indian merchants would have been pleased to have more competitors in foreign commerce. So Roe was welcomed in the Mughal Court but, contrary to his expectations, probably did not receive the honour due to an ambassador of a prominent country. Although he was successful in making a favourable impression on the Emperor, he was irked by the inferior status accorded to him. He reported later to the Company:[263]

> "An ambassador lives not in fit honour here. A meaner agent would, among these proud moors, better effect your business."

As regards how to run the "business," Roe advised the Company as follows:[264]

> "The best way to do your business in it [India] is to find some Mogul, that you may entertain for 1000 rupees a year, as your solicitor at court. He must be authorised by the king, and then he will serve you better than ten ambassadors. Under him you must allow 500 rupees for another at your port, to follow the Governor and customers, and to advertise his chief at court. These two will effect all; for your other smaller residencies are not subject to much inconveniency."

The final settlement which Roe was able to make with the Mughal Emperor in September 1618 was not exactly what he had come to get, namely, a charter of rights from the Emperor himself, but he obtained a public declaration by the Emperor of his amity towards the East India Company. Henceforth, the merchants were given liberty to trade "freely" in India, to live in a rented house on shore, to govern themselves and to bear arms when they went abroad in the city. No payments beyond the normal dues were to be demanded of them. The Portuguese were invited to co-operate in an "open trade;"—exactly what the Indian interests, when they were in a position to assert it, would have liked it to be. But this was also the thin end of the wedge which ultimately led to the complete conquest of India by the British.

English influence in India began to spread in easy stages. Before Roe left India in February 1619, the English East India Company had established factories at Surat, Agra, Ahmadabad and Broach. All these were placed under the control of the President and Council of the Surat factory, who had also the power to control the Company's trade with the Red Sea Ports and Persia. Surat became the depot for cotton, muslins, saltpetre, indigo and dyestuffs collected from all parts of the interior. English factories were also started at Broach and Baroda with the object of purchasing at first hand the piece-goods manufactured in the localities. The purpose of having a factory at Agra was mainly to sell broad-cloth to the officers of the Imperial Court and to buy indigo, the best quality of which was manufactured at Biyana.

In 1668, Bombay was transferred to the East India Company by Charles II (who had got it from the Portuguese as a part of the dowry for marrying Catherine of Braganza) at an annual rent of £ 10. Bombay grew more and more prosperous, and became so important that in 1687 it superseded Surat as the chief settlement of the English on the west coast of India.

Expanding its influence in the south-eastern part of India was not however so easy for the Company. Here the Mughal Power was less firmly established; therefore, the English had to face formidable opposition from the Dutch who had earlier settled in this part of India. On the south-eastern coast, the English had established in 1611 a factory at Masulipatam, the principal port of the kingdom of Golconda, in order to purchase the locally woven piece-goods. These goods they used to export to Persia and Bantam. But being much troubled there by the opposition of the Dutch and the frequent demands of the local officials, they opened another factory in 1626 at Armagaon, a few miles north of the Dutch settlement of Pulicat.

At Armagaon also the English were put to various inconveniences, and so they turned their attention again to Masulipatam. And now, by means of their usual craft, they managed to secure from the Sultan of Golconda the "Golden Firman" in 1632, one of the notable "concessions" secured by the Company in this period. According to this *firman*, the English were allowed to trade freely in the ports belonging to the kingdom of Golconda on payment of duties worth 500 pagodas (a coin current in South India), or the equivalent of about Rs. 1,750 per year. A fixed amount of custom duty, irrespective of the volume of trade, when the trade was flourishing, was certainly beneficial to the Company, and so it managed to have the condition repeated in another *firman* issued in 1634.

The *firman* however did not relieve the Company from the demands of local officers, to which all other merchants were subjected. The English Company, therefore, looked for a more advantageous place, and in 1639 obtained the lease of Madras from the ruler of Chandragiri, representative of the ruined Vijayanagar Empire. There it built a fortified factory which came to be known as Fort St. George. Fort St. George soon superseded Masulipatam as the headquarters of the English settlements on the Coromandel Coast. Later, this place figured prominently during the English conquest of South India, as has been noted in connection with the Carnatic Wars.

The next stage in the growth of English influence was expansion in the east. Factories had been started at Hariharpur in the Mahanadi Delta and at Balasore (both within the present state of Orissa) in 1633. In 1651 a factory was established at Hugli (Bengal), and soon others were opened at Patna (Bihar) and Cassimbazar (Bengal). In 1658, all the settlements in Bengal, Bihar and Orissa, and on the Coromandel Coast, were made subordinate to Fort St. George in Madras. The principal articles of trade of the Company in Bengal during this period were silk, cotton piece-goods, saltpetre and sugar.

In Bengal also the Company tried to receive more trading privileges. In this province the staples of commerce could not be purchased near the coast, but had to be procured from places lying far up the waterways of the province. Like all other merchants, the Company was therefore subject to payment of tolls at the custom-posts. In 1651, Sultan Shuja, the Mughal Governor of Bengal, issued a *firman* (royal command) or a *nishan* (letter of authority) granting the Company the privilege of trading in return for a fixed annual payment of duties worth Rs. 3,000. Another order, granted in 1656, laid down that "the factory of the English Company be no more troubled with demands of customs for goods imported or exported either by land or by water, nor that their goods be opened and forced from them at underrates in any places of government by which they shall pass and repass up and down the country; but that they buy and sell freely, and without impediment."[265] How such grants were obtained is evident from the fact that in a later communication, to be referred to subsequently, the Court of Directors themselves spoke of such *firmans* (or as they put it, *phirmaund*) as "purchased."

However, although the Company thus managed to receive such unique privileges, the successors of Sultan Shuja in Bengal did not consider the order to be binding on them, probably because it was merely a *nishan* from Sultan Shuja and not a *firman* from the Emperor. For the obvious reason that such privileges affected the Treasury, and also being granted to only one merchant company became a gross indication of partiality, they demanded that the English, in view of their increasing trade, should pay duties similar to other merchants. The Company, however, secured another *firman* or *nishan* in 1672 from the Governor of Bengal, Shaista Khan, granting exemption from the payment of duties. Furthermore, the Emperor Aurangzeb issued a *firman* in 1680, ordering that none should molest the Company's people for customs or obstruct their trade, and that "of the English nation, besides their usual custom of 2 per cent of their goods, more 1½ jezia or poll-money, shall be taken."[266] For this royal command the Company had to spend Rs. 50,000 as bribes to the Mughal officers; but "by this the trade of the English was made custom-free in all places except Surat."[267]

In spite of these *firmans*, however, the Company's agents in all places—Bombay, Madras and Bengal—could not escape from the demands of the local customs officers and their goods were occasionally seized. The customs officers need not be blamed for their action, for it was not unusual with the servants of the Company to smuggle goods of their own for private inland trade in India, and to this were added the goods of their compatriots making money in India as private inland traders. Since it was the duty of the custom-officers to levy duties on such goods, and since, being aware of the artifices of these private traders, they could not always be sure that the goods in question belonged strictly to the Company, it is not unlikely that on several occasions the Company's goods were also assessed by them. But, true to their policy, instead of checking such abuses by its own servants (for reasons to be explained later), the Company now decided to protect itself by force. The reason for taking such a decision was obvious. As mentioned before, the Company was then under the impression that the Mughal Power would not be able to retaliate. So, as a first step, it thought it necessary to have a fortified settlement at Hugli, just as had already been built at Madras.

Hostilities broke out between the Mughal Power and the English Company on the sack of Hugli by the latter in October 1686. But the English were "obliged to retire from Hoogly, after they had cannonaded it with the fleet, and took shelter at Chutanuttee, afterwards Calcutta, till an agreement with the Nabob, or additional forces, should enable them to resume their stations."[268] But, as happened in Bombay in the same period, the Mughals were still much stronger than the English Company had anticipated. While the English had stormed Hijli and the Mughal fortifications at Balasore, and they themselves burnt the town (although the Company had established a factory there), the properties of the Company at Patna and Cassimbazar were seized. The English were now in a deplorable state. They had to go down the Ganges to a fever-stricken island at the mouth of the river,* wherefrom they opened negotiations with the Mughals. Because the Mughals were interested in the Company's trade, in view of the income to the State Treasury, the negotiations ended favourably to the English. In September 1687, "an accommodation was effected and the English were allowed to return to Hoogly with their ancient privileges."[269] But now the English had further realized the importance of settling nearer to the sea; so they "obtained leave to build a factory at Calcutta, which they preferred, as more secure and accessible to shipping."[270]

* Worthy of note is their refuge at a place opening to the sea, which was always of strategic importance to the Company.

The Company however did not become a peaceful trading body, which it never was and could not be on account of its inherent policy and historical character. In 1688, hostilities were renewed when a fresh naval force was sent from London with orders to seize Chittagong. This attempt also ended in failure.

These rash and premature actions on the part of the Company stopped when, after assessing their relative strength, the President and Council of Bombay concluded peace with the Mughal Emperor in 1690. An English factory was established at Sutanuti; and under the orders of the Mughal Emperor, Ibrahim Khan, who was the successor of Shaista Khan in the government of Bengal, issued a *firman* in February 1691 granting the Company exemption from the payment of custom-duties in return for Rs. 3,000 a year. In other words, the status quo of 1651 was re-established.

But although the Company was forced to accept these terms of trade, it did not, by any means, give up its consistent policy of securing undue privileges through clever manoeuvreing and, in the last resort, by military strength. Owing to the rebellion of Sobha Sing, a *zemindar* or revenue farmer in the district of Burdwan, the Company got an excuse to fortify its new factory in Sutanuti in 1696. In 1698, on payment of Rs. 1,200 to the previous proprietors, the Company was granted the right of revenue farming, or *zemindari*, of the three villages of Sutanuti, Kalikata and Govindapur. In 1700, the English factories in Bengal were placed under the separate control of a President and Council, established in the new fortified settlement which was henceforth named Fort William, "in compliment to the then reigning king of England."[271] The city took the anglicised name of Calcutta from the name of the village Kalikata, which is still the Bengali name for the city.

Such was the position of the Company in India while the Mughal Empire was still a powerful entity, and politically had the control over practically the whole of India. It is important to note that by the end of the seventeenth century, the English Company had securely settled down at three strategic points in India, viz. Surat or Bombay in the west, Madras in the south, and Calcutta in the east. From

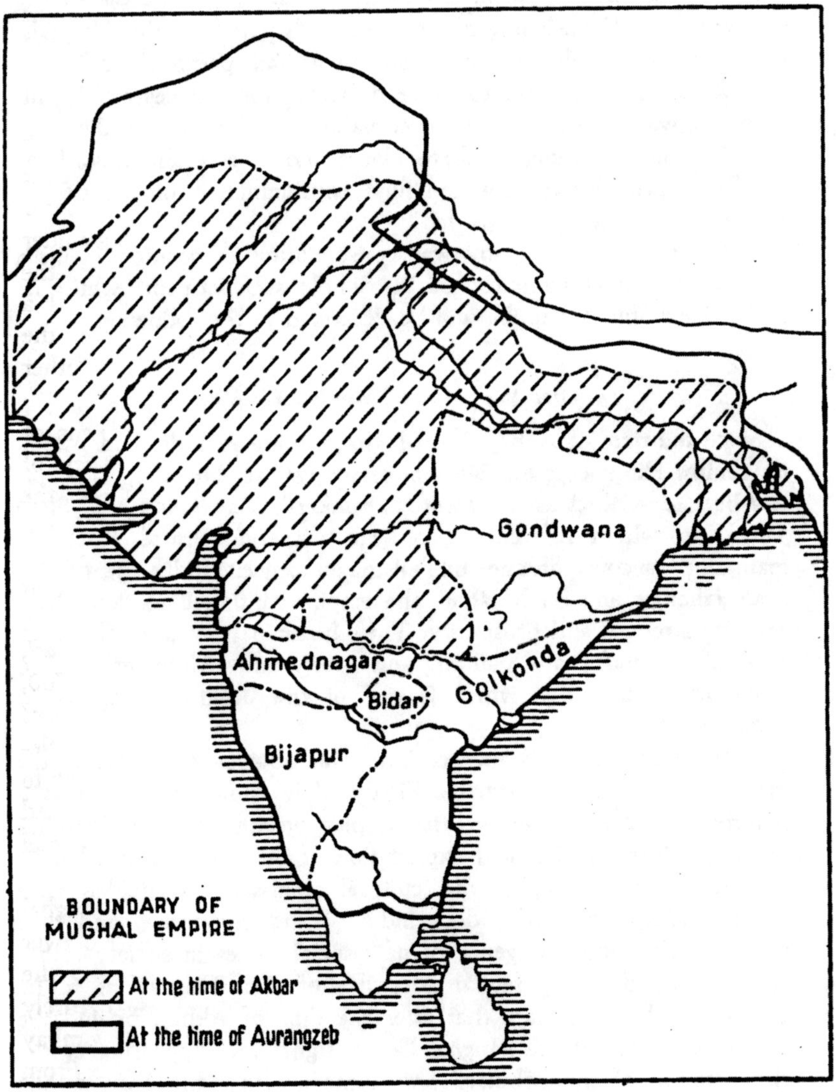
Gondwana
Ahmednagar
Golkonda
Bidar
Bijapur
BOUNDARY OF
MUGHAL EMPIRE
At the time of Akbar
At the time of Aurangzeb

these vantage points, fortified and having immediate access to the sea where the English power remained undisputed by the Mughals, the Company could not only spread to all parts of India for commercial activities and to make overtures for "concessions," but, while the way to escape in any eventuality was always at its disposal, at the opportune moment these places could serve the English as excellent spring-boards for the final consummation of the desires of merchant capital.

In this way the Company was consolidating its position in India prior to the final conquest of the whole subcontinent, which its policy inevitably led to, as will be described in the following.

5. Disintegration of Mughal Empire

Since the time of Akbar, the Mughal Empire in India had passed its zenith. His successors were of lesser calibre. His son, Jahangir, has been described as a "talented drunkard." Jahangir's son, Shah Jahan, to whom reference has been made as Prince Khurram, maintained a court of unexampled magnificence. Under the rule of both Jahangir and Shah Jahan, the empire continued to flourish in seeming strength and prosperity. Their lavish patronage of the Arts, especially of music and painting and poetry and architecture, led to a cultural renaissance which is one of the brightest chapters in Indian history.

Such a cultural renaissance of India was obviously not due to the mere whims of two monarchs. Firstly, they could indulge in such luxuries because of their greater surplus wealth resulting from increasingly intensified feudal exploitation of the peasants and handicraftsmen; and, secondly, this cultural renaissance coincided with the flourishing state of India's industry and commerce, and thus reflected more the emergence of new social forces in society rather than of the decaying feudal attributes of life. This seems to be corroborated by the fact that after the time of Akbar, behind the pomp and show of the Mughal Court, signs were appearing of the degeneration of the nobility. This came out into the open during and after the reign of the third successor of Akbar, and became an important factor in the disintegration of the Mughal Empire and the full expression of the role of British merchant capital in India. In the words of three reputed historians of India.[272]

> "With abundant resources at their disposal, the rich naturally indulged in luxury and intemperance, and the apprehension of escheat of the wealth and property of the nobles at death destroyed their incentive to thrift. Excessive addiction to wine and women was a very common vice among the aristocrats. ...They lived in highly decorated palatial buildings and amused themselves with outdoor sports as well as indoor games. ...The nobles originally possessed qualities which made them efficient servants of the State so long as it retained its vigour, but they began to lose their old usefulness, and grew more demoralised, with the closing years of the reign of Shah Jahan. Further deterioration set in during the reign of Aurangzeb and in the eighteenth century. The rivalries and conspiracies of the selfish and debased nobility of the later period, besides casting a malign influence on social life, were largely responsible for the political disorders of the age."

In the Mughal Empire, "every officer of the State was entitled to receive an income defined precisely in cash, out of which he had ordinarily to maintain a specified force of cavalry, available for the service of the ruler at any time."[273] But, instead of paying them the salaries, "the most distinctive institution of the period" was to assign to each of these officials "the revenue of an area estimated to yield the income due to him."[274] This form of assignment of revenue had become so important in Mughal administration that in 1647, "revenue aggregating 190 millions of rupees was assigned, while thirty millions were reserved for the treasury."[275] Evidently, this institution gave the nobles ample scope for a luxurious living, and to degenerate in sensuality and lasciviousness with the loss of vigour in Mughal rule, which also affected their usefulness. And while they thus degenerated, they could also simultaneously consolidate their position by the virtually hereditary grant entitled *altamgha,* which, contrary to the usages at the time of Akbar when the assignments were at the most for the life-time of a noble, was first introduced in India by Jahangir and were "made profusely" in the eighteenth century.[276] At any rate, the biggest nobles in the Mughal Court could thus make a bid to capture supreme power in the eighteenth century when the Mughal Empire was falling to pieces; and in this period of extreme confusion in India's political field the English Company finally emerged as the ruler of the subcontinent. In short, the decaying feudal forces of society neither provided the basis for the cultural renaissance which India witnessed in this period nor could they maintain their hold over India for long.

On the other hand, it appears that while the marked increase in India's wealth in this period from her industrial and commercial progress (which, it stands to reason, had a very significant bearing upon the cultural renaissance in this period) was due to the growing influence of the Indian mercantile class, it could neither rise above the feudal forces of the country nor could it by that time have a decisively upper hand over the European merchants, and specially over the English Company, which was probably the strongest at that time. This was evidently the most opportune moment for the European mercantile bourgeoisie to unfold fully their designs over India; and in this process the English Company—of the two rivals in India at that time, namely the English and the French—, became ultimately victorious. Thereby, the normal course of social development of India was cut short and reverted for two centuries. Palme Dutt noted:[277]

"The internal wars which racked India in the eighteenth century after the decline of the Moghul Empire represented a period of inner confusion (comparable in some respects to the Wars of the Roses in England or the Thirty Years War in Germany) necessary for the break-up of the old order and preparing the way, in the normal course of evolution, for the rise of bourgeois power on the basis of the advancing merchant, shipping and manufacturing interests in Indian society. The invasion, however, during this critical period of the representatives of the more highly developed European bourgeoisie, with their superior technical and military equipment and social-political cohesion, thwarted this normal course of evolution, and led to the outcome that the bourgeois rule which supervened in India on the break-up of the old order was not Indian bourgeois rule, growing up within the shell of the old order, but foreign bourgeois rule, forcibly superimposing itself on the old society and smashing the germs of the rising Indian bourgeois class. Herein lay the tragedy of Indian development, which thereafter became a thwarted or distorted social development for the benefit of a foreign bourgeoisie."

To return to this critical period in India's history, it has already been noted how from the last days of the fifteenth century the prosperity of the Indian merchants became linked up with the commercial pursuits of the European merchants. At first this was particularly marked in south India, where the Portuguese persevered to oust the Arab traders and assume the virtual monopoly of ocean-going commerce. The sixteenth century saw that the European merchants had a significant role to play in the large-scale commercial transactions of the Bahmani and Vijayanagar kingdoms as well as of Golconda and other states and territories in this part of India; and there the Indian merchants could not do without them, namely, first the Portuguese, then the Dutch, and lately the English and the French. In north India also the Indian merchants were closely connected in their business transactions with the European merchants, and especially with the English East India Company in later years. As it is reported:[278]

"The increasing demand for Indian cotton cloth in England led to a more intensive activity of merchants and weavers. The demand for Indian calico increased from 1619 onwards. Purchases were made at Agra of calico 'woven in other localities, chiefly Oudh' (W. H. Moreland: *From Akbar to Aurangzeb*, 1923, London, p. 127). The towns of Dariyabad and Khairabad in Avadh came into prominence as centres of manufacture. Lucknow developed into another centre of exchange. In 1638–39, Agra sent 2,823 pieces of cotton cloth to England; in 1639–40, this number increased to 12,122 and in 1640–41, it increased further to 23,550. In the same years, Gujarat had been exporting 38,883, 13,660, and 18,918 pieces respectively (ibid., p. 129). Agra thus beat Gujarat in export trade and the pieces exported were made mostly in Avadh. . . . Moreland comments: 'The London market was thus definitely opened to the weavers of Northern India.'

According to Manrique, Agra had a population of six lacs (600,000) in 1640. Clive had compared Dacca with London and the population of Dacca in his time was only 1½ lacs (150,000). Agra indeed was one of the biggest trading centres of Asia and therefore of the world. 'There is no Nation in all the

East but hath some commerce or other at their place,' wrote Mandelslo (Pant: *The Commercial Policy of the Moghuls*, p. 204).

Agra was also a big centre of saltpetre industry. Stone quarries were worked at Fatahpur and Biana was rich in indigo. Iron mines were worked at Gwalior and all these centres were linked together through a centralised authority."

Also,

"Bernier [1656—1668] observes: 'There is in *Bengale* such a quantity of cotton and silk, that the Kingdom may be called the common storehouse for those two kinds of merchandise, not of Hindoustan or the Empire of the *Great Mogul* only, but of all the neighbouring kingdoms, and even of Europe'. ... Moreland writes on the authority of Tavernier that, about the middle of the seventeenth century, the total production of silk in Bengal was 'about 2½ million pounds out of which one million pounds were worked up locally, ¾ million were exported raw by the Dutch and ¾ million distributed over India, most of it going to Gujarat, but some being taken by merchants from Central Asia.' ... Saltpetre, used chiefly as an ingredient for gunpowder in India and also exported outside by the Dutch and English traders, was manufactured in widely distributed parts of India during the seventeenth century, particularly in Peninsular India and the Bihar section of the Indo-Gangetic region. Bihar henceforth enjoyed a special reputation for the manufacture of this article till the first half of the nineteenth century, and it was in high demand by the Europeans for use in wars in their countries."[279]

In conditions of such rapid progress, the Indian merchants went a step forward. Manufacture had by then begun to develop and it was leading to the eventual alienation of the product from the producer by the merchant-capitalists. Shifting from their previous position of only being interested in buying goods cheap from the artisans and peasants and selling them dear to the European merchants, the Indian merchants were also encouraging production in a way similar to the *verlag* system of Germany or the "putting-out" system current in England in "the later half of the sixteenth and the early seventeenth century."[280] This development has already been noted in regard to north and south India. What is of particular importance to note here is the *social* significance of such a shift. It is, therefore, of some relevance to quote the following comment which has been made in regard to this feature in production and exchange of commodities in India in those days.

> "The merchant-capitalist advanced funds to the weavers with which they bought the necessary material and supported themselves while at work. Thus, when they handed over their products to the merchant-capitalists, they were no longer owners of their own produce. The product was alienated from the producer. The merchant-capitalist derived not the usual profit out of buying cheap and selling dear; he was already exploiting the labour-power of the producer."[281]

The rising *entrepreneurs*, however, were at the earliest stage of development; and their orientation was almost entirely towards the foreign merchants, on whom depended ultimately their realization of profit. In eastern India, for instance, there were the *Dadni* merchants who were so called as they were paid advances by the European companies in order that they in their turn could advance money to the weavers in conformity with the "putting-out" system which had come into vogue. These *Dadni* merchants worked for the English as well as for the French and the Dutch Companies in the seventeenth and the first half of the eighteenth century.

This collaboration between the Indian and the European merchants, of course, did not mean that the time had come when the latter could dictate their own terms. Thus, referring to the *Dadni* merchants, it has been noted:[282]

> "From the internal evidence of British records it appears that the *dadni* merchants themselves were not very eager to do business for the English East India Company and considered that the provision of goods for the French and the Dutch was more lucrative and more convenient."

Evidently, the foreign merchants had not yet reached the stage when they could have "matters all their own way," and so they had to take careful note of the Indian traders who were "generally subtle and clever," as Moreland remarked.[283] But at the same time it should not be forgotten how definitely the socio-economic life of the country was geared to external trade *via media* the European

Companies, and particularly the English Company. This would be evident from the following account of the situation at the close of the seventeenth century when with the disintegration of the Mughal Empire the general unsettled condition so badly affected agriculture, industries and trade that "for some time trade came almost to a standstill." As it has been stated following the above remark:[284]

> "During the years 1690–98, the English could not procure sufficient cloths for their shipping. 'Thus ensued,' observes the historian of Aurangzeb, 'a great economic impoverishment of India—not only a decrease of the 'national stock,' but also a rapid lowering of mechanical skill and standard of civilisation, a disappearance of art and culture over wide tracts of the country.'"

It appears thus from whatever little information is available on the subject and from such indirect observations as that above that while the Indian merchants were growing stronger every day, they were not yet in a position to provide any opposition to the English Company when it finally decided to usurp political power in India.

On the other hand, there is some evidence to suggest that the Indian mercantile class might have reckoned that its immediate prosperity and its eventual growth in influence and power lay with the well-being of the European merchant companies, and especially of the English Company in later years when the Portuguese and the Dutch powers in India had paled into insignificance and between the remaining two, viz. the English and the French, the former was emerging stronger particularly in Bengal and some other parts of northern India. Possibly, the Indian merchants (like the Indian rulers) were unable to fathom the underlying motive of merchant capital in this "buying country," and so they took the European merchant companies as their allies and found in them their chance of progress under the current state of affairs. Whatever it is, one cannot fail to take note of the fact that, irrespective of the subjective attitude of the Indian mercantile class to the European merchant companies, some of the Indian merchants certainly allied themselves to the interests of the English Company. Indeed, how trustworthy they appeared before the English Company would be evident from the fact that during the last years of the seventeenth century (1689–1698), after the Company had declared its intention of striving for political power in India, the Court of Directors sent instruction to India from London:[285]

> "... instead of multiplying European agents in India, natives, and especially Armenians, should be employed: 'because,' to use the words of Mr. Bruce, copying or abridging the letters of the Court, 'that people could vend English woollens, by carrying small quantities into the interior provinces, and could collect fine muslins, and other new and valuable articles, suited to the European demands, *better* than any agents of the Company could effect, under any phirmaund [*firman* or royal command] or grant which might be eventually purchased."

The Armenians referred above were those who had finally settled down in India and were absorbed in the Indian business community.[286] How effectively these Armenians, and the "Hindus, Mussulmans and other subjects of Calcutta" served the cause of the English Company during its last hostility with the Nawab of Bengal (since when the Company became the king-maker in India) is suggested by the fact that the treaty which the first puppet Nawab, Mir Jafar, signed with the representatives of the Company included the payment of 2,700,000 rupees for the losses alleged to have been sustained by these people during the hostilities.[287]*

It is also worthy of mention in this connection that it may not be quite fortuitous that the prime movers from the Indian side in the conspiracy launched by the Company to overthrow the last independent Nawab of Bengal (of which more will be said later) were those who were foremost in banking and commerce in that period. Jagat Seth, who was probably the brain behind the conspiracy from the Indian side, was a reputable banker; his name signified: "The Banker of the World." Omichand or Amirchand,

---

* For some details regarding the role of the Armenian merchants in enhancing the influence of the English Company in India, one may consult Narendra K. Sinha's *The Economic History of Bengal* (reference 282), Appendix A.

who played the biggest part in the conspiracy from Calcutta–the seat of the Company in Bengal–, was "one of the wealthiest native merchants resident at Calcutta."[288] Mir Jafar himself was the Pay Master General of the Nawab's Forces.

However, it should be understood at the outset that nothing definite can be said about the role of the Indian mercantile class in this critical period of India's history until further knowledge is obtained about them. Yet the above facts should be borne in mind, from which it appears that some belonging to this class, at any rate, took the side of the English in the endeavours of the European mercantile bourgeoisie to capture power in India. That some Indian merchants were, on the other hand, working with the French is suggested by the fact that during the period of hostilities between the English and the French in the fifth decade of the eighteenth century, the former captured some ships belonging to the Indian merchants on the plea that they were carrying merchandise for the French Company. Furthermore, it is worthy of note that while some Indian merchants might have taken the side of Indian rulers, at least in one case that is known it was because of receiving previously unfavourable treatment from the English mercantile bourgeoisie. Thus, up to 1750, the English Company's Investments (or goods purchased) in Bengal were provided by *Dadni* merchants of the country who received advances and contracted to deliver the goods at the principal settlement. But after that date a new measure was adopted to provide the Investment by direct agents of the Company who were also Indians but employed for this purpose as servants of the Company. It was reported that the *Dadni* merchants worked against the English Company in the Court of the Nawab of Bengal during the fateful years which resulted in the emergence of the Company as the ruler of the *subah* of Bengal, and then of the whole of India.[289]

Thus, on the whole, the statement may be justified that there was some collusion between the Indian merchants and their European contemporaries, although to what extent it affected the situation is yet to be investigated. This, however, may be safely stated that the Indian bourgeoisie had not yet developed to the stage necessary to deal a shattering blow to India's feudal society, of which the Mughal nobility was obviously the foremost representative.

What then were the *main* causes at that time, as far as it is known today, which led to the disintegration of the Mughal Empire, the termination of India's feudal epoch, and of her normal course of social development? One of the foremost was the acute agrarian trouble which had set in during the rule of Aurangzeb, the successor of Shah Jahan to the throne of India, because of "the ruination of the great mass of the peasants by feudal exploitation, coupled with enslavement by usurers' capital."[290]

Since the death of Akbar, direct assessment of each cultivator for revenue was allowed to lapse, for his successors were not efficient enough to continue with the process. Assessment of the entire village gradually became the rule as in the pre-Sher Shah period, but with this difference that in the meanwhile the headmen were turned into some sort of civil servants of the State instead of remaining as previously the representatives of the village communities. That the headmen had turned into autocrats became fully manifest during the reign of Arangzeb.

"The other abuse was oppression of the weaker peasants by the village headmen, who had to distribute the amount of the assessment over individuals. The method of distribution in each village was determined by local custom, but manipulation was always possible in practice, and the Ministry suspected, again not unreasonably, that headmen were favouring themselves and their friends, to the prejudice of the peasants outside their circle."[291]

Besides such "other abuse," there was the more important one, that is, the State now demanded much greater rent than before. At the time of Akbar, a one-third share of the crop was the normal revenue; now it had become in general one-half. It has been reported:[292]

"Under pressure to increase the revenue, the practice had grown up of making sanguine assessments, more than could in fact be realised; then, as the year progressed, reports would come in of injury to the crops from drought, frost, hail and other calamities, injuries which involved a reduction in the assessments originally made. The Revenue Ministry considered, not unreasonably, that many of the calamities reported were fictitious, devised in order to get the local officials out of the difficulty caused by the original over-assessment, and stringent orders were issued to ensure that the controlling officers should be supplied with adequate information, and should closely scrutinise all reports of the kind. The effect of these orders is matter for conjecture, but the necessity for their issue is significant of the pressure which had been exerted to bring assessments to the highest possible figure."

And, apart from such burdens on the peasantry, there were the "incidents of unauthorised cesses, levies and other exactions by local officers."[293] As the historian of Aurangzeb wrote referring to the "last days of Aurangzīb's rule."[294]

"The general unrest naturally caused a falling off in the rent collection from the peasants. Then, the frequent changes of officers and transfers of their jagirs prevented them from gaining knowledge of the tenantry, establishing relations with them, and spreading the inevitable arrears of a lean year gently over a number of fat years. It is difficult to imagine a system more ruinous to the peasants and therefore in the long run more harmful to the State also, than the actual administration of Mughul *jagirs*. It ended in a mad looting of the peasants by rival jagirdars' agents or successive agents of the same jagirdar. . . . As for the latter, Bhimsen gives a lurid picture of it: 'There is no hope of a jagir being left with the same officer next year. When a jagirdar sends a collector to his jagir, he first takes an advance from the latter by way of loan. This collector, on arriving in the village, fearing lest a second man who had given a larger loan to the jagirdar was following (to supplement him), does not hesitate to collect the rent with every oppression. ... The ryots have given up cultivation; the jagirdars do not get a penny.' (*Dil.* ii. 139a—140a). The same ruinous policy was followed in revenue collection in the Crownlands, as we learn from the despatches of the subahdar of Orissa. (*Studies in Mughal India*, 223):"

The sum-total results was:[295]

"The detailed provisions in Aurangzeb's orders leave no room for doubt that in the opening decade of his reign the administration was already seriously concerned about the scarcity of peasants and their readiness to abscond, topics which do not emerge in the literature of Akbar's time. They thus confirm in the essential points the description of the agrarian situation given by the French physician, François Bernier, whose experience was gained during this period. His observations, made during eight years' residence at the Mughul court, led him to the conclusion that agriculture was declining in consequence of the 'execrable tyranny' which the peasants were experiencing at the hands of officials, farmers, and assignees alike; and that many of them were either absconding to other regions, especially the domains of the chiefs, where conditions were more tolerable, or were abandoning the land in order to work as servants in the towns or with the army. It may be taken therefore as an established fact that by this time the danger foreseen by the early Islamic jurists had become a reality; that agricultural production was being diminished by the excessive burden laid upon the peasants' shoulders; and that the efforts of the administration to increase the revenue were in fact leading in the direction of a progressive decline."

Added to the situation was the excessive religious zeal of Aurangzeb. A man of tireless energy, but narrow-minded, puritanical and bigoted, he reversed the policy laid down by Akbar and for fifty years toiled unceasingly to impose upon all, Hindu and Moslem alike, conformity to the religious principles of Islam, as interpreted by himself and the Moslem sect of the Sunnis to which he belonged. His attacks were mainly against the Hindus who formed the great majority of the Indian population, representing all classes and occupations in society. He reimposed the capitation tax, Jezia, which was not insignificant in amount; "in Gujarat it was expected to form 4 per cent of the total revenue."[296] He also imposed special and additional taxes on Hindu traders.

"In 1665 Aurangzeb introduced religious discrimination by charging 5 per cent on goods imported and exported by Hindus and 2½ per cent on those by the Muslims. Not content with this, he remitted the custom duties on the Muslims in 1668. To make good the loss, the duties on the Hindus were raised to 5 per cent. Sometime about 1672 this was found unworkable—Muslim traders imported and exported the goods belonging to Hindu traders free, charging a 'consideration' for their services. This probably led to the reduction of the duty on the Hindus to 2½ per cent. But in 1680 the duties on the Muslims were again imposed at 2½ per cent and raised on the goods of the Hindu merchants to 5 per cent."[297]

Probably Aurangzeb also reimposed the pilgrimage tax for the Hindus, as some European writers claim,[298] and in any case he made the rich Hindus pay heavily to keep their places of worship open or not to have them destroyed by his expeditions sent from time to time for the purpose.[299]

Far from succeeding, Aurangzeb's attempt to turn India into an orthodox Moslem State only hastened the decline of the Mughal Empire. All-round oppression of the people in their economic, social and religious life resulted in many places in mass-uprisings of the Hindus against the Mughal Power led by the leading people of the community.

> "By these measures Aurangzeb aroused the enmity of the exploiting section of the Hindus—the priests, the usurers and the secular feudal lords—and gave them the opportunity of summoning the mass of the Indian craftsmen and peasants to a religious war against the Mohammedans."[300]

In Maharastra, under the leadership of their great leader Sivaji, the people were already fighting against Mughal tyranny from the time of Shah Jahan's rule; and this became particularly insistent after Aurangzeb usurped the throne in 1658 by imprisoning his father and getting rid of his brothers.

> "The backbone of Shivaji's army was composed of the peasantry, who belonged to two low castes, named *Maratha* and *Kunbi*."[301]

In 1664 Sivaji assumed royal title, and henceforth, for all practical purposes, Maharastra fell out of the Mughal Empire. As Marx wrote:[302]

> "1668 und 1669: *Sevaji settles his kingdom; macht advantageous treaties mit den Rajputs und anderen Nachbarn.*
>
> 1669. So die Mahrattas a nation, governed by an independent sovereign."

Later, Aurangzeb spent many long years in fighting the powerful and intractable opposition of the Marathas, but with no success. In 1674 Sivaji assumed the title of *Chhatrapati*; the rule and influence of Sivaji spread over large parts of the Deccan and the Carnatic.

Next the Rajputs were alienated. As Marx noted:[303]

"1678: *Schließlich entfremdet er die besten Krieger in seiner Armee, die Rajputs* durch his *conduct gegen Witwe und Kinder* ihres großen chief: *Rajah Jeswant Singh,* der 1678 †. *Durga Das,* des Rajah's Sohn, plotted mit *Prinz Akber,* Aurangzeb's son, marched gen Delhi mit 70,000 *Rajputs.* Die combination broken by intrigue und defection und die army disbanded vor irgend einer action; *Akber* und *Durga Das* flüchteten zu den *Mahrattas* unter *Sambaji, Sohn* des famosen *Sevaji.*"

Some coinciliation was later made with the Rajputs.

"1681: *Frieden* in *Mewar und Marwar,* nachdem der Kampf zwischen beiden parties in desultory way fortgedauert."[304]

But with the more pronounced cracks in the edifice of the Mughal Empire, the Rajputs maintained their oppositional role.

Also, in the Punjab, the Sikhs who had formed themselves into a sect through the Bhakti movement and created a common platform for the Hindu and Moslem masses, now armed and organized themselves to resist Aurangzeb's tyranny. As it has been stated:[305]

"The sect of the Sikhs, formed at the beginning of the 16th Century, created at first the opposition of the merchants, and partly of the usurers in the north Indian towns against the feudal order. The founder of the sect, Nanak (1469–1538), and the 'Gurus' (literally: teachers) who followed him as head of the Sikhs, not only condemned the caste system and proclaimed the equality of all Sikhs in the sight of God, but also preached the rejection of force and of the oppression by the Padishahs. The Padishahs, particularly Akbar, bestowed large grants of land on the Sikh-Guru in the 16th Century. They intended thereby to use for their own interests the influence of the head of the Sikhs among the ordinary people. The successive Gurus of the Sikhs became peculiar spiritual feudal lords, who possessed unlimited powers over the members of the sect. At the beginning of the 17th Century the demands of the Sikh-Gurus, not only to spiritual but also to secular power led to the first conflict with the Mogul administration.

From the second half of the 17th century, in the period of growing class conflicts, there were changes both in the class composition of the Sikh community, and the aims of the movement. The ruined peasants and craftsmen became the main force of this movement. After a number of splits, the sect was cleansed of the merchants and usurers, and the armed anti-feudal fight commenced. Under the leadership of Guru Govind Singh

(1675—1708) power passed to the Khalsa, the community of the Sikhs, the caste differences between Sikhs were wiped out, and a complete break was made with orthodox Hinduism. The Sikhs began an armed struggle for a 'real government' in order to become masters of their land and the soil.

The persecution of members of the sect began. In 1705 the united forces of the Moguls and the Hindu Rajahs beat the Sikhs and captured their fortress Anandpur. Govind was forced to flee. Shortly before his death in 1708 he named the peasant Banda as his successor, and bequeathed him the task of continuing the fight against the Moguls."

And the peaceful Jats, who lived on cultivation in North India, also rose in rebellion from 1669.

"The rising of the Jats, the caste of peasants in the Agra-Delhi area, continued, with a few interruptions, throughout the entire second half of the 17th Century (1669, 1671—72, 1686—91, 1705). After 50 years of struggle the Jats drove the Jagirdars, the vassals of the Moguls, together with the tax-collectors, from many districts near to the capital of the Mogul State."[306]

In short, everywhere in the empire discontent grew out of the oppression of the people and the sectarian policy of Aurangzeb. Where the people could gather enough strength, they rose against the tyranny; and, otherwise, discontent spread and went deeper into society. Referring to the year 1670, Marx noted:[307]

"*Seit dieser Zeit decline of Aurangzeb's influence*; all parties irritated against him; seine *Mogulsoldaten* wütend wegen seiner faulen Mahratta-züge; *die Hindus, weil er die 'Jezia' erneuert und sie persecutes on all sides.*"

Such was the situation in India during Aurangzeb's rule. With his death in 1707, the glory of the Mughals faded. Their empire fell to pieces, civil war broke out, the powerful ones of the decadent nobility emerged bidding for supreme power, and a multitude of adventurers and independent principalities ruled by adventurers sprang up in every part of the country. Utter confusion prevailed everywhere.

Taking advantage of the fights between the sons and grandsons of Aurangzeb to secure the throne at Delhi, the *subah* of the Deccan became independent under Nizam-ulk-Mulk, who, as noted before, played a significant role during the Carnatic Wars. His grandfather had migrated to India about the middle of the seventeenth century and entered the service of Aurangzeb. His father was also in the imperial service during the reign of Aurangzeb; and Nizam-ul-Mulk himself was also appointed to a small command at the age of thirteen. Skilfully consolidating his position during the days of turmoil following the death of Aurangzeb, in 1724 he virtually became independent and laid foundation to the Hyderabad State in the Deccan.

Similarly, the *subah* of Oudh (Avādh) became semi-independent in this period. This subah then comprised not only modern Oudh but also some territory to its west and some districts near Allahabad and Cawnpore. It thus formed a large piece of the Mughal Empire, and its alienation, even if only *de facto*, for it still accepted suzerainty of the Mughal Emperor, dealt another severe blow to the might of the Empire. Its Nawab, Shuja-ud-Daula, who came into the picture in 1754, had to play a significant role in the history of northern India in the first phase of British expansion in India.

The *subah* of Bengal also became semi-independent during the rapid disintegration of the Mughal Empire. Murshild Quli Jafar Khan, who was appointed by Aurangzeb as Governor of Bengal Subah in 1705, was a strong ruler. He made attempts to prevent the abuse of *dastak* or free passes by the servants of the English Company, about which something has already been said and more follows in the next chapter. After his death in 1727, his son-in-law Shuja-ud-din Khan succeeded him in the government of Bengal. During his regime, in 1733, the Bihar *subah* was annexed to Bengal. The semi-independent state of Bengal also had thus enlarged itself while the Mughal Empire was crumbling to pieces.

Later the son of Shuja-ud-din Khan came to the *masnad*, or the seat of Bengal. Then, one of his employees, Alivardi Khan, who killed the new Nawab, ascended the throne of Bengal. Alivardi Khan was followed by his favourite grandson who was known as Siraj-ud-Daula. By this time, the Nawab of Bengal was virtually the independent ruler of Bengal, Bihar and Orissa. Siraj-ud-Daula was the last independent ruler who lost his throne to the English in the battle of Plassey in 1757.

Besides the rise to power of such *nawabs* and *nizams*, who were in control of large territories, the rulers of many vassal states also began to consider themselves somewhat independent of the Mughal Power. Notable amongst them was the Nawab of Arcot who ruled over the Carnatic region, that is, the Coromandel Coast and its hinterland, and eventually became the stooge of the English Company, as the Carnatic Wars described before revealed.

Bold adventurers were also aspiring to become rulers in this uncertain period. One of them was Hyder Ali who was previously a general in the army of the Hindu kingdom of Mysore. Later he became its ruler by means of his genius and bold leadership. Hyder Ali formed a serious rival to the English conquest of the Deccan, and his son Tipu Sultan became one of the most dangerous foes of the English in South India, as will be discussed later.

The important point to note about all these rising *nawabs* and generals is that all of them intended to maintain the feudal order of the society. They acknowledged the suzerainty of the Mughal Emperor, and the lesser ones, at least formally, showed their allegiance to the Emperor's representatives, as was seen in the case of relation between the Nawab of Arcot and the Nizam-ul-Mulk during the Carnatic Wars. But the fond hope of all of them was to become independent powers in the course of time, as was rightly remarked by Shelvanker (quoted earlier).

At the same time, when these *nawabs* were coming into the political picture of India, the Rajputs and the Jats were assuming independent power in northern India. The principal Rajput States, like Mewar (Udaipur), Marwar (Jodhpur) and Amber (Jaipur) had sympathy with the Mughal Empire before the reign of Aurangzeb. Aurangzeb alienated them, as noted before, and after his death they tried to throw off their allegiance. The son of Aurangzeb, who ascended the throne after him with the title of Bahadur Shah, at first brought the Rajputs to submission. But in 1708 they departed from the Emperor's camp and formed a league against him. In view of the

Sikh rising in the north of Sirhind, Bahadur Shah pacified the Rajputs by conciliatory measures. But during the disorders that followed his death, Ajit Singh of Jodhpur invaded the imperial territories. Finally, in 1714, he concluded peace with the Emperor, and gave one of his daughters in marriage to him. Henceforth, the chiefs of Jodhpur and Jaipur played an important part in Delhi politics, and "by opportune aloofness or adherence they had added to their possessions a large portion of the Empire."[308] Ajit Singh remained the Governor of Ajmer and Gujarat till 1721. During the reign of Muhammad Shah, the great-grandson of Aurangzeb, Jay Singh II of Jaipur was appointed the Governor of Surat; later, he also became the Governor of Agra.

> "In this way the country from a point sixty miles south of Delhi to the shores of the Ocean at Surat was in the hands of these two Rajas, very untrustworthy sentinels for the Mughuls in this exposed frontier."[309]

Towards the close of the reign of Aurangzeb, predatory bands of the Jats under individual village-headmen carried out depredations round Delhi and Agra and increased their power. But in 1721 they lost their power to the hands of the Rajput chiefs who henceforth controlled these areas. But, later, under the leadership of Badan Singh and his adopted son, Suraj Mal, the Jats extended the authority of the Bharatpur kingdom over the districts of Agra, Dholpur, Mainpuri, Hathras, Aligarh, Etawah, Meerut, Rhotak, Farrukhnagar, Mewat, Rewari, Gurgaon and Muttra.

It has been noted before that during the reign of Aurangzeb the Sikhs were rising against his tyranny. After the death of the Emperor, they marched northwards and captured the province of Sirhind. The country lying between the Sutlej and the Jumna next fell into their control. But Bahadur Shah managed to drive them away to the hills north of Lahore. However, after the death of Bahadur Shah, they virtually reoccupied Sirhind. They were again defeated by the Mughals in 1715, and a large number of them were killed. But the military power of the Sikhs could not be completely destroyed. Later, they came to control large territories formerly belonging to the Mughal Empire.

Thus the Mughal Power was attacked from all sides, and big sections of the empire were either directly cut off or these *de facto* maintained an independent status.

Of all these Indian Powers which were carving out their portions from the Mughal Empire, the strongest was the Maratha's. The Marathas, with their base at Poona, made a bid for empire, and the successively weakened Mughal Emperors had to sanction, after about the middle of the eighteenth century, Maratha supremacy in large tracts of the Deccan and the Hindustan proper (that is, the Indo-Gangetic Plain). But for their internal quarrels about the leadership of the Maratha Confederacy, there would have been the possibility that the Marathas would have proved successful in completely ousting the Mughals and becoming a stronger rival to the English Company in its designs to conquer India than they actually were. There can be no doubt that in later years only they proved to be the most formidable opponent to the English Company.

To complete this brief account of the disintegration of the Mughal Empire, it is worthy of note that the empire was crumbling not only owing to internal disorders fomented by the family struggle of the sons and grandsons of Aurangzeb for the throne. Other reasons were the intrigues which set in among the Mughal nobility who, realizing their opportunity, played at king-making in order to make the position of one faction supreme in the empire at the cost of others; the attempts of the officers of the Mughal Administration (Governors in distant regions) and lesser fry to assume sovereignty and extend their power in this confusion; and the uprisings of the masses against the most powerful feudal authority (although such uprisings were often led by feudal elements in these societies, such as among the Marathas). There was also another factor which hastened the decline of the empire, viz. foreign invasions from 1738 onwards.

During the reign of strong Mughal rulers, the northwest frontier of India was well-guarded. But after the death of Aurangzeb the frontier-defence weakened markedly due to internal troubles leading to corruption and inefficiency. Finding thus a suitable moment, Nadir Shah of Persia invaded India in 1738, and his victorious army reached

Delhi, the capital of Mughal India. Wherever he and his army went, they devastated the country and plundered the people. The Mughal Emperor could not offer any resistance at all. Nadir Shah's invasion thus aimed a serious blow at Mughal Power from the outside. Nadir Shah's death in 1747 did not relieve the Mughal Emperors from further invasions. Misfortunes were still awaiting them. After the assassination of Nadir Shah, one of his officers named Ahmed Shah, an Afghan chief of the Abdali clan, rose to power and succeeded in establishing himself as the independent ruler of Afghanistan. Ahmad Shah Abdali, while accompanying Nadir to India, had seen with his own eyes "the weakness of the Empire, the inbecility of the Emperor, the inattentiveness of the ministers, the spirit of independence which had crept among the grandees."[310] So, after establishing his power at home, he led several expeditions into India from 1748 to 1767. These were something more than mere predatory raids; they further expedited the collapse of the Mughal Empire.

Such was the situation in India in the first half of the eighteenth century, when while the Mughal Empire was going to pieces and its strength was ebbing away, the English Company was more and more consolidating its position and coming out as the strongest military power.

6. Company and Collapse of Mughal Power

It has already been described how during the later half of the seventeenth century the English Company spread over India and consolidated its position in the western, southern and eastern regions. At the same time, taking advantage of the political disorders in the country, it began to come out more openly to establish its position by territorial acquisitions. Marx wrote:[311]

"The paramount power of the Great Moghul was broken by the Moghul Viceroys. The power of the Viceroys was broken by the Mahrattas. The power of the Mahrattas was broken by the Afghans (with the first blow in 1761 at the hands of Ahmad Shah referred to earlier—R. K. M.), and while

all were struggling against all, the Briton rushed in and was enabled to subdue them all."

On the pretext of long warfare between the Imperial (Mughal) forces and the Marathas and the other Deccan States, the Maratha raids on Surat in 1664 and 1670, the weak government of the Mughal Viceroys in Bengal, and the disturbances caused by the Malabar pirates, the East India Company rapidly developed its military strength. The President at Surat and Governor of Bombay, Gerald Aungier, wrote to the Court of Directors of the Company in London, "the time now requires you to manage your general commerce with the sword in your hands."[312] In December 1687 the Court of Directors wrote to the Chief of Madras, "to establish such a politic of civil and military power, and create und secure such a large revenue to secure both ... as may be the foundation of a large, well grounded, secure English domain in India for a long time to come."[313]

It is of interest to stress again that the above statement from the Court of Directors of the Company showed clearly that, as early as in the last decades of the seventeenth century, conquering India as a logical culmination of the mercantile policy of the merchant bourgeoisie was in their mind and it came out directly when any suitable moment for executing such a task became apparent.

In pursuance of this policy of conquest, in December 1688, the Company blockaded Bombay and the Mughal ports on the western coast. It seized many Mughal vessels and sent its captains to the Red Sea and Persian Gulf in order to "arrest the pilgrimage traffic to Mecca."[314] But the English had then underestimated the force of the Mughal Power which was still formidable enough to exercise its control. The representatives of the Company, being in a very difficult situation, at last appealed for pardon to Aurangzeb. The Emperor not only pardoned the English but in February 1690 also granted a licence for English trade when the English agreed to restore all the captured Mughal ships and to pay Rs. 150,000 in compensation.

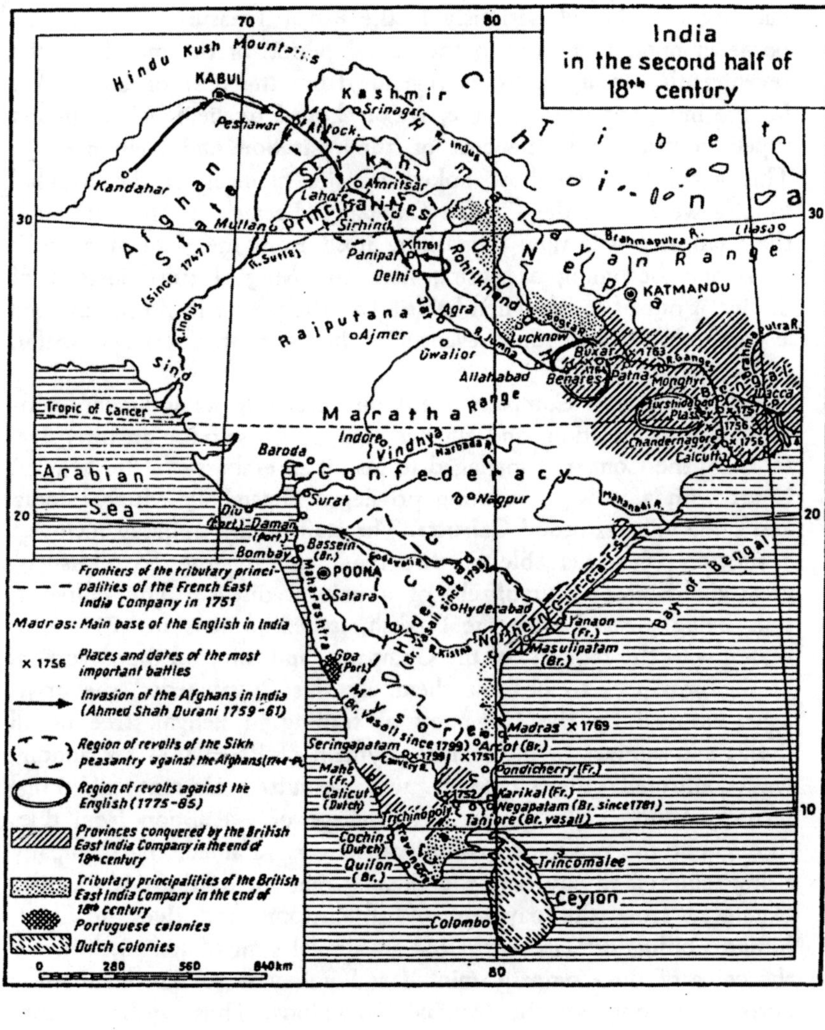
India
in the second half of
18th century
Hindu Kush Mountains
KABUL
Peshawar
Attock
Kashmir
Srinagar
Kandahar
Afghan State (since 1747)
Sikh principalities
Lahore
Amritsar
Multan
Sirhind
Panipat
Delhi
Tibet
Himalaya
Nepal
KATMANDU
Brahmaputra R.
Oudh
Rohilkhand
Agra
Lucknow
Rajputana
Ajmer
Gwalior
Allahabad
Benares
Buxar
Patna
Monghyr
Bengal
Dacca
Murshidabad
Plassey
Chandernagore
Calcutta
Sind
Tropic of Cancer
Maratha Confederacy
Indore
Vindhya Range
Baroda
Narbada R.
Arabian Sea
Surat
Nagpur
Mahanadi R.
Diu (Port.)
Daman (Port.)
Bombay
Bassein (Br.)
POONA
Satara
Maharashtra
Hyderabad (Br. vasall since 1798)
Hyderabad
Godavari R.
R. Kistna
Northern Circars
Yanaon (Fr.)
Masulipatam (Br.)
Bay of Bengal
Goa (Port.)
Mysore (Br. vasall since 1799)
Seringapatam
Madras ×1769
Arcot (Br.)
Mahe (Fr.)
Calicut (Dutch)
Pondicherry (Fr.)
Karikal (Fr.)
Negapatam (Br. since 1781)
Tanjore (Br. vasall)
Trichinopoly
Cochin (Dutch)
Quilon (Br.)
Travancore
Trincomalee
Ceylon
Colombo
Frontiers of the tributary principalities of the French East India Company in 1751
Madras: Main base of the English in India
× 1756 Places and dates of the most important battles
Invasion of the Afghans in India (Ahmed Shah Durani 1759–61)
Region of revolts of the Sikh peasantry against the Afghans
Region of revolts against the English (1775–85)
Provinces conquered by the British East India Company in the end of 18th century
Tributary principalities of the British East India Company in the end of 18th century
Portuguese colonies
Dutch colonies
0 280 560 840km

As mentioned before, probably an important reason behind this softened attitude of the Emperor was that the lack of trade at Surat had begun to be felt seriously in the Royal Treasury. It should be borne in mind that even in the earlier period of the middle of the seventeenth century customs revenue from the port of Surat, "by far the most important source, was reckoned to yield half a million rupees a year, after the cost of administration had been met."[315] This again indicates how linked up the finances of the Mughal Empire were with the English Company. Because of this, although the Company was now unmasking itself from the pose of a meek lamb and becoming a roaring lion, the Mughal ruler instead of driving it out of India, when he still had the power to do so, effected a compromise, and thus eventually brought about the downfall of the empire.

Meanwhile, the Company went on spreading its influence, consolidating its position, and further equipping itself for an offensive. In 1715, the Company managed to install an embassy in the Mughal Court with a view to securing privileges throughout Mughal India and some villages round Calcutta. The staff of the embassy included a surgeon who was able to cure the then Emperor, Farrukhsiyar, great-grandson of Aurangzeb, of a painful disease. The Emperor, thus being pleased with the English, issued *firmans* in 1717 complying with the requests of the Company, and directed the governors of the provinces to observe them. By this Royal order, the privileges enjoyed by the Company of trading in Bengal, free of all duties and subject to the annual payment of Rs. 30,000 per annum, was confirmed; the Company was permitted to rent additional territory round Calcutta; its old privilege of exemption from dues throughout the province of Hyderabad was retained, the Company being required to pay only the existing rent for Madras; it was also exempted from the payment of all customs and dues at Surat, hitherto obligatory, in return for an annual sum of Rs. 10,000; and the coins of the Company minted at Bombay were allowed to have currency throughout the Mughal Dominions. Thus, with the connivance of the Mughal Emperor, the Company emerged as a strong power. The historian Orme truly described the *firmans* of 1716–1717 as the "Magna Charta of the Company."[316]

In Bengal, Murshid Quli Jafar Khan, of whom mention has already been made as a strong and able governor who had already assumed semi-independent status, opposed the grant of the additional villages to the English. Still, the other rights secured by the Emperor's *firman* greatly furthered the interests of the Company. Its trade prospered markedly in Bengal. The importance of Calcutta increased so much that it came to have a population of 100,000 by 1735. The Company's shipping at the port during the ten years following the embassy of 1715 amounted to ten thousand tons a year.

On the western coast of India, the Company's trade did not prosper so well immediately after the Emperor's *firman* was granted. It suffered from the quarrels between the Marathas and the Portuguese, and the ravages of the Maratha sea-captains who dominated the coast between Bombay and Goa from two strongholds, Gheria and Suvarndrug. But here also the Company did not peacefully acquiesce to the situation. During 1715–1722, the Company built a wall round Bombay and increased the number of their armed ships, and their military strength in all other respects. After that the Company's power in Bombay began to prosper. In 1744, the town had a population of about 70,000. In 1739, the Company concluded a treaty with the Marathas, and in alliance with the Peswa, the *de facto* head of the Maratha Confederacy, launched attacks against the Maratha sea-captains. Suvarndrug was captured in 1752, and Gheria in 1757.

At Madras also the Company on "peaceful commerce" was on "excellent terms" both with the Nawab of Arcot, the ruler of the Carnatic region (who in course of time became the Company's puppet, as noted before), and his overlord, the Subahdar of the Deccan (who also later was reduced to a similar status vis-a-vis the Company). In 1717, the Company took possession of five towns near Madras, which its Governor of Madras from 1698 to 1709 had originally obtained from the Nawab of Arcot in 1708. In 1734, the

Company also secured Vepery and four other hamlets. Its base in the south-eastern part of India was thus strongly developed.

In this way, during the disintegration of the Mughal Empire in the last decades of the seventeenth and the early decades of the eighteenth centuries, two strong powers rose up in India. These were the Marathas and the English. Only these two were powers that had to be reckoned with.

But there was an important difference between the two. Although, as against the decadent outlook of the Mughal nobility now aspiring for power, the Marathas, being inspired by the teachings of the Bhakti movement, were imbued with a new spirit of "self-reliance, courage, perseverance, a stern simplicity, a rough straight-forwardness, a sense of social equality, and consequently pride in the dignity of man as man,"[317] they were no less dominated by the essentially feudal orientation of their leaders. It may also be of interest to note here what an eminent Indian historian has remarked with regard to the Marathas in those days:[318]

> "The chief defect of the Marathas, which has disastrously reacted on their political history, is their lack of business capacity. This race has produced no great banker, trader, captain of industry, or even commissariat organiser or contractor."

Moreover, the germs of the prevailing putrition in India's political sky were making in-roads into the Marathas. Dissensions were raising their head within the Maratha Confederacy and making it weaker. Also, some of the Marathas were already turning into predatory adventurers, a feature particularly noteworthy in the second half of the eighteenth century.

The English, on the other hand, were governed by a single objective of finally stabilizing their mercantile interests at this most opportune moment in India. In addition, from the First Carnatic War (1744–48) they had learnt two important lessons, namely, (1) complete rottenness of the Indian political situation, and (2) superiority of European forces to that of the Indian powers at that time, provided they were treated separately one after another. Moreover, their unique privilege as a sea-power vis-a-vis all Indian powers (including the Marathas) was very favourably demonstrated in the First Carnatic War. From all such respects, therefore, there was a great difference between the Marathas and the English; and this difference between the two rising powers in India could greatly help the English Company in its eventual conquest of the whole of the subcontinent.

For such a consummation of the eternal desire of merchant capital, the Company henceforth instilled forceful weight to its demands for "concessions," keeping in mind the lessons it had learnt from the First Carnatic War. The first application of this lesson was in Bengal, wherefrom started the victorious march of the Company in India.

7. Conquest of Bengal

It has been mentioned earlier that in 1717 the English Company had received a *firman* from the Mughal Emperor by which it obtained freedom of trade for its goods for export and import and the right of issuing *dastaks* or passes for such goods. This had a serious effect on the government finances, for in those days, as in many other countries, the transit of goods by roads and navigable rivers was subject to inland duties in India. But now the goods which the Company imported from Europe, and those which they purchased in India for export were permitted to pass through the country without payment of duties. A *dastak* signed by the English President of any settlement of the Company or by chiefs of English factories was shown at the toll-house, and protected the Company's merchandise from all duties.

This arrangement, while fulfilling the Company's motto of buying cheap, meant a sharp depletion of the Government Treasury in Bengal particularly, for in that province most commodities had to be fetched from inland and so inland duties for trading were an important source of revenue to the Government. All the Nawabs after 1717 therefore felt very strongly against it, and in 1756 Nawab Siraj-ud-Daula, who had recently become the Nawab after the death of his grandfather, Alivardi Khan, decided to reduce the power of the English to the extent of driving them out of Bengal unless they were satisfied to trade on the footing they had before they had obtained the *firman* from the Mughal Emperor.

It is likely that Siraj-ud-Daula was moved to take this step from a political motive also. It has been reported that before his death Alivardi Khan told him:[319]

> "My life has been a life of war and stratagem: for what have I fought, to what have my councils tended, but to secure you, my son, a quiet succession to my *subadari*? My fears for you have for many days robbed me of sleep. I perceived who had power to give you trouble after I am gone hence. ... Keep in view the power the European nations have in the country. This fear I would also have freed you from if God had lengthened my days.—The work, my son, must now be yours. Their wars and politics in the Telinga country [southern India] should keep you waking. On pretence of private contests between their kings they have seized and divided the country of the King [the Mughal] and the goods of his people between them. Think not to weaken all three together [the English, French, and the Dutch]. The power of the English is great; ... reduce them first; the others will give you little trouble, when you have reduced them. Suffer them not, my son, to have fortifications or soldiers: if you do, the country is not yours."

That Alivardi Khan had also the same intention was evident from his letters to Watts, the agent of the English Company, about which J. Z. Holwell (once Acting-Governor of the Company in Calcutta) wrote to the Court of Directors in London on November 30, 1756, that he "had long meditated to destroy the forts and garrisons of the Europeans, and to reduce their trade on the footing of the Armenians."[320] For obvious reasons, this move of the Indian rulers to equate the European merchants with the general run of traders in India, Armenians included, was strongly resented by the "peaceful" East India Company. Therefore, although following the advice of his grandfather, Siraj-ud-Daula tried to curb the growing power of the English, his intentions did not materialize in the end.

The intentions of the English, on the other hand, were all too apparent by their latest moves. But why Siraj-ud-Daula could not curb their power, and had ultimately to surrender his throne and also his head to a puppet of the English has a little history behind it.

This may be outlined in some detail, for, in a certain sense, the story of the English conquest of Bengal brings out almost all the features of India at that time, and also gives a graphic account of the manoeuvres of the English Company – of the guile and flattery of its officers, their meanness and cowardice. Eulogistic British writers have often praised Clive as a great hero, because the battle of Plassey went in the Company's favour. But, as will be realized from the following, looked at objectively, the battle of Plassey was nothing better than a cowardly act of hitting the adversary "below the belt," after having drained off his vitality by conspiracy. This tale may best be told in the words of three reputable historians of India, and so is given below.[321]

"Like the Deccan, Bengal was under a Subahdar who nominally acknowledged the suzerainty of the Mughul Emperor of Delhi, but was to all intents and purposes an independent king. Like the Deccan, too, Bengal lacked any political strength or stability. Conspiracies and revolutions were the order of the day and corruption and inefficiency sapped the vitality of the State. ...

'Alivardi had no male heir. His three daughters were married to three sons of his brother. Siraj-ud-daulah, the son of his youngest daughter, was his chosen successor, but the arrangement was naturally disliked by the two other sons-in-law, who were governors respectively of Dacca and Purnea. It was inevitable that they should be centres of plots and conspiracies by scheming persons. Although both of them died towards the close of 'Alivardi's reign, Ghasiti Begam, the widow of the former, and Shaukat Jang, the son of the latter, pursued their policy up to the very end. Ghasiti was ably supported by her *Diwan* [Minister] Rajballabh, who really carried on affairs in the name of the princess.

Amidst these troubles 'Alivardi died on 9th April, 1756, and Siraj-ud-Daula ascended the throne without any difficulty. But although his succession was unopposed, his troubles indeed were great. In addition to the hostile activities of Rajballabh and Shaukat Jang, he found himself implicated in a bitter dispute with the English Company.

Even when Siraj-du-daulah was administering the State during the illness of 'Alivardi, the relations between the Nawab and the English had been anything but friendly. The main cause of the dispute was the additional fortification of Calcutta, which the English had recently undertaken, ostensibly as a measure of precaution against the French. The recent events in the Carnatic were certainly calculated to rouse the suspicion of the Nawab against any such measure. The manner in which it was done increased the wrath of the Nawab still further. The English not only mounted guns on the old fort but also commenced to build additional fortifications without the permission or even the knowledge of the Nawab. The fact was that the English discounted, like many others, the chances of Siraj-ud-daulah's accession to the throne, and were therefore eager to court the favour of Rajballabh, the leader of the opposing party, with surer chances of success. This explains why at the request of Watts, their agent at Cassimbazar, the English agreed to give protection to Rajballabh's son Krishnadas, who fled to Calcutta with his family and treasure. They knew full well that this step was calculated to provoke the wrath of Siraj-ud-daulah against them. There is no doubt also that Siraj-ud-daulah construed the event as proving the complicity of the English in the schemes of Rajballabh against him.

The contemporary historian, Orme, writes: 'There remained no hopes of Alivardy's recovery; upon which the widow of Nawajis (i.e. Ghasiti Begam) had quitted Muxadabad (the capital city of Murshidabad) and encamped with 10,000 men at Moota Ghill (Moti jhil), a garden two miles south of the city, and many now began to think and to say that she would prevail in her opposition against Surajo Dowla (Siraj-ud-daulah). Mr. Watts therefore was easily induced to oblige her minister and advised the Presidency (of Calcutta) to comply with his request.'

Indeed, the rumour was widely spread in Murshidabad that the English had espoused the cause of Ghasiti Begam. Dr. Forth, attached to the factory of Cassimbazar, visited 'Alivardi about a fortnight before his death. While he was talking with the Nawab, Siraj-ud-daulah came in and reported that he had information to the effect that the English had agreed to help Ghasiti Begam. The dying Nawab immediately questioned Forth about this. Forth not only denied the charge but disavowed on behalf of his nation any intention to interfere in Indian politics.

This denial had but little effect on the mind of Siraj-ud-daulah which was already embittered against the English over the question of fortification. Immediately after his accession to the throne, he communicated his views to Watts, the chief of the English factory at Cassimbazar, in remarkably plain language. The Nawab pointed out that he looked upon the English only as a set of merchants and they were welcome as such, but he disapproved of their recent fortifications and insisted on their immediate demolition. The Nawab also sent envoys to Calcutta with similar instructions and a demand for the surrender of Rajballabh's family, but they were dismissed with scant respect by the English governor. This incredible conduct can only be explained by a tenacious belief that Rajballabh would ultimately succeed against Siraj-ud-daulah.

The first concern of Siraj-ud-daulah after his accession to the throne was, therefore, to remove the great internal danger that threatened his safety. By a masterly stroke, which has not been sufficiently recognised in history, he succeeded in quietly removing Ghasiti Begam to his own palace, without any bloodshed. The English now came to realise their mistake. Excuses and apologies were offered for their late conduct. But Siraj-ud-daulah was not the man to be satisfied by mere hollow promises. He wrote a letter to Mr. Drake, the governor of Calcutta, repeating his orders to demolish the additional fortifications. For the time being he could do no more, for although Ghasiti Begam had been suppressed, Shaukat Jang, the governor of Purnea, still remained the centre of a revolutionary conspiracy against him. The Nawab rightly concluded that he must remove this danger before he could adopt a strong policy towards the English. Accordingly he marched towards Purnea. When he reached Rajmahal, the reply of Governor Drake reached him. It was couched in polite language, but contained no indication that he would comply with the Nawab's request. The Nawab immediately changed his mind, and returned to Murshidabad, in order to begin a campaign against the English in good earnest. The letter of Drake evidently convinced him that he had more to fear from the inveterate enmity of the British than anything that Shaukat Jang could do against him.

Once having taken the decision, Siraj-ud-daulah acted with unwonted energy. The return journey from Rajmahal commenced on 20th May. He reached Murshidabad on 1st June and on 4th June seized the English factory at Cassimbazar. On 5th June he marched against Calcutta and reached there on the 16th. Three days later, Governor Drake, the Commandant and many prominent Englishmen abandoned the fort to its fate and sought their own safety on board the ships. Next day, i.e. on 20th June, Fort William surrendered to Siraj-ud-daulah after a feeble resistance.

The capture of Calcutta will ever remain memorable in history on account of the so-called Black Hole episode, which occupies a prominent place in the narrative of Holwell. According to his version, 146 English prisoners were confined during the night in a small room, known as the Black Hole, 18 feet long by 14 feet 10 inches wide. One hundred and twenty-three died of suffocation, and 23 miserable survivors alone remained to tell the tale of that tragic summer night.

The truth of this story has been doubted on good grounds. That some prisoners were put into the Black Hole and a number of them, including those wounded in the course of the fight, died there, may be accepted as true. But the tragic details, designed to suit a magnified number of prisoners, must almost certainly be ascribed to the fertile imagination of Holwell, on whose authority the story primarily rests. In any case, it is agreed on all hands that Siraj-ud-daulah was not in any way personally responsible for the incident.*

Leaving his general Manikchand in charge of Calcutta, Siraj-ud-daulah returned to Murshidabad. Shaukat Jang had in the meantime procured from the titular Mughul Emperor of Delhi the formal *Sanad* for the Subahdarship of Bengal and made no secret of his intention to make a bold bid for the viceregal throne. He no doubt relied upon the help of disaffected chiefs of Bengal like the banker Jagat Seth and the general Mir Jafar. But before they could agree upon any general plan, Siraj-ud-daulah marched against Shaukat Jang and defeated and killed him.

It reflects no small credit upon the young and inexperienced Nawab that he could get rid of his three powerful enemies within a few months of his accession to the throne. A superficial observer might well have regarded the future with equanimity, and perhaps even the Nawab was led into a false sense of security. But if he had been a true statesman he should not have been unaware of the dangers and difficulties ahead.

It was, for instance, sheer ineptitude to expect that the English would retire from Bengal after their first defeat without making fresh efforts to retrieve their situation. For, although small in number, the possession of the sea gave them a decided advantage in any warfare with the Nawab as it kept open the way for retreat when pressed hard, and the means of securing fresh supplies of resources, either from home or from other settlements in India. If the Nawab had fully realised this fact he would have continued his hold upon Calcutta in order to keep the English permanently in check.

The Nawab would perhaps have devoted his serious attention to this problem and evolved suitable measures if his own house were in order. But that was the chief plague-spot. Bengal, like most other provincial States, lacked almost every element that makes a State strong and stable. It had only recently emerged as a semi-independent kingdom; and no tradition or attachment bound the people to the ruling house. The theoretical powers of the Emperor of Delhi still existed, and the case of Shaukat Jang showed

---

* Marx in his *Chronological Notes on India* (reference 1) wrote about the Black Hole incident as follows (cf. Section: *Events in Bengal: 1755—1773*):

"*Evening 21 June 1756* reissen die Handelsjingling etc. aus; in der Nacht fort verteidigt durch *Holwell* 'by the light of the burning factories,' fort stormed, garrison taken prisoners, *Suraj gab orders all the captives should be kept in safety till the morning*; die *146 men*, (accidentally it seems) aber crushed into a room 20 feet square und mit but one small window; *am andern Morgen* (von *Holwell selbst* das Zeug erzählt) nur noch 23 am Leben, ihnen *erlaubt to sail down the Hoghly*. Dies '*das Black Hole of Calcutta*,' worüber the *English hypocrites* so viel sham scandal bis dato machen. *Suraj-u-dowla* zurück nach *Moorshedabad; Bengal* nun *completely and effectually cleared of the English intruders*."

what practical use could be made of them. The common people were too accustomed to revolutions to trouble themselves seriously about any change in the government, while the more influential chiefs shaped their policy with a view to their own interests alone. ...

The discomfited English leaders knew the situation in Bengal well enough, and, having experienced the force of the Nawab's arms, they sought to retrieve their position by exploiting the internal situation. After the fall of Calcutta, they had taken refuge in Fulta, and from this place they carried on intrigues with the leading persons whom they knew to be hostile to the Nawab. The attempt of Shaukat Jang to seize the throne opened up new hopes to them. They sent him a letter with presents 'hoping he might defeat Siraj-ud-daulah.' When that hope failed they won over to their cause Manikchand, the officer in charge of Calcutta, Omichand, a rich merchant of the city, Jagat Seth, the famous banker, and other leading men of the Nawab's court. At the same time they made appeals to the Nawab to restore their old privileges of trade in Calcutta. This appeal, backed by the support of the interested advisers, induced the Nawab to consent to an accommodation with the English.

In the meantime warlike preparations were being made by the Madras Council. As soon as they received the news of the capture of Calcutta, they decided upon sending a large military expedition. Fortunately, a fully equipped army and navy which had been made ready for an expedition against the French were immediately available. After some discussion it was resolved to send the expedition under Clive and Admiral Watson. The expedition set sail on 16th October and reached Bengal on 14th December. The Nawab was evidently quite ignorant of this. While the English fugitives at Fulta were lulling his suspicions by piteous appeals, and his treacherous officers and advisers were pleading the cause of the 'harmless traders,' Clive and Watson arrived at Fulta with the force from Madras. It is only fair to note that the English at Fulta were perhaps equally ignorant of the help sent from Madras, and did their very best to induce Clive to desist from warlike operations against the Nawab, who was ready to concede their reasonable demands. But Clive and Watson paid no heed to the proposals of their compatriots in Fulta. On 17th December Watson addressed a letter to the Nawab asking him not only to restore the ancient 'rights and immunities' of the Company but also to give them a reasonable compensation for the losses and injuries they had suffered. The Nawab appears to have sent a pacific reply, but it probably never reached Watson. Clive marched towards Calcutta. Manikchand made a pretence of war and then fled to Murshidabad. Clive recovered Calcutta on 2nd January, 1757, without any serious fighting. The English then plundered Hugli and destroyed many magnificent houses in that city.

Even after these provocations, Siraj-ud-daulah came to Calcutta and concluded the Treaty of 'Alinagar (9th February, 1757), conceding to the English practically all their demands.* This pacific attitude of Siraj-ud-daulah, offering such a strange contrast to his earlier policy, is difficult to explain. It has been suggested that a night attack on his camp by Clive terrified him into a humble submission. But that attack, according to Orme, was a great failure for which Clive was taken to task even by his own soldiers. Besides, the letters written by Siraj-ud-daulah, even before he reached Calcutta, contained proposals of peace similar to those to which he afterwards agreed. It is probable that the known treacherous designs of his own officers and the apprehension of an invasion from the north-west induced him to settle with the English at any cost.

Whatever may be the right explanation, it is quite clear that from this time onward Siraj-ud-daulah displayed a lack of energy and decision at almost every step. The outbreak of the Seven Years' War introduced a new element into the situation. The English naturally desired to conquer the French possession of Chandernagore. Siraj-ud-daulah very reasonably argued that he could never allow one section of his subjects to be molested by another. When the English made preparations for sending an expedition to Chandernagore he accused them of violating the Treaty of 'Alinagar and loudly proclaimed his determination never to sacrifice the French. Yet he did nothing to protect the French and Chandernagore was easily conquered by Clive and Watson in March, 1757. It is admitted by the English themselves that the Nawab had a large force near Chandernagore under Nanda

* The treaty which promised more favourable terms to English trade, even allowed the Company "to fortify Calcutta in such a manner as they shall esteem proper for their defence, without any hindrance or obstruction," and "that restitution be made to the Company of their factories and settlements at Calcutta, Kasimbazar, Dacca, etc., which have been taken from them. That all money and effects taken from the English Company, their factors or dependents, at the several settlements, and *Aurangs* (collecting stations for goods or sub-factories), be restored in the same condition. That an equivalent in money be given for such goods as are damaged, plundered, or lost, which shall be left to the Nawab's justice to determine" (cf. Aitchison, *Treatis and Sanads*, 4th Ed. i., 181). Not only his strength relative to that of the Company, but his prestige as a Nawab was also thus seriously undermined. And this treaty put an end to the Nawab's wishes of reducing the English Company to the same footing as other merchants—Indian or foreign, for the treaty also noted that "all goods belonging to the English Company, and having their *Dastak*, do pass freely by land or water, in Bengal, Behar, and Orissa, without paying any duties or tolls of any kind whatsoever; and that the Zemindars (District Collectors of land-revenue). Chaukidars (Collectors of Customs), Guzarbans (Collectors of ferry-tolls), etc., offer them no kind of molestation upon this account." (*ibid.*)

Kumar, the Faujdar of Hugli, and if he had not moved away they could not have conquered the French city. It is almost certain that Nanda Kumar was bribed, but it does not appear that the Nawab had given any definite orders to Nanda Kumar to resist the English.

The Nawab, gallantly enough, afforded shelter to the French fugitives at his court, and refused to drive them away even when the English offered in exchange military help against a threatened invasion of Bengal by the heir-apparent to the Mughul Empire. Generosity and prudence alike must have dictated the course of policy which the Nawab pursued, for in any war with the English the French support would have been of inestimable value to him.

The English fully understood the danger of the situation. While the war was going on with the French, a Nawab of Bengal with sympathy for the French cause was an element of potential danger. A French force from Pondicherry might join the Nawab and renew in more favourable circumstances the policy of expelling the English which Dupleix had so brilliantly initiated in the Carnatic.

Hence the English leaders were bent upon replacing Siraj-ud-daulah by a Nawab more amenable to their control. A conspiracy was set on foot with the help of the disaffected chiefs, and it was ultimately resolved to place Mir Jafar upon the throne of Bengal. Mir Jafar and Rai Durlabh, the two generals of the Nawab, as well as Jagat Seth, the rich banker, all joined in the plot. A regular treaty was drawn up (10th June) which stipulated, among other things, the reward to be given to the Company and to their chief servants in Calcutta for their military help. A difficulty arose at the last moment. Omichand, who acted as the intermediary, asked for a large share of the plunder, and Clive silenced him by a forged copy of the treaty in which Omichand's demands were admitted. As Watson refused to sign this treaty his signature was forged at the instance of Clive.*

---

* Torrens noted: "The unsuspecting Hindoo was satisfied; but when the time came for settling accounts among the conspirators, Clive bade an interpreter inform the old man of the trick of which he had been the dupe—that the treaty containing his name was a sham, and that having asked too much, he was to have nothing. Stunned at this ruin of his golden dreams, Omichand fell to the ground insensible. He slowly recovered, but remained for the rest of his days an idiot." (cf. Torrens, W. M.—*Empire in Asia—How We came by It: A Book of Confessions*, Trübner & Co., London, 1872, p. 39)

Even such dishonour among the thieves did not come in for any condemnation. Mill noted a hundred years later: "Not an Englishman, not even Mr. Orme, has yet expressed a word of sympathy or regret." (cf. reference 261, Vol. III, p. 136, n.)

Narendra K. Sinha is of the opinion that although Omichand was cheated by Clive, the "story of Amirchand's becoming insane is a pure figment of imagination." (cf. reference 282, p. 241.)

The Nawab displayed a lamentable lack of decision and energy in this critical moment.* After having drawn upon himself the wrath and inveterate hostility of the English by his support to the French fugitives, he ultimately agreed to send them away on the advice of his treacherous ministers. At the time of their departure the French gave him friendly warning of the conspiracy, which was evidently patent to everybody save the Nawab. His eyes were not opened until he came to know of the secret treaty. Even then he failed to act vigorously. Had the Nawab promptly imprisoned Mir Jafar, the other conspirators would have been struck with terror and the plot might perhaps have come to nothing. The Nawab's courage, however, failed. Far from taking any energetic measures, he himself paid a visit to Mir Jafar (15th June) and made pathetic appeals to him in the name of 'Alivardi Khan. Mir Jafar gave him most solemn assurances of support and the Nawab was apparently satisfied. He hastily began to make preparations for the war, with Mir Jafar as commander of his forces.

Three days before this interview the English forces had left Calcutta on their expedition against the Nawab. So thoroughly did treachery pervade all ranks of the Nawab's army, that little or no real opposition was offered to the English even by the garrisons at Hugli or Katwa. On the night of 22nd June Clive reached the mango grove of Plassey, on the bank of the Bhagirathi, where the Nawab was already entrenched with his troops.

The battle broke out on the morning of the 23rd June. On the Nawab's side Mir Jafar and Rai Durlabh stood still with their large armies, and only a small force under Mohanlal and Mir Madan, backed by a French officer, took part in the battle. Had Mir Jafar loyally fought for the Nawab the English forces might have easily been routed. Even the small advance party made the situation too critical for the English. After half an hour's fighting Clive withdrew his forces behind the trees. At eleven o'clock he consulted

* Probably it was influenced by the fact that the French were not strong enough, and the vitality of Siraj-ud-Daula's Government was sapped by the treacherous intrigues among his ministers and officers, as stated above. While Bussy did not come to the assistance of the Nawab, that the Nawab's uncle and Pay Master, Mir Jatar, had an eye on the throne did not pass unnoticed by the English. The situation for the young Nawab, who had just passed his teens, was indeed pathetic. Since the time of signing the treaty with Siraj-ud-Daula, and, in fact, since the time before he ascended the throne of Bengal, the English were conspiring to overthrow him. They found in him an enemy who would not bow down to their will and pleasure. And since now they had considerable strength and the internal situation of Bengal was most congenial to all kinds of conspirators, they wanted to have one of "their" own men as the Nawab. It can be truthfully said that after the battle of Plassey the English Company became the greatest king-maker in India. They put up "suitable" kings wherever they wanted them to protect and expand their interest.

his officers. It was resolved to maintain the cannonade during the day and to attack the Nawab's camp at midnight. Unfortunately a stray shot killed Mir Madan and this so unnerved the Nawab that he sent for Mir Jafar and accepted his treacherous advice to recall the only troops which were fighting for him. What followed may be best described in the words of a contemporary historian, Ghulam Husain, the author of the *Siyar-ul-mutakherin*:—

> 'By this time Mohanlal who had advanced with Mir Madan, was closely engaged with the enemy; his cannon was served with effect; and his infantry having availed themselves of some covers and other grounds, were pouring a quantity of bullets in the enemy's ranks. It was at this moment he received the order of falling back, and of retreating. He answered: 'That this was not a time to retreat; that the action was so far advancea, that whatever might happen, would happen now; and that should he turn his head, to march back to camp, his people would disperse, and perhaps abandon themselves to an open flight.' Siraj-ud-daulah, on this answer, turned towards Mir Jafar, and the latter coldly answered: 'That the advice he had proposed was the best in his power; and that as to the rest, His Highness was the master of taking his own resolutions.' Siraj-ud-daulah, intimidated by the General's coldness, and overcome by his own fears and apprehensions, renounced his own natural sense, and submitted to Mir Jafar's pleasure; he sent repeated orders, with pressing messages, to Mohanlal; who at last obeyed, and retreated from the post to which he had advanced.
>
> 'This retreat of Mohanlal's made a full impression on his troops. The sight of their General's retreat damped their courage; and having at the same time spied some parties which were flying (for they were of the complot), they disbanded likewise, and fled, every one taking example from his neighbour; and as the flight now had lost all its shame, whole bodies fled although no one pursued; and in a little time the camp remained totally empty. Siraj-ud-daulah, informed of the desertion of his troops, was amazed; and fearing not only the English he had in his from his neighbour; and as the flight now had lost all its shame, whole all firmness of mind. Confounded by that general abandonment, he joined the runaways himself; and after marching the whole night, he the next day at about eight in the morning arrived at his palace in the city.'

Siraj-ud-daulah reached Murshidabad on the morning of the 24th. The news of his defeat created the utmost panic and confusion in the city. He made an effort to collect his forces, but both men and officers fled pell-mell in all directions. In vain did he lavish considerable treasures to induce the troops to stand by him, and then, finding no other way, he fled with his wife Lutf-un-nisā and one trusted servant.

Mir Jafar reached Murshidabad on the 25th and Clive followed him a few days later. Mir Jafar was proclaimed Subahdar of Bengal. In a few days news arrived of the capture of Siraj-ud-daulah. He was brought back to the capital and immediately murdered by the orders of Miran, the son of Mir Jafar. Thus the treacherous conspiracy of Mir Jafar was brought to a triumphant conclusion."

Having thus ascended the throne as the puppet *nawab* of the English, Mir Jafar signed a treaty with the Company by which the latter received undisputed right to trade in Bengal, Bihar and Orissa. This meant virtually the whole of eastern India. The Company also received a *zemindari* or the right to revenue-farming over a large tract of land south of Calcutta, which is still known as the District of 24 Parganas. Furthermore, the puppet nawab assured the Company that he "will not erect any new fortifications below Hugli, near the River Ganges," and that when demanded "the English assistance" he would be "at the charge of the maintenance of them;" and, in addition to such promises, he paid a total sum of Rs. 17,700,000 for the redress of the Company, for the maintenance of its forces, and for the redress of the English, Armenians, Hindus and Muslim inhabitants of Calcutta, with the understanding that the money was "to be disposed by them (that is, Clive and other Company officers) to whom they think proper."[322]

8. Control of Upper Gangetic Plain

After the conquest of Bengal, there were no powers, foreign or Indian, to oust the Company from India. With such a rich possession as Bengal, Bihar and Orissa, the English Company could easily crush the French Power in India (successive Carnatic Wars); and after having dealt the decisive blow to French aspirations in India, the efforts of the Company after the later half of the eighteenth century were to bring the Indian territories under full control, the territories which were then ruled by various kings, *nawabs*, and adventurers. Proceeding prudently in this venture, the first objective of the Company was to build a wall of defence against the Maratha power.

So, to safeguard its newly-acquired territory of eastern India against the incursions of the Marathas or of the Afghans, the Company first spread its domination over the Subah of Oudh (Avādh), which, as noted earlier, was the most important semi-independent State in northern India in those days.

This was not a difficult task. When, in 1763, the Company's army drove Mir Kasim out of Bengal (Mir Kasim had replaced Mir Jafar as the Nawab of Bengal because of the latter's incompetence in meeting the demands of the Company and its officers but eventually proved hostile to the Company's rule, as it will be explained in the next chapter), and when the Nawab of Oudh came to his aid, the united forces were utterly defeated by the English at Buxar in 1764. Buxar finally rivetted the shackles of the Company's rule upon Bengal, and furthermore placed Oudh at the mercy of the English. By the treaty of 1765, which followed the war, the Nawab of Oudh, who was also titular Vizier or Minister of the Mughal Emperor since 1761, became a dependent of the Company. Henceforth, it was a matter of policy to maintain a close alliance with Oudh, "with a view to utilising it as a bulwark against the incursions of the Marathas or of the Afghans."[323]

The Emperor of Delhi also now fell into the hands of the English. The feeble descendant of the Great Mughals was now a homeless wanderer, but was still recognized as the titular sovereign of India. All the kings and chiefs in the vast subcontinent still owed nominal allegiance to him, and all pretended to derive from him their power in the kingdoms and provinces which they conquered by force of arms. The English also imitated their example. In 1765, the Company obtained from the Emperor a Charter, making the Company the Dewan or Administrator of the Subah of Bengal. The English thus obtained a legal status, and also formally took upon themselves the responsibility of administering the province which they had conquered eight years before.

9. Anglo-Mysore Wars

Next, the English paid their attention to Mysore where Hyder Ali and later his son, Tipu Sultan, were a source of danger to the rising power of the British in India. And thus followed the Anglo-Mysore Wars, in which, like in all wars of the English with the Indian Powers, the Indian side won compaigns but lost the battle.

While the Carnatic was distracted by wars and Bengal was entering into her ignoble days, Hyder Ali steadily rose to power in Mysore. Originally an adventurer, he entered the service of the prime minister of Mysore, who had made himself the practical dictator over the titular Hindu ruler of the State. Though uneducated and illiterate, Hyder Ali has been said to have been the most capable military commander that India produced in the later half of the eighteenth century. Taking advantage of the prevailing distractions in the south, he increased his power and soon supplanted his former patron. He extended his territories by conquering Bednore, Sunda, Sera, Canara and Guti, and by subjugating the quasi-military chiefs of South India—the Poligars, who were essentially revenue-farmers.

The rapid rise of Hyder naturally excited the jealousy of the Marathas, the Nizam of Hyderabad, and the English; and they formed a tripartite alliance against Hyder. But in the first Anglo-Mysore War Hyder was victorious. He devastated the Carnatic and appeared within a few miles of Madras. The Company was struck with panic, and made peace with the terrible invader in 1769. This, however, was not the end. A second Anglo-Mysore war broke out in 1780, and in this Hyder was defeated. But his strength was not broken. Hyder Ali died in 1782, and the war ended with a peace with his son, Tipu Sultan, in 1783.

Two more wars were fought against the Mysore Sultan Tipu, for he was making alliance with the French and his rich possession remained an eye-sore to the English, the Marathas and the Nizam. Again there was a tripartite alliance between these enemies of Tipu in the third Anglo-Mysore war of 1790–92. Tipu fought bravely, and by his military and diplomatic skill averted a complete disaster.

Ultimately he was forced by circumstances to sign the Treaty of Seringapatam in 1792, by which he had to surrender half of his dominions. The allies divided the territory among themselves, the English receiving the most important areas. It has been remarked that these "were cessions of considerable importance in adding to the strength and compactness of the Company's territories."[324] Moreover, Tipu was made to pay an indemnity of more than three million pounds and to send two of his sons as hostages to the English Company.

In the fourth and the last Anglo-Mysore war Tipu tried to regain his position. Meanwhile, he had added fortifications to his capital, and reorganized his forces. He also took help from the French when they were involved in a deadly war with the English in Europe. He even sent emissaries to Arabia, Kabul, Constantinople, Versailles and Mauritius, inviting them to send volunteers to come forward to help him "in expelling the English from India."[325] The English, on the other hand, revived their triple alliance, although this time the Marathas remained rather cool. The war that followed was of a very short duration, but quite decisive. Tipu fell in 1799 in the defence of his capital, which was then plundered by the English troops.

Mysore was now at the disposal of the English. A portion was offered to the Marathas if they would form a subsidiary alliance, but they declined. This policy of "subsidiary alliance" is worth explaining in detail to show why the Marathas were clever enough to refuse this offer. At the time when the wars of Napoleon Bonaparte were influencing British policy in Europe, William Pitt was subsidizing the Great Powers to maintain armies against Napoleon. Lord Mornington, afterwards Marquis of Wellesley, who came to India in 1798 as the Governor-General of the Company, introduced this policy of Pitt in India, but with an important variation. Instead of paying subsidies to the Indian princes, Wellesley obtained it from them for maintaining contingents of the British army in their dominions. This at once brought money to the Company and kept the Indian princes under British control. This astute policy of the British in India came to be known as the policy of "subsidiary alliance."

Thus, by refusing to be drawn into this noose, the Marathas showed their wisdom. Later, of course, the Maratha Peshwa placed his neck in it, just as it adorned all the vassals of the Company, including the Nawab of Oudh.

To return to the story of the annexation of Mysore, another portion of it was given to the Nizam of Hyderabad who was fool enough to fall into the trap. Subsequently it was taken back by the Company in lieu of the British contingent forced upon him to safeguard the interests of the British in the Deccan, lest the French make any move to re-enter the political arena of India. This is actually how the policy of "subsidiary alliance" worked.

And then what remained of Mysore was formed into a little kingdom without any outlet to the sea, and the old Hindu house was restored. The new State of Mysore became virtually a dependency of the English, the same fate as that of the *subah* of Oudh and other provinces and states which had shown their independence with the decline of the Mughal Empire but were cleverly annexed by the British in course of time.

A subsidiary treaty which the new ruler of Mysore had to accept provided for the maintenance of a "protecting British force within the kingdom" (the same "subsidiary alliance!"), and it was also enjoined that the ruler must pay a subsidy to the English which would be increased "in time of war."[326] Furthermore, the Governor-General of the Company was "empowered to take over the entire internal administration of the country if he was dissatisfied on any account with its government."[327] In the words of the British contemporary writer, Thornton, the Governor-General of the Company thus "acted wisely in not making Mysore ostensibly a British possession. He acted no less wisely in making it substantially so."[328]

The settlement of Mysore secured for the Company substantial territorial, economic, commercial, and military advantages. Previous to it, in 1788, the English had secured from the Nizam of Hyderabad the town of Guntur which was the only outlet of that state to the sea. Now the State of Mysore was also similarly crippled, while the acquisition of its parts by the English extended the Company's dominion "from sea to sea across the base of the peninsula," encompassing the new kingdom of Mysore on all sides except in the north. And when in 1800 the Nizam transferred his acquisitions from Mysore to the Company, this kingdom "was entirely encircled by the Pax Britannica."[329]

Such an achievement of the Governor-General of the Company was enthusiastically applauded in England. As mentioned earlier, he was elevated to the rank of Marquis in the peerage of Ireland, and his general, Harris, was made a baron.

The fall of Tipu Sultan also removed another serious concern of the English. The French menace in India now disappeared completely. They could not any more make serious attempts to regain their lost position. The Marathas, however, remained the chief concern of the English, but they were also soon liquidated as will be seen from the following account of the Anglo-Maratha Wars.

10. Anglo-Maratha Wars

During the period in which successive stages of the Anglo-Mysore wars were conducted, hostilities broke out between the English and the Marathas, which lasted till the second decade of the nineteenth century, ending in the complete collapse of the Marathas. The most powerful rival of the English was thus eliminated.

As described earlier, the treaty of 1765 with the Nawab of Oudh was meant primarily as a bulwark against Maratha invasions in northern India. The English further strengthened the arrangement by the Benares Treaty of 1773. This was particularly necessary when in 1770–71 the vagrant Emperor of Delhi, Shah Alam II, the Mughal, (who was previously brought under British control in 1765 by the offer of Kora and Allahabad from the Subah of Oudh as his personal possession and was simultaneously pensioned off by the promise of the payment to him of an annual tribute of Rs. 2,600,000 for the English possession of the Subah of Bengal), placed himself under Maratha tutelage. By this new treaty of Benares, Kora and Allahabad were taken away from the Mughal, his pension was stopped, and simultaneously Oudh was virtually reduced to a state of vassalage in order to maintain an efficient defence against any possible Maratha invasion. Then followed the Ruhela War which has been noted before.

Very soon, besides these defence preparations, an opportunity arrived for the English to take a direct move vis-a-vis the Marathas. As elsewhere in India the internal quarrels among the Indian princes and chiefs gave the English the chance to intervene in their internal affairs, so it happened in the case of the Marathas also. There were two claimants to the post of Peshwa, the head of the Maratha Confederacy; and the Bombay Government of the Company did not miss the opportunity to enter into a treaty in 1775 to help one of them. This started the first Anglo-Maratha war. In this war, however, the English could not make spectacular gains. They captured Ahmedabad and Gwalior, but the war failed in its objective. The ally of the British retired on a pension, while Salsette and some other islands which were in significant positions in western India fell into the hands of the Company under the peace of 1782.

Maratha power remained a headache for the English, and so a second Anglo-Maratha war soon followed. Fortunately for the English, the Peshwa was hard pressed by other Maratha chiefs, and their internal quarrels thus finally compelled him to seek the Company's aid. A "subsidiary alliance" was concluded in 1802, and the Peshwa was placed on his throne with the help of British troops. The Company thus gained a foot-hold among the Marathas. But the other Maratha chiefs, Sindia, Holkar and Bhonsla, were taken aback by this introduction of British power in their dominions; and then followed what is known as the Second Maratha War. General Wellesley, who was afterwards known as the Duke of Wellington, crushed the armies of Sindia and Bhonsla in the battles of Assye and Argaon in 1803, and Lord Lake triumphantly entered Delhi in the same year and defeated Sindia's troops at Laswari. But Holkar who was playing a waiting game now joined in. Thus the interminable war with the many-headed Maratha Confederacy continued. This alarmed the Directors of the Company, and so for the time being they adopted the policy of letting the Marathas alone.

The final offensive against the Marathas was undertaken in the second decade of the nineteenth century. But before dealing decisively with the Marathas, the Company first consolidated its position still further. A war with Nepal during 1814–16 brought the independent Nepalese Government into submission. According to a treaty signed in 1816, the Nepalese gave up their claims to places in the lowlands along their southern frontier, ceded to the Company the districts of Garwal and Kumaon west of Nepal, withdrew from Sikhim, and agreed to receive a British Resident at Khatmandu. These were indeed important gains for the English, for the northwestern frontier of their dominions now reached the mountains, and thus henceforth they had greater facilities for communications with the regions of Central Asia.

Next came the wars with the Pindaris and Pathan hordes which led to the extension of British supremacy over Rajputana and Central India. The Pindaris were described as "swarms of Afghan, Jat and Maratha condottieri–who had offered their service to any chief who paid them."[330] The Pindaris mainly dwelt in Central India and were employed as auxiliary forces in the Maratha armies and enjoyed the protection of Maratha chiefs like Sindia and Holkar. In 1794, Sindia granted them some settlements in Malwa near the Narmada. By the end of 1817, the Company succeeded in expelling the Pindaris from Malwa and "by the close of January, 1818, they were practically exterminated."[331]

After this came the suppression of the Pathans. Many Pathans at this time took to the habits of a predatory horde like the Pindaris. They generally served as military adventurers under one of the Rajput or Maratha chiefs of the time. The English managed to isolate the most important of their chiefs, Amir Khan, from the others in November 1817, and made him the Nawab of Tonk. After that there was no problem in suppressing the Pathans.

Then came the third and final war with the Marathas. As noted before, the Peshwa had concluded a subsidiary alliance with the Company in 1802, but he soon realized its implications and chafed under the restraint. At last he threw off all disguise, and other

Maratha chiefs joined him. But it was too late. The Peshwa was beaten off at Khirki, Bhonsla's army was defeated at Sitabaldi, and Holkar's army was crushed at Mehidpur. The Peshwa's dominions were annexed in 1817, and formed into the province of Bombay. He himself was captured in the following year, and retired on pension. Minor Maratha chiefs–Sindia, Holkar, Bhonsla and Gaekwar, were allowed to "rule" in their own "States" under the imperial power of the Company. As in all other states, they were also shorn off their political and military powers.

11. Remaining Indian Powers

British moves, as in a game of chess, followed successively one after another. Their next move was to extend their paramountcy over Rajputana and Central India. This was easy. The lords of Rajputana had once stood as serious rivals to the Mughal supremacy in India; but now they were utterly bankrupt. Their land, distracted by dynastic quarrels, had become the prey to external aggressions of the Marathas, the Pindaris and the Pathans, resulting in anarchy, plunder, economic ruin, and moral degradation. Therefore, when the Company had vanquished the leading Indian powers, the Rajput leaders readily acknowledged British supremacy. The whole of Rajputana and Central India soon fell under the control of the Company which lorded over the numerous small states, some rearranged from the old ones and some newly-created to make room for the Company's stooges.

Thus, the close of the eighteenth and the beginning of the nineteenth century saw the fall of those Indian powers which arose or revived on the decline of the Mughal Power and contended for political supremacy or local sovereignty. Simultaneously, the English Company became the paramount power over a dominion extending from the Himalayas to Cape Comorin, and from the Sutlej to the Brahmaputra.

For the complete possession of India and fortification of her frontiers there remained only the Sikhs in the Punjab, the Sindhis, the

Pathan and Baloch tribes in the north-west, the Afghans beyond the Khyber Pass, and the Burmese and the Assamese to the east of the Brahmaputra. In course of time all these territories were brought under control, and "friendly" ties were established with the Afghans. By the first Anglo-Burmese War of 1824–26, Assam, Cachar and Manipur became practically the protectorates of the Company; Sind was conquered in 1843; the Punjab was annexed as the result of the Anglo-Sikh Wars lasting over 1848–52; and the English extended their domination over Burma in the later wars during the second half of the nineteenth century. The Company thus became the unchallenged master of India.

Meanwhile, the weaker States were dealt with more summarily, and the Company was not very particular in its methods. The Raja of Benares was disposed of in 1794; the Nawab of Surat died in 1799, his brother was retired on pension and his State was annexed by the Company; the Raja of Tanjore was set aside, his brother resigned his powers to the Company and retired on pension; the Nawab of the Carnatic died in 1801 but his successor declined to abdicate, so another prince was set up in his place who, following the example of others, gave his kingdom to the Company and retired on pension; the Nawab of Bengal was pensioned off earlier; and the boy-*nawab* of Farakkabad who was about to attain his majority, was also made to transfer the State to the Company and was retired on pension. The same procedure continued.

Even the large State of Oudh was not treated differently. The State of Benares which formed a part of the dominion of the Nawab of Oudh was taken away from him in 1775, and, as has been noted before, Kora and Allahabad were taken away even earlier (1765) for nothing in return, and were sold back to the Nawab after a few years (1773) for five million rupees. Later, the Nawab was asked either to make over the civil and military administration of his kingdom to the Company or to enter into the bondage of "subsidiary alliance" ceding one-half of his kingdom for the maintenance of the British contingent forced upon him. He was compelled to accept the latter proposal, and again ceded Allahabad and other districts to the Company in 1801. Finally, in 1856, the State of Oudh was annexed to British India, and the Nawab disappeared for good.

In the last ten years of the Company's rule in India after 1848, many Indian States were liquidated. Lord Dalhousie who was then the Governor-General of the Company in India annexed "about 150,000 square miles previously ruled by dependent princes."[332] Gone were the Maratha realm of the Bhonsla family in Nagpur, the States of Sattara, Jhansi, and others. In the case of some of them the reason was purely to further strengthen direct British hold on India. Thus, regarding the annexation of Nagpur and Sattara it has openly been admitted that "imperial considerations weighed with him (Lord Dalhousie)," for, "they were placed right across the main lines of communication between Bombay and Madras and Bombay and Calcutta."[333]

In this period the British not only liquidated many Indian states, but further curtailed the power of the others, and by reducing the pension of the deposed princes made their position still worse. Thus, the British acquired further territories from the Indian rulers who had failed to pay regularly the stipulated sum to the Company for being a party to the scheme of "subsidiary alliance" and therefore maintaining the British contingent forced on their territory to guard the interests of the British. Because of this, in 1853, the cotton-producing province of Berar was taken away from the Nizam of Hyderabad in lieu of the subsidy.

Meanwhile, the huge pensions paid to several dethroned or degraded rulers were drastically revised or abolished. Notable among them were the ex-Peshwa (who had been made the Raja of Bithur), the nominal Nawab of Bengal, and the nominal Nawab of the Carnatic. Henceforth, the expropriated wealth of India could be enjoyed by the British alone.

In those days the English thought that they had no more need of their "Indian allies," and so could dispose of them on the slightest pretext or stop their pensions without any ceremony. But the Indian Revolt of 1857–58, which the English contemptuously described as the Sepoy Mutiny and Marx in his *Chronological Notes on India* acclaimed as "die Sepoy Revolution,"[334] showed them the usefulness of maintaining the remaining princes, *nawabs* and *maharajas* as a buffer between them and the Indian people, while their "States" depended in all essentials on the wishes of the British Residents imposed upon them. Lord Canning quite candidly remarked in his Minute of 30th April, 1860."[335]

> "The safety of our rule is increased, not diminished, by the maintenance of native chiefs well affected to us. Should the day come when India shall be threatened by an external enemy, or when the interests of England elsewhere may require that her Eastern Empire shall incur more than ordinary risk, one of our best mainstays will be found in these Native States. But to make them so we must treat their chiefs and influential families with consideration and generosity, teaching them that, in spite of all suspicion to the contrary, their independence is safe, that we are not waiting for plausible opportunities to convert their country into British territory."

But how "independent" these Indian "rulers" were has already been evident from the conditions under which the "ruler" of Mysore was invested with the title of *Maharaja* by the Company. He had not only to maintain a "protecting British force within the kingdom" and pay a subsidy to the Company which would be increased "in time of war," but the Governor-General of the Company was "empowered to take over the entire internal administration of the country if he was dissatisfied on any account with its government." And neither Mysore was any exception, nor was the dependence of the "native rulers" on British administration curtailed in later years. Indeed, it so remained the policy of the foreign rulers in regard to the "Native States" of India, which were rearranged or created with their allies at the top of state-administrations, that these "rulers" had no real power at all and had to serve in many ways the interests of the supreme government. As later evidence brought to light quite clearly, this was the first wall of defence that the British built in India against the natural desire of her people to become free from feudal domination (which was more manifest in the "Native States" than in British India) and proceed on a normal course of development.

It may, therefore, be of some interest to note here what Marx had written regarding the "Native States" as early as in 1853:[336]

"After the British intruders had once put their feet on India and made up their mind to hold it, there remained no alternative, but to break the power of the native princes by force or by intrigue. Placed with regard to them in similar circumstances as the ancient Romans with regard to their allies, they followed in the track of Roman politics. 'It was,' says an English writer, 'a system of fattening allies as we fatten oxen, till they were worthy of being devoured.' After having won over allies in the way of ancient Rome, the East India Company executed them in the modern manner of Change-Alley. In order to discharge the engagements they had entered into with the Company, the native princes were forced to borrow enormous sums from Englishmen at a usurious interest. When their embarrassment had reached the highest pitch, the creditors got inexorable, 'the screw was turned' and the princes were compelled either to concede their territories amicably to the Company, or to begin war; to become pensioners on their usurpers in one case or to be deposed as traitors in the other. At this moment the Native States occupy an area of 699,961 square miles—with a population of 52,941,263 souls*, being, however, no longer allies, but only the dependents of the British Government upon multifarious conditions and under the various forms of the subsidiary and of the protective systems. These systems have in common the relinquishment, by the Native States of the right of self-defence, of maintaining diplomatic relations, and of settling the disputes among themselves without the interference of the Governor-General.

All of them have to pay a tribute, either in hard cash, or in a contingent of armed forces commanded by British officers. The final absorption or annexation of these Native States is at present eagerly controverted between the reformers who denounce it as a crime and the men of business who excuse it as a necessity.

In my opinion the question itself is altogether improperly put. As to native *States,* they virtually ceased to exist from the moment they became subsidiary to or protected by the Company. If you divide the revenue of a country between two governments, you are sure to cripple the resources of the one

* Up to the end of the British Period of India's history, there were 562 Indian States, covering an area of 598,138 square miles, or nearly two-fifths of the total area of India: and these States contained a total population of 78,996,854, that is, roughly less than a quarter of the total population of India. (cf. Panikkar, K. M.—*Indian States,* Oxford Pamphlets on Indian Affairs, Oxford, 1944, p. 3.)

and the administration of both. Under the present system the native States succumb under the double incubus of their native administration and the tributes and inordinate military establishments imposed upon them by the Company. The conditions under which they are allowed to retain their apparent independence are, at the same time, the conditions of a permanent decay, and of an utter inability of improvement. Organic weakness is the constitutional law of their existence, as of all existence living upon sufferance. It is, therefore, not the native States, but the native Princes and Courts about whose maintenance the question revolves. Now, is it not a strange thing that the same men who denounce 'the barbarous splendours of the Crown and Aristocracy of England' are shedding tears at the downfall of Indian Nabobs, Rajahs and Jagirdars, a great majority of whom possess not even the prestige of antiquity, generally usurpers of very recent date, set up by the English intrigue. There exists in the whole world no despotism more ridiculous, absurd and childish than that of these Schazennas and Schariars of the Arabian Nights. The Duke of Wellington, Sir J. Malcolm, Sir Henry Russel, Lord Ellenborough, General Briggs, and other authorities have pronounced in favour of the *status quo* but on what grounds? Because the native troops under English rule want employment in the petty warfares with their own countrymen, in order to prevent them from turning their strength against their own European masters. Because the existence of independent states gives occassional employment to the English troops. Because the hereditary princes are the most servile tools of English despotism, and check the rise of those bold military adventurers with whom India has and ever will abound. Because the independent territories afford a refuge to all discontented and enterprising native spirits....

As to the pensioned Princes, the £ 2,468,969 assigned to them by the British Government on the Indian revenue is a most heavy charge upon a people living on rice, and deprived of the first necessaries of life. If they are good for anything, it is for exhibiting royalty in its lowest stage of degradation and ridicule. Take, for instance, the Great Moghul, the descendent of Timour Tamerlane. He is allowed £ 120,000 a year. His authority does not extend beyond the walls of his palace, within which the royal idiotic race, left to itself, propagates as freely as rabbits. Even the police of Delhi is held by Englishmen, above his control. There he sits on the throne, a little shrivelled yellow old man, trimmed in a theatrical dress, embroidered with gold, much like that of the dancing girls of Hindostan. On certain State occasions, the tinsel-covered puppet issues forth to gladden the hearts of the loyal. On his days of reception strangers have to pay a fee, in the form of guineas, as to any other *sallimbanque* exhibiting himself in public; while he, in his turn, presents them with turbans, diamonds, etc. On looking nearer at them, they find that the royal diamonds are like so many pieces of ordinary glass, grossly painted and imitating as roughly as possible the precious stones, and jointed so wretchedly, that they break in the hand like ginger-bread.

The English money-lenders, combined with English aristocracy, understand, we must own, the art of degrading Royalty, reducing it to the nullity of constitutionalism at home and to the seclusion of etiquette abroad. And now, here are the Radicals, exasperated at this spectacle!"

Thus, by using its characteristic "tools of trade"—fair or foul, subversive or open—, by the middle of the nineteenth century the Company emerged as the undisputed ruler of India, while two-fifths of India's territory remained "independent" under Native Rulers.* As Marx remarked in 1853:[337]

"As to its exterior, India was now finished. It is only since 1849, that one great Anglo-Indian empire has existed."

---

* It should not however be understood that during the whole process of its onslaught, the Company did not come across any opposition from the Indian people. At first, when the Company was playing at "king-making," they might have taken it as only a change of dynasties, and so did not trouble themselves much. But soon they came to realize that they had fallen victim to a new system of oppression and exploitation. And after this there arose active opposition of the people in all parts of India. In the beginning, this took the character of sporadic peasant revolts. The eighteenth century was particularly marked by them; such as in Dinajpur and Rangpur, at Benares, in Oudh, in the Northern Circars, etc. But this century also marked the Sannyasi Revolt of Bengal (1760—1774), which took the character of armed united resistance of the artisans and peasants under the leadership of a socio-religious sect. The people fought with country-made firearms and even field-pieces, and caused a good deal of panic and anxiety to the Company. Then, in the first half of the nineteenth century, there were a series of revolts, such as the Bareilly rising of 1816; the Kol revolt of 1831—32 in Bihar; several uprisings in Chota Nagpur and Palamau; the revolts of the Bengal peasantry under the leadership of Titu Mir and Didu Mir in 1831 and 1847, respectively; peasant uprising in Mysore in 1830—31; the uprisings of the Moplah in south India after 1836; the Santhal Insurrection of 1855—56; and others. As has been reported:

"These risings testify to the general ferment in the British Empire in India, the last and the most severe being the Mutiny of 1857—1859, which shook its mighty fabric to its very foundation." (reference 107, p. 772)

All these revolts were ruthlessly suppressed by the Company with inhuman terror and oppression, of which, however inadequate, information are available in government documents and historical literatures. And the Company could so smash the people's opposition to its rule of pillage and destruction because of possessing superior

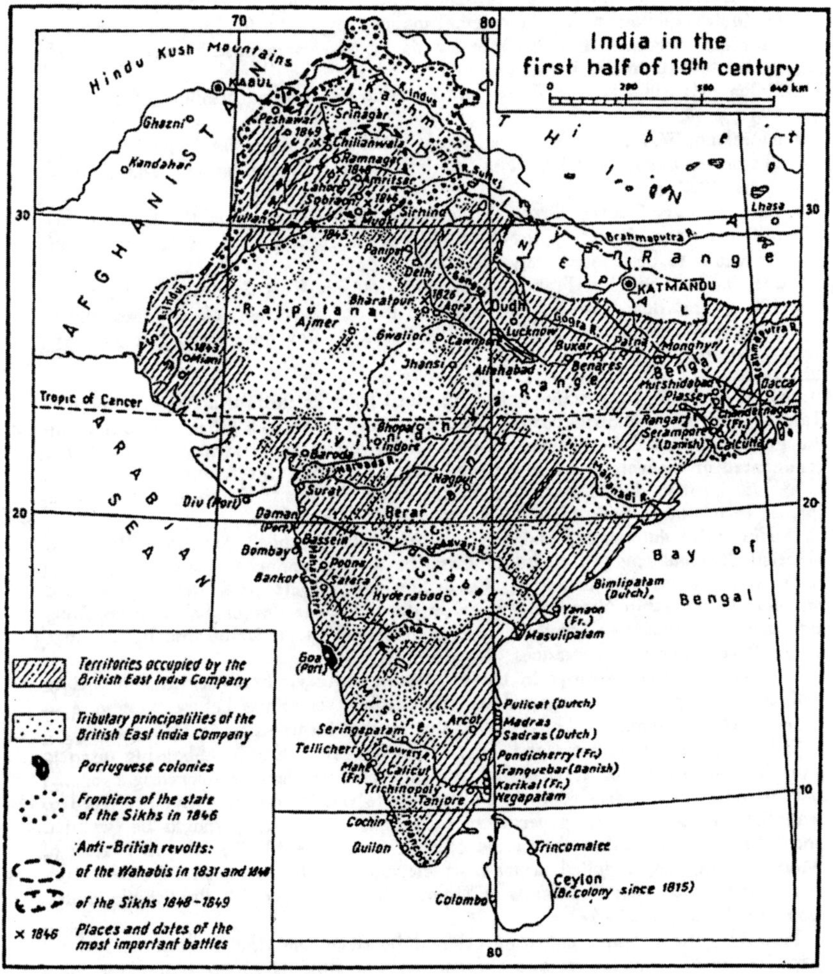
India in the
first half of 19th century
Territories occupied by the British East India Company
Tributary principalities of the British East India Company
Portuguese colonies
Frontiers of the state of the Sikhs in 1846
Anti-British revolts:
of the Wahabis in 1831 and 1848
of the Sikhs 1848–1849
× 1846 Places and dates of the most important battles
Hindu Kush Mountains
KABUL
Ghazni
Kandahar
AFGHANISTAN
Peshawar
Srinagar
Chilianwala
Ramnagar
Lahore
Amritsar
Sobraon
Sirhind
Multan
Mudki
Panipat
Delhi
Bharatpur
Agra
Oudh
Rajputana
Ajmer
Miani
Gwalior
Cawnpore
Lucknow
Buxar
Patna
Monghyr
Jhansi
Allahabad
Benares
Bengal
Murshidabad
Plassey
Dacca
Chandernagore (Fr.)
Serampore (Danish)
Calcutta
Tropic of Cancer
ARABIAN SEA
Bhopal
Indore
Baroda
Surat
Nagpur
Berar
Diu (Port.)
Daman (Port.)
Bassein
Bombay
Poona
Satara
Bankot
Hyderabad
Bimlipatam (Dutch)
Yanaon (Fr.)
Masulipatam
Bay of Bengal
Goa (Port.)
Pulicat (Dutch)
Madras
Sadras (Dutch)
Arcot
Seringapatam
Tellicherry
Mahé (Fr.)
Calicut
Pondicherry (Fr.)
Tranquebar (Danish)
Karikal (Fr.)
Negapatam
Trichinopoly
Tanjore
Cochin
Quilon
Trincomalee
Ceylon (Br. colony since 1815)
Colombo
Tibet
Lhasa
Brahmaputra R.
NEPAL
KATMANDU
Himalaya Range
Vindhya Range
Deccan
Mysore
Kashmir
70
80
30
20
10

Notes and References

1 Marx, Karl—*Chronologische Auszüge über Ostindien* (Chronological Notes on India), Photo-copy of the original manuscript in the Institute for Marxism-Leninism, Berlin. (All underlined words in Marx's manuscript are italicized in the extracts in this book.)

2 Collis, Maurice—*British Merchant Adventurers,* William Collins of London, 1942, p. 17.

3 Moreland, W. H.—*The Revenue System of the Mughul Empire,* "The Cambridge History of India," Vol. IV, "The Mughul Period," Cambridge at the University Press, 1937, p. 450.

4 Parliamentary Papers, Great Britain—*The Fifth Report from the Select Committee on the Affairs of the East India Company,* ordered by the House of Commons to be printed, July, 28, 1812, p. 85.

5 See, for instance, Dr. Francis Buchanan's *Journey from Madras, etc.* (London, 1807); the Board of Revenue's letter to the Governor of Madras, dated 25th April, 1808; the Minute of the Board of Revenue, dated 5th January, 1818; etc.

---

arms and because of the active help it received from its faithful allies—the "Native Rulers," and the landlords created by it, especially in Bengal, Bihar and Orissa by the Permanent Land Settlement of 1793. Referring to these loyal "rulers," Marx commented in connection with the Sepoy Revolt of 1857 (cf. reference 1):

"*Sindia* loyal to the 'English dogs,' nicht so his '*troopers;*' *Rajah of Patialah*—for shame!—sends large body of soldiers in aid of the English! ...

During July, August, September 1858: Sir Colin Campbell, Sir Hope Hunt and General Walpole engaged to hunt down the more prominent rebels and take *all forts* whose possession disputed; *die Begum made some final stands,* then fled *mit dem* Nana Sahib über Rapti river, in die territories des English dogman *Jung Bahadur, of Nepaul;* er erlaubt den English die rebels to pursue into his country, so die 'last bands of desperadoes dispersed;' ..."

In almost all the uprisings in the nineteenth century, these elements in society actively participated in hunting down the patriots, sometimes before they were so ordered by the Company. Thus, during the Santhal Insurrection of 1855—56:

"Many of the zamindars (landlords) in the Bhagalpur and neighbouring districts lent their elephants for service with the different detachments operating over the battle-front. They expressed their willingness 'to receive no hire;' but preferred to lend the elephants to the government only desiring that they should be 'well-fed and taken care of during the period of their employment.' The Nawab Nazim of Murshidabad, too, supplied 'a train of elephants at his personal expense.'" (cf. Natarajan, L.—*Peasant Uprisings in India: 1850—1900*, People's Publishing House, Bombay, 1953, pp. 26—27)

However, the people's anger at colonial bondage, and the consequent ruthless exploitation of their labour and the country's wealth, flared up again and again throughout the nineteenth century and the early years of the twentieth. And then by the second decade of the twentieth century it emerged as the mighty all-India movement for freedom—to which the British Power had to succumb finally.

6 cf. *The Minute* of Holt Mackenzie, dated 1st July, 1819; and Charles Metcalfe's *Minute*, dated 7th November, 1830.

7 cf. Mountstuart Elphinstone's *Report on the Territories Conquered from the Peswa*, submitted to the Governor-General in October 1819; and paragraphs 26, 27, 30 and 32 of Captain Robertson's administrative report, dated 10th October, 1821.

8 cf. paragraph 28 of the report

9 Baden-Powell, B. H.—*The Land System of British India*, Oxford at the Clarendon Press, 1892, Vol. I, p. 3.

10 *loc. cit.* 4, pp. 80, 47—48, 17

11 Marx, Karl—*Capital: A Critical Analysis of Capitalist Production*, Volume I, George Allen & Unwin Ltd., London, 1949, pp. 350—352.

12 See, for instance, *The Vākāṭaka-Gupta Age* edited by Ramesh Chandra Majumdar and Anant Sadashiv Altekar, The Bharatiya Itihas Parishad, Banaras, 1954, Chapter XIV; *The Classical Age* edited by R. C. Majumdar and A. D. Pusalker, Bharatiya Vidya Bhavan, Bombay, 1954, Chapters XVI, XXII, etc.; *The Age of Imperial Kanauj* edited by R. C. Majumdar and A. D. Pusalker, Bharatiya Vidya Bhavan, Bombay, 1955, Chapters X, XIII, etc.; *State & Government in Ancient India* by A. S. Altekar, Motilal Banarsidass, Banaras, 1949, Chapter XI, etc.; *A History of South India* by K. A. Nilakanta Sastri, Oxford University Press, London, 1955, Chapter XIII; etc.

13 Majumdar, R. C. and Altekar, A. S. (editors)—*The Vākāṭaka-Gupta Age*, The Bharatiya Itihas Parishad, Banaras, 1954, p. 266.

14 *ibid.*, p. 266

15 Majumdar, R. C. and Pusalker, A. D. (editors)—*The Classical Age*, Bharatiya Vidya Bhavan, Bombay, 1954, p. 353.

16 *loc. cit.* 13, pp. 266—267

17 Altekar, A. S.—*State & Government in Ancient India*, Motilal Banarsidass, Banaras, 1949, p. 176.

18 *loc. cit.* 13, p. 266

19 ibid., pp. 266—267

20 *loc. cit.* 17, p. 70

21 *ibid.*, p. 70

22 *loc. cit.* 13, p. 252

23 *loc. cit.* 17, p. 70

24 Sastri, K. A. Nilakanta—*A History of South India*, Oxford University Press, London, 1955, p. 157.

25 *ibid.*, p. 315

26 loc. *cit.* 12, and Niharranjan Ray's *Bangaleer Itihas*, Book Emporium, Calcutta, 1951, Chapters 5, 8, etc.

27 Ray, Niharranjan—*Bangaleer Itihas*, Book Emporium, Calcutta, 1951, pp. 212—213, 217—221, 235, 242, 244, 247—249, 251—253, etc.

28 This point has been treated in some detail in the book entitled *The Dynamics of a Rural Society: A Study of the Economic Structure in Bengal Villages* by the present writer, Akademie Verlag, Berlin, 1957.

29 *loc. cit.* 13, pp. 331—332 (Dr. A. S. Altekar's investigation into the *Social and Economic Condition* in the Vākāṭaka-Gupta Age)
30 *ibid.*, pp. 332—333
31 *ibid.*, p. 332
32 *ibid.*, p. 332
33 *ibid.*, p. 333
34 *loc. cit.* 17, p. 197
35 *loc. cit.* 13, p. 256
36 Mahalingam, T. V.—*Administration and Social Life under Vijayanagar*, University of Madras, 1940, p. 75.
37 *loc. cit.* 24, p. 315
38 *ibid.*, p. 315
39 *ibid.*, p. 315
40 *loc. cit.* 13, p. 332
41 cf. Dr. Francis Buchanan's (later Buchanan-Hamilton) *Journey through Madras* and other manuscripts in the Commonwealth Office Library, London.
42 *loc. cit.* 24, p. 315
43 For details regarding India's physical isolation and its effect on the Indian society, see, for instance, *The Population of India and Pakistan* by Kingsley Davis, Princeton University Press, USA, 1951, pp. 12—13.
44 For details on the racial and ethnic characteristics of the Indian people, their courses of migration, etc., see, for instance, B. S. Guha's *An Outline of Racial Ethnologie of India* in "Outline of Field Sciences of India," Indian Science Congress Association, Calcutta, 1937; etc.
45 *ibid.* See also K P. Chattopadhyay's *History of Indian Social Organisation*, Journal of Royal Asiatic Society of Bengal, Calcutta, 1935; Christian Lassen's *Indische Alterthumskunde*, Verlag von H. B. Koenig, Bonn, 1847, Erster Band, Zweites Buch; etc.
46 See, for instance, K. P. Chattopadhyay's *History of Indian Social Organisation*, Journal of Royal Asiatic Society of Bengal, Calcutta, 1935.
47 See, for instance, Nirmal Kumar Bose's *Democracy and Social Change in India*, Bulletin of the Ramakrishna Mission Institute of Culture, October, 1955, p. 234 ff.
48 Marx, Karl—*The British Rule in India*, New York Daily Tribune, June 25, 1853.
49 Regarding the importance of rainfall to the well-being of the agrarian society of India, see, for instance, *loc. cit.* 43, pp. 10—12.
50 *loc. cit.* 12, etc.
51 *loc. cit.* 41, etc.
52 See, for instance, D. D. Kosambi's *The Basis of India's History* (I), Journal of the American Oriental Society, USA, Vol. 75, No. 1, 1955. It is worthy of note that Mountstuart Elphinstone drew a similar conclusion in his book entitled *The History of India: The Hindu and Mahometan Periods*, John Murray, London, 1866, p. 75.
53 See, for instance, Niharranjan Ray's *Bangaleer Itihas* (*loc. cit.* 27), Chapter 5; J. F. Hewitt's *The Communal Origin of Indian Land Tenures*, Journal of the Royal Asiatic Society of Great Britain and Ireland, 1897, pp. 628—641; John

D. Mayne's *A Treatise on Hindu Law and Usage*, Higginbotham & Co., Madras and Stevens and Haynes, London, 1888, pp. 6, 217 ff.; Christian Lassen's *Indische Alterthumskunde* (loc. cit. 45), zweiter Band, 1852, pp. 721 ff.; Emile Senart's *Les Castes dans l'Inde*, Librairie Orientaliste Paul Geuthner, Paris, 1927; H. S. Maine's *The Village Communities in the East and the West*, London, 1876; etc.

54 *loc. cit.* 17, p. 237

55 Kosambi, D. D.—*The Basis of India's History* (I), Journal of the American Oriental Society, USA, Vol. 75, No. 1, 1955, p. 35.

56 cf. Sir Charles Metcalfe's *Minute*, dated 7th November, 1830, printed in the *Report of Select Committee of House of Commons*, British Parliament, 1832, Vol. III, Appendix 84, p. 331.

57 For a more detailed discussion on the *jati*-division of society and its relation to the village community system, see the present writer's *The Dynamics of a Rural Society* (*loc. cit.* 28), Chapter 2.

58 For details, see, for instance, H. H. Risley's *The Tribes and Castes of Bengal*, Bengal Secretariat Press, Calcutta, 1891; W. Crooke's *The Tribes and Castes of N. W. Provinces and Oudh*, Calcutta, 1896; John C. Nesfield's *Brief View of the Caste System of the North-Western Provinces and Oudh*, Allahabad, 1885; D. C. J. Ibbetson's *Outlines of Panjáb Ethnography*, Government publication, Calcutta, 1883; R. V. Russel and H. Lal's *The Tribes and Castes of the Central Provinces of India*, 1916; R. E. Enthoven's *Tribes and Castes of Bombay*, Bombay 1920—1922; L. K. A. Iyer and H. V. Nanjundayya's *The Mysore Tribes and Castes*, Bangalore, 1928—1935; L. K. A. Iyer's *The Cochin Tribes and Castes*, Madras, 1909—1912; L. K. A. Iyer's *The Travancore Tribes and Castes*, Trivandrum, 1937—1941; E. Thurston and K. Rangachari's *Castes and Tribes of South India*, Madras, 1909; etc.

59 Senart, Émil—*Les Castes dans l'Inde*, Librairie Orientaliste Paul Geuthner, Paris, 1927, p. 176.

60 See, for instance, P. V. Kane's *History of Dharmaśāstra*, Bhandarkar Oriental Research Institute, Poona, Vol. II, Part 1 (1941), Chapters II and III; S. V. Ketkar's *History of Caste in India*, Taylor & Carpenter, Ithaca, N.Y., USA, 1909, p. 5 ff.; Herman Oldenberg's *Zur Geschichte des indischen Kastenwesens*, Zeitschrift der Deutschen Morgenländischen Gesellschaft, Band 51, Leipzig, 1897, pp. 267—290; etc.

61 On the nature and extent of "Aryanization" of south India, see, for instance, *loc. cit.* 24, Chapter IV.

62 *loc. cit.* 55, p. 36 ff.

63 *ibid.*, p. 43

64 *loc. cit.* 27, Chapter 6

65 Maine, H. S.—*Ancient Law*, George Routledge & Sons, London, 1907, pp. 217—219.

66 See, for instance, *loc. cit.* 55; *loc. cit.* 46; *loc. cit.* 27, Chapter 6; *loc. cit.* 59, pp. 234—236, etc.; J. Jolly's Beiträge zur indischen Rechtsgeschichte, Zeitschrift der Deutschen Morgenländischen Gesellschaft, Band 50, Leipzig, 1896, pp. 507—518; U. N. Ghoshal's *Social Condition* in "The Classical Age" (*loc.*

cit. 12), p. 555 ff.; Christian Lassen's *Indische Alterthumskunde*, Erster Band (*loc. cit.* 45), pp. 801 ff., 817 ff.; etc.

67 See, for instance, *loc. cit.* 55; *loc. cit.* 59, pp. 218—222, 234—236, etc.; J. Jolly's *Beiträge zur indischen Rechtsgeschichte* (*loc. cit.* 66), pp. 512—513; Christian Lassen's *Indische Alterthumskunde*, Zweiter Band (*loc. cit.* 53), pp. 728—729; etc.

68 Kane, P. V.—*History of Dharmaśāstra*, Bhandarkar Oriental Research Institute, Poona, Vol. II, Part 1 (1941), Chapter II.

69 Probably basing their views on the formation of *jatis* mainly in the way mentioned in the text, some authorities are found inclined to consider the *varnas* as "castes" and the *jatis as* "half-castes." Ketkar held this view in his *History of Caste in India* (loc. *cit.* 60), but in a later publication entitled *An Essay on Hinduism* (Luzac and Company, London, 1911) he seems to have modified this opinion. Kane, on the other hand, has all along considered *jatis* as "sub-castes" (*loc. cit.* 68, Vol. II, Part 1 [1941], pp. 28, 33, 36, 44, 47, 48, 51, 55, 58, 69, 100, 103, etc.).

70 *loc. cit.* 27, pp. 305—306, 311, etc.

71 *ibid.*, Chapter 6; *loc. cit.* 46

72 *loc. cit.* 27, p. 263 ff.

73 *ibid.*, p. 266 ff.

74 *ibid.*, pp. 277—278, 289—290, 315—320, etc.

75 *ibid.*, pp. 253 and 278 (English rendering by the present writer)

76 *loc. cit.* 68, Vol. II, Part 1 (1941), Chapter III; *loc. cit.* 17, p. 41; etc.

77 See, for instance, *loc. cit.* 68, Vol. II, Part 1 (1941), p. 423, Vol. IV (1953), pp. 213—216; J. Jolly's *Beiträge zur indischen Rechtsgeschichte* (*loc. cit.* 66), *lichen Indien zu Buddha's Zeit*, Verlag für Orientalische Literatur, Kiel, 1897, pp. 213—216; J. Jolly's *Beiträge zur indischen Rechtsgeschichte* (loc. *cit.* 66), p. 513; Christian Lassen's *Indische Alterthumskunde* (loc. *cit.* 45), Band I, pp. 801 ff., Band II (*loc. cit.* 53), pp. 728—729, etc.; Max Weber's *Grundriß der Sozialökonomik*, Verlag von J. C. B. Mohr (Paul Siebeck), Tübingen, 1947, III. Abteilung — *Wirtschaft und Gesellschaft*, pp. 248—249, etc.; *loc. cit.* 17, p. 245 ff.; *loc. cit.* 59, p. 222 ff.; etc.

78 *loc. cit.* 68, Vol. II, Part 1 (1941), p. 155, Vol. III (1946), p. 881; etc.

79 It may be of interest to note here that because the caste system had once a useful role to play in Indian society and afterwards it became an obstacle to India's further development, in the early years of British rule in India diametrically opposite opinions were voiced on this institution by several authorities on India. Thus, Abbé J. A. Dubois wrote in his *Hindu Manners, Customs and Ceremonies* (translated by Henry K. Beauchamp and published in Oxford at the Clarendon Press, 1953, pp. 28—29):

"I believe caste division to be in many respects the *chef-d'oevre*, the happiest effort, of Hindu legislation. I am persuaded that it is simply and solely due to the distribution of the people into castes that India did not lapse into a state of barbarism, and that she preserved and perfected the arts and sciences of civilization whilst most other nations of the earth remained in a state of barbarism ... Caste assigns to each individual his own profession or calling; and the handing down of this system from father to son, from generation to generation, makes it impossible for any person or his descendants to change the condition of life which the law assigns to him for any other. Such an institution was probably the only means that the most clear-sighted prudence could devise for maintaining a state of civilization amongst a people endowed with the peculiar characteristics of the Hindus."

Similarly, Meredith Townshend remarked in *Asia and Europe* (Archibald Constable & Co., London, 1901, p. 72):

"I firmly believe caste to be a marvellous discovery, a form of socialism which through ages has protected Hindoo society from anarchy and from the worst evils of industrial and competitive life—it is an automatic poor-law to begin with, and the strongest form known of trades union—but Cristianity demands its sacrifices like every other creed, and caste in the Indian sense and Christianity cannot co-exist."

On the other hand, H. S. Maine stated emphatically that—

"... division of society into classes which at a particular crisis of social history is necessary for the maintenance of the national existence degenerates into the most disastrous and blighting of all human institutions—*Caste*." (*loc. cit.* 65, p. 16)

Evidently, the above-mentioned authorities failed to examine the institution of caste system in the light of progressive development of a society according to which an institution which was useful at one time can become retrogressive afterwards. Because of this, they were either all praise or all condemnation for the Indian caste system. As opposed to such judgements, it is therefore worth noting what others have said on the basis of studying the institution in a historical perspective. Thus, looking at the evolution of the Indian caste system in the light of India's historical development, S. A. Dange wrote about the period when the institution was useful to Indian society (cf. *India from primitive communism to slavery*, People's Publishing House Ltd., New Delhi, March 1955, pp. xii, xviii—xix):

"The household community with the growth in population and development of production soon breaks up and grows into a village community. The slave groups become the *Heena Jatis* of the village community and the members of the household community taking to different trades according to their choice or skill or need become crystallised into different castes. In this process the *Varnas* lose their validity and castes replace them in the structure of the new organisation—the village community....

The coming into existence of the village community, with its hereditary division of labour by castes, developed the productive powers of society. Each caste and sub-caste, specialising in its own craft, developed it to the highest pitch possible for handicrafts. On the basis of the growth of productivity, also grew the surplus extracted by the ruling classes and the state. From this surplus were maintained the public works of irrigation and also those monuments of architecture, as have been preserved to us. The rich culture, the flowering of art and literature of the Gupta Empire, the vast irrigation works (one of the water works of Kashmir was built by an untouchable builder-engineer), the big trade and commerce of the mediaeval eras—all were the achievements of our productive powers developed by the village community, its agriculture and handicrafts and the special projection of the latter in the towns of the mediaeval kingships."

But the institutions of village community and the caste systems also contained germs of obstruction to future development of India, for they did not give scope for the productive forces to develop further and for new relations of production to be inaugurated as demanded by the society in later times. Therefore, describing the situation when the village community system was being destroyed in the early years of British rule in India, Marx remarked (*loc. cit.* 48):

"Now, sickening as it must be to human feeling to witness those myriads of industrious patriarchal and inoffensive social organisations disorganised and dissolved into their units, thrown into a sea of woes, and their individual members losing at the same time their ancient form of civilisation, and their hereditary means of subsistence, we must not forget that these idyllic village communities, inoffensive though they may appear, had always been the solid foundation of Oriental despotism, that they restrained the human mind within the smallest possible compass, making it the unresisting tool of superstition, enslaving it beneath traditional rules, depriving it of all grandeur and historical energies. We must not forget the barbarian egotism which, concentrating on some miserable patch of land, had quietly witnessed the ruin of empires, the perpetration of unspeakable cruelties, the massacre of the population of large towns with no other consideration bestowed upon them than on natural events, itself the helpless prey of an aggressor who deigned to notice it at all. We must not forget that this undignified, stagnatory, and vegetative life, that this passive sort of existence evoked on the other part, in contradistinction, wild, aimless, unbounded forces of destruction and rendered murder itself a religious rite in Hindustan. We must not forget that these little communities were contaminated by distinctions of caste and by slavery, that they subjugated man to external circumstances, instead of elevating man the sovereign of circumstances, that they transformed a self-developing social state into never changing natural destiny, and thus brought about a brutalising worship of nature, exhibiting its degradation in the fact that man, the sovereign of nature, fell down on his knees in adoration of *Hanuman*, the monkey, and *Sabbala* the cow.

England, it is true, in causing a social revolution in Hindustan, was actuated only by the vilest interests, and was stupid in her manner of enforcing them. But that is not the question. The question is, can mankind fulfil its destiny without a fundamental revolution in the social state of Asia? If not, whatever may have been the crime of England she was the unconscious tool of history in bringing about that revolution."

80 See, for instance, Richard Fick's *Die Sociale Gliederung im Nordöstlichen Indien zu Buddha's Zeit* (*loc. cit.* 77), p. 20 ff.; U. N. Ghoshal's *Social Conditions* in "The Age of Imperial Kanauj" (*loc. cit.* 12), p. 373; Vincent A.

Smith's *The Oxford History of India*. Oxford at the Clarendon Press, 1923, p. 8 ff.; *loc. cit.* 27; *loc. cit.* 59; etc.

81 See, for instance, E. A. Gait's *Caste* in the "Encyclopaedia of Religion and Ethics", edited by James Hastings and John A. Selbie, New York, 1911; L. S. S. O'Malley's *Indian Caste Customs,* Cambridge University Press, Great Britain, 1932; etc. For interesting details regarding the little known Khoja sect in the Moslem community, one may consult Syed Mujtaba Ali's *The Origin of the Khojāhs and their Religious Life Today*, Buchdruckerei Richard Mayr, Würzburg, Germany, 1936.

82 Suleykin, D. A.—*Basic Questions on the Periodisation of Ancient Indian History*— Д. А. Сулейкин — Основные вопросы периодизации истории древней „Индии" — Учёные записки Тихоокеанского института, том II, Изд. АН СССР, Москва-Ленинград 1949, стр. 177—192.

83 *loc. cit.* 12; *loc. cit.* 27; *loc. cit.* 46; *loc. cit.* 53; *loc. cit.* 55; *loc. cit.* 58; *loc. cit.* 66; *loc. cit.* 77; etc.

84 *loc. cit.* 17, p. 172 ff

85 This point was particularly stressed by Fick in *loc. cit.* 77; Senart in *loc. cit.* 59; Oldenberg in *loc. cit.* 60; Jolly in *loc. cit.* 66.

86 *loc. cit.* 68, Vol. II, Part 1 (1941), Chapter II, etc.

87 *loc. cit.* 17; *loc. cit.* 46; etc.

88 *loc. cit.* 53; *loc. cit.* 58; etc.

89 *Manusmrti*, translated by Georg Bühler under the title "The Laws of Manu," Oxford at the Clarendon Press, 1886, Chapter X, *slokas* 81—82.

90 *ibid.*, Chapter X, *sloka* 95

91 *ibid.*, Chapter X, *slokas* 83, 85

92 *ibid.*, Chapter X, *slokas* 98—100

93 *ibid.*, Chapter X, *slokas* 123, 121

94 See, for instance, *loc. cit.* 68, Vol. II, Part 1 (1941), Chapters III and IV, which give details regarding the duties, disabilities and privileges of the usurping, producing and serving castes, as reflected by the injunctions given for each *varna* by different authorities on *Dharmaśāstra.*

95 *loc. cit.* 17; *loc. cit.* 24; *loc. cit.* 68, Vol. II, Part 1 (1941), Chapters II—IV; etc.

96 *loc. cit.* 17, p. 245

97 *loc. cit.* 68, Vol. II, Part 1 (1941), Chapters III and IV, Vol. IV (1953), Chapters I—VI

98 *loc. cit.* 17, pp. 38—39, 61, 110—111, 124, 132, 238, etc.

99 *loc. cit.* 89, Chapter X, *slokas* 76, 79, Chapter I, *sloka* 91

100 *ibid.*, Chapter I, *sloka* 100, Chapter IX, *sloka* 418, Chapter X, *sloka* 129

101 *ibid.*, Chapter I, *slokas* 88—91, Chapter II, *slokas* 31—32, Chapter IV, *slokas* 3, 60—61, 253—254, Chapter VII, *slokas* 24, 80—85, 113—122, 127—138, Chapter VIII, *slokas* 398—399, 410—418, Chapter X, *slokas* 74—129; etc.

102 See, for instance, *loc. cit.* 68 (4 volumes).

103 *loc. cit.* 17; *loc. cit.* 24; *loc. cit.* 29; etc.

104 Marx, Karl — *Grundrisse der Kritik der politischen Ökonomie (Rohentwurf): 1857—1858*, Dietz Verlag, Berlin, 1953, pp. 399—400.

105 Shelvanker, K. S.—*The Problem of India*, Penguin Books, England, 1943, pp. 77—80.
106 Takahashi, H. K.—*A Contribution to the Discussion* in "The Transition from Feudalism to Capitalism: A Symposium," An Arena Publication, Fore Publications Ltd., London, 1954, p. 35.
107 Majumdar, R. C.; Raychaudhuri, H. C.; Datta, Kalikinkar—*An Advanced History of India*, MacMillan, London, 1953, p. 395.
108 *loc. cit.* 9, Vol. I, pp. 188, 182—183
109 *loc. cit.* 17, p. 187
110 Moreland, W. H.—*The Agrarian System of Moslem India*, 1929, p. 12; quoted in *loc. cit.* 36, pp. 78—79.
111 *loc. cit.* 107, p. 395, etc.
112 See, for instance, *ibid.*, pp. 330, 333, 394, etc.; *loc. cit.* 36, pp. 79—81; W. H. Moreland's *From Akbar to Aurangzeb*, 1923, p. 272 ff.; etc.
113 *loc. cit.* 107, pp. 307—308; Vincent A. Smith's *The Oxford History of India* (*loc. cit.* 80), p. 248; Khwājah Nīzāmuddīn Ahmad's *The Tabaqāt-i-Akbarī*, translated by B. De, Bibliotheca Indica, No. 225, Asiatic Soc. of Bengal, Calcutta, 1927, pp. 168—169; etc.
114 Aḥmad, Khwājah Nizāmuddīn—*The Tabaqāt-i-Akbarī*, translated by B. De, Bibliotheca Indica, No. 225, Asiatic Soc. of Bengal, Calcutta, 1927, p. 169.
115 *loc. cit.* 107, pp. 312—313
116 *ibid.*, p. 314
117 *ibid.*, p. 319
118 *ibid.*, p. 330
119 *ibid.*, pp. 335, 340
120 *ibid.*, p. 341
121 *ibid.*, p. 425
122 Smith, Vincent A.—*The Oxford History of India*, Oxford at the Clarendon Press, 1923, p. 327.
123 *loc. cit.* 3, p. 457
124 *ibid.*, p. 455
125 Anonymous—*On the Formation of the Hindustani Nationality and the Problems of its National Language*, "*Indian Literature*," People's Publishing House, Bombay, 1953, No. I, p. 5.
126 Sharma, Sri Ram—*Mughal Government and Administration*, Hind Kitabs Limited, Bombay, 1951, p. 260.
127 *loc. cit.* 3, p. 456
128 *ibid.*, p. 463
129 *loc. cit.* 1
130 *loc. cit.* 36, p. 83
131 *loc. cit.* 122, p. 296
132 *loc. cit.* 123, p. 457
133 *ibid.*, p. 458
134 *loc. cit.* 36, p. 75
135 *loc. cit.* 24, p. 316
136 *loc. cit.* 126, pp. 83—84

137 See, for instance, *loc. cit.* 13, pp. 329—330; *loc. cit.* 15, pp. 586—590; *loc. cit.* 24, p. 316; *The Age of Imperial Kanauj*, edited by R. C. Majumdar and A. D. Pusalkar (*loc. cit.* 12), pp. 399—403; etc.
138 *loc. cit.* 107, pp. 397—398, 572, 575, etc.; *loc. cit.* 24, pp. 322—325; etc.
139 *loc. cit.* 107, p. 571
140 Anonymous—*Geschichte Indiens*, "Große Sowjet-Enzyklopädie", Rütten & Loening, Berlin, 1955, p. 23.
141 Engels, F.—*Anti-Dühring*, Foreign Languages Publishing House, Moscow, 1947, p. 463.
142 Marx, Karl—*Capital: A Critique of Political Economy*, Charles H. Kerr & Co., Chicago, 1909, Vol. III, p. 701.
143 *loc. cit.* 24, p. 10
144 *ibid.*, p. 11
145 Rawlinson, H. G.—*The Rise of the Marāthā Empire* in "The Cambridge History of India: The Mughul Period", Cambridge at the University Press, Vol. IV, 1937, p. 426
146 Sarkar, Jadunath—*Shivaji and His Times*, M. C. Sarkar & Sons, Calcutta, 1919, pp. 13—14
147 *loc. cit.* 107, p. 205
148 Raghavendrachar, H. N.—*Madhva in* "History of Philosophy: Eastern and Western", edited by S. Radhakrishnan, George Allen & Unwin Ltd., London, 1952, Vol. I, p. 336.
149 Bhatt, Govindlal Hargovind—*Vallabha* in "History of Philosophy: Eastern and Western" (*loc. cit.* 148), Vol. I, p. 356.
150 Eliot, Sir Charles—*Hinduism and Buddhism*, Routledge & Kegan Paul Ltd., London, 1954, Vol. II, p. 243, n 2.
151 Tagore, Rabindranath—*One Hundred Poems of Kabir*, India Society, London, 1914.
152 Chari, P. N. Srinivasa—*Rāmānuja in* "History of Philosophy: Eastern and Western" (*loc. cit.* 148), Vol. I, p. 320.
153 *loc. cit.* 107, p. 405
154 *ibid.*, p. 406
155 *loc. cit.* 150, Vol. II, p. 272
156 *ibid.*, Vol. II, p. 254
157 For details regarding the nature of this movement, its social basis, and its leaders, etc., see, for instance, D. Mishew's *The Bulgarians in the Past*, Librairie Centrale des Nationalités, Lausanne, 1919, p. 60 ff; Jack Lindsay's *Byzantium into Europe*, The Bodley Head, London, 1952, pp. 244—253; etc.
158 Tawney, R. H.—*Religion and the Rise of Capitalism*, Pelican Books, England, 1948, p. 120.
159 Anonymous—*Politische Ökonomie: Lehrbuch*, Akademie der Wissenschaften der UdSSR, Institut für Ökonomie, Dietz Verlag, Berlin, 1955, pp. 71—72.
160 *loc. cit.* 24, p. 327 ff., p. 404 ff.
161 *loc. cit.* 150, Vol. II, p. 245
162 *ibid.*, Vol. II, p. 245
163 *loc. cit.* 149, p. 356

164 See, for instance, *loc. cit.* 24, Chapter XIV; *loc. cit.* 36, Chapter X; *loc. cit.* 107, p. 377 ff.; etc.
165 Sen, Dinesh Chandra—*The History of the Bengali Language and Literature*, Calcutta University Press, 1911.
166 *loc. cit.* 150, Vol. II, p. 245
167 *ibid.*, Vol. II, p. 245
168 *loc. cit.* 107, p. 407
169 *ibid.*, p. 407
170 *loc. cit.* 150, Vol. II, p. 258
171 *loc. cit.* 165, p. 170
172 See, for instance, A. M. Djakow's *Zur Frage der nationalen Zusammensetzung der Bevölkerung Indiens*, German translation of the study published in Wissenschaftliche Aufzeichnungen des Fernöstlichen Instituts, Izd. Adad. Nauk., Moscau/Leningrad, 1947, S. 223—330.
173 Gover—*The Folk-songs of Southern India*, Trübner & Co., London, 1872, p. 275.
174 *loc. cit.* 151
175 *loc. cit.* 150, Vol. II, p. 251
176 Diakov, A.—*Historical Significance of Sectarian Movements in India in the XV—XVII Centuries*, Papers presented by the Soviet Delegates at the XXIII. International Congress of Orientalists at Cambridge in 1954, Moscow, 1954, pp. 19—20.
177 *loc. cit.* 125, p. 3
178 *ibid.*, p. 2
179 loc. cit. 24, pp. 316—317, 318
180 *loc. cit.* 125, p. 4
181 *ibid.*, p. 5
182 Haig, Sir Wolseley—*Sher Shāh and the Sūr Dynasty. The Return of Humāyūn.* Chapter III in "The Cambridge History of India: The Mughul Period," Cambridge at the University Press, Vol. IV, 1937, p. 57.
183 Vidyalankar, Satyaketu—*Pataliputra ki katha*, Allahabad, 1949, p. 652; quoted in *loc. cit.* 125, p. 5.
184 *loc. cit.* 125, p. 6
185 *loc. cit.* 182, p. 57
186 *loc. cit.* 126, p. 268
187 loc. cit. 107, pp. 574—575
188 *ibid.*, p. 570
189 *ibid.*, p. 570
190 Catrou, F. F.—*The General history of the Mogol Empire from it's Foundation by Tamerlane to the late Emperor Orangzeb: Extracted from the Memoirs of M. Manouchi, A Venetian, and Chief Physician* to Orangzeb *for above Forty Years*, Jonah Bowyer, London, 1709, p. 229.
191 *loc. cit.* 24, p. 319
192 *loc. cit.* 107, p. 375
193 loc. *cit.* 24, p. 317
194 *loc. cit.* 107, pp. 397, 572
195 *ibid.*, p. 382

196 *ibid.*, pp. 380, 402—403
197 Sarkar, Jadunath—*History of Aurangzeb*, M. C. Sarkar & Sons, Calcutta, 1916, Vol. III, pp. 348—349.
198 *loc. cit.* 114, p. 170
199 *ibid.*, p. 170
200 *loc. cit.* 107, p. 318
201 *ibid.*, pp. 354, 402
202 *ibid.*, p. 354
203 *loc. cit.* 165, pp. 12, 14, 170, 184, 201, 203, etc.
204 *loc. cit.* 107, p. 402
205 *ibid.*, p. 402
206 *ibid.*, p. 402
207 Taylor, Meadows—*Manual of the History of India*, Longmans, London, 1895; quoted in *loc. cit.* 122, p. 296
208 Quoted in *loc. cit.* 107, p. 403
209 *loc. cit.* 1
210 *loc. cit.* 126, p. 65
211 *loc. cit.* 1
212 *loc. cit.* 126, p. 180
213 *ibid.*, pp. 168—169
214 *loc. cit.* 122, p. 357 ff.
215 *loc. cit.* 190, p. 151
216 *ibid.*, p. 154
217 See, for instance, *Túzak-i-Jahāngīri*, English Translation by W. H. Lowe, Asiatic Society of Bengal, Calcutta, "Bibliotheca Indica" Series, 1889.
218 *loc. cit.* 122, p. 388
219 *loc. cit.* 190, p. 219
220 *ibid.*, p. 220
221 *loc. cit.* 122, p. 370
222 *loc. cit.* 126, p. 5
223 Smith, Vincent A.—*Akbar: The Great Mogul*, Oxford at the Clarendon Press, 1919, p. 411.
224 Panth, D.—*The Commercial Policy of the Moguls*, Bombay, 1930, p. 109 ff.
225 *ibid.*, p. 165
226 *ibid.*, p. 165 ff.
227 *ibid.*, pp. 195, 197
228 *ibid.*, p. 211
229 *loc. cit.* 2, p. 18; etc.
230 *loc. cit.* 3, p. 450
231 *loc. cit.* 224, p. 211
232 *loc. cit.* 107, p. 479
233 *loc. cit.* 125, p. 6
234 *ibid.*, p. 8
235 *loc. cit.* 107, pp. 572—574
236 *loc. cit.* 24, p. 320
237 Quoted in *loc. cit.* 24, p. 321.

238 *loc. cit.* 24, pp. 321—322
239 *ibid.*, pp. 322—325
240 *ibid.*, p. 320
241 *loc. cit.* 107, p. 575
242 *ibid.*, p. 574
243 *loc. cit.* 24, p. 324
244 *loc. cit.* 125, p. 9
245 *loc. cit.* 107, p. 575
246 See, for instance, *loc. cit.* 13, pp. 308—312, 329—330, etc.; *loc. cit.* 15, pp. 589—592, 615—616, 626—627, etc.; *The Age of Imperial Kanauj* (*loc. cit.* 12), pp. 401—404, 411 ff.; *loc. cit.* 24, pp. 128, 134—136, 320, etc.; etc.
247 *loc. cit.* 126, p. 148
248 *loc. cit.* 107, p. 375
249 *loc. cit.* 24, p. 306
250 Burn, Sir Richard—*Jahāngīr* in "The Cambridge History of India: The Mughul Period", Cambridge at the University Press, Vol. IV, 1937, p. 162.
251 *loc. cit.* 176, p. 20
252 Quoted in *loc. cit.* 24, p. 324.
253 *loc. cit.* 24, p. 324
254 *loc. cit.* 250, p. 162
255 *ibid.*, p. 162
256 *ibid.*, p. 162
257 Sarkar, Sir Jadunath—*Aurangzīb* in "The Cambridge History of India: The Mughul Period," Cambridge at the University Press, Vol. IV, 1937, p. 308.
258 *ibid.*, p. 308
259 *loc. cit.* 24, p. 321
260 *loc. cit.* 107, p. 383
261 Mill, James—*The History of British India*, James Madden, London, 1858, Vol. III, p. 60.
262 *loc. cit.* 3, p. 466
263 *loc. cit.* 261, Vol. I, p. 24
264 *ibid.*, pp. 24—25
265 Quoted in *loc. cit.* 107, p. 639.
266 *ibid.*, p. 639
267 *loc. cit.* 261, Vol. I, p. 55, n 2
268 *ibid.*, Vol. I, p. 85
269 *ibid.*, Vol. I, p. 85
270 *ibid.*, Vol. I, p. 101, n 1
271 Thornton, Edward—*A Gazetteer of the Territories under the Government of the East India Company and of the Native States on the Continent of India*, Wm. H. Allen & Co., London, 1854, Vol. I, p. 241.
272 *loc. cit.* 107, pp. 566—567
273 *loc. cit.* 3, p. 455
274 *ibid.*, pp. 455—456
275 *ibid.*, p. 467
276 *ibid.*, p. 467

277 Dutt, R. Palme—*India Today*, People's Publishing House, Bombay, 1949, pp. 95—96.
278 *loc. cit.* 125, pp. 8—9
279 *loc. cit.* 107, p. 573
280 Dobb, Maurice—*Studies in the Development of Capitalism*, George Routledge & Sons Ltd., London, 1946, pp. 18, 138, etc.
281 *loc. cit.* 125, p. 9
282 Sinha, Narendra, K.—*The Economic History of Bengal: From Plassey to the Permanent Settlement*, Vol. I, Das Gupta & Sons, Calcutta, 1956, p. 7.
283 Quoted in *loc. cit.* 107, p. 576
284 *loc. cit.* 107, p. 576
285 *loc. cit.* 261, Vol. I, p. 89
286 One may consult *loc. cit.* 282, Appendix A, for some interesting details regarding "The Armenian Traders in Bengal," for instance.
287 Muir, Ramsay—*The Making of British India: 1756—1858*, Longmans, Green & Co., London, 1917, p. 58.
288 Macaulay, T. B.—*Lord Clive* in "Critical and Historical Essays," Vol. IV, Tauchnitz, Leipzig, Vol. No. CLXXXVIII.
289 Anonymous—*Historical Sketch on the Taxes on the English Commerce in Bengal from 1633 until 1820*, Mss. Eur. D. 283 in The Commonwealth Office Library, London, p. 137.
290 *loc. cit.* 140, p. 25
291 *loc. cit.* 3, p. 470
292 *ibid.*, p. 470
293 *ibid.*, p. 470
294 Sarkar, Jadunath—*History of Aurangzib*, Longmans, Green & Co., London, 1924, Vol. V, p. 452.
295 *loc. cit.* 3, p. 471
296 *loc. cit.* 126, p. 65
297 *ibid.*, p. 59
298 *ibid.*, p. 65
299 *ibid.*, p. 65 ff.
300 *loc. cit.* 140, p. 26 (Translation by the writer)
301 *loc. cit.* 146, p. 18
302 *loc. cit.* 1
303 *ibid.*
304 *ibid.*
305 *loc. cit.* 140, pp. 26—27 (Translation by the writer). For details, one may consult Joseph Davey Cunningham's *A History of the Sikhs from the Origin of the Nation to the Battles of the Sutlej*, John Murray, London, 1849.
306 *loc. cit.* 140, pp. 27—28 (Translation by the writer)
307 *loc. cit.* 1
308 Quoted in *loc. cit.* 107, p. 540.
309 Quoted in *loc. cit.* 107, pp. 540—541.
310 Quoted in *loc. cit.* 107, p. 534.

311 Marx, Karl—*The Future Results of British Rule in India,* New York Daily Tribune, August 8, 1853.
312 Quoted in *loc. cit.* 107, p. 638.
313 Quoted in *loc. cit.* 107, pp. 638—639.
314 Quoted in *loc. cit.* 107, p. 639.
315 *loc. cit.* 3, p. 450
316 Quoted in *loc. cit.* 107, p. 642.
317 Quoted in *loc. cit.* 107, p. 511.
318 *loc. cit.* 146, p. 20
319 *loc. cit.* 287, pp. 40—41
320 *ibid.*, p. 40
321 *loc. cit.* 107, pp. 655—665
322 *loc. cit.* 287, pp. 58—59
323 *loc. cit.* 107, p. 691
324 Quoted in *loc. cit.* 107, p. 688.
325 *loc. cit.* 107, p. 712
326 *ibid.*, p. 714
327 *ibid.*, p. 714
328 Quoted in *loc. cit.* 107, p. 714.
329 Quoted in *loc. cit.* 107, p. 714.
330 Dutt, Romesh—*The Economic History of India under Early British Rule,* Routledge & Kegan Paul Ltd., London, 1950, p. 12.
331 *loc. cit.* 107, p. 725
332 *loc. cit.* 287, p. 340
333 Quoted in *loc. cit.* 107, p. 768.
334 *loc. cit.* 1
335 Quoted by W. M. Torrens in his book entitled *Empire in Asia—How We Came by It: A Book of Confessions,* Trübner & Co., London, 1872, p. 358.
336 Marx, Karl—*The Native States,* New York Daily Tribune, July 25, 1853.
337 Marx, Karl—*The East India Company,* New York Daily Tribune, July 11, 1853.

CHAPTER 5

COMPANY AS THE RULER

With reference to the British rule in India, beginning from the conquest of Bengal in 1757, Marx wrote in 1853:[1]

> "England has to fulfil a double mission in India: one destructive, and the other regenerating—the annihilation of old Asiatic society, and the laying the material foundations of Western society in Asia.
>
> Arabs, Turks, Tartars, Moguls, who had successively over-run India, soon became *Hinduised*, the barbarian conquerors being, by an eternal law of history, conquered themselves by the superior civilisation of their subjects. The British were the first conquerors superior, and therefore inaccessible to Hindu civilisation. They destroyed it by breaking up the native communities, uprooting the native industry, and by levelling all that was great and elevated in the native society. The historic pages of their rule in India report hardly anything beyond that destruction. The work of regeneration hardly transpires through a heap of ruins. Nevertheless it has begun."

What Marx characterized as the "regenerating" mission of England in India will be briefly stated in the next chapter while touching upon the interests of British industrial capital in India, for, as Marx indicated at the same time as writing the above lines, it was the need of British industrial capital that laid down "the material premises" for the regeneration of India. What will be discussed in this chapter is the "destructive" mission of England, which was essentially the role of the East India Company as the organized body of British merchant capital. This chapter will thus show *why* and *how,* along with the subjugation of different parts of India as the logical culmination of the cherished dreams of British merchant capital, the Company as the ruler devitalized India during its government over a hundred years in all, and led the people towards destitution.

It should, however, be mentioned at the outset that the following account by no means gives an exhaustive or even a complete picture of the activities of the East India Company as the ruler of India. New facts are constantly coming to light as a result of intensive researches into the social and economic history of India during those days. In recent times more and more Indian as well as foreign scholars are delving into the "true" story of the Company's role in Indian society after it became the master of the subcontinent. In the light of such researches some points made in this chapter have, or may in the future, become clearer and fully established, while some others may need modification in regard to their relative importance in unfolding the role of the Company in different parts of India. But, on the whole, it may be justified to state that, although based primarily on earlier researches, this chapter will provide a general description of the *modus operandi* of the Company to fulfil the governing desire of merchant capital and also to go beyond that in order to live on the conquered people as rent-receivers. Thus, on the one hand, this chapter will show how the English mercantile bourgeoisie with their moorings on the decadent feudal structure of their own society thrived on subjugated India, and, on the other, it will indicate how Indian society underwent a course of retrogression under the Company's rule with the forced destruction of its progressive forces and the disintegration of its economy.

1. Ruination of Artisans

With "the typical aim of the monopolist companies of Merchant Capital, to make a profit by securing a monopoly trade in the goods and products of an overseas country," as Palme Dutt wrote, the governing objective of the Company was "not the hunt for a market for British manufactures, but the endeavour to secure a supply of the products of India and the East Indies (especially spices, cotton goods and silk goods), which found a ready market in England and Europe, and could thus yield a rich profit on every successful expedition that could return with a supply."[2] But, until the Company usurped political power in India, the commercial transactions were faced with a grave difficulty. This was because, firstly, British industries in those days were poor in development and could not offer much to India in exchange for Indian goods, and, secondly, the woollen goods, which were virtually the only commodity of quality which the Company could offer, were not in any great demand in the tropical climate of India. So, in the pre-conquest days, while the "concessions" helped the Company much in "buying cheap," still its business had to be conducted mainly in exchange for silver which the English "obtained by the sale of the slaves in the West Indies and Spanish America."[3]

This situation underwent a qualitative change after the Company captured Bengal, and eventually the whole of India. Henceforth, "methods of power could be increasingly used to weight the balance of exchange and secure the maximum goods for the minimum payment."[4] As noted before, the European mercantile bourgeoisie never drew a sharp margin between trade and plunder; the original Merchant Adventurers of England often combined trade with piracy. Now, whatever margin there had been between trade and plunder began to grow conspicuously thin. The merchants were now rulers. Thus, being "favourably placed in relation to the individual producer, whether weaver or peasant, to dictate terms favourably to himself," the Company was now "able to throw the sword into the scales to secure a bargain which abandoned all pretence of equality of exchange."[5] The policy of the Company was established to extract from the Indian producers as much as possible, and to give them in return virtually nothing or so meagre a remuneration that they ultimately became unable to maintain even the reproductive rate of the economy. This decision of the Company, pursued with unwavering resolution, was first put into practice in Bengal after 1757, and in the course of time it spread all over India with the subjugation of her territory, directly or indirectly, by the Company.

In the beginning, the artisans were most drastically affected by this policy. Export of cotton and silk goods from India, "which no western looms could rival,"[6] was then the main item of the Company's trade. So, orders were sent out to force Indian artisans to work in the Company's factories. On frequent occasions the artisans were not allowed to leave the "factory" until they had fulfilled the commitments they were obliged to undertake by intimidation and oppression. Also, the Commercial Residents of the Company were legally vested with extensive powers over villages and communities of Indian weavers to make them work for the Company irrespective of what they received in return. In many places it became a general rule that the artisans could not undertake work for anyone other than the Company. In short, the artisans were turned into bond slaves of the Company.

How terrible were the sufferings of the Indian artisans under the Company's rule can be glimpsed from the following extract from the pen of an English merchant "who saw things with his own eyes."

> "Inconceivable oppressions and hardships have been practised towards the poor manufacturers and workmen of the Country, who are, in fact, monopolized by the Company as so many slaves. ... Various and innumerable are the methods of oppressing the poor weavers, which are duly practised by the Company's agents and *gomastas* [Indian sub-agents] in the country; such as by fines, imprisonments, floggings, forcing bonds from them, etc., by which the number of weavers in the country has been greatly decreased. ...
>
> In this situation of things, as the trade of the Company increased, and with it the inland trade of individuals also in a much greater proportion, those evils, which at first were scarcely felt, became at last universal throughout the Bengal provinces: and it may with truth be now said, that the whole inland trade of the country, as at present conducted, and that of the Company's investment for Europe in a more peculiar degree, has been one continued scene of oppression: the banefull effects of which are severely felt by every weaver and manufacturer in the country, every article produced being made a monopoly; in which the English, with their *banyans* [Indian agents] and black *gomastas,* arbitrarily decide what quantities of good, each manufacturer shall deliver, and the *prices* he shall receive for them. ...
>
> But for the better understanding of the nature of these oppressions, it may not be improper to explain the methods of providing an *investment* of piece

goods, as conducted either by the Export-warehouse-keeper and the Company's servants at the subordinate factories, on the Company's account, or by the English gentlemen in the service of the Company, as their own private ventures. In either case, factors, or agents called *gomastas* are engaged at monthly wages by the gentleman's *banyan*. These are dispatched, with a *parwana* (authorisation) from the Governor of Calcutta, or the chief of a Subordinate (subordinate factory) to the *zemindar* [Indian revenue-farmer] of the district where the purchases are intended to be made; directing him not to impede their business, but to give them every assistance in his power. Generally a proportion of such goods as it is imagined can be sold advantageously in the said districts, are also dispatched, with the Company's *dastak*, and consigned to these *gomastas*. Upon the *gomasta's* arrival at the *aurang*, or manufacturing town, he fixes upon a habitation, which he calls his *kachari*; to which, by his *peons* and *harkaras* he summons the brokers, together with the weavers; whom he makes to sign a bond for the delivery of a certain quantity of goods, at a certain time and price, and pays them a part of the money in advance. The assent of the poor weaver is in general not deemed necessary, for the *gomastas*, when employed on the Company's investment, frequently make them sign what they please; and upon the weavers refusing to take the money offered, it has been known that they have had it tied to their girdles, and then have been sent away with a flogging. The brokers, who are usually and necessarily employed by the *gomastas*, as knowing and having accounts with all the weavers of the respective districts, are often as much oppressed as the weavers; but when separately employed they always make the latter pay for it. A number of these weavers are generally also registered in the books of the Company's *gomastas*, and not permitted to work for any others; being transferred from one to another as so many slaves, subject to the tyranny and roguery of every succeeding *gomasta*. The cloth, when made, is collected in a warehouse for the purpose, called a *khatta*; where it is kept marked with the weaver's name, till it is convenient for the *gomasta* to hold a *khatta*, as the term is, for assorting and fixing the price of each piece. The roguery practised in this department is beyond imagination, but all terminates in the defrauding of the poor weaver; for the prices which the Company's *gomastas* fix upon the goods, are in all places at least fifteen per cent, and in some even forty per cent less than the goods so manufactured would sell for in the public Bazar, or market, upon a free sale. The weaver, therefore, desirous of obtaining the just price of his labour, frequently attempts to sell his cloth privately to others, particularly to the Dutch and French *gomastas*, who are always ready to receive it. This occasions the English Company's *gomasta* to set his peons over the weaver to watch him, and not infrequently to cut the piece out of the loom when nearly finished. ...

Weavers, also, upon their inability to perform such agreements as have been forced upon them by the Company's agents, universally known in Bengal by the name of Mutchulcahs, have had their goods seized and sold on the spot to make good the deficiency; and the winders of raw silk, called Nagoads, have been treated also with such injustice, that instances have been known of their cutting off their thumbs to prevent their being forced to wind silk."[7]

The above account refers particularly to the Subah of Bengal, where the oppression of the English merchants in the first phase of their victorious intoxication was probably most severe. The puppet Nawab of Bengal complained to the Company's Governor in Calcutta in a Memorandum, dated May 1762:[8]

"They forcibly take away the goods and commodities of the Reiats [peasants], merchants, etc., for a fourth part of their value; and by ways of violence and oppressions they oblige the Reiats, etc., to give five rupees for goods which are worth but one rupee."

Thus, the ever-present desire of the merchant bourgeoisie–to buy cheap and sell dear–attained consummation when the Company became the master of Bengal. And this motto was established with full vigour whenever a new patch of territory came under the Company's rule, and from wherever it could obtain its exportable goods. The result was obvious. In 1834–35, the Governor-General of the Company reported to London:[9]

"The misery hardly finds a parallel in the history of commerce. The bones of the cotton-weavers are bleaching the plains of India."

2. Liquidation of Traders

Along with thus turning the Indian artisans "out of this 'temporal' world," as Marx remarked caustically,[10] proceeded the liquidation of the Indian merchants. Monopolizing Indian products for the English meant that the Indian merchants could no longer survive. Only those could maintain their profession who acquiesced in becoming the underlings of the Company or of its servants engaged in private inland trade in India or of the private English merchants residing in India for the same purpose. Otherwise, they had to find a new source of livelihood. Not only were the Indian merchants prohibited from buying commodities directly from the producers, which were monopolized by the English, but the agents of the Company and its servants forced such goods on the Indian merchants at a price higher than the prevailing one. These features, again, were most marked in the Subah of Bengal, where the Company and its servants had their first "taste of blood." In 1762, it was reported from the once prosperous district of Bakherganj in Bengal by one Sergeant Brego:[11]

> "A gentleman sends a Gomastah here to buy or sell; he immediately looks upon himself as sufficient to force every inhabitant either to buy his goods or sell him theirs; and on refusal (in case of non-capacity) a flogging or confinement immediately ensues. This is not sufficient even when willing, but a second force is made use of, which is to engross the different branches of trade to themselves, and not to suffer any person buy or sell the articles they trade in; and if the country people do it, then a repetition of their authority is put in practice; and again, what things they purchease, they think the least they can do is to take them for a considerable deal less than another merchant, and oftentimes refuse paying that; and my interfering occasions an immediate complaint. These, and many other oppressions more than can be related, which are daily used by the Bengal Gomastahs, is the reason that this place is growing destitute of inhabitants; every day numbers leave the town to seek a residence more safe, and the very markets, which before afforded plenty, do hardly now produce anything of use, ..."

In the same year, the Collector of Dacca, also previously a very prosperous district in Bengal, wrote to the Governor of the Company in Calcutta:[12]

> "In the first place, a number of merchants have made interest with the people of the factory, hoist English colours on their boats, and carry away their goods under the pretence of their being English property, by which means the Shah-bunder and other customs are greatly determined. Secondly, the Gomastahs of Luckypoor and Dacca factories oblige the merchants, etc., to take tobacco, cotton, iron, and sundry other things, at a price exceeding that of the bazaar [market], and then extort the money from them by force;

besides which they take diet money for the peons, and make them pay a fine for breaking their agreement. By these proceedings the Aurungs and other places are ruined."

Reporting on such activities of the English merchants and their Indian agents, Sergeant Bergo and the Collector of Dacca further noted that the agents did not pay rent for the lands they occupied and sometimes the English merchants hat even organized their own police force, which they sent to seize from the people whatever they wanted. As a result of such vandalism, many flourishing industrial places and market towns, like the two noted above, were ruined;[13] and the Indian merchants, who preferred to remain independent and not become accomplices of the Company or its official or the other English merchants in their nefarious deeds, had to give up their traditional calling.

Besides this monopolization of trade by the Company, the Indian merchants suffered from another serious discrimination practised against them. This related to the customs duties to be paid in internal trade, of which mention has already been made. In Bengal, opposition to this discrimination took a political character, and revealed to the full the dishonest policy of the Company and the insatiable greed of its servants. It has therefore been described below in some detail.

It has been noted before that in India the servants of the Company in their personal capacity indulged in private inland trade. The Company connived at it, for it was an indirect source of income to the Company itself. The employees of the Company used to get a salary of only ten to twenty pounds per annum, and for that, while abroad, they had to sign a bond for good behaviour of five hundred to a thousand pounds, so that they would not aspire for positions like that of Samuel White and other rivals of the Company. Naturally, the employees looked at the salary as no more than a retaining fee, and from the beginning looked to make their income from private inland trade, which the terms of Indentures of the Company's servants show as fully recognized by the Company itself.[14] Needless to say, following the footsteps of the Company, its servants were also guided by the policy of buying cheap, and, as mentioned before, in the pre-conquest days, used to make gross misuse of the *dastak* or the free pass to which only the Company was entitled in order to carry its goods duty-free. Now, when the Company *de facto* became the ruler of the Subah of Bengal, its servants began to abuse the terms of trade on an even bigger scale. Openly as private traders they *claimed* exemption from duties, to which as laid down in the Treaty only the Company was entitled, and "began to trade in the articles which were before prohibited, and to interfere in the affairs of the country."[15]

Naturally this meant a marked depletion of the Treasury of Bengal. Therefore, Mir Kasim, who as an efficient *nawab* had replaced Mir Jafar in 1760 and had duly paid back to the Company and its servants all the "dues" which they claimed under the Company's "treaty" with Mir Jafar for making him the Nawab of Bengal, began to protest against this unjust curtailment of income to his treasury and the unfair discrimination displayed against the Indian merchants when in the same private trade the English officials could transport their goods duty-free. The situation was indeed very serious. As has been reported:[16]

> "The country traders were ruined; the Nawab's revenues declined; and the servants of the Company monopolised the trade and reared colossal fortunes."

So heavy was this oppression of the English merchants that Harry Verelst, who succeeded Clive as Governor in 1767, noted:[17]

> "A trade was carried on without payment of duties, in the prosecution of which infinite oppressions were committed. English agents or Gomastahs, not contented with injuring the people, trampled on the authority of government, binding and punishing the Nabob's officers whenever they presumed to interfere. This was the immediate cause of the war with Meer Cossim."

As mentioned above, eventually, receiving no redress from the Company, Mir Kasim fell out with the English and brought his own downfall. But, before his rupture with the English, Mir Kasim presented a strong remonstrance against the oppression of the Company's servants in a letter to the English Governor, dated 26th March, 1762:[18]

"From the factory of Calcutta to Cossim Bazar, Patna, and Dacca, all the English chiefs, with their Gomastahs, officers, and agents, in every district of the government, act as Collectors, Renters, Zemindars, and Taalookdars [estate-holders], and setting up the Company's colours, allow no power to my officers. And besides this, the Gomastahs and other servants in every district, in every Gunge [a market town], Perganah [part of a district], and Village, carry on a trade in oil, fish, straw, bamboos, rice, paddy, betel-nut, and other things; and every man with a Company's Dustuck in his hand regards himself as not less than the Company."

Indeed, such was the zeal of the servants of the Company to maintain their "rights" that "an Armenian merchant had been accused of purchasing a small quantity of saltpetre for the use of the Nawab; this was deemed an infringement of the Company's rights, and Ellis [the Company's representative at Patna, and great supporter of 'free trade' for the English only] had him seized and sent in irons to Calcutta."[19]

Undoubtedly, the complaints of Mir Kasim were just. Even Clive, who was no better than other servants of the Company in extorting "presents" from the "Nawab" of Bengal and himself was interested in the inland trade, noted:[20]

"The trade has been carried on by free merchants, acting as *gomastas* to the Company's servants, who, under the sanction of their names, have committed actions which make the name of the English stink in the nostrils of a Hindu or a Mussulman; and the Company's servants thanselves have interfered with the revenues of the Nawab, turned out and put in the officers of the government at pleasure, and made every one pay for their preferment."

Yet the Company paid no attention to Mir Kasim's complaints. So long as the subjugated *nawab* met its demands of "tributes" and "trading rights", the Company did not care a penny for the welfare of the State and had no objection to its servants fattening on the well-being of the Indians; on the contrary, it suited the Company to pay low emoluments to its officers.

Some servants of the Company, however, felt the seriousness of the situation, and realized that it could take a dangerous turn for the Company. Thus, Warren Hastings, then a Member of the Governor's Council at Calcutta, wrote to the Governor on the 25th of April, 1762:[21]

> "I beg leave to lay before you a grievance which loudly calls for redress, and will, unless duly attended to, render ineffectual any endeavours to create a firm and lasting harmony between the Nabob and the Company. I mean the oppression committed under the sanction of the English name. ... I have been surprised to meet with several English flags flying in places which I have passed, and on the river I do not believe I passed a boat without one. By whatever title they have been assumed (for I could trust to the information of my eyes without stopping to ask questions), I am sure their frequency can bode no good to the Nabob's revenues, the quiet of the country, or the honour of our nation, but evidently tends to lessen each of them. A party of Sepoys who were on the march before us afforded sufficient proofs of the rapacious and insolent spirit of those people where they are left to their own discretion. Many complaints against them were made me on the road, and most of the petty towns and Serais [inns] were deserted at our approach and the shops shut up from the apprehension of the same treatment from us. You are sensible, Sir, that it is from such little irregularities, too trivial perhaps for public complaint and continually repeated, that the country people are habituated to entertain the most unfavourable notions of our government."

Mir Kasim also further protested to the Governor in a letter written in May 1762:[22]

> "In every Perganah, every village, and every factory, they (the Company's Gomastahs) buy and sell salt, betel-nut, ghee, rice, straw, bamboos, fish, gunnies, ginger, sugar, tobacco, opium, and many other things, more than I can write, and which I think it needless to mention. ... The officers of every district have desisted from the exercise of their functions; so that by means of these oppressions, and my being deprived of my duties, I suffer a yearly loss of nearly twenty-five lakhs of Rupees [equivalent to £ 250,000—R. K. M.]"

Henry Vansittart, the Governor, realized how serious was the situation. Although he was "unwilling to give up an advantage which had been enjoyed by them, in a greater or less degree, for five or six years,"[23] he was wise enough to go to see the Nawab in Monghyr in order to settle matters amicably. The meeting resulted in an agreement, of which the most important points were: (a) the Company's right to trade duty-free to remain as before, but (b) by every other person duties would have to be paid according to rates to be particularly settled and annexed to the agreement.

The other officers of the Company, however, vehemently protested against such an agreement. Three of them declared in January 1763:[24]

> "... the regulations proposed by him (Vansittart) are dishonourable to us as Englishmen, and tend to the ruin of all public and private trade."

And they were in the majority, as the interests of almost all the English "gentlemen" were involved in the private inland trade. So, on the 1st of March, 1763, the General Council of the Company in Calcutta asserted that the Company's servants had the right to carry on internal trade duty-free; and that, as an acknowledgement to the Nawab, a duty of 2½ per cent would be paid on salt alone, instead of 9 per cent on all articles to which Vansittart had agreed.

On hearing of this decision, Mir Kasim did the most generous thing he could do at the time. He sacrificed his revenues and abolished all inland duties, so that as far as his government was concerned his subjects–the Indian merchants–might at least trade on equal terms with the servants of the Company and other English merchants. But the General Council again protested! They considered the repeal of all duties as a breach of faith towards the English nation, and they demanded that the duties on the Indian merchants be restored while they themselves would continue to enjoy the right of "free trade." Mill wrote on the occasion:[25]

> "The conduct of the Company's servants, upon this occassion, furnishes one of the most remarkable instances upon record, of the power of interest to extinguish all sense of justice, and even of shame."

Mir Kasim resisted the claim, and the result was war. Although he fought bravely, Mir Kasim was defeated by the superiority of British arms, and Mir Jafar—incompetent but obedient—was reinstated on the throne.*

The English went on enjoying the exclusive privilege in the internal trade. Even though the Directors of the Company prohibited it in their letter of the 8th February, 1765, their orders were disregarded by the Company's servants in India. So determined were they in pursuing this lucrative business that when Clive came to India for the third time in 1765, on the 18th of September of that year he "executed an indenture, jointly with other servants of the Company, to carry on the trade regardless of the orders of the Company."[26] But now this form of trade affected the interests of the Company itself, for from 1765 it had undertaken civil administration of the Subah of Bengal, and so the financial affluence of Bengal's Treasury was of direct concern to the Directors in London. Hence, in their letter of the 17th of May, 1766, they refused to sanction Clive's scheme for continuing with the trade under regulations framed by him. Yet this order was disregarded by the servants of the Company on the pretence of contracts formed and advances made, and the inland trade was kept going for another two years.

By then, the big merchants of India were practically wiped out in Bengal and elsewhere. When in the first decade of the nineteenth century Dr. Francis Buchanan, a medical officer of the Company, conducted socio-economic surveys in the Company's territories in India, both south and north, as ordered by the Governor-General of the Company and the Court of Directors from London, he hardly mentioned the presence of big Indian merchants.[27] Perhaps typical of the situation was the following account of the position in the district of Dinajpur in Bengal as obtained from his survey.[28]

---

* Indeed, this was always the dilemma of the foreign rulers in India. They could not use the efficient and at the same time loyal men for a long time. They had to choose, and obviously they chose the latter, resulting in misery and misrule of the people.

"A great portion of the trade of the District had passed from the hands of native traders to that of the Company. There were no longer any Saudagars or great native merchants in the District. 'One family, indeed, has acquired immense wealth in that line, and for nine generations the forefathers of Baidyanath Mandal carried on an extensive commerce with great reputation and propriety. The present head of the family has given up trade, has made large purchases of land, and is just as much despised as his forefathers were respected.'

Smaller merchants, called Mahajans, with capitals from Rs. 2000 to Rs. 25,000 [equivalent to £ 200 to £ 2,500--R. K. M.], residing in the District, exported rice, sugar, molasses, oil, and tobacco, and imported salt, cotton, metals, and spices. The whole number of fixed shops in the District did not amount to 2000, but open markets were numerous. Petty traders were called Paikars. Gold had become scarce, the Kuldar Rupee of Calcutta was the usual currency, and Cowrie shells were largely used."

Gone were the days of prosperity and mounting influence of the Indian merchants. Henceforth, they were allowed to exist only as petty intermediaries between the English and the Indian artisans and peasants, in the form of *baniyans* and *gomastahs* of the former. The future of the independent development of the Indian mercantile class was thus cut short by the Company and its servants because of their insatiable greed.

On the other hand, taking its birth in the womb of English merchant capital in India, from the time it came into the world this "colonial" variety of Indian merchants had a stunted and abnormal growth. Subservient to the needs of the English, as against those of the Indians (the two could not be reconciled), these *baniyans* and *gomastahs* could prosper only through roguery and anti-popular activities. "Righteous" indignation of the English "reformers" has often fallen on their heads, though of course it is seldom made clear that these creatures were the first product of the monstrous machine of colonial exploitation introduced by the Company in India.

3. Reforms or Retrogression?

Simultaneously with the liquidation of Indian traders and the ruination of artisans went the introduction of some "reform measures" in India. Complete chaos and anarchy are not conducive to maintaining the interests of any ruling power in any country. Therefore, during the Company's rule in India, while on the one hand the means of extracting the wealth and resources of the country were piled one upon the other and caused extreme misery and oppression to the Indian people (beginning with the destruction of the previously growing class of merchants and artisans to the disintegration of India's economic life as will be discussed later in this chapter), on the other hand some "reform measures" were introduced in order to stabilize the Company's rule in all aspects of Indian life. But, significantly enough, two of the most important "reform measures" taken in the last quarter of the eighteenth century and the early part of the nineteenth century supported, directly or indirectly, the decadent forces in society.

When the Company emerged as the ruling power, first in the Subah of Bengal and then, in due course, all over India, Indian society was in the transitional phase from feudalism to the next higher stage in social development. Progressive forces were then jostling against decadent ones, and naturally, therefore, it would have been difficult for some foreigners to have had a clear insight at once into the workings of the social forces in Indian society at that time. Hence, it remains an open question whether the "reform measures" introduced at the onset of the Company's rule were deliberately intended to encourage the decadent forces or not. But, apart from such a discussion (which will be briefly touched upon on a following page), the fact remains that throughout the British period of India's history the consistent policy of the foreign rulers remained to stabilize somehow their rule in India, and afterwards make it durable, without necessarily giving proper attention to the interests of the people brought under subjugation. This point has been clarified in many studies on British India, and glimpses of this policy will be obtained in the course of the present discussion. From this it will be seen that the regeneration of the decadent forces and their renewed grip on Indian society were the logical outcome of some "reform measures" which might or might not have been introduced to have that function in particular.

The upshot was that along with the destruction of the growing class of merchants and artisans, which formed the economic basis of the progressive forces emerging in Indian society during her period of transition, these "reform measures" put a serious check on the further growth of progressive forces in the social and ideological spheres of Indian life. In fact, the sum-total effect of such a policy as pursued by the Company during its rule and also afterwards by the foreign rulers, as stated above, was that Indian society was first led towards retrogression instead of towards future progress, and then it remained backward in many ways.

To give a short account of two major "reform measures" introduced during the Company's rule, which affected Indian society adversely, the basis for the first one was laid with the full assumption by the Company of the government of the Subah of Bengal. In a way, it is true to say that this was introduced by Warren Hastings during his Governorship (1772–74) and Governor-Generalship (1774–86) of the Company's territory in India. In 1765, Clive had taken over the civil administration of the Subah of Bengal in the name of the Company from the Great Mughal at Delhi; but the collection of the revenue and the government of the country remained, as before, in the hands of the Nawab's officials. This resulted in chaos, for, as it will be explained later, while the Company was the real power and the Nawab its puppet, it remained undefined upon whom the real responsibility of administration rested. Also the collection of the revenue which was paid over to the Company, after paying the tribute to the Great Mughal and a fixed sum to the Nawab of Bengal as the expenses of collection, did not fulfil the main objective of this new arrangement, namely, "to bolster up the finances of the Company, which had suffered from the maintenance of armies."[29] Instead of enriching the Company, "for the yield was very disappointing; within five years the Company was on the verge of bankruptcy."[30] So further experiments were tried by "appointing English supervisors to see that the native collectors did not appropriate the funds;" but "the attention of the supervisors was concentrated on their own private trade, and the only result of their appointment was to turn them into tyrants of districts."[31] Under these circumstances, "the Company resolved to take over, not the government of Bengal, but the actual collection of the revenues," and "to carry out this change they appointed (1772) Warren Hastings" as the Governor of Bengal.[32] Hastings was, no doubt, one of the ablest representatives of the Company, who, like his efficient predecessor Clive, looked after the interests of the Company as well as his own. Therefore, while he was ultimately responsible for terrible sufferings and oppression of the Indian people, as they were vividly described during his impeachment in the British Parliament, within two years of his Governorship the affairs of the Company was "once more thriving" and the Directors in London "were full of delight."[33] But Hastings had also done something contrary to the wishes of the Court of Directors at that time, which however was fully endorsed later by the Company. He "actually assumed control of the government of Bengal" and "laid the real foundations of the British power in India."[34] As a shrewd and efficient Governor, he had realized at the outset that in the long run the Company's interest lay not merely in taking over the collection of the revenue from Indian hands but also in assuming full control of the administration at the same time, and that for this purpose it was necessary to have some knowledge of the inner workings of Indian society in order to stabilize the Company's rule therein. Therefore, he took a personal interest in codifying Hindu and Muhammedan laws, for he "was convinced that they formed the only sound basis of a reinvigorated system."[35] At the beginning, Hastings' viewpoint was seriously challenged by those "Reformers in England" who believed that "Indian law had no value" and therefore "the greatest boon they could render to India was the introduction of English law."[36] But "the British Government gradually worked back to his point of view," so that the "Act of 1833 authorised a codification of Indian law such as Hastings had begun at his own expense" and the "Proclamation of 1858 promised respect for and maintenance of Indian customs as a fundamental principle."[37] Thus, Hastings "saw what his successors only slowly learnt, that if the British power in India was to be lasting it must become an Indian power."[38] But, curiously enough, whether genuinely interested in supporting the laws and customs of the Indian people or not, what Warren Hastings and his successors persisted in putting forward as Indian laws and custom took the direction of patronizing religious orthodoxy instead of encouraging the liberal ideas which had gained ground in Indian society in the previous period and which, as described in the previous chapter, were ushering in a progressive life in India with a permanent rapproachment between the Hindus and Moslems and the eradication of decadent customs and institutions.

Under Hastings' direct support and personal initiative, the laws for the Hindus were codified according to the Brahminical doctrine as contained in the *Dharmasastras*, and that for the Moslems according to the orthodox interpretation of Islam. Selected Brahmin *pandits* from different parts of the Subah of Bengal were brought to Calcutta where they were employed for two years in order to prepare a compendium of Hindu Law in Sanskrit on the basis of orthodox religious works starting with *Manusmṛti*.[39] The manuscript was then translated into Persian and from Persian into English by N. B. Halhead, whereby presented by Warren Hastings to the Court of Directors of the East India Company and published in 1776 it came to be known as Halhead's *Gentoo Code*. Likewise, Hastings employed "learned professors of the Mahomedan law, for translating from the Arabic into the Persian tongue, a compendium of their law, called *Hedaya*,"[40] and thus Islamic orthodoxy also had the possibility to re-establish itself with new vigour within the Moslem community.

The 1781 Act of Settlement directed that all matters relating to inheritance, succession and contract were to be determined "in the case of Mohammedans by the laws and usages of Mohammedans and in the case of Gentoos by the laws and usages of Gentoos; and where only one of the parties shall be a Mohammedan or Gentoo by the laws and usages of the defendant."[41] Moreover, although the above Act specifically referred to inheritance, succession and contract, "judicial interpretation" of the Act extended its application to "all family and religious matters" of the two communities; so that its provisions were commented upon as "the first recognition of the Warren Hastings rule in the English statute Law."[42] And it is of further interest to note in this connection that: "In organizing the judicial system in the mofussil, Warren Hastings had made a rule that as regards inheritance, marriage, caste and other religious usages and institutions the laws of the Koran were to be administered for the Mohammedans and the laws of the Shastra for the Hindus."[43] This rule, first enacted in Calcutta in 1781, was extended to Madras in 1802, and to Bombay in 1827. In course of time, along with the Company's conquest of all parts of India, it embraced the whole of the subcontinent.

Evidently, this course of reform had a far-reaching consequence in Indian society, for it led to the revival of those forces among the people which had lost their usefulness with the further evolution of society and had thus become even reactionery in character. It is true that one should not underestimate the fact that even up to the time India came under British rule religious orthodoxy had an important bearing on the society. But it is equally true that, as described in the last chapter, new values had also emerged in contradistinction to the orthodoxy of Brahminism and Islam and that they were rapidly leading to the liberalisation of the Hindu and the Moslem views of life and towards a happy, peaceful and permanent rapproachment of all communities in India on the basis of *humane* qualities as enunciated by the proponents of the Bhakti movement and as encouraged in various ways by several Indian rulers in different parts of the subcontinent and in different generations. But henceforth these ideas received a severe battering. On the other hand, not only in the economic sphere was the growing stratum of artisans and traders reduced to non-entity, but in the social and ideological spheres of society Brahminism and Islamic orthodoxy reasserted themselves with the support they received from the ruling authority.

It is still a debatable point whether or not Hastings was prompted by a genuine desire to uphold Indian laws and custom, which, however, he thought to have been embodied only in orthodox religious works of the Hindus and Moslems. It has been asserted that: "One of Hastings' root principles was that Indian law and custom should be as far as possible preserved and respected."[44] It is also known that Warren Hastings defended the "Indian system" when "he learnt that the wiseacres of 1773 proposed to introduce English law, to be administered by a new Supreme Court."[45] His letter in this connection to Lord Mansfield, "the greatest of English lawyers," rings a sincere note when he wrote:[46]

> "Among the various plans which have been lately formed for the improvement of the British interests in the provinces of Bengal, the necessity of establishing a new form of judicature, and giving laws to a people who were supposed to be governed by no other principle of justice than the arbitrary wills, or uninstructed judgements, of their temporary rulers, has been frequently suggested; and this opinion I fear has obtained the greater strength from some publications of considerable merit in which it is too positively asserted that written laws are totally unknown to the Hindus or original inhabitants of Hindustan. From whatever cause this notion has proceeded, nothing can be more foreign from truth. I presume, my Lord, if this assertion can be proved, you will not deem it necessary that I should urge any argument in defence of their right to possess those benefits under a British and Christian administration which the Mahomedan government has never denied them. It would be a grievance to deprive the people of the protection of their own laws, but it would be a wanton tyranny to require their obedience to others of which they are wholly ignorant, and of which they have no possible means of acquiring knowledge. ... With respect to the Mahomedan law, which is the guide at least of one fourth of the natives of this province, your Lordship need not be told that this is as comprehensive, and as well defined, as that of most states in Europe, having been formed at a time in which the Arabians were in possession of all the real learning which existed in the western parts of this subcontinent."

But at the same time one cannot fail to note that when political exigencies demanded otherwise, Hastings himself had no qualms to go against what he supported as Indian laws and custom. Although, as Macaulay wrote referring to the Hindus, "according to their old national laws, a Brahmin could not be put to death for any crime whatever," Hastings, as "the real mover in the business," sent his adversary in Bengal, Nanda Kumar, "a Brahmin of the Brahmins," to the gallows in May 1775.[47] And it is of particular importance to note that not only has Nanda Kumar's conviction by the Supreme Court been considered by reputable historians as a "miscarriage of justice" and that "the jurisdiction of the Supreme Court over the indigenous population was doubtful," but while Hastings with such apparent sympathy had pleaded for Indian laws and custom one year earlier, Nanda Kumar was tried according to the English law and moreover "the English law making forgery a capital crime was not operative in India till many years after Nanda Kumār's alleged forgery had been committed."[48] Yet Hastings remained unperturbed, and it has been reported that a few years later he referred to Judge Impey (who pronounced the death sentence on Nanda Kumar and about whom Macaulay wrote that: "No rational man can doubt that he took this course in order to gratify the Governor-General") as the person "to whose support he was at one time indebted for the safety of his fortune, honour, and reputation."[49]

Thus there are certainly reasons to doubt that it was a matter of *principle* with Hastings to champion Indian laws and custom or even that his intention was to preserve and respect only those laws and custom of the Indian people which could fit in with the progressive development of society. For it remains a fact that his support went to orthodoxy and not to the growing liberal ideas in the social and ideological life of the Indian people. The latter ones could have been codified and thus a basis could have been created for further progress in Indian society; a basis which during their reign Akbar and several other progressive Indian rulers endeavoured to lay down by giving stress to secular laws and customs of the people and also by listening to the proponents of the Bhakti movement, as Akbar did with Dadu in order to cement a lasting friendship between the Hindu and the Moslem communities. And, if

Akbar (also a newcomer in India and two centuries earlier) could find out which way the Indian society was moving at a time when the Mughal rule had not yet attained stability, why should such an understanding have been unattainable for such a wise representative of the East India Company as Warren Hastings, when there is other evidence to indicate that the English Company had the best appreciation of the forces working in Indian society in those days and took definite measures to destroy such forces as were opposed to its interests or moulded them in its favour?

Indeed, whatever might have been the subjective attitude of Warren Hastings in supporting religious orthodoxy in Indian society, additional evidence (as described in the following pages) bears out that the consistent policy of the Company was not necessarily to institute real reforms in Indian society and to give a filip to the progressive forces therein, but while ruling out chaos from the country to secure support from the decadent forces in order to establish the stability of its rule in India.

Obviously, such a policy could not lead to "meeting and mingling together" of the Hindus and Moslems irrespective of their religious beliefs, which as a goal was cherished by the previous progressive rulers of India like Akbar and others and which was considered as "peculiarly instructive" by writers like Sir John Marshall. As it has been stated in a recent publication of the Government of India: "Legislative recognition given to the differences based on religion and caste may have been responsible to some extent for holding the two major communities apart."[50]

Moreover, the policy of the new ruling power was to drive a new wedge between these two largest communities in India. This became particularly manifest by the fact that while standing by Islamic orthodoxy, in order to counter-balance the still existing political power of the Mughals and other Moslem rulers and their underlings in India, until "their power was securely established," the British rulers gave particular support to Brahminism for then they had a great "use for the higher castes against the Mahomedan," as the Census Commissioner of Bengal for 1951 stated so candidly.[51] Indeed, this was such an obvious feature of the Company's rule in India that even those foreigners who believed that the "awakening" of India came from British rule admitted that during those days decadent and obscurantist customs were deliberately encouraged in India and the Brahminical doctrine and the practices of the high-caste Hindus were deliberately supported and patronized by the rulers "for the stability of their position." Farquhar noted, for instance:[52]

"In order to understand their attitude, we must realize that their only object was trade, and that it was purely for the safeguarding of their trade that they had interfered with the politics of the land. In consequence, they regarded themselves as in every sense the successors of the old rulers and heirs to their policy and method, except in so far as it was necessary to alter things for the sake of trade. There was another point. They had won their territory by means of an Indian army composed mainly of high-caste Hindus, who were exceedingly strict in keeping all the rules of caste and of religious practice. Further, every competent observer was deeply impressed with the extraordinary hold Hinduism had upon the people. Every element of life was controlled by it. In consequence, the Government believed it to be necessary, for the stability of their position, not merely to recognize the religions of the people of India, but to support and patronize them as fully as the native rulers had done, and to protect their soldiers from any attempt to make them Christians. Accordingly, they adopted three lines of policy from which, for a long time, they stubbornly refused to move:

a. They took under their management and patronage a large number of Hindu temples. They advanced money for rebuilding important shrines and for repairing others, and paid the salaries of the temple officials, even down to the courtesans, which were a normal feature of the great temples of the South. They granted large sums of money for sacrifices and festivals and for the feeding of Brahmans. Salvoes of cannon were fired on the occasion of the greater festivals; and government officials were ordered to be present and to show their interest in the celebrations. Even cruel and immoral rites, such as hook-swinging, practised in the worship of the gods, and the burning of widows, were carried out under British supervision. In order to pay for all these things, a pilgrim-tax was imposed, which not only recouped the Government for their outlay, but brought them a handsome income as well. Reformers in England and India found it a long and toilsome business to get this patronage of idolatry by a Christian Government put down. The last temple was handed over as late as 1862.

b. They absolutely refused to allow any missionary to settle in their territory. Carey got a footing in Bengal by becoming an indigo-planter; and he was not able to devote his whole time and energy to Christian work, until he settled at Serampore, twelve miles north of Calcutta, under the Danish flag. Many missionaries, both British and American, landed in India, only to be deported by the authorities. This policy was reversed by Act of Parliament in 1813.

c. They refused to employ native Christians in any capacity, and they enforced all the rigours of Hindu law against them. In the Bengal army, if any native soldier wished to become a Christian, he was forcibly prevented by the authorities; or, if by any chance he became baptized, he was expelled from the service. This fierce prejudice was so strong even at the time of the Mutiny that the services of thousands of Indian Christians were refused by the Government....

We can see how it is that men in business and in government have come to believe that we had better not touch the religion and civilization of India, that it is impossible to alter them, or to produce any lasting influence on Indian thought, and that every attempt to introduce change is bad for the people, on the one hand, and a grave danger to British trade and government, on the other.

It is well to notice that from time to time men of scholarship and character have held to the old policy and ideas in these matters. Horace Hayman Wilson, the famous Sanskrit scholar, was opposed to Bentinck's abolition of *sati*, and seriously believed that it would cause the Government grave difficulty.... Many noteworthy persons, and masses of business men throughout the nineteenth century have been opposed to educating the Indian. Lord Ellenborough, when Governor-General,

> regarded the political ruin of the English power as the inevitable consequence of the education of the Hindus.

Many a business men in Calcutta echoes this belief to-day, but no serious statesman holds such an opinion. Here is how the attitude of the people of Calcutta to missions was described in 1812:

> All were convinced that rebellion, civil war, and universal unrest would certainly accompany every attempt to promote missionary enterprise, and, above all, that the conversion of a high-caste native soldier would inevitably mean the disbanding of the army and the overthrow of British rule in India."

It is evident from the above that Farquhar was preoccupied with the spread of Christianity in India. But, apart from a discussion on whether conversion to Christianity was the way to a progressive development of the Indian people, it is well worth stressing the above-quoted features of British rule in India, as to how the decadent forces and obscurantist customs were supported by the foreign rulers in order to circumvent "a grave danger to British trade and government." For this policy obstructed the growth of the previously developing progressive forces in the social and ideological aspects of Indian life, and, on the other hand, kept India backward in many ways with the preservation and even reimposition of decayed social forms and institutions.

It will be remembered that in the period of transition as described in the last chapter many social and ideological measures were propagated by the rising forces of progress in Indian society and they were recommended and encouraged by several Indian rulers like Akbar and others. But under the Company's rule most of them went overboard.

For instance, Akbar persevered to abolish the practice of widow-burning among the high-caste Hindus. But whether he was successful or not in this endeavour, it is important to state that, although even *Manusmṛti* (the most important of all the standard *Dharmasastras* of the Hindus) did not enjoin this custom, basing on other *Dharmasastras* the *Gentoo Code* stated categorically that: "It is proper for a Woman, after her Husband's Death, to burn herself in the Fire with his Corpse; every Woman, who thus burns herself, shall remain in Paradise with her Husband Three *Crore* and Fifty *Lacks* of Years, by Destiny."[53] And, even under the rule of what was until 1829; it being "carried out under British supervision."

Several distinguished persons in Indian society at that time, such as Ram Mohan Roy, were against this practice. But the ruling authority was so adamant to maintain it in order to have the continued support of the decadent forces in Indian society for their rule that Ram Mohan Roy had to plead in person before the Court of Directors of the Company in London, while even a great savant like Wilson "was opposed to Bentinck's abolition of *sati*, and seriously believed that it would cause the Government grave difficulty." Naturally, the outcome was as one could expect. On the basis of documented facts and figures Altekar stated that "the Satī custom could not have been in much greater vogue in the Hindu and Muslim periods than it was in the first quarter of the 19th century."[54]

Similarly, Akbar had tried to prevent child-marriage. But, again, whether his attempts were successful or not, thanks to the support given to Hindu orthodoxy during the Company's rule and even later, child-marriage went on in full swing in Indian society. It has been worked out from the studies of Indian "castes and tribes" made in the last decades of the nineteenth and the early part of the twentieth century that out of the total of 560 "castes and tribes" for which the requisite information was available, 37.3 per cent practised only child-marriage, 31.4 per cent practised both child and adult marriage, and only 31.3 per cent practised solely adult marriage.[55]

Furthermore, it is worthy of note that under the domination of Hindu orthodoxy many of the low castes and those tribals which had come within the pale of "civilized" society took to the practise of child-marriage, although previously adult-marriage was the general rule with them. Thus it has been worked out from the same sources as for the above figures that while 51 per cent of the total of 318 high-castes (for which the relevant information was available) practised child-marriage, 31 per cent practised both child and adult marriage, and 18 per cent only adult marriage, the corresponding proportions for the total sample of 224 low-castes (including untouchables, detribalized aboriginals, undefined religious groups and Moslem castes) were 19, 32 and 49 per cent, respectively.[56]

How pernicious was this form of acculturation between the "lower sections of the community" and the dominant Hindu orthodoxy, and how belatedly a legal measure was enacted by the British Government by the Sarda Act of 1929 to fix the minimum marriageable age for girls at 14 and for boys at 18 (which, in fact, only followed "the actual practice of the advanced middle classes of society"), will be further evident from the following extract from Altekar's studies on *The Position of Women in Hindu Civilisation* in 1938:[57]

"8 or 9 was the usual marriageable age of girls at the advent of the British rule. With the introduction of western ideas and civilisation the educated sections of society began to feel the necessity of deferring marriages to a more advanced age. Social conferences began to advocate the cause of post-puberty marriages during the nineties of the last century, but their efforts were not appreciably successful till the beginning of the 20th century. The terrible havoc caused by the plague advanced the marriageable age of girls from 8 to 12 or 13. Society, however, was still afraid to cross openly the fateful age of puberty. The gradual disruption of the joint family system, the progressive realisation of the usefulness of female education, and above all, the hard necessities of the economic struggle for existence have now induced the advanced sections of Hindu society to throw over-board the Smriti injunctions, and to openly adopt post-puberty marriages. If, on account of economic factors, youths find it necessary to postpone marriage to the age of 24 or 25, they have naturally to choose their partners in life who are at least 16 or 17 at the time of the marriage. The Sarda Act, which has laid down 18 and 14 as the minimum legal age of marriage for boys and girls respectively, follows the actual practice of the advanced middle classes of society. Of course early marriages still prevail in lower sections of the community, and working on the data of the census of 1921, the Age of Consent Committee of 1929 computed that about 39% of girls were married before the age of 10....

The passing of the Sarda Act in 1929, penalising the marriages of girls before the age of 14, produced a reaction in the orthodox section of Hindu society, some members of which proceeded to openly break the law."

Also, like widow-burning and child-marriage, under the Company's rule the same was the state of affairs in regard to widow remarriage as well as divorce. Akbar had permitted Hindu widows to remarry; but, following the recommendation for undergoing *sati*, it was recorded in the *Gentoo Code* that, if after the death of her husband, a woman "cannot burn, she must, in that Case, preserve an inviolable Chastity; if she remains always chaste, she goes to Paradise; and if she does not preserve her Chastity, she goes to Hell."[58] Naturally, pursuant to such a strong sanction against widow remarriage, life-long widowhood remained in force in Hindu society. The upshot was that, after her marriage as a child, even if the husband died before the girl had attained maturity to enter into a conjugal life, she was to remain a virgin widow all her life and undergo all the penance and hardship associated with the rigorous life of a Hindu widow as recommended in the *Dharmasastras*.

Against such a cruel custom, the great Brahmin *pandit* of Bengal, Iswar Chandra Vidyasagar, had to plead for a long while with the Company's representatives in Calcutta and had to launch a campaign for a legal permission for widow remarriage before a law was made in 1856, "permitting widow remarriage under certain conditions."[59] Yet, among other reasons, since orthodoxy fully dominated society and went on dominating it, not only widow remarriage remained as a rare phenomenon among the high-caste Hindus and divorce was quite out of the question, but among the low-castes, Hinduised aboriginals, etc., widow remarriage was more and more restricted and the system of divorce was also gradually abolished, as the above-mentioned studies of Indian "castes and tribes" have distinctly recorded.

In such a vicious atmosphere as produced by the support given to orthodoxy, many other decadent and obscurantist customs prevailed in society, or they revived with renewed vigour. For instance, *kulinism*, which as an institution is said to have been elaborated in Bengal by Ballala Sena and his son, Lakshmana Sena, in the twelfth century, now became a scourge in society. The Brahmin families began to marry their daughters to the "purest", that is, to the *kulin* Brahmins, whereby it became not uncommon for a *kulin* Brahmin to marry dozens of wives and sometimes even hundreds. The wives stayed life-long with their parents as grass widows, while the apostle of purity undertook his regular business rounds and visited them for short periods according to the plan he had chalked out on the basis of the register he kept of the names and villages of all his fathers-in-law. Against such an abject degradation of women in society, Iswar Chandra Vidyasagar and many other progressive Indians launched severe onslaughts; but, although because of their campaigns as well as because of the growing economic difficulties this monstrous custom while flourishing during the Company's rule gradually fell into disuse, polygamy remained a lawful practice till the end of British rule in large parts of India. Only in a free and sovereign India was polygamy legally forbidden all over the Republic (and the minimum marriageable age for girls was raised to 16 years and for boys to 19 years) by the Hindu Marriage Act 25 of 18th May, 1955.[60]

Furthermore, it should again be stressed that the renewed role of Brahminism in society not only meant that Hindu orthodoxy revived its grip on the caste-Hindus, but following the course of acculturation in a society dominated by Brahminical ideology, it went on bringing in those aboriginals within its sphere who were coming into the pale of "civilisation." Alfred Lyall spoke of "the gradual Brahminising of the aboriginal, non-Aryan, or caste-less tribes" of India;[61] and it is of interest to note that, as found by the authorities who studied the "castes and tribes" of British India, one of the most important features of this course of Brahminising was the transformation of those people into low castes within the Hindu community.

With the emergence of new forces in society as described in the last chapter, the non-Hindu and non-Moslem aboriginal peoples (along with many in the above two communities) were veering round to the Bhakti cult in the previous centuries. But henceforth they came more and more under the Brahminical cult; and although these people did not totally give up the liberal teachings of the Bhakti movement and supported in some ways the views of Vaishnabism and such other schools of the Bhakti cult, nevertheless in course of time they began to emerge as distinct castes within the Hindu fold just as the earlier aboriginals were undergoing the process in the hey-day of feudalism in India. Thus the caste system, (which having passed the usefulness it had in the feudal times as supplying the frame-work to the Indian social organization had come under severe attacks in the fifteenth to the seventeenth centuries from the movements of the people because it impeded further progressive development), was re-established with renewed vigour with the consistent support Brahminism received from the ruling authorities.

The upshot was that not only among the caste-Hindus the regenerated force of Brahminism enforced the position of individuals as cogs in the wheel of the caste-machinery with little scope for the expression of individual initiative and aspirations, but also those aboriginals who henceforth came within "civilised" society began to lose whatever social and ideological freedom they had before. In the process of Hinduisation, they began to prohibit widow remarriage and divorce, adopt child-marriage, and occupy a low position in society with all the peculiar restrictions of inter-dining, inter-marriage, touchability and others. It was such a transformation in their life that Verrier Elwin has aptly characterized it as: "A Loss of Nerve."[62]

And this process of transformation as well as the maintenance of caste-distinction in society was further stabilized by another "reform" enacted in the last decade of the eighteenth and the early years of the nineteenth century. For reasons to be explained in the next chapter, definite forms of land settlements were made in British India at this time. These settlements varied somewhat in details, as will be described in Chapter 6; but they had a common characteristic, namely, whether directly introduced at the time of the "land reforms" or not, henceforth landlordism began to emerge all over India.

It has been discussed in the previous chapter that whether or not land alienation and transfer took place in Indian society in the past, landlordism (and particularly absentee landlordism) was not a feature of the Indian society in those days. That such remained as the state of affairs until the early years of British rule in India is attested from British *Parliamentary Papers*. The famous *Fifth Report* of British Parliament on the affairs of the East India Company described in 1812 how the village communities still functioned in India; and even for Bengal, where it was asserted by some that the presence of *zemindars* indicated that landlordism existed there from earlier times, it specifically stated that the *zemindars* were "herediatry superintendents of the land."[63] Moreover, while discussing the land settlements made under the Company's rule, the *Fifth Report* categorically recorded:[64]

"... the leading members of the supreme government appear to have been, at an early period of the transactions now commencing, impressed with a strong persuasion of the proprietory right in the soil possessed by the Zemindars, or if the right could not be made out, consistently with the institutions of the former government, that reason and humanity irresistibly urged the introduction of it. ...

In the progress and conclusion of this important transaction, the government appeared willing to recognize the proprietory right of the Zemindars in the land; not so much, from any proof of the existence of such right, discernible in his relative situation under the Mogul government, in its best form, as from the desire of improving their condition under the British government, as far as it might be done consistently with the permanency of the revenue and with the rights of the cultivators on the soil."

And that:[65]

"The sale of land by auction, or in any other way, for realizing arrears of land revenue, appears to have been unusual, if not unknown in all parts of India, before its introduction by the British government into the Company's dominions."

Evidently, landlordism did not exist in India before, and also land was not definitely and legally established as private property in the sense that it could be sold (or auctioned) freely and could be used as a property by absentee landlords, until these features were introduced in Indian society under the Company's rule. But what "reason and humanity irresistibly urged" did not lead to the betterment of the cultivators. Instead of fostering "the rights of the cultivators on the soil," the introduction of "the sale of land by auction, or in any other way, for realizing arrears of land revenue" eventually led to the growth of a landowning class all over India at the expense of the common peasantry, although landlordism was directly established only in some regions with the enforcement of the *Permanent Zemindary Settlement*.

This was so because when the agrarian crisis set in in India with the constant exploitation by the foreign interests as well as by their local agents and from the neglect of looking after the improvement of the agrarian economy by the parasitic rent-receivers, the peasants more and more came to a state where they could not maintain even the mere reproductory rate of the economy; and under such dire circumstances the only course left to them for survival was either to mortgage their holdings (and thus lose them in course of time in lieu of the unpaid burden of usurious interests and the principal borrowed) or to sell them outright.[66] Thereafter, as in the words of Montgomery Martin, India was turned into the "Agricultural Farm of England,"[67] in the absence of any other available source of livelihood the "unpeasantised" peasants could not but live on the agrarian economy as sharecroppers or agricultural labourers while clinging on to the last to tiny patches of land they might still possess.

Thus the economic power of society decisively went over to the landlords, many of whom, significantly enough, belonged to the high-castes; while the bulk of the poor cultivators, sharecroppers, agricultural labourers, and the so-called "menial servants" in rural society belonged to the low-castes.[68] In this way, the caste structure was telescoped into the economic structure of society which developed in British India, and thereby the former claimed stability and simultaneous existence so long as the landlords dominated rural society.

Indeed, the permeation of the caste-ideology over all in society, that is, "the social hierarchy is divinely ordained and that equality is not only contrary to experience but is impossible because each man's state of life is predermined by his actions in past lives," was particularly to the advantage of the landowning class which had to keep the vast mass of disintegrating peasantry under its control and thus continue with the parasitic living as rent-receiver from the multitude of tenants and sharecroppers. Therefore, apart from some enlightened individuals breaking out of their circle and aligning themselves with the progressive currents in society, the landlords as a class gave consistent support to Brahminism and to the most important social institution it fostered, namely, the caste system. As O'Malley remarked in 1932:[69]

"In the past it [caste system] has helped to save Hindu society from disintegration and Hindu culture from destruction. Through successive conquests and revolutions it has been a stable force, and its stabilizing influence is not without political importance at the present time, when the communist movement is said to be a menace to India. A system which is permeated by religion is utterly opposed to the Bolshevist doctrine of a war upon religion. The idea of a class war is alien to a people which believes that the social hierarchy is divinely ordained and that equality is not only contrary to experience but is impossible because each man's state of life is predetermined by his actions in past lives.

Many thoughtful Indians are therefore strongly in favour of the caste system on the ground that it is a bulwark of society against revolutionary assault."

It will not, therefore, be an exaggaration to state that while in the feudal epoch of India's normal development the "myriads of industrious patriarchal and inoffensive social organisations" of the village community system "were contaminated by distinctions of caste and slavery" and thereby "they subjugated man to external circumstances, instead of elevating man the sovereign of circumstances,"[70] henceforth under the Company's rule, while the village communities disintegrated, landlordism developed, and the caste system received a new lease of life with the support given to Hindu orthodoxy by the ruling power as well as by the landowning class. And, as it had done in the past, again the caste-distinction asserted its role in society and persevered to turn "a self-developing social state into never changing natural destiny."[71]

In fact, by means of such "reform measures" as described in the previous pages, in many ways the Company brought in a phase of "secondary feudalism" in India. Under the Company's rule, not only did the "native" rulers openly persist in maintaining a feudal control over two-fifths of the geographical area of the subcontinent, but in British India also the landlords, with the privileges they obtained "so entirely on their side," dominated Indian society and throve as parasitic rent-receivers. The disintegrating peasantry, on the other hand, remained under their control and were enmeshed in the decadent caste-ideology fully subscribed to and propagated by the top stratum of society.

In 1812, the *Fifth Report* had remarked with reference to the "land reforms" introduced in the Company's dominions in India that: "If any deviations from the established usages of the natives should occur, in what was intended to be done, the advantage was still so entirely on their side, particularly in regard to the landholder, that it was presumed they would at once sufficiently perceive the benefit intended, and not object to it, because the mode of introducing it was new, nor regret the abolition of practices injurious to them, on account of their having been of long standing."[72] And, as the reaction of the "landholders" made it clear, the "benefit" conferred on them was not lost sight of. Perhaps typical of their attitude was the declaration made by the President of the Bengal Landowners' Association in his Address to the British Viceroy in 1925, viz.: "Your Excellency can rely on the ungrudging support and sincere assistance of the landlords."[73]

As the political history of British India has repeatedly shown, all over the subcontinent such support and assistance were consistently given by the bulk of the landlords (except some individuals, as stated before) to the foreign rulers against the developing movement of the Indian people for freedom and democracy, progress and prosperity. Not only did the landowning class form the driving force behind the communal organizations of Hindu and Moslem reaction, which had a splintering effect on the movements organized by the Indian National Congress—the platform for all freedom-loving Indians in British India—and not only did the landlord section of Indian society generally take up the leadership of several other pro-government organizations formed in the first half of the present century in order to oppose the Indian National Congress, but also specifically as a body of "landholders" the landowning class came out clearly in support of British rule in India. When the first All-India Landholder's Conference has held in 1938, the Maharaja of Mymensing (a big landlord of Bengal) declared in his Presidential Address that "if we are to exist as a class" then "it is our duty to strengthen the hands of the Government."[74]

Thus, on the one hand, politically playing second fiddle to the foreign rulers and economically living a parasitic life on the toils of the disintegrating peasantry, and, on the other, remaining strong adherents to the decadent and obscurantist customs and to the reactionary caste-ideology in social life, the "landholders" as a class obstructed progress in Indian society.

Such then were the outcome of two major "reform measures" introduced in India during the Company's rule. The first regenerated religious orthodoxies and gave special support to Brahminism. Thereby, it not only kept both the Hindu and the Moslem communities backward without giving them the possibility to come to a permanent rapproachment on the basis of the liberal ideas propagated in the previous centuries, but also helped Hindu orthodoxy to spread again its tentacles to those "non-Aryan, or casteless tribes" which were not yet within its fold. Thus, with the revival and further elaboration of Hindu orthodoxy, caste-practices and caste-ideology became again rampant in Indian society. And, by leading to the evolution of landlordism in society, the second "reform measure" gave additional vigour to caste-distinction and stability to the institution of the caste system in British India. Retrogression thus set in in India society, where landlordism became the scourge of the people all over India,[75] and the caste system as well as decadent and obscurantist customs prevailed in their social organization.

Significantly enough, the round of life which was thus enforced for the Indian people became later a matter of publicity for the foreign rulers in order to indicate the innate primitive life and backward outlook of the Indian masses; an outlook which in spite of their consistent efforts, they asserted, forbade them from "granting" self-government to India. For instance, the Indian Statutory Commission of 1928 remarked:[76]

> "Any quickening of general political judgement, any widening of rural horizons beyond the traditional and engrossing interest of weather and water and crops and cattle, with the round of festivals and fairs and family ceremonies, and the dread of famine or flood—any such change from these immemorial preoccupations of the average Indian villager is bound to come very slowly indeed."

But measures to lift society out of the morass it was made to sunk into were hardly at all taken during the British rule. It was left to the Republic of India to initiate progress in society by launching the first and the second five year plans to change the "face of India," and by enacting progressive social legislations. Thus, on the 12th of April, 1955, "Lok Sabha" [of the Indian Parliament] passed the Constitution (Fourth Amendment) Bill, defining the State's power to acquire and requisition private property, and fix the amount of compensation to be paid;" on the 15th of April of the same year, "150-year old Zamindari system of landownership ended in West Bengal;" on the 28th of April, 1955, "Lok Sabha passed bill making practise of 'untouchability' a criminal offence;"[77] and the *Caste Distinction Removal Bill* of 1954 is now pending in Parliament which "is stated to be the first step in the direction of removing all caste distinctions and the fostering of a casteless Hindu society in the interest of the solidarity of the nation."[78]

There is hardly any doubt, therefore, that the two major "reforms" made during the Company's rule did not really lead to progress of Indian society. On the contrary, they fostered and intensified backwardness in social, economic and ideological aspects of Indian life. Referring to such a policy pursued throughout the British rule in India, Palme Dutt had remarked that: "A policy which in practice fosters and maintains the division and backwardness of a subject people, and even by its administrative methods intensifies these evils, while in public it loudly proclaims these evils as a melancholy proof of the incapacity of the people for unity and self-government, condemns itself."[79] And, indeed, there is no exaggeration in the following caustic comment made by Marx with reference to these reforms and the spoliation of India by the Company and its representatives, about which a brief account is given in the following pages. Marx wrote:[80]

"The profound hypocrisy and inherent barbarism of bourgeois civilisation lies unveiled before our eyes, turning from its home, where it assumes respectable forms, to the colonies, where it goes naked. They are the defenders of property, but did any revolutionary party ever originate agrarian revolutions like those in Bengal, in Madras, and in Bombay? Did they not, in India, to borrow an expression of that great robber, Lord Clive himself, resort to atrocious extortion, when simple corruption could not keep pace with their rapacity? While they prated in Europe about the inviolable sanctity of the national debt, did they not confiscate in India the dividends of the *rajahs*, who had invested their private savings in the Company's own funds? While they combated the French revolution under the pretext of defending "our holy religion," did they not forbid, at the same time, Christianity to be propagated in India, and did they not, in order to make money out of the pilgrims streaming to the temples of Orissa and Bengal, take up the trade in the murder and prostitution perpetrated in the temple of Juggernaut? These are the men of "Property, Order, Family, and Religion."

4. Disintegration of Indian Economy

Not only were the industries and trade of India devitalized in the first phase of the Company's rule and not only was the social life in India led towards retrogression instead of towards progress, but the exploitation by the Company and its servants attacked the very basis of the Indian economy. India up till the eighteenth century was a great manufacturing as well as a prosperous agricultural country, and the products of Indians looms supplied the markets of Asia and Europe. But, although, as mentioned before, a new system of exploiting the labour of the artisans by the rising *entrepreneurs* was coming into existence especially in the eighteenth century, in general the Indian economy was based on the "domestic union of agricultural and manufacturing pursuits," and "these two circumstances had brought about, since the remotest times, a social system of particular features—the so-called *village system* which gave to each of these small unions their independent organisation and distinct life."[81] In short, the village community system was still the prevailing social system of India. But, now "it was the British intruder who broke up the Indian hand-loom and destroyed the spinning wheel," and eventually "thus produced the *only social* revolution ever heard of in Asia."[82]

India had previously seen many despotic rules, and had undergone many kinds of oppression. But the rule of the Company attacked the very base of her economic foundation. For the Indian people, "the springs of their industry were stopped, the sources of their wealth were dried up;"[83] and this ruination of the artisans and traders had a far-reaching effect on agriculture, firstly because the artisans in the villages were also partly peasants, and, secondly, because the peasants were also equally oppressed by the agents of the English to supply them the crops they demanded at a nominal or no price at all, and, thirdly, henceforth agriculture became the only source of livelihood for the mass of Indian people.

How terribly English oppression affected the village economy is evident from the following extract from the writings of the same Englishman "who saw things with his own eyes:"

> "For the Ryots, who are generally both landholders and manufacturers, by the oppressions of Gomastahs in harassing them for goods are frequently rendered incapable of improving their lands, and even of paying their rents; for which, on the other hand, they are again chastised by the officers of the revenue, and not unfrequently have those harpies been necessitated to sell their children in order to pay their rents, or otherwise obliged to fly the country."[84]

It was not only the native Gomastahs who oppressed the peasantry as a part of the Company's policy in occupied India. In this sphere the direct role of the Company and its officers was even worse. How destructive their policy was the renowned economist Adam Smith noted as follows while denouncing the monopoly rule of merchant capital and comparing the colonial policy of the Dutch East India Company in the East Indies and that of the English East India Company in Bengal.

> "The English and Dutch companies, though they have established no considerable colonies, except the two above mentioned*, have both made considerable conquests in the East Indies. But in the manner in which they both govern their new subjects, the natural genius of an exclusive company has shown itself most distinctly. In the spice islands the Dutch are said to burn all the spiceries which a fertile season produces beyond what they expect to dispose of in Europe with such a profit as they think sufficient. In the islands where they have no settlements, they give a premium to those who collect

* The two colonies referred to were the Cape of Good Hope and Batavia where the Europeans had settled down, and so in those days these two places were regarded as colonies as differentiated from other conquered territories on the coast of Africa and the East Indies with which Adam Smith was dealing in the above extract.

the young blossoms and green leaves of the clove and nutmeg trees which naturally grow there, but which this savage policy has now, it is said, almost completely extirpated. Even in the islands where they have settlements they have very much reduced, it is said, the number of those trees. If the produce even of their own islands was much greater than what suited their market, the natives, they suspect, might find means to convey some part of it to other nations; and the best way, they imagine, to secure their own monopoly is to take care that no more shall grow than what they themselves carry to market. By different arts of oppression they have reduced the population of several of the Moluccas nearly to the number which is sufficient to supply with fresh provisions and other necessaries of life their own insignificant garrisons, and such of their ships as occasionally come there for a cargo of spices.... The English company have not yet had time to establish in Bengal so perfectly destructive a system. The plan of their government, however, has had exactly the same tendency. It has not been uncommon, I am well assured, for the chief, that is the first clerk of a factory, to order a peasant to plough up a rich field of poppies, and sow it with rice or some other grain. The pretence was, to prevent a scarcity of provisions; but the real reason, to give the chief an opportunity of selling at a better price a large quantity of opium, which he happened then to have upon hand. Upon other occasions the order has been reversed; and a rich field of rice or other grain has been ploughed up, in order to make room for a plantation of poppies; when the chief foresaw that extraordinary profit was likely to be made by opium. The servants of the Company have upon several occasions attempted to establish in their own favour the monopoly of some of the most important branches, not only of the foreign, but of the inland trade of the country."[85]

The urban economy was also no less affected. Prosperous territories, towns and market-places became desolate, and only the ruins of a prosperous past stood witness to the devastation wrought by the Company and its servants, and its army and other appendages. In northern India, of the places where the Company had strong influence from the beginning, the manufacturing towns of Dacca, Murshidabad and Surat are worthy of note. In 1757, Clive found the town of Murshidabad at least equal in prosperity to the city of London, if not greater. But in 1840, Sir Charles Trevelyan reported:[86]

"The peculiar kind of silky cotton formerly grown in Bengal, from which the fine Dacca muslins used to be made, is hardly ever seen; the population of the town of Dacca has fallen from 150,000 to 30,000 or 40,000, and the jungle and malaria are fast encroaching upon the town. ... Dacca, which was the Manchester of India, has fallen off from a very flourishing town to a very poor and small one; the distress there has been very great indeed."

Montgomery Martin reported in the same year to the same Select Committee of the House of Commons enquiring into the affairs of the East India Company:[87]

"The decay and destruction of Surat, of Dacca, of Murshedabad, and other places where native manufactures have been carried on, is too painful a fact to dwell upon. I do not consider that it has been in the fair course of trade; I think it has been the power of the stronger exercised over the weaker."

Sir Henry Cotton noted in 1890:[88]

"In 1787 the exports of Dacca muslin to England amounted to 30 lakhs (three millions) of rupees; in 1817 they had ceased altogether. ... Families which were formerly in a state of affluence have been driven to desert the towns and betake themselves to the villages for a livelihood. ... This decadence had occurred not in Dacca only, but in all districts."

It was not only in northern India that such shattering of the Indian economy took place. In the south, the situation was no better, as the following extract from the *Ninth Report of the Committee of Secrecy Appointed by the House of Commons—7 December 1772 to 30 June 1773*—testifies. The extract refers to the evidence given before the Committee by one witness, George Smith, who arrived in India in 1764, and spent twelve years, from 1767 to 1779, in Madras.[89]

"Being asked what was the state of trade at Madras at the time when he first knew it, he said it was in a flourishing condition, and Madras one of the first marts in India. Being asked in what condition did he leave it with respect to trade, he replied at the time of his leaving it, there was little or no trade, and but one shop belonging to the place. Being asked in what state the interior country of the Karnatic was with regard to commerce and cultivation when he first knew it, he said at that period he understood the Karnatic to be in a well-cultivated and populous condition, and as such consuming a great many articles of merchandise and trade. Being asked in what condition it was when he left Madras with respect to cultivation, population, and internal commerce, he said in respect to cultivation, greatly on the decline, and also in respect of population; and as to commerce, exceedingly circumscribed."

The destruction wrought by the Company was even more pronounced in Tanjore. The place was renowned for its prosperity, and, until the Carnatic Wars and thereafter, the English had no great influence there. But in 1782 Mr. Petrie in his evidence before the Committee of Secrecy of the House of Commons reported:[90]

> "Before I speak of the present state of Tanjore country, it will be necessary to inform the Committee that not many years ago that province was considered as one of the most flourishing, best cultivated, populous districts in Hindustan. I first saw this country in 1768, when it presented a very different picture from its present situation. Tanjore was formerly a place of great foreign and inland trade; it imported cotton from Bombay and Surat, raw and worked silks from Bengal, sugar, spices, etc., from Sumatra, Malacca, and the eastern islands; gold, horses, elephants, and timber from Pegu, and various articles of trade from China. It was by means of Tanjore that a great part of Haidar Ali's dominions and the north-western parts of the Mahratta empire were supplied with many European commodities, and with a species of silk manufacture from Bengal, which is almost universally worn as a part of dress by the natives of Hindustan. The exports of Tanjore were muslins, chintz, handkerchiefs, ginghams, various sorts of long-cloths, and a coarse printed cloth, which last constitutes a material article in the investments of the Dutch and the Danes, being in great demand for the African, West Indian, and South American markets. Few countries have more natural advantages than Tanjore; it possesses a rich and fertile soil, singularly well supplied with water from the two great rivers Cavery and Coleroon, which, by means of reservoirs, sluices, and canals, are made to disperse their waters through almost every field in the country; to this latter cause we may chiefly attribute the uncommon fertility of Tanjore.... Such was Tanjore not many years ago, but its decline has been so rapid, that in many districts it would be difficult to trace the remains of its former opulence....
>
> At this period (1771), as I have been informed, the manufactures flourished, the country was populous and well cultivated, and the inhabitants were wealthy and industrious. Since the year 1771, the era of the first siege [described in Chapter 4—R. K. M.], until the restoration of the Raja the country having been during that period twice the seat of war, and having undergone revolutions in the government, trade, manufactures, and agriculture were neglected, and many thousands of inhabitants went in quest of a more secure abode."

Thus, in peace or during wars, the security, prosperity and progress of the countries were stopped; the people moved from one place to another to escape the ravages of the Company's rule; and when the surviving ones settled down permanently, they had nothing else to depend upon but agriculture as their only source of living. The logical conclusion was overpressure in agriculture, which went on gathering momentum throughout the British Period of India's history. In 1840, Sir Charles Trevelyan reported to the House of Commons Select Committee:[91]

> "We have swept away their manufactures; they have nothing to depend on but the produce of their land, ..."

In 1880, the Famine Commission of the Government admitted:[92]

> "At the root of much of the poverty of the people of India and of the risks to which they are exposed in seasons of scarcity lies the unfortunate circumstance that agriculture forms almost the sole-occupation of the masses of the people."

5. "Well-being" of the People

While the economy of India thus began to disintegrate with the onset of the Company's rule, the policy of the Company "to make hay while the sun shines" blocked all sources of revival of the old economy. Marx wrote:[93]

> "There have been in Asia, generally, from immemorial times, but three departments of government, that of finance, or the plunder of the interior, that of war, or the plunder of the exterior; and, finally the department of public works. ... Now, the British in East India accepted from their predecessors the department of finance and of war, but they have neglected entirely that of public works."

The result was that while the English did not foster any new industry or revive the old industries of India, so that the people were left with no other source of living but agriculture, the agrarian economy itself faced a serious situation with the total neglect of the department of public works.

In ancient India it was the duty of the State to look after the central irrigation system, on which depended the agricultural prosperity. During the first half of the eighteenth century, in the period of utter confusion in India, many of the immense irrigation works were not properly cared for. Now, when "peace" was brought to these territories with the extension of the Company's rule, the people expected that the administration would now revive the irrigation system. But since the attitude of the Company was, as characteristically put by Clive (himself one of the big sharers in the spoils)—"let us get what we can today, let tomorrow take care for itself"[94]—that expectation never came true. As a result, these irrigation systems, spread all over India, were soon transformed into historical ruins.

In Bengal Sir William Wilcocks, the renowned hydraulic engineer, who made a scientific study of the ancient system of irrigation in Bengal, discovered that—

> "innumerable small destructive rivers of the delta region, constantly changing their course, were originally canals which under the English regime were allowed to escape from their channels and run wild. Formerly these canals distributed the flood waters of the Ganges and provided for proper drainage of the land, undoubtedly accounting for that prosperity of Bengal which lured the rapacious East India merchants there in the early days of the eighteenth century. ... Some areas, cut off from the supply of loam-bearing Ganges water, have gradually become sterile and non-productive; others, improperly drained, show an ... accompaniment of malaria. Nor has any attempt been made to construct proper embankments for the Ganges in its low course, to prevent the enormous erosion by which villages and groves and cultivated fields are swallowed up each year."[95]

The same was the state of affairs in other parts of India. Dr. Francis Buchanan frequently came across ruins of irrigation reservoirs during his surveys in the first decade of the nineteenth century. Some of them were "seven or eight miles in length and three in width," from which water was "let out in numerous small canals to irrigate fields in the dry season."[96] But, so little attention was paid by the Company even in the later phase of its rule to reviving the ancient public works or to building new ones that as late as in 1851–52 less than one per cent of the gross revenue from the three Presidencies of

Bengal, Madras and Bombay were spent on "roads, canals, bridges, and other works of public necessity."[97]

No wonder then that the over-pressed agrarian economy, failing to maintain even the previous rates of production, and being further over-burdened by ever-increasing land-tax demanded by the Company and extracted from the starving peasantry with unexampled vigour (as it will be described in the following pages), led to chronic famine conditions. But, consoling themselves with the knowledge that famines were not formerly unknown in India, the officials of the Company as well as the Court of Directors in London hardly ever took adequate measures to relieve the famine-stricken people. As a result, the virulence with which the famines began to set in with a clock-work regularity, and the epidemics which they brought in their trails (in addition to malaria and such diseases which became endemic in India—thanks to the turning of her fertile lands into bogs, swamps and marshes with the destruction of the irrigation systems), took ever-mounting tolls of lives. Hardly any statistics are available of the total deaths from the repeated famines which ravaged the plains of India—Bengal, Bihar, Orissa, Benares, Oudh, Madras, Mysore and other parts of north and south India—in the eighteenth century, except that the famine deaths in Bengal in 1770 alone were estimated at ten millions! And, in the first half of the nineteenth century, while the Company was still in power and was supposed to have become more "humanitarian," 1,400,000 famine deaths were recorded.[98] Referring to the Bengal famine of 1770, the Calcutta Council of the Company, while taking no steps to ameliorate the conditions of the people, wrote to the Court of Directors in London:[99]

> "The famine which has ensued, the mortality, the beggary, exceed all description."

It would scarcely be an exaggeration to state, as several studies on India during the Company's rule have shown, that this became the general rule for the whole of British India under the government of the East India Company.

6. "Economic Drain" from India

Perhaps the worst effect of the Company's rule, which again was inherent in its policy, was to take away India's wealth and resources to England without providing her with anything in return. This was characterized by the Indian historians and economists of the early twentieth century as the "economic drain" on India. How serious was this phenemenon of the Company's rule (which continued unabated throughout the British Period of India's history) would be realized from the fact that even under the worst government that India had in former times the situation was different. The vast sums which the Afghan and Mughal Emperors spent on their armies went to support great and princely houses, as well as hundreds of thousands of soldiers and their families whose attachment to society was not lost, as it was by Indian soldiers under British rule. The gorgeous palaces and monuments the Indian rulers built, as well as the luxuries and displays in which they indulged, fed and encouraged the manufacturers and artisans of India. Nobles and Commanders of the army, Subahdars, Dewans, and Kazis, and a host of inferior officers in every province and every district, followed the example of the Court; and mosques and temples, roads, canals and reservoirs, guest houses on the road-sides and other buildings, etc., attested to their interest in the country's welfare, their wide liberality to the people, and even to their vanity as efficient rulers and officers. In any case, under wise rulers as well as under foolish kings, the proceeds from the people in the forms of taxes and tributes flowed back to them and fructified their trade and industries. But from the beginning of the British rule a profound change came over India. In 1783, in his speech on Fox's East India Bill in the British Parliament, as follows the famous English orator, Edmund Burke, described this "perpetual drain from India" during the Company's rule:[100]

"The Asiatic conquerors very soon abated of their ferocity, because they made the conquered country their own. They rose or fell with the rise and fall of the territory they lived in. Fathers there deposited the hopes of their posterity; the children there beheld the monuments of their fathers. Here their lot was finally cast; and it is the normal wish of all that their lot should not be cast in bad land. Poverty, sterility, and desolation are not a recreating prospect to the eye of man, and there are very few who can bear to grow old among the curses of a whole people. If their passion or avarice drove the Tartar lords to acts of rapacity or tyranny, there was time enough, even in the short life of man, to bring round the ill effects of the abuse of power upon the power itself. If hoards were made by violence and tyranny, they were still domestic hoards, and domestic profusion, or the rapine of a more powerful and prodigal hand, restored them to the people. With many disorders, and with few political checks upon power, nature had still fair play, the sources of acquisition were not dried up, and therefore the trade, the manufactures, and the commerce of the country flourished. Even avarice and usury itself operated both for the preservation and the employment of national wealth. The husbandmen and manufacturer paid heavy interest, but then they augmented their fund from whence they were again to borrow. Their resources were dearly bought, but they were sure, and the general stock of the community grew by the general effect.

But under the English Government all this order is reversed. The Tartar invasion was mischievous, but it is our protection that destroys India. It was their enmity, but it is our friendship. Our conquest there, after twenty years, is as crude as it was the first day. The natives scarcely know what it is to see the grey head of an Englishman; young men, boys almost govern there, without society, and without sympathy with the natives. They have no more social habits with the people than if they still resided in England; nor, indeed, any species of intercourse but that which is necessary to making a sudden fortune, with a view to a remote settlement. Animated with all the avarice of age, and all the impetuosity of youth, they roll in one after another; wave after wave, and there is nothing before the eyes of the natives but an endless, hopeless prospect, of new flights of birds of prey and passage, with appetites continually renewing for a food that is continually wasting. Every rupee of profit made by an Englishman is lost for ever to India."

Thus, the British, as "the first conquerors superior, and therefore inaccessible to Hindu civilisation," destroyed it "by breaking up the native communities, uprooting the native industry, and by levelling all that was great and elevated in the native society."[101] Simultaneously, by taking out the wealth of the country throughout the Company's rule (as well as in the later period), they left no course open for a progressive development of India until, in the words of

Marx in 1853, "in Great Britain itself the now ruling classes shall have been supplanted by the industrial proletariat, or till the Hindus themselves shall have grown strong enough to throw off the English yoke altogether."[102]

To give a brief account of this economic drain from India during the Company's rule, in the first stage after the battle of Plassey it took the character of indiscriminate loot and plunder. Those were the days when, in the words of the pious Clive himself, the Company and its servants "thought of nothing but the present time, regardless of the future," and therefore their actions concentrated on the "immediate division of the loaves and fishes."[103] So, with the establishment of Mir Jafar on the throne of Bengal in 1757, the looting began.

Acquisitions were made not only in the sphere of "trade," as it has been described before. Tributes to the Company and its servants from the puppet Indian rulers (which in the last analysis came from the Indian people) was another important variation adopted from the very start. When in 1757 Mir Jafar became the Nawab of Bengal, in addition to a million pounds to the Company, half a million to the "English inhabitants of Calcutta," and the sum of £ 270,000 for the Hindus, Mussulmans, Armenians, and other subjects of Calcutta,–which were all specified in the Treaty–, the new Nawab had to make large gifts to the principal servants of the Company. The Select Committee of the House of Commons of 1772 estimated the total amount of these gifts at £ 1,238,575; out of which the "hero" Clive received £ 31,500 besides a rich *jaigir* or an estate for revenue-farming which was estimated to bring in £ 27,000 a year.[104] When Clive had left England he was a poor man. But now fortune smiled on him. He himself reported later that "fortunes of £ 100,000 have been obtained in two years."[105] Quite candidly he told the Select Committee of the House of Commons of 1772:[106]

"I never sought to conceal it, but declared publicly in my letters to the Secret Committee of the India Directors that the Nabob's generosity had made my fortune easy, ... What pretence could the Company have to expect, that

I after having risked my life so often in their service, should deny myself the only opportunity ever offered of acquiring a fortune without prejudice to them, who it is evident would not have had more for my having had less?"

The Indian historian, R. C. Dutt, commented on this statement:[107]

"It never struck Clive that the treasure belonged neither to the Company nor to him, but to the country, and should have been devoted to the good of the people."

To the virtuous Clive, however, this was not only of no concern at all, but while describing in the House of Commons,

"in vivid language the situation in which his victory had placed him; a great prince dependent on his pleasure; an opulent city afraid of being given up to plunder; wealthy bankers bidding against each other for his smiles; vaults piled with gold and jewels thrown open to him alone. ... 'By God, Mr. Chariman', he exclaimed, 'at this moment I stand astonished at my own moderation'."[108]

One should note in the above extract the writer's (T. B. Macaulay's) characteristic defence of the English character. Like the great majority of the representatives of the ruling power, Macaulay was confident of "the lower standard of Indian morality;" discovered regarding the "Bengalee" that: "Courage, independence, veracity, are qualities to which his constitution and his situation are equally unfavourable;" and remarked that: "What the horns are to the buffalo, what the paw is to the tiger, what the sting is to the bee, what beauty, according to the old Greek song, is to woman, deceit is to the Bengalee."[109] But, as regards the Englishman Clive, the situation was of course different. Everything was opened to him; there was no persuasion, no intimidation, no force applied to the puppet Nawab and the merchants and bankers of Bengal!

And, neither was Clive the only person who gained by the "gifts" made out of Bengal's wealth, nor was this the only occasion. Long before Macaulay set foot in India, the representatives of the Company collected many more "presents," which were recorded in British *Parliamentary Papers* and so could not have passed unnoticed by eminent writers and historians like Macaulay.

After three years of "reign," Mir Jafar was set aside on grounds of "incompetence," and Mir Kasim was installed on the throne in 1760. This Nawab again made presents to the English officials to the tune of £ 200,269, out of which the Governor Vansittart (who had replaced Clive, received £ 58,333. To the Company itself Mir Kasim agreed to pay the balance which Mir Jafar had left unpaid; to make a present of Rs. 500,000, or £ 50,000, as a contribution towards the Company's wars in south India (whereby the Company subjugated another part of India); and further assigned the revenues of three districts of Bengal–Burdwan, Midnapur and Chittagong–for a regular income of the Company."[110]

Again, this was not the last round of loot. Three years later, when Mir Kasim was thrown out and Mir Jafar reinstated in 1763, the presents amounted to £ 500,165. After two more years, when Mir Jafar died and his illegitimate son, Najim-ud-Daula, was hastily put on the throne (as the Directors of the Company now wanted to stop such accumulation of fortunes to their servants), further presents came in to the extent of £ 230,356.[111]

It should further be noted that this extraction of £ 2,169,665 within a period of only eight years did not represent the total sum obtained as "presents" from Bengal. In addition, the servants of the Company claimed more, and as restitution obtained within the same period £ 3,770,833.[112] Even taking £ 5,940,498 (thus obtained in all in the eight years after the Company captured power) as the total sum extracted as "gifts" from the Subah of Bengal, (for no account is available in figures of the direct extraction from the people–the peasants, artisans and traders), it represented more than four times the revenue collection of the Nawab in the year 1765–66 according to Bengali calender ending in April, when £ 1,470,000 were so collected. Such was the magnitude of this colossal plunder; and it should be further borne in mind that all that was extracted, directly or indirectly, from the people and the puppet *nawabs* was taken away to England to fructify that country while leading the country and the people supplying the "tributes" towards destitution.

This form of vandalism, however, could not continue for long. As mentioned above, the acquisition at the enthronment of Najim-ud-Daula had to be made hastily and the General Council propped him up much too quickly in order to reap the last harvest, for the share-holders of the Company were not feeling amicably towards such fortunes going to their employees. Those at the helm of the Company were, of course, not governed by any philantropic whim towards the Indians. On the contrary, their self-interest dictated this move; that is, to replace such spontaneous plunder of the "goose laying golden eggs" by a more regular system of exploitation, which would be to the advantage of the Company only.

Of the two main reasons which governed this decision of the Company, the first one was that the former employees of the Company were coming out as rivals to their former masters when they returned to England with great fortunes. Noteworthy amongst such ex-servants was Clive who, on his return from India, decided to enter Parliament in order to oppose the Company.

> "His purchases of land seem to have been made in a great measure with that view, and, after the general election of 1761, he found himself in the House of Commons, at the head of a body of dependents whose support must have been important to any administration."[113]

Clive also wanted to get into the Court of Directors of the Company. So, he "himself laid out a hundred thousand pounds in the purchase of stocks, which he then divided among nominal proprietors on whom he could depend, and whom he brought down in his train, to every discussion and every ballot."[114] And, Clive was no exception; "others did the same, though not to quite so enormous an extent."[115] Hence, in order not to impair their strength further, the ring of Directors desired that the employees of the Company should not grow into millionaires by means of extracting "presents" from India.

The second reason of the Company was probably even more important. In increasing measure, it was usurping all the rights of government in India; hence, the depletion of revenue would now affect the Company directly, and not just the puppet *nawabs*. Even before the Company fully undertook the civil administration of Bengal, the importance of such a measure was revealed to the Directors by the comparatively smaller fortuness the Company had amassed since the subjugation of Bengal in 1757. Already in 1763, L. Scrafton, a member of Clive's Council at Calcutta, wrote:[116]

"These glorious successes have brought near three millions of money to the nation; for, properly speaking, almost the whole of the immense sums received from the Soubah (of Bengal) finally centres in England. So great a proportion of it fell into the Company's hands, either from their own share, or by sums paid into the treasury at Calcutta for bills and receipts, that they have been enabled to carry on the whole trade of India (China excepted) for three years together, without sending out one ounce of bullion. Vast sums have been also remitted through the hands of foreign companies, which weigh in the balance of trade to their amount in our favour with such foreign nations."

Because in this way "the dearest dream of the merchants of the East India Company was thus realized: to draw the wealth out of India without having to send wealth in return,"[117] the Company in order to complete its mission in India decided now to take up full economic control of the territory already under political subjugation.

For these two purposes, viz. to stop the employees from extorting great sums of money from the *nawabs* and to take full control over the Subah of Bengal, the Directors of the Company despatched Clive for the third time to India in 1765. On arrival in India, the first thing that Clive did was to obtain from the tottering Mughal Emperor a charter making the East India Company the Dewan or the Civil Administrator of the Subah of Bengal. For, though the "Great Mughal" had no real power, he was still the titular sovereign of India and therefore his charter gave the Company a legal status in the country. And this was the beginning of the scheme of the "British moneyocracy," as Marx described them, to convert India into its landed estate and organize systematic extraction of the wealth and resources of the people and the country. Henceforth, over and above the "trading zeal" of the Company was added the "pound of flesh" motive of Shylock. Ever-increasing land-tax imposed on the people and collected with extraordinary efficiency, without hardly in any way caring for the welfare of their economy, sucked at the very vitals of the people. Hunger and famine, pestilence and epidemics became the order of the day in once flourishing lands of India. And, while India and her people were thus continually impoverished, this was the beginning of the *organized* Economic Drain from India, which swelled in bulk and amounted to colossal figures in course of time. With this blood money of India was built the industrial England; and thus were planted the edifices of the great "Victorian" Civilisation, referring to which Marx wrote in a letter to Engels on October 8, 1858: "We cannot deny that bourgeois society has experienced its sixteenth century a second time."[118]

This form of extracting India's wealth by the policy of estate-farming is best described by considering different parts of India separately in the order of application of the Company's policy to these areas. As mentioned above, the policy was first put into practice in the Subah of Bengal in 1765; then it was gradually extended to the whole of northern India. In South India, it was first applied in the Carnatic, and then spread over other parts. It reached Bombay, the Deccan, and the Punjab during the last days of the Company's rule, as everywhere the exploitation began in the wake of subjugating these territories. In the following sections, therefore, the situation in different parts of India during the Company's rule has been described in the above order.

7. Estate-Farming in Bengal

In a letter to the Court of Directors from Calcutta, dated 30th September, 1765, Clive wrote:[119]

"Your revenues, by means of this acquisition, will, as near as I can judge, not fall far short for the ensuing year of 250 lacks [25,000,000] of Sicca Rupees, including your former possessions of Burdwan, etc. Hereafter they will at least amount to twenty or thirty lacks more. Your civil and military expenses in time of peace can never exceed sixty lacks of Rupees; the Nabob's allowances are already reduced to forty-two lacks, and the tribute to the King [the Mughal] at twenty-six; so that there will be remaining a clear gain to the Company of 122 lacks of Sicca Rupees, or £ 1,650,900 sterling."

Thus, the Subah of Bengal was entered into the Company's ledger book as a rich estate, a source of profit. In the period that followed, the land revenue was extracted with the utmost vigour, and simultaneously trade and manufacture declined under the system of monopoly and coercion. Hardly any consideration was paid to the welfare of the people.

Considering the period from the financial years, May–April, of 1765–66 to 1770–71, the Gross Collection was £ 20,133,579; the Net Revenue after deducting the tribute to the Mughal, allowance to the Nawab of Bengal, charges of collection, salaries, commissions, etc., was £ 13,066,761; the Total Expenditure–civil, military, buildings, fortifications, etc.,–was £ 9,027,609; and the Net Balance in six years was £ 4,037,152.[120] The figures show that nearly one-third of the net revenue of the Subah was actually remitted out of the country. The actual drain was, however, much larger, for a large portion of the civil and military expenses consisted of the pay of English officials who sent all their savings out of the country.

Furthermore, the vast fortunes amassed by those who had excluded the Indian merchants from their legitimate trades and industries were annually sent out of India. The actual drain from the Subah may therefore be correctly represented by the figures for imports and exports from the year 1765. Total figures for the entire period of six years is not available; but in the three years of 1766, 1767 and 1768 only, goods and treasures to the value of £ 6,311,250 were exported from the Subah, while the imports amounted to only £ 624,375.[121] In other words, the country sent out about ten times what it received.

Such gross expropriation of the country's wealth and the total neglect of its economy led to chronic want. Eventually it burst forth in a virulent famine in 1770 with a seasonal failure of rain and the manipulation of grain-stocks by the profit-hunting English officials and the Indian agents. The situation has been described as follows.[122]

> "Early in 1769 high prices gave an indication of an approaching famine, but the land-tax was more rigorously collected than ever. 'The revenues were never so closely collected before' (Resident at the Durbar, 7th February 1769. India Office Records, quoted in Hunter's *Annals of Rural Bengal*, London, 1868, p. 21 note). Late in the year the periodical rains ceased prematurely, and the Calcutta Council in their letter of the 23rd November to the Court of Directors anticipated a falling off of the revenues, but specified no relief measures to be undertaken. On the 9th May 1770 they wrote: 'The famine which has ensued, the mortality, the beggary, exceed all description. Above one-third of the inhabitants have perished in the once plentiful province of Purneah, and in other parts the misery is equal. 'On the 11th September they wrote: 'It is scarcely possible that any description could be an exaggeration of the misery the inhabitants .. have encountered with. It is not then to be wondered that this calamity has had its influence on the collections; but we are happy to remark they have fallen less short than we supposed they would.' On the 12th February 1771 they wrote: 'Notwithstanding the great severity of the late famine and the great reduction of people thereby, some increase has been made in the settlements both of the Bengal and the Behar provinces for the present year.' On the 10th January 1772 they wrote: 'The collections in each department of revenue are as successfully carried on for the present year as we could have wished.'"

The above remarks on the land-tax collection should be read while keeping in mind that according to the officially-made estimate (which is usually an under-estimate), about one-third of the population of Bengal, or about ten million people, had died in this famine of 1770.

Furthermore, it is worthy of note that while the Company did not take any measure to ameliorate the distress of the people, their sufferings were heightened by the actions of the officials of the Company and their agents. These creatures not only monopolized the grain in order to make high profits from the hunger of the dying people, but they compelled the cultivators to sell even the seed requisite for the next harvest. The Court of Directors was apparently incensed by this method of "profiting by the universal distress" and suggested the infliction of "the most exemplary punishment,"[123] but when their own pounds, shillings and pence were concerned they did not indulge in any act of benevolence. Warren Hastings, the Governor of Calcutta, wrote to the Court of Directors on the 3rd of November, 1772:[124]

> "Notwithstanding the loss of at least one-third of the inhabitants of the province, and the consequent decrease of the cultivation, the nett collections of the year 1771 exceeded even those of 1768. ... It was naturally to be expected that the diminution of the revenue should have kept an equal pace with other consequences of so great a calamity. That it did not was owing to its being violently kept up to its former standard."

Such was the character of exploitation of Bengal in the first years of the Company's government.

In later years, when the Company took over the entire administration to itself, the system of exploitation was better organized and more intensified. In 1765, with the grant of the Dewani to the Company, Clive had organized a sort of dual government in which the collection of revenues, administration of justice and all other transactions were still made under the cover of the Nawab's authority and through his officers; while the Company was the real ruler of the country, and its servants "practised unbounded tyranny for their own gain, overawing the Nawab's servants and converting his tribunals of justice into instruments for the prosecution of their own purposes."[125] Such a situation however could not continue for long. As the Governor Verelest wrote to the Directors of the Company on the 16th December 1769:[126]

> "We insensibly broke down the barrier betwixt us and Government, and the native grew uncertain where his obedience was due. Such a divided and complicated authority gave rise to oppressions and intrigues unknown at any other period; the Officers of Government caught the infection, and being removed from any immediate control, proceeded with still greater audacity."

Therefore, as stated before, in order to come out of the chaos, in 1772 Warren Hastings decided to make over the administration directly to the English officials, and a committee was formed of the

Governor and four members of his Council to look after the management of the revenues and the administration of justice. Calcutta, instead of Murshidabad where the Nawab resided, became henceforth the capital of Bengal, and soon that of the whole of India under the Company's rule.

About this time, to be exact in 1773, Lord North's Regulating Act was passed in the British Parliament, whereby a substantial control of Parliament over the Company was enforced, the individual officers of the Company were strictly forbidden to extort tributes from the Indian rulers for their personal gain, and the internal trade in India carried on by the servants of the Company and other Englishmen was abolished unless they had received licences from the Company. These measures of 1773 were further enforced by Pitt's India Act of 1784. Hence, from the time the Company undertook full control of the Subah of Bengal, estate-farming became the principal avenue for extracting India's wealth, and eventually the Company's policy in the whole of India was directed to this end.

Previous to 1772, when the Subah was administered formally by the Nawab's officers, the Company had introduced a new system of land settlement in Burdwan and Midnapur soon after it had acquired these districts from Mir Kasim in 1760. The system was as follows:[127]

> "The lands were let by public auction for the short term of three years. Men without fortune or character became bidders at the sale; and while some of the former farmers, unwilling to relinquish their habitations, exceeded perhaps the real value in their offers, those who had nothing to lose advanced yet further, wishing at all events to obtain an immediate possession. Thus numberless harpies were let loose to plunder, whom the spoil of a miserable people enabled to complete their first year's payment."

This method of profiting through the intermediary of unscrupulous agents was now established over the whole of the Subah. A land-settlement for five years was adopted in 1772, and instead of asking the previous revenue-farmers to continue as before, settlements were made by auction with a view to realize the highest possible revenue. The result was obvious.

"Bidders at the auction had been led by the eagerness of competition to make high offers, had squeezed the cultivators of the soil, and had yet failed to pay the promised revenue."[128]

Simultaneously, the traditional revenue-farmers who had bid along with the agents of the English officials were ruined.

"The Rajah of Nuddea survived the famine so much in default, that he was glad to surrender his estates to his son. . . . The young Rajah of Beerbhoom was thrown into jail for arrears of land-tax; while the aged Rajah of Bishenpoor was only let out of a debtor's prison when his end visibly drew nigh. . . . The ruin of the Hindu gentry excited little pity or forbearance."[129]

The Company, however, instead of relaxing its extortion and coming to the aid of the ruined people and the old revenue-farmers, decided in 1774 to employ its direct agents—the Indian "Amils"—in each district. These Amils virtually became the revenue-farmers, and, on the threat of imprisonment and torture (which were not infrequently put into practice), extracted whatever the people and the traditional revenue-farmers had in order to fill the coffers of the Company and their own.

When the five years' settlement came to an end in 1777, the auction system was somewhat modified, and preference was given to ancient revenue-farmers. But, henceforth it was decided to let out the estates not for five years, but annually. This was done for 1778, 1779 and 1780. In 1781 a Committee of Revenue was formed which continued with the one-year settlement as before, but increased the land-revenue by £ 260,000.[130] Furthermore, this time a new incentive was given to the Company's officials to extort the utmost from the people.

". . . the Collectors were encouraged to replenish the exchequer by the grant of a percentage on their collections, in addition to their salaries. How this bribe succeeded may be estimated from a fact mentioned by Lord Cornwallis, that one collector, with a salary of 1000 rupees a month (£ 1200 a year) had an income of at least £ 40,000 a year."[131]

By such ever-increasing demand for land-tax the people were led towards destitution; and while the English officials and their Indian agents gained substantially by the Company's policy, those of the ancient revenue-farmers who had some consideration for the people were led to the verge of ruin in order to meet the demands of the Company. And if they could not meet the demands regularly, the rapacious agents were let loose on the estates in order to plunder the people and the revenue-farmers alike, and thus to meet the demands of the Company and fill their own pockets. This one can realize from the available account of the three largest estates in Bengal, namely, Burdwan with its annual revenue of over £ 350,000, Rajshahi with that of over £ 260,000, and Dinajpur with that of over £ 140,000.

"Dinajpur suffered most. An unscrupulous and rapacious agent, Debi Sing, was appointed from Calcutta to manage this estate during the minority. Debi Sing had been guilty of tyranny in Purnea and in Rungpur, and had been removed from his previous employment, and branded in the Company's records; but he was chosen as a proper agent when the object was to screw up the revenues of Dinajpur during a minority. Debi Sing proved himself equal to the task. With a cruelty perhaps unparalleled even in Bengal in the eighteenth century, he imprisoned the Zemindars and flogged the cultivators in order to raise the revenue. Women were not exempted from his tyranny, and insult and indecent outrage were added to the tortures of the stake and the lash.

The oppression of Debi Sing drove the suffering cultivators of Dinajpur from their homes and villages. They attempted to leave the district, but bands of armed soldiers drove them back. Many fled into the jungles, and large numbers of the most passive and submissive race of cultivators on earth were goaded to rebellion. The insurrection spread through Dinajpur and Rungpur; soldiers were called in, and then followed punishments and cruel executions. Mr. Goodlad, the English chief of the district, described the rising as the greatest and most serious disturbance which had ever happened in Bengal; the cruel severity by which it was suppressed was also perhaps unexampled in Bengal.

The story of Burdwan is less tragic, because the great wrong fell on the territorial house, and not to any great extent on the people. Maharaja Tilak Chand had died in 1767, and the succession of the minor son, Tej Chand, had been allowed and confirmed. Lalla Umi Chand, a friend of the family, had been appointed administrator of the estate by the deceased Zemindar; but John Graham, the British chief of the district, forced on the widow Rani a rapacious and unscrupulous manager in Braj Kisor. The Rani, as far as a woman could, endeavoured to stop his dishonesty, and refused him the great seal of the estate.

'My son's seal', she said in a petition to Warren Hastings in 1774, 'was in my own possession; and as I affixed it to no paper without first perusing it, Braj endeavoured by every method to get it into his own hands, which I constantly persisted in refusing him. Upon this, in the Bengal year 1179 (A. D. 1772), Braj Kisor, having prevailed upon Mr. Graham to come to Burdwan, took from me my son Tej Chand, then nine years of age, and confined him in a separate place under a guard. In this situation, through affliction and apprehension, having remained more than seven days without sustenance to the absolute endangering my life, and finding no resource, I gave up the seal.'

The letter went on to say, that after thus obtaining the seal of the estate, Braj Kisor wasted the wealth of the estate, embezzled a large sum of money, and refused to submit any accounts. The Rani with her son was in dread of her life, and prayed to be allowed to proceed to Calcutta to reside in safety.

Clavering, Monson, and Francis, members of the Governor-General's Council, asked for an inquiry into the charge of embezzlement against Braj Kisor and John Graham. ... The dissensions in the Council, however, prevented a proper inquiry, and Warren Hastings defended John Graham. 'Such inconsiderable presents,' wrote Clavering, Monson, and Francis, 'as the Governor-General says Mr. Graham received, could never have created the immoderate fortune he is known to possess.'

'I am totally unacquainted,' replied Hastings, 'with Mr. Graham's fortune; I know not on what foundation the majority style it immoderate. I thought it incumbent to vindicate him from the calumnies of the Burdwan Rani.'

For the rest, the Burdwan estate was heavily assessed. ...

The new revenue system introduced by Warren Hastings, and the five-years' settlements made in 1772, affected Rajshahi as they affected every other estate in Bengal. The Governor and Council, in their letter of the 31st December 1773, remarked that 'Rani Bhavani, the zemindar of Rajshahi, proved very backward in her payments.' And on the 15th March 1774 they determined to make 'a declaration to the Rani, that if she did not pay up the revenue due from her to the end of the Bengal month of Magh (10th February) by the 20th Phalgun (1st March), we should be under the necessity of depriving her of her zemindari, and putting it into the possession of those who would be more punctual in fulfilling their engagements with Government.' In another letter, dated 18th October 1774, the Governor-General 'resolved to dispossess her both of her farm and her zemindari, and of all property in the land, and to grant her a monthly pension of 4000 rupees (£ 400) during life, for her subsistence.'

Among the many petitions which the aged Rani submitted to avert this disgrace and humiliation, there are some which are of more than usual interest. In one of these petitions she recounted the history of her estate since the five-years' settlement of 1772, the oppressions committed by the farmer, Dulal Roy, who had been appointed, and the depopulation of the country in consequence.

'In the year 1179 (A. D. 1772), the English gentlemen of the Sircar (Government) did blend all the old rents of my land together, and did make the Ziladari Mathote (exactions on tenants) and other temporary rents perpetual. ... I am an old Zemindar; and not being able to see the griefs of my Ryots, I agreed to take the country as a farmer. I soon examined the country, and found there was not enough in it to pay the rents. ...

'In Bhadra, or August 1773, the banks broke, and the Ryots' ground and their crops failed by being over-flowed with water. I am a Zemindar, so was obliged to keep the Ryots from ruin, and gave what ease to them I could, by giving them time to make up their payments; and requested the gentlemen (English officials) would, in the same manner, give me time, when I would also pay up the revenue; but not crediting me, they were pleased to take the Cutchery (rent-collection office) from my house, and bring it away to Motijhil, and employed Dulal Roy as a servant and Sazawal, to collect the revenue from me and the country. ...

'Then my house was surrounded, and all my property inquired into; what collections I had made as farmer and Zemindar were taken; what money I borrowed and my monthly allowances were all taken; and made together Rs. 2,258,674 (£ 226,000).

'In the new year 1181 (A. D. 1774), for the amount of Rs. 2,227,824 (£ 223,000) the country was given in farm to Dulal Roy, taking from me all authority. Then Dulal Roy and Paran Bose, a low man, put on the country more taxes, viz., another Ziladari Mathote (exaction on tenants), and Assey Jzaffer, loss of Ryots' desertion taken from present Ryots etc. These two men issued their orders, and took from Ryots all their effects, and even seed grain and ploughing bullocks, and have depopulated and destroyed the country. I am an old Zemindar; I hope I have committed no fault. The country is plundered, and the Ryots are full of complaints. ...'

Pran Krishna, son of Rani Bhavani, submitted other petitions, and there were many revenue consultations. Philip Francis protested against the practice of European servants holding farms in the names of their Banians or Indian agents. 'The country,' he said, 'belongs to the natives. Former conquerors contended themselves with exacting a tribute from the land. ... Every variation hitherto introduced from the ancient customs and establishments of the country appears to have been attended with fatal consequences, insomuch that I understand it to be the general opinion, that at least two-thirds of the whole surface of Bengal and Behar are in a state of total depopulation. The timid Hindoo flies from the tyranny which he dare not resist.'

In the end, the majority of the Council resolved in 1775 'to deprive Raja Dulal Roy of the farm of Rajshahi, and that the Rani be reinstated in possession of her lands in farm.'

Hastings never entirely approved of this decision; ... Large slices of the old Rajshahi estates were curved out to create a flourishing estate for Kanta Babu, the Banyan of Warren Hastings."[132]

The severity of this form of exploitation from the fertile lands of Bengal will be fully realized from the following table which gives the land-revenues demanded and collected from the Subah of Bengal since the sixteenth century.[133]

Year	Particulars	Land-revenues in £	
		Demanded	Collected
1582	Todar Mall's Settlement	1,070,000	Probably less
1658	Sultan Shuja's Settlement	1,312,000	Probably less
1722	Jaffar Khan's Settlement	1,429,000	Probably less
1728	Suja Khan's Settlement	1,425,000	Probably less
1762–63	Mir Kasim's Rule		646,000
1763–64	Mir Jafar's Second Rule		762,000
1764–65	Mir Jafar's Second Rule		818,000
1765–66	First Year of Dual Government		1,470,000
1771–72	Last Year of Dual Government		2,341,941
1771–72 to 1778–79	Yearly average during Company's Direct Rule		2,577,078
1790–91	Company's Direct Rule		2,680,000

The table shows that before the British conquest of the Subah of Bengal the revenue demand had not very much altered over a century and a half. Moreover, it should be borne in mind that in those days there was a sharp difference between what the Indian rulers *wanted* to collect, as laid down in the Settlement Records, and what they *actually* received. The latter figure was usually below the mark, even though during the last days of Mughal administration land-tax used to be collected with greater rigour and increasing oppression of the people, as has been noted in the previous chapter. This was so because, firstly, the revenue-farmers and the Government Collectors did sometimes pay heed to the requests of the distressed peasantry for suspension or remission of their taxes in case of natural calamities and such reasons, and, secondly, the collecting apparatus of the Indian rulers was never so well organized as that of the Company. Therefore, it is likely that the people of the Subah in those days had to contribute even less to the State coffer than the above figures suggest. Moreover, this suggestion is further supported by the figures of land-revenue actually collected during the rule of puppet *nawabs*; in which case, of course, there was the additional factor that because of reckless vandalism of the Company officials and their agents the people could not contribute much to the Government Treasury, and following the traditional usages the Indian rulers could not enforce it too much. Yet the table shows that the revenue collection began to mount steadily from Mir Kasim's rule to the first and the second years of Mir Jafar's second installation on the throne; and then the situation changed drastically from the year the Company undertook civil administration of the Subah. In the first year of the "Dual Government" the revenue collection was nearly double that of the previous year. In the next six years it further rose by 59 per cent. And it went on rising, so that the collection of 1790–91 was nearly double the assessments of Jafar Khan and Shuja Khan, even though these were the *highest amounts desired* by the Indian rulers in the pre-British days. It should further be noted that it was three times the collections made in the last year of Mir Jafar's rule, and nearly double the collection made in the first year of the Company's Dewani (1765–66). No wonder then that Bengal–once the Granary of the East–became empty; hunger and famine, death and disease stalked the country.

And the worst calamity in this situation was that virtually the whole of the revenue of the Subah was drained out of the country, and did not, in any shape, return to the people in order to fructify their trade, their industries and their agriculture. The Select Committee of the House of Commons reported in 1783:[134]

> "Notwithstanding the famine of 1770, which wasted Bengal in a manner dreadful beyond all example, the Investment by a variety of successive expedients, many of them of dangerous nature and tendency, was forcibly kept up. ... The goods from Bengal, purchased from the territorial revenues, from the sale of European goods, and from the produce of the monopolies ... were never less than a million sterling, and commonly nearer £ 1,200,000. This million is the lowest value of the goods sent to Europe, for which no satisfaction is made. About £ 100,000 a year is also remitted from Bengal on the Company's account to China, and the whole of the product of that money flows into the direct trade from China to Europe. Besides this, Bengal sends a regular supply in time of peace to those Presidencies (in India) which are unequal to their own establishments."

In short, Bengal became the *Kam Dhenu*, the wish-fulfilling cow, of the English by means of which they not only harvested fortunes from India but also carried on their China trade without any payment from England.

The Select Committee further reported:[135]

> "When an account is taken of the intercourse, for it is not commerce, which is carried on between Bengal and England, the pernicious effects of the system of Investment from revenue will appear in the strongest point of view. In that view, the whole exported produce of the country, so far as the Company is concerned, is not exchanged in the course of barter, but it is taken away without any return or payment whatever."

This exhaustion of the country and of the people reached such an extent only three decades after the Company's rule began in 1757 that the Governor-General Lord Cornwallis declared in 1789:[136]

> "I may safely assert that one-third of the Company's territory in Hindustan is now a jungle inhabited only by wild beasts."

Comments would be superfluous.

8. Extraction from Northern India

The same rule of fleecing the country and the people was enacted in Northern India during the latter part of the eighteenth and early nineteenth centuries. It has been noted before how the Company made presents of other people's property in order to gain its own ends, and then returned the same property to its original owner at a larger price when the necessity of pleasing the third party was over. The illustrative case in this respect was the State of Oudh, which occupied practically the whole of Northern India, east of Delhi and west of the Subah of Bengal. From this State, Kora and Allahabad were first taken away by the Treaty of 1765, (which the Nawab of Oudh had to sign after his defeat at the hands of the Company along with Mir Kasim), and handed over to the Emperor of Delhi to bring the latter under control of the Company and obtain from him the right of civil administration of the Subah of Bengal. Eight years later, in 1773, when the defunct Mughal Emperor was found to be aligning himself with the Marathas instead of to the Company, these two territories were taken back from him and "sold" to the Nawab of Oudh for Rs. 4,500,000, or the equivalent of about £ 450,000. This, however, was not the only price the Nawab of Oudh and his satelites had to pay for their vassalage to the Company. Heavier and more ruthless ones followed in succession. And they had the same characteristics as in the case of the Subah of Bengal, namely, first, extortion of colossal tributes from the Indian rulers until they were sucked dry, and then collection of ever-increasing land-revenues under the direct auspices of the officials of the Company.

To describe only the most prominent cases of such tyranny and oppression, it is best to quote the words of a reputable economist-historian of India. The State of Benares is described first.[137]

"Among the many little States into which Northern India was divided in the eighteenth century, none was more flourishing and prosperous, according to the testimony of all eye-witnesses, than Benares. The people were industrious, agriculture and manufactures flourished, and Raja Balwant Sing had his capital in that sacred city which was revered by all Hindus in all parts of India.

Balwant Sing died in 1770, and his liege lord, the King of Oudh, known as the Vizir, confirmed his son, Chait Sing, in succession on receipt of a succession fee and on a slight increase of the revenue previously paid. The East India Company had interested themselves in this succession, and in a general letter to the Directors, dated 31st October 1770, the Governor of Bengal wrote that 'the Vizir's readiness in complying with this our recommendation and request has offered us great satisfaction, and is a circumstance the most pleasing, as it must give strength to the opinions of the several Powers in Hindustan of the strict friendship subsisting between the English and him.'

The King of Oudh, Suja-ud-Daula, himself died in 1775, and Warren Hastings, then Governor-General, took advantage of the death of the old ally of the British to extend British dominion and power. In 1775 a new treaty was ratified between his son and successor, Asof-ud-Daula, by which Benares was ceded to the East India Company, and Raja Chait Sing became a vassal of the British.

'The cession of Benares and the other territories of the Raja Chait Sing, wrote the Governor-General to the Directors in August 1775, 'to the Company, we flatter ourselves, will prove perfectly agreeable to your ideas, as it conveys a valuable acquisition to the Company. ... The revenue which accrues from this acquisition amounts to Rs. 2,372,656 (£ 237,000), and will be paid by the Raja in monthly payments as a neat tribute, without rendering any account of his collections, or being allowed to enter any claims for deduction.'

Three years after this the unfortunate Chait Sing comprehended the full import of the change of his masters. 'War having been declared between the Courts of Great Britain and France,' wrote Warren Hastings to Chait Sing in July 1778, 'by the former on the 18th March ... I am to request of you, in my own name and that of the Board as a subject of the Company, bound to promote their interest on every occasion, to contribute your share of the burden of the present war' [which was Rs. 500,000 or £ 50,000 annually —R. K. M.]. ...

A second year's contribution of five lakhs (£ 50,000) was demanded from Chait Sing, then a third year's contribution of five lakhs, and then a fourth year's contribution, besides expenses of troops. He was reprimanded for failure of payment and then arrested; and when his people attacked the Company's guards, his fate was sealed. He fled from his estate; his sister's son, Mahip Narayan, was seated in his place with a large increase of the revenue demand; and the administration was controlled by the Governor-General's own agents.

The administration was a ghastly failure—not because Warren Hastings was a less able administrator than Bulwant Sing and Chait Sing, under whom Benares had flourished—but because the increased revenue demand under the new administration crushed the agricultural industry of the State.

The first deputy whom Hastings appointed for the Raja was dismissed for the offence of not making punctual payments. The second accordingly acted upon the 'avowed principle that the sum fixed as the revenue must be collected.' Lands were over-assessed, collections were made with the utmost harshness, the population was plunged into misery, and the country was desolated by a terrible famine in 1784."

In later years also the ruthless extraction of land revenue from the State of Benares went on. In 1794 it was taken directly under the Company's rule; the Raja of Benares being allowed to maintain his right of revenue-farming over a small tract which had formed the patrimony of his family.

While Benares was thus ransacked, the situation in Oudh itself was no better, especially since Asof-ud-Daula became the Nawab in 1775.

"When Asof-ud-Daula ascended his father's throne, Warren Hastings extended the power of the East India Company in Oudh. The old treaty with Suja-ud-Daula was modified, and a new treaty was made with Asof-ud-Daula, 'by which the latter eventually and necessarily became a vassal of the Company.'

This vassalage was the ruin of Oudh. Colonel Hanny, who was sent up to Oudh by Hastings in command of a brigade, shared with many of his countrymen of those days the desire to make the best of his opportunities, and to rear a rapid fortune in his new station. The practice of the assignment of the land revenues, which had proved so fatal in Madras and elsewhere, was pursued in Oudh. Colonel Hanny exercised civil and military powers in Oudh, and became the farmer of the revenues of Barraich and Gorakpur. Rents were increased; collection were made with every circumstance of cruelty and coercion; the people fled from their fields and villages; the country became desolate.

Asof-ud-Daula saw the ruin he had brought on himself. In 1779 he wrote to the British Government: 'From the great increase of expense, the revenues were necessarily farmed out at a high rate, and the deficiencis followed yearly. The country and cultivation is abandoned.' The Nawab accordingly protested against fresh assignments for the new brigade, declaring that the troops were quite useless to him, and were the cause of loss in the revenues and of confusion in the affairs of his government.

The Calcutta Council deliberated on this important communication. Philip Francis, ..., recorded a characteristic Minute.

'I have not been long enough in the habits of dominion to see anything offensive or alarming in the demand made by an independent prince to be relieved from the burden of maintaining a foreign army, which, it is notorious, have devoured his revenues and his country under colour of defending it...' ...

In the eyes of Warren Hastings, the pecuniary loss which would be inflicted on the Company by withdrawing the battalions had greater weight than the miseries imposed on the people of Oudh. The Nawab, he said, was the vassal of the Company, and the troops 'cannot be withdrawn without imposing on the Company the additional burden of their expense.' ...

The demands of the British Government in 1780 stood at £ 1,400,000. How the Governor-General recalled Bristow from Lucknow and sent Middleton as Resident; how the Nawab was helped to rob his mother and his grandmother, the Begams of Oudh, to meet the demands of the Company's Government; and how a large sum of money was extorted from them with every circumstance of oppression and indignity, are matters of history which it is unnecessary to narrate in these pages. The condition of the cultivators of Oudh is of far greater importance for the purposes of the present work than the more dramatic story of the wrongs of the royal house.

The facts which were deposed to at the celebrated impeachment of Warren Hastings relating to the collection of rents from the impoverished tenantry are sufficiently dismal. It was stated that the defaulters were confined in open cages, and it was replied that confinement in such cages under the Indian sun was no torture. It was stated that fathers were compelled to sell their children, and it was replied that Colonel Hanny had issued orders against such unnatural sales. Large masses of the people left their villages and fled the country, and troops were employed to prevent their flight. At last a great rebellion broke out; farmers and cultivators rose against the unbearable exactions; and then followed horrors and executions with which the untrained tillers of the soil are put down by the infuriated soldiery.

Colonel Hanny was then recalled from Oudh, and the rebellion was quelled, but Oudh was in a state of desolation. Captain Edwards visited Oudh in 1774 and in 1783. In the former year he had found the country flourishing in manufactures, cultivation and commerce. In the latter year he found it 'forlorn and desolate.' Mr. Holt, too, stated that Oudh had fallen from its former state, that whole towns and villages had been deserted, and that the country carried the marks of famine. A severe famine actually visited the province in 1784, and the horrors of starvation were added to the horrors of misgovernment and war."[138]

The same state of affairs continued in the later years. The British province of India, formerly called the North-Western Provinces and Oudh (which later became the United Provinces, and now Uttar Pradesh), was acquired by the Company in successive stages. As mentioned before, Benares and some adjoining districts were annexed by Warren Hastings in 1775 and in 1794 it came under direct Company's rule. Allahabad and some other districts were "ceded" by the Nawab of Oudh to the Company in 1801 under pressure from Lord Wellesley, and were at first called "Ceded Districts or Provinces." Agra and the Basin of the Ganges and the Jumna were conquered by the Company in the Maratha War of 1803, and were at first called, "Conquered Provinces." And the remaining portion of Oudh was annexed by Lord Dalhousie in 1856, by pensioning off the Nawab who had by then outlived his usefulness. Along with thus subjugating different parts of the province, land-revenues were successively increased, and the extraction mounted on an ascending scale.

As regards the "Ceded Districts," the Nawab's land-revenue assessment was Rs. 13,523,474. In the first year of possession, the Company's assessment was Rs. 15,619,627; in the second year, Rs. 16,162,786; and in the third year, Rs. 16,823,063.[139] Bearing in mind the essential difference between an Indian ruler's assessment, which was generally higher than what was actually collected, and the Company's assessment, of which not a farthing was abated during the collection, it will be realized how steeply the land-revenue demand rose within the first three years. Mr. Dumbleton, a Collector in this territory, remarked that the settlement of 1802 "pressed beyond a reasonable demand;"[140] a polite statement on the situation, no doubt.

Also for the "Ceded and Conquered Provinces," afterwards considered together, it is seen how the land-revenues were constantly increased. In 1807 it was £2,008,955; from this figure it steadily increased to £2,892,789 in 1818.[141]

And then for the North-western Provinces as a whole the land-revenue collections increased from £4,018,344 in 1834–35 to £4,478,417 in 1836–37.[142] But now the Company had reached the limit. All forms of tyranny and coercion failed; the people could not pay more. In 1837–38 the collection came down to £ 3,765,973.[143] Later also, in 1838–39, the revenue-demand for "Northern India" was set at £ 4,554,899, but the collection was £ 3,630,215.[144] So it continued for the next few years during which the demand was a little relaxed and the collection was more rigorously undertaken. As a result, in 1847–48, the demand was for £ 4,292,166, and the collection was £ 4,248,582.[145] In this way the people of Northern India went on building the Company's fortune.

9. Usury and Estate-Farming in South India

After the Third Carnatic War, ending in 1763, the Company's direct control over the whole of the eastern seaboard stretching northwards from Madras to the Subah of Bengal and some territories round Madras was no more disputed. At the same time, the existence of Muhammad Ali as the Company's puppet Nawab of the Carnatic was also universally accepted. And then began in full scale the extraction of south India's wealth by the Company and its officials.

Unlike Mir Kasim, Muhammad Ali was a man of no character. He left his own capital Arcot to live amidst the luxuries of the British town of Madras. Also, instead of being able to liquidate the "claims" of the Company, as Mir Kasim did, he drifted more and more into debt. Moreover, he made assignments of his land-revenues to his British moneylenders, viz. the officials of the Company, until virtually the whole of his "kingdom" passed into the hands of his creditors.

Incidentally, a comparison of Mir Kasim and Muhammad Ali showed that a strong "ruler" had no place in the scheme of the Company's rule, while a weak "ruler" was permitted to live and to borrow and to pay the interest out of the revenue of his "kingdom"–all of which, of course, were shipped to England. In the following, therefore, this sordid picture may be described in some details, and this is best done in the words of the noted economist-historian, R. C. Dutt:[146]

"Under the administration of this feeble potentate the Company found it easy to extend its influence and power. The Company did not stand forth as the Dewan of the Karnatic, as they had done in Bengal in 1765. On the contrary, Mahomed Ali remained nominally the Dewan or revenue administrator, as well as the Nizam or military governor, while the Company virtually enjoyed all real power. The military defence of the country was undertaken by the Company, and a part of the Nawab's revenues was assigned for this purpose. The demands of the Company increased with their wars, and the Nawab came to adopt the strange method of borrowing from the servants of the Company in order to meet the demands of the Company.

What was still more significant and fatal was the security which the Nawab offered for these private debts. Unable or unwilling to draw from his own hoards, he readily delivered up to his private creditors the revenues of his territories. The cultivators of the Karnatic passed from the rule of the Nawab's agents to the rule of British money-lenders. The crops that grew in the fields were subject to the inalienable claims of British creditors. The collections which were made by the Nawab's servants, often under coercion and the use of the whip, were handed over to the British servants of the Company in order to be remitted to Europe. The whole of the Karnatic resembled an egg-shell with its contents taken out. The fields and villages of Southern India were converted into a vast farm, and the tillers tilled and the labourers toiled in order that all the value of the produce might be annually exported to Europe. ... The country became poorer, industries and trades declined. ...

The servants of the Company, comprising members of the Madras Council, were building up large fortunes from their loans to the Nawab, and were not anxious to keep the Court of Directors fully informed of their doing. Under the orders of the Court of Directors, however, they had consolidated their loans into one loan of 1767 at the moderate rate of 10 per cent interest, and they even expressed a hope, from time to time, that the Nawab would pay off his loan. It was neither their interest, however, nor that of the effete and inefficient Nawab, to close the transaction; and it was never closed. And when the full official account of the transaction at last reached the Directors in 1769, their anger knew no bounds."

The righteous indignation of the Court of Directors was of course not dictated by the misery and sufferings of the Indian people, but by the fact that these dealings of the servants of the Company with the puppet Nawab affected the interests of the Company itself. Thus, in a letter to the Superintending Commissioners, dated 23rd March 1770, the Court of Directors wrote:[147]

"The said Governor and Council have, in notorious violation of the trust reposed in them, manifestly preferred the interest of private persons to that of the Company, in permitting the assignment of the revenues of certain valuable districts to a very large amount from the Nawab to individuals which ought to have been applied towards the discharge of the Nawab's debt to the Company: the impropriety of which conduct is the more striking as those revenues, in a very great degree, owe their existence to the protection of the Company (!); and by such unnatural application of the said revenues, although the care and expense of protecting the Karnatic falls principally on the Company, the prospect of paying off the vast sums owing to us by the Nawab is postponed."

R. C. Dutt commented on this note of the Directors:[148]

"The assignment of revenues appeared 'unnatural' to the Court, not because it impoverished the country, but because it postponed the prospect of the Nawab's repaying his debt to the Company."

The debt to the Company, incurred solely to build the Company as a political power in south India and to enrich it, was not however immediately made amenable to the Company's interests. On behalf of the Company Warren Hastings endeavoured to effect a conciliation between its interests and that of its officials in Madras. But it was of no avail, for "the Nawab, who was a tool in the hands of his private creditors, was endeavouring to create influence in England against the Company, and in favour of his creditors;" and, as will be seen below, his creditors also, "who amassed vast fortunes from the rents of the assigned districts, were soon able to qualify a large number of votes, and to make themselves masters of the Court of Directors."[149]

To continue with this sordid story of greed and avarice, of corruption and conspiracies within the Company's administration, which were inevitable outcomes of the very basis of the role of English merchant capital in India:

"In the meantime the Nawab had nearly exhausted the resources of his own kingdom by assignments to his creditors, and began to cast longing eyes on the rich state of the Raja of Tanjore. In the treaty which had been concluded between the British and Haidar Ali in 1769, the Raja of Tanjore had been recognised as an ally of the British. But even the Court of Directors became covetous of the wealth of their 'ally,' and gave a willing ear to the proposals of Mahomed Ali to rob Tanjore in order to repay his debts to the Company.

'It appears most unreasonable to us,' wrote the Directors, 'that the Raja of Tanjore should hold possession of the most fruitful part of the country, which can alone supply an army with subsistence, and not contribute to the defence of the Karnatic...'

This was a broad hint, and was acted upon. Tanjore was besieged in 1771, and saved itself only by the payment of £ 400,000. But this only whetted the appetite of the Nawab, and his friends the British were easily led to think that 'it is dangerous to have such a power in the heart of the province.' Tanjore was besieged again and captured on the 16th September 1773; the unfortunate Raja and his family were taken prisoners in the fort; and his dominions were transferred to the Nawab.

Never was a flourishing and prosperous state so reduced within a few years of misgovernment as the State of Tanjore after it passed under the government of the Nawab. Regarding it as a hostile and conquered country, Mahomed Ali multiplied his exactions upon the people, made assignments of its revenues to his British creditors, and ruined its trade and industries; and within a few years Tanjore, the garden of Southern India, became one of the most desolate tracts on the eastern coast."[150]

Tanjore, however, did not remain for a long time in the hands of the Nawab of Arcot. In 1776, the Raja of Tanjore was reinstated; but now the interests of the Company came in conflict with that of its officials.

"Among the many creditors of the Nawab of Arcot, one Paul Benfield had obtained an unenviable prominence. He had come out to India in 1763 in the Company's service as a civil architect, but had succeeded better as an architect of his own fortunes by usury. When the Raja of Tanjore was reseated on his throne, Benfield claimed that he had assignment upon the revenues of Tanjore to the amount of £ 162,000 for money lent to the Nawab, and that for money lent to individuals in Tanjore he had assignments upon the standing crops to the amount of £ 72,000. The incident throws a strong light on the times. Benfield was still a junior servant of the Company drawing a few hundred pounds a year, but he kept the finest carriages and horses in Madras, and he claimed a fabulous sum from the Nawab. The revenues of a rich state and the standing crops of a nation of agriculturists were supposed to be hypothecated for the satisfaction of his claim.

Lord Pigot (Governor of Madras) laid Benfield's claims before the Board. Benfield was unable to produce vouchers, but urged that the Nawab would admit his debt. The Board resolved by a majority that Benfield's claims against individuals had not been sufficiently explained, and that the assignments of the Nawab on the revenues of Tanjore were not admissible. Benfield was not satisfied, and he had friends and resources. His claims were again brought before the Council, and admitted. Lord Pigot's proposal to send Russel as Resident to Tanjore did not satisfy the majority of members. Colonel Stuart, who was supposed to have agreed to manage Tanjore affairs in the interest of the creditors, was chosen. Lord Pigot resisted the majority, and on the 24th August 1776 he was arrested by Colonel Stuart and imprisoned."[151]

In 1777, Lord Pigot died in prison, before the orders of the Court of Directors to release him and send him back to England reached Madras. And before the next Governor, Sir Thomas Rumbold, reached Madras in the next year, two more loans were contracted by the Nawab in 1777 in favour of the Company's officials.

"The Nawab was persuaded to discharge his useless cavalry, but had no money to pay them. Taylor, Majendie, and Call offered to advance £ 160,000 if the Company's sanction were given to the debt, and this was done. Assignments of revenues were of course made, and the Nawab's manager complained to him two years after.

'The entire revenue of those districts is by your Highness's order set apart to discharge the Tuncaws granted to the Europeans. The Gomastas of Mr. Taylor ... are there in order to collect those Tuncaws, and as they receive all the revenue that is collected, your Highness's troops have seven or eight months' pay due which they cannot receive.'

A third loan of over two million pounds sterling was also consolidated in this eventful year, 1777, and Sir Thomas Rumbold, on his arrival at Madras, wrote of this new loan with just indignation."[152]

But now these creditors were economically and politically in a secure position in England, and so they could openly override the interests of the Company.

"And when the matter came for final settlement in the House of Commons, the influence created by those creditors in the House was so great, that all the supposed claims, fraudulent or otherwise, were admitted without inquiry.

Paul Benfield, the greatest and most successful of the creditors, used the vast wealth he had accumulated in India in creating parliamentary influence in England. He returned eight members to Parliament including himself, and he was a powerful and influential man whom the Ministry did not care to offend. 'It was to hold the corrupt benefit of a large parliamentary interest, created by the creditors and creatures, fraudulent and not fraudulent, of the Nawab of Arcot, that ... the Ministry of 1784 decided that they should all, whether fraudulent or not fraudulent, receive their demands.'"[153]

The role of Paul Benfield and his associates in England, as portrayed by the great orator Edmund Burke in his speech in the British Parliament on the Nawab of Arcot's debt, gives a glimpse into one side of British political life in those days, to which some reference has been made in a previous chapter. To quote from this speech noted for its scathing sarcasm:[154]

"Paul Benfield is the grand parliamentary reformer. What region in the empire, what city, what borough, what county, what tribunal in this kingdom, is not full of his labours. In order to station a steady phalanx for all future reforms, this public-spirited usurer, amidst his charitable toils for the relief of India, did not forget the poor rotten constitution of his native country. For her he did not disdain to stoop to the trade of a wholesale upholsterer for this House, to furnish it, not with the faded tapestry figures of antiquated merit, such as decorate, and may reproach, some other Houses, but with real solid, living patterns of true modern virtue. Paul Benfield made (reckoning himself) no fewer than eight members in the *last* Parliament. What copious streams of pure blood must he not have transfused into the veins of *the present*! ...

It was, ..., not possible for the minister to consult personally with this great man [for Benfield was in India]. What then was he to do? Through a sagacity that never failed him in these pursuits, he found out in Mr. Benfield's representative his exact resemblance. A specific attraction, by which he gravitates towards all such characters, soon brought our minister into a close connexion with Mr. Benfield's agent and attorney; that is, with the grand contractor (whom I name to honour) Mr. Richard Atkinson: a name that will be well remembered as long as the records of this house, as long as the records of the British treasury, as long as the monumental debt of England, shall endure! This gentleman, Sir, acts as attorney for Mr. Paul Benfield. Every one who hears me is well acquainted with the sacred friendship and the mutual attachment that subsist between him and the present minister. As many members as chose to attend in the first session of this parliament can best tell their own feelings at the scenes which were then acted...

Every trust, every honour, every distinction was to be heaped upon him [Atkinson]. He was at once made a Director of the India Company; made an Alderman of London; and to be made, if ministry could prevail (and I am sorry to say how near, how very near they were to prevailing), representative of the capital of this kingdom. But to secure his services against all risk, he was brought in for a ministerial borough. On his part he was not wanting in zeal for the common cause. His advertisements show his motives, and the merits upon which he stood. For your minister, this worn-out veteran submitted to enter into the dusty field of the London contest; and you all remember that in the same virtuous cause, he submitted to keep a sort of public office, or counting-house, where the whole business of the last general election was managed. It was openly managed, by the direct agent and attorney of Benfield. It was managed upon Indian principles, and for an Indian interest. This was the golden cup of abominations; this the chalice of the fornications, of rapine, usury, and oppression, which was held out by the gorgeous Eastern harlot; which so many of the people, so many of the nobles of this land, had drained to the very dregs."

To go back to the state of affairs in south India, following the great whales, like Paul Benfield, came the shoals of fishes. The other creditors now preferred their claims against the Nawab to the tune of £20,390,570. But, by this time, the Nawab was pensioned off and Tanjore was also annexed by the Company. So, any further payments to be made had to be from the Company's Treasury. The Company therefore now behaved just as it did with the inland trade of Bengal. After an inquiry, only £1,346,796 was declared valid; the rest of more than nineteen million pounds was now declared as fraudulent and invalid.[155]

Meanwhile, the country was reduced to utter desolation by usurious transactions with the Nawab of Arcot and the direct revenue administration of the Northern Circars by the Company. In the latter, in successive stages, the land-revenues were increased by more than fifty per cent. For instance, the revenue-farmer of Peddapore paid £37,000 under the Mughals, but his revenue was increased by Rumbold to £56,000; and "similar enhancements were made in all zemindaries except one poor estate."[156] Moreover, how even the "virtuous" officials of the Company made their fortunes in the meanwhile was made known by the dismissal of Rumbold himself when it was pointed out that he had remitted £ 164,000 to Europe within two years of service in Madras.[157]

Thus, the whole of southern India under the Company's dominion was in a wretched state. And added to that were the Anglo-Mysore wars. So, "the people fled to the woods, fields were left uncultivated, villages were burnt and destroyed;" and "these accumulated misfortunes, coupled with the impoverishment of the people, brought on the widespread and terrible famine of Madras in 1783."[158]

Yet, land-tax was collected with the utmost rigour, and it went on increasing in bulk. Within twelve years from 1767–68 to 1778–79, the total net revenue of the Madras Presidency increased by 30 per cent from £ 381,330 to £ 494,208.[159] In 1792, some more territories, like the districts of Salem and Krishnagiri were added to the Madras Presidency, the next addition being in 1800 when the country between the rivers Krishna and Tumbhadra was annexed; and within this period of seven years the land-revenue again increased by 15 per cent from the already very high figure of £ 742,760 in 1792–93 (nearly double the total net revenue of 1778–79) to £ 856,666 in 1798–99.[160] In the next two years the Company "acquired the richest and fairest portions of that great territory" which formed the British Province of Madras, and within that period the land-revenue had already increased by 24 per cent, from £ 883,539 in 1799–1800 to £ 1,095,972 in 1801–02.[161]

So it went on in southern India throughout the Company's rule; and, needless to say, all the extracted wealth went out of India without in any way benefiting the disintegrated economy of the country and the impoverished people. Only during the twelve years 1767–68 to 1778–79, the cargoes which went from the Madras Presidency to Europe as the Company's Investments, that is, "commodities and merchandise purchased out of the revenues for sale in Europe," was valued at prime cost at more than two million pounds sterling![162]

10. India — "Agricultural Farm of England"

Like in northern, eastern and southern India, wherever else the Company extended its power its policy became to extract as much as possible from the territory and the people in the form of land-tax. Thus, with the destruction of her industry and trade, firstly, India was reduced to become only, or mainly, an agrarian country, and, secondly, she was transformed into the revenue-producing agricultural farm of England. To complete this picture after having described the state of affairs in Bengal, Benares, Oudh and south India, a brief account is given below for Bombay, the Deccan, the Punjab, and central India.

In 1811 the dominions of the last of the Maratha Peswa came into the hands of the Company and formed the substantial part of the British Province of Bombay. In 1821, the Governor of Bombay, Mountstuart Elphinstone, recorded a Minute on the land-revenue arrangements at Broach. In this he wrote:[163]

> "The general principle is to take half of the money produced by the sale of the crops, and leave the rest to the Ryot. ... An increase of four lakhs and a half (£ 45,000) has taken place this year."

On the same day, Elphinstone wrote another Minute on the land-revenue operations in Ahmedabad and Kaira.[164]

> "In the Ahmedabad Zilla (district), the number of villages that have been let to the highest bidder, the consequent detection of all sources of revenue, and in some cases the raising of the Bigoties by Panchyats granted at the suggestion of the farmer, have a tendency to strain the revenue to the highest pitch."

In the same year he had recorded another Minute on Surat in which he wrote:[165]

> "If I were to decide on the present condition of the people in this Collectorship, I should pronounce it to be very much depressed. The Ryots seem to be ill-clothed and ill-lodged, ..."

In the Deccan, Mr. Chaplin succeeded Elphinstone as the Commissioner. From his reports of November 1821 and August 1822 it is seen that the payments of the *ryots* or peasants were fixed by the Company's servants with reference to their cultivation and the receipts of former times, but the levy of the State demand was henceforth much more vigorous than before. In 1817 the "revenue of the newly acquired territory was £ 800,000; in 1818 it was raised to £ 1,150,000, and in a few more years to £ 1,500,000."[166] Also, under the Company's rule, "the village officials were allowed less and less power of interference; the Company's servants liked to come in closer contact with each individual cultivator; and the Village Communities virtually disappeared in a few years in Bombay, as they had disappeared in Madras," and elsewhere.[167]

Taking the province of Bombay as whole, of which the territory remained virtually unaltered during this period, the land-revenue increased from £ 868,047 in 1817 to £ 1,818,314 in 1820–21, or an increase of 109 per cent.[168] This was only the beginning.

The survey settlements recommended by Elphinstone were undertaken by Pringle of the Bombay Civil Service in 1824–28, and the settlements were conducted on untrue and exaggerated estimates of the produce of the soil. As the Bombay Administration Report of 1872–73 noted, it led to disastrous results.

> "From the outset it was found impossible to collect anything approaching to the full revenue. (The Government demand was 55 per cent of the net produce—R. K. M.) In some districts not one half could be realised. ... Every effort, lawful or unlawful, was made to get the utmost out of the wretched peasantry, who were subjected to torture, in some instances, cruel and revolting beyond all description, if they would not or could not yield what was demanded. Numbers abandoned their homes, and fled into the neighbouring Native States. Large tracts of land were thrown out of cultivation, and in some Districts no more than a third of the cultivable area remained in occupation."[169]

Naturally, the system had to be abandoned, as it was killing the goose which laid the golden eggs; and a survey was commenced in 1835, which was the beginning of the revenue system finally adopted for the Bombay Province. But this new system also gave hardly any relief to the oppressed people. The principles of the new settlement were as follows.

"Firstly, that it was based on the assessment of each field separately, and not of holdings or villages collectively; Secondly, that it granted long leases for thirty years instead of the short leases which had preceded; and Thirdly, that it abandoned the basis of produce-estimates, and substituted the estimated value of lands as the basis of assessment."[170]

Quite characteristically, the principles involved an elaborate scale for the distribution of the District Revenue demand among a million fields contained in the District according to a fictitious geological value of the land, but prescribed no limit to that demand. And it let loose swarms of "Classers of the Soil," paid ten or twelve shillings a month, to determine the depth and nature of the soil in each field in order to fix its relative value! On the other hand, in this system,

"The cultivator had no voice in the settlement of the Land-Tax; he was called upon, after the demand was settled, to pay it or to quit his ancestral land and starve."[171]

Sir G. Wingate noted in 1850:[172]

"There can be little doubt that the over-estimate of the capabilities of the Deccan, formed and acted upon by an early collector, drained the country of its agricultural capital."

How very real this impoverishment of the country was, and the precarious condition of the people, was attested by a young officer of the Bombay Province, Goldfinch, while reporting to the Parliamentary Committee on the 20th June, 1853.[173]

"The assessment was fixed by the Superintendent of Survey, without any reference to the cultivator; and when those new rates were introduced, the holder of each field was summoned to the Collector and informed of the rate at which his land would be assessed in future; and if he chose to retain it on those terms, he did; if he did not chose. he threw it up."

With such provisions for the good of the people, the land-revenue of Bombay increased from £ 868,047 in 1817–18 to £ 1,858,525 in 1837–38;–an increase of 114 per cent![174]

So it went on during the Company's rule, and in every part of India where the Company set its foot. Thus the Company annexed a portion of the Punjab in 1846, and the whole of the Punjab was fully occupied in 1849; and, as elsewhere, with the conquest of the Punjab, a British garrison was placed there with the stipulation that "the Lahore State was to pay to the British Government £ 220,000 a year."[175] Also, Kashmir was separated from the Punjab and was given to one Golab Singh by the Company at the price of £ 750,000. And then the Company began extorting land-taxes from the people. Between 1847–48 and 1850–51 the land-revenue of the Punjab increased from £ 820,000 to £ 1,060,000; in 1851–52, it stood at £ 1,060,989; and in 1856–57 and 1857–58 (the last two years of the Company's rule) the collections were £ 1,452,000 in each year.[176] Furthermore:

> "The fall in prices added to the distress of the cultivators now required to pay their revenue in money. The complaints during the year 1851 on the part of the agriculturists was loud and general."[177]

In this way, throughout India revenue collections went on at an increasing tempo. In Central India, within a period of only five years from 1819 to 1824, the gross revenue increased by 26 per cent while the territory under the Company's control remained the same as before.[178]

11. The "particular kind of melancholy" under Company's Rule

Needless to say, such enhanced taxation as described in the foregoing pages affected the Indian people very severely and led them towards destitution. Bishop Heber, who toured India during 1824–26 and possessed a fair mind, noted:[179]

> "Neither Native nor European agriculturist, I think can thrive at the present rate of taxation. Half the gross produce of the soil is demanded by Govern-

ment, and this, ... is sadly too much to leave an adequate provision for the present, even with the usual frugal habits of the Indians, and the very inartificial and cheap manner in which they cultivate the land. Still more is it an effective bar to anything like improvement; it keeps the people, even in favourable years, in a state of abject penury; and when the crop fails in even a slight degree, it involves a necessity on the part of the Government of enormous outlays in the way of remission and distribution, which, after all, (as these outlays are in so magnaminous a scale!—R. K. M.) do not prevent men, women, and children dying in the streets in droves, and the roads being strewed with carcasses."

No doubt, under the Company's government India was in a dismal state, which could not pass unnoticed by any observer who was interested in finding out the true state of affairs. And there is also no doubt that the situation could have been improved and the society put on a progressive footing, if the ruling power had been interested in doing so. Heber, for instance, came to the conclusion:[180]

"I am convinced that it is only necessary to draw less money from the peasants, and to spend more of what is drawn within the country, to open some door to Indian industry in Europe, and to admit the natives to some greater share in the magistracy of their own people, to make the Empire as durable as it would be happy."

But the policy of the Company was different. As its guiding principle was to extract to the highest possible limit the wealth of India and send it off to England, it was neither interested "to draw less money from the peasants" nor "to spend more of what is drawn within the country." Some idea of the extent to which India was deprived of her wealth because of this policy is obtained from the excess of India's exports over imports during the Company's rule. According to available figures for the later part of the Company's rule, from 1834 to 1855, India's external trade consistently showed an export-surplus, which ranged from 20 per cent of the total imports in 1852 to 78 per cent in 1836–37; the average percentage-figure being 39.[181] The total value thus drained away from India in merchandise and treasures without any replacement amounted to £ 89,211,185 in 21 years, or a yearly average of £ 4,248,152.[182]

Referring to the colossal drain from India in the manner noted above, and in other ways, as will be described below, Montgomery Martin, an Englishman with genuine sympathy for the Indian people, wrote in 1838:[183]

"For half a century we have gone on draining from two to three and sometimes four million pounds sterling a year from India, which has been remitted to Great Britain to meet the deficiencies of commercial speculations, to pay the interest of debts, to support the home establishment, and to invest on England's soil the accumulated wealth of those whose lives have been spent in Hindustan. I do not think it possible for human ingenuity to avert entirely the evil effects of a continued drain of three or four million pounds a year from a distant country like India, and which is never returned to it in any shape."

But the Company was not concerned with "the evil effects of a continued drain of three or four million pounds a year from a distant country like India, and which is never returned to it in any shape." On the contrary, instead of ameliorating the distress of the Indian people and introducing progressive measures in their economic organization, the Company went on putting additional burdens on the already impoverished people in order to consolidate its position in the territories possessed as well as to spread its influence further through expeditions and wars, while paying at the same time high dividends to its shareholders in England, tributes to the British Government since 1769, and bribes to influential persons in its mother country, as has been described earlier. Thereby the so-called "Indian Debt" came into existence, about which the well-known economist-historian R. C. Dutt noted:[184]

"The whole of the Public Debt of India, built up in a century of the Company's rule, was created by debiting India with the expenses incurred in England, which in fairness and equity was not due from India."

But, fair or foul, "Indian Debt" was established as an important feature of the Company's financial operations, and it went on increasing in bulk with the extension of the Company's rule in India.

"The total Indian Debt, bearing interest, was a little over 7 millions in 1792, and had risen to 10 millions in 1799. Then followed Lord Wellesley's wars, and the Indian Debt rose to 21 millions in 1805, and stood at 27 millions in 1807. It remained almost stationary at this figure for many years, but had risen to 30 millions in 1829, the year after Lord William Bentinck's arrival in India. That able and careful administrator was the only Governor-General under the East India Company who made a substantial reduction in the Public Debt of India, and on the 30th April 1836 the Indian Debt was £ 26,947,434. ...

But from 1840—41 Lord Auckland's unfortunate Afghan War began to tell one the finances of India, and the total Debt of India rose from 34½ millions to 43½ millions by 1844—45. ...

The annexation of Sindh by Lord Ellenborough, and the Sikh Wars of Lord Hardinge and Lord Dalhousie brought fresh liabilities, and the total Debt of India rose to 55 millions by 1850—51. There was a fluctuation after this, and endeavours were made to reduce the Debt, but it rose in the last year of Lord Dalhousie's administration to 59½ millions. The Mutiny which occurred in 1857 raised the Debt in one year by 10 millions, so that on April 30, 1858, the total Debt of India stood at 69½ millions sterling."[185]

Regarding the mechanism of this "Indian Debt," R. C. Dutt remarked in his *Economic History of India in the Victorian Age*:[186]

"A very popular error prevails in this country [England in 1903] that the whole Indian Debt represents British capital sunk in the development of India. It is shown in the body of this volume that this is not the genesis of the Public Debt of India. When the East India Company ceased to be rulers of India in 1858, they had piled up an Indian Debt of 70 millions. They had in the meantime drawn a tribute from India, financially an unjust tribute, exceeding 150 millions, not calculating interest. They had also charged India with the cost of Afghan wars, Chinese wars, and other wars outside India. Equitably, therefore India owed nothing at the close of the Company's rule; her Public Debt was a myth; there was a considerable balance of over 100 millions in her favour out of the money that had been drawn from her."

The British side, however, did not look at the matter from this viewpoint either during the Company's rule or afterwards. Therefore, after 1813, it became a permanent feature of the Company's finances to remit in addition to the export-surplus a part of the extracted wealth of India as "home charges" to England. These "home charges" included, besides other forms of expenditure, payments of interests on the "Indian Debt" and other startling items, such as "that India should pay £ 12,000 per annum for the Persian Mission."[187] In 1814–1815, £ 2,446,016 was drawn out of India through these avenues; steadily it increased to £ 3,090,582 in 1836–37; and in 1851, on the eve of the fall of the Company, it stood at £ 6,162,043.[188] Montgomery Martin had written as early as in 1838:[189]

> "This annual drain of £ 3,000,000 on British India amounted in thirty years, at 12 per cent (the usual Indian rate) compound interest to the enormous sum of £ 723,997,917 sterling; or, at a low rate, as £ 2,000,000 for fifty years, to £ 8,400,000,000 sterling! So constant and accumulating a drain even on England would have soon impoverish her; how severe then must be its effects on India, where the wages of a labourer is from two pence to three pence a day?"

But, naturally, no heed was paid to appeals from noble-minded persons in England, such as Martin and his like. The yearly drain went on mounting higher and higher, so that the total tribute drawn out of India during the Company's rule assumed a frightening dimension. During the twenty-four years of the last phase of the Company's rule, from 1834–35 to 1857–58, only the years 1855, 1856 and 1857 showed a total import-surplus of £ 6,436,345.[190] This, of course, did not indicate that the foreign rulers had changed their policy. On the contrary, this was due to the fact that some British capital flowed into India in these years to build railways in order to prepare her for exploitation by British industrial capital in the next phase when agrarian India's position vis-a-vis industrial Britain's as a country producing raw materials for British industries and buying British-made goods in return was assured. However, even including these three years in the account, it is seen that in the last twenty-four years of the Company's rule the total tribute which was drained from India in the form of "Home Charges" and "excess of Indian exports" amounted to the colossal figure of £ 151,830,989.[191] This works out at a yearly average of £ 6,325,875, or roughly half the annual land-revenue collections in this period!

India was thus bled white during the Company's rule, without hardly giving her any possibility to restore her economy. To "open some door to Indian industry in Europe," as pleaded by Bishop Heber, was therefore quite out of the question, and, for obvious reasons, the government of their country could not be handed over to the Indian people. On the other hand, as explained before, in the social and ideological aspects of life also India was led towards retrogression over and above the devitalisation of her economy. There is scarcely any doubt, therefore, that the Company's rule was certainly a different one from what India had experienced before, as Burke had stressed so forcefully. To India, her old world was lost; but also the new forces which, as described in the previous chapter, were arising in society in the transitional phase of her development were destroyed. This imparted a "particular kind of melancholy" to the Indian society under the Company's rule, which cannot be explained merely by a good and a bad government. For India had experienced both good and bad governments many times before; and, as the past history of India had shown, while she suffered under a bad government, her economy was restored and the society prospered and progressed again under a good government. But now, under the Company's rule, the very basis of her society underwent transformation. As Marx noted:

"... the oppression and neglect of agriculture, bad as it is, could not be looked upon as the final blow dealt to Indian society by the British intruder, had it not been attended by a circumstance of quite different importance, a novelty in the annals of the whole Asiatic world."[192]

This novelty was that a new system—the colonial system of bondage and exploitation—was brought into India by a foreign power which never made it its home. Therefore, in the wake of fulfilling its governing desire to ensure and augment merchant capitalist's profit, and later to thrive on the subjugated people as rent-receivers while maintaining its moorings on the decadent feudal structure of its own society, the organized body of British merchant capital was not so much concerned with what happened in the colony so long as its returns to the home country were satisfactory. On the other hand, this process of profit-gathering necessitated the disintegration of the "entire framework of Indian society," as has been explained in the foregoing pages. Hence, with few qualms and no effect upon themselves, which they would have felt if they formed a part of the society like the previous rulers, the British, as "the first conquerors superior, and therefore inaccessible to Hindu civilisation," could turn back the wheel of progress for a time "by breaking up the native communities, uprooting the native industry, and by levelling all that was great and elevated in the native society." And the execution of this policy, "without any symptoms of reconstruction yet appearing," imparted a "particular kind of melancholy" to the sufferings of the Indian people and separated India, "ruled by Britain, from all its ancient traditions, and from the whole of its past history." As Marx commented upon the Company's rule in India in 1853:[193]

> "I share not the opinion of those who believe in a golden age of Hindustan, without recurring, however, like Sir Charles Wood, for the confirmation of my view, to the authority of Khuli Khan. But take, for example, the times of Aurangzeb, or the epoch, when the Mogul appeared in the North, and the Portuguese in the South; or the age of Mohammedan invasion, and of the Heptarchy in Southern India; or, if you will, go still more back to antiquity, take the mythological chronology of the Brahmin himself, who places the commencement of Indian misery in an epoch even more remote than the Christian creation of the world.
>
> There cannot, however, remain any doubt but that the misery inflicted by the British on Hindustan is of an essentially different and infinitely more intensive kind than all Hindustan had to suffer before. I do not allude to European despotism, planted upon Asiatic despotism, by the British East India Company, forming a more monstrous combination than any of the divine monsters startling us in the temple of Salsette.
>
> This is no distinctive feature of British colonial rule, but only an imitation of the Dutch, and so much so that in order to characterise the working of the British East India Company, it is sufficient to literally repeat what Sir Stanford Raffles, the English governor of Java, said of the Dutch East India Company....
>
> All the civil wars, invasions, revolutions, conquests, famines, strangely complex, rapid and destructive as the successive action in Hindustan may appear, did not go deeper than its surface. England has broken down the entire framework of Indian society, without any symptoms of reconstitution yet appearing. This loss of his old world, with no gain of a new one, imparts a particular kind of melancholy to the present misery of the Hindu and separates Hindustan, ruled by Britain, from all its ancient traditions, and from the whole of its past history."

Yet, with characteristic complaceny, arrogance, and hypocrisy, Lord Dalhousie, the last full-term Governor-General of the Company in India, declared on the eve of leaving the colony:[194]

> "My parting hope and prayer for India is, that, in all time to come, these reports from the Presidencies and Provinces under our rule may form, in each successive year, a happy record of peace, prosperity, and progress."

The answer to such pious hopes and prayers was given by the Indian people in the next year, when the Revolt of 1857, led by the Indian soldiers with support from the masses, shook the bastion of the Company's rule.*

Notes and References

1 Marx, Karl—*The Future Results of British Rule in India*, New York Daily Tribune, August 8, 1853.
2 Dutt, R. P.—*India Today*, People's Publishing House, Bombay, 1949, pp. 96—97.
3 Knowles, L. C. A.—*Economic Development of the Overseas Empire*, p. 74; quoted in *loc. cit.* 2, p. 97.
4 *loc. cit.* 2, p. 98
5 *ibid.*, p. 98
6 Muir, Ramsay—*The Making of British India: 1756—1858*, Manchester at the University Press, 1917, p. 89.

---

* Typical of its propaganda regarding India, the cause of the Indian Revolt of 1857, contemptuously described by the English as the Sepoy Mutiny, was given by the Company and its historians as the religious superstition of the Hindu and Muslim soldiers in the Company's army, who objected to tearing the paper-coverings of the newly-issued cartridges for their rifles, the cartridges being (though the Company denied it at that time) greased with pig-fat or cow-fat. But reputable historians have proved conclusively that the inflammable material for the revolt was produced by the Company itself through its inhuman oppressions of the people in all spheres of life and cruel servitude of the Indian soldiers in its army. And, as Atchison remarked, "On this inflammable material the too true story of the cartridges fell as a spark on dry timber" (quoted in "An Advanced History of India", by R. C. Majumdar, H. C. Raychaudhuri, and Kalikinkar Datta, Macmillan, London, 1953, p. 775). So, the soldiers, supported by the common people, rose up in revolt, but the superior arms of the ruling power and the support it received from some of their puppet "Indian rulers" and landlords led it to victory after mass annihilation. Furthermore, as retaliatory measures, the representatives of a professedly superior civilisation demanded the legalisation of punishments like "flaying alive, impalement, or burning of the murderers," and a "ruthless and indiscriminate policy of vengeance." (quoted, ibid., 779).

7 Bolts, William—*Considerations on Indian Affairs*, London, 1772, pp. 73, 83, 191—194; quoted in *loc. cit.* 6, pp. 89—92.
8 Anonymous—*Historical Sketch on the Taxes on the English Commerce in Bengal from 1633 until 1820*, Mss. Eur. D. 283 in The Commonwealth Office Library, London, p. 55.
9 Quoted by Karl Marx in *Capital: A Critical Analysis of Capitalist Production*, Vol. I, George Allen & Unwin Ltd., London, 1949, p. 432.
10 Marx, Karl—*Capital: A Critical Analysis of Capitalist Production*, George Allen & Unwin Ltd., London, 1949, Vol. I, p. 432.
11 Quoted by R. C. Dutt in *The Economic History of India under Early British Rule*, Routledge & Kegan Paul Ltd., London, 1950, pp. 23—24.
12 *ibid.*, pp. 24—25
13 See, for instance, the English Chief at Malda, Mr. Gray's letter, dated January 7, 1764, and that of Mr. Senior, the English Chief at Cassimbazar, dated March 24, 1764, to Mr. Vansittart (cf. *loc. cit.* 8, p. 63).
14 *loc. cit.* 7, p. 112
15 Vansittart, Henry—*A Narrative of the Transactions in Bengal*, Vol. I, p. 24; quoted in *loc. cit.* 11, pp. 19—20.
16 Dutt, R. C.—*The Economic History of India under Early British Rule*, Routledge & Kegan Paul Ltd., London, 1950, p. 19.
17 Verelst, Harry—*View of Bengal*, p. 48; quoted in *loc. cit.* 16, p. 20.
18 *loc. cit.* 8, p. 52
19 *loc. cit.* 16, pp. 20—21
20 Malcolm, Sir John—*Life of Robert Lord Clive*, 1836, Vol. II, p. 379; quoted in *loc. cit.* 6, p. 76.
21 *loc. cit.* 8, p. 53
22 *ibid.*, p. 55
23 Quoted by James Mill in *The History of British India*, James Madden, London, 1858, Vol. III, p. 234.
24 Quoted in *loc. cit.* 16, p. 28.
25 Mill, James—*The History of British India*, James Madden, London, 1858, Vol. III, p. 237.
26 *loc. cit.* 16, p. 40
27 See, for instance, the manuscripts of Dr. Francis Buchanan in the Commonwealth Office Library, London, and some of their published editions, like *A Survey of the Zilla of Dinajpoore*.
28 *loc. cit.* 16, p. 250, giving extracts from Buchanan's studies
29 *loc. cit.* 6, p. 5
30 *ibid.*, p. 5
31 *ibid.*, p. 5
32 *ibid.*, p. 5
33 *ibid.*, p. 5
34 *ibid.*, pp. 5, 6
35 *ibid.*, p. 8
36 *ibid.*, pp. 7—8
37 *ibid.*, p. 8

38 *ibid.*, p. 8
39 Cf. *A Code of Gentoo Laws, or, Ordinations of the Pundits, from a Persian Translation, made from the Original, written in the Shanscrit Language*, London, 1776, pp. 26—28.
40 From Warren Hasting's despatch from India to the Court of Directors of the Company in London, dated February 21, 1784; quoted in *loc. cit.* 6, pp. 151—152.
41 Anonymous—*Social Legislation: Its Role in Social Welfare*, Issued on behalf of The Planning Commission, Government of India, New Delhi, 1956, p. 16.
42 *ibid.*, p. 16
43 *ibid.*, pp. 16—17
44 *loc. cit.* 6, p. 143
45 *ibid.*, p. 144
46 From Warren Hasting's letter to Lord Mansfield, dated March 21, 1774; excerpts from the letter reproduced in *loc. cit.* 6, pp. 144—145.
47 Macaulay, Thomas Babington—*Warren Hastings* in "Critical and Historical Essays, contributed to The Edinburgh Review," Tauchnitz, Leipzig, Vol. No. CLXXXVIII, 1850, pp. 254, 256—257.
48 Majumdar, R. C.; Raychaudhuri, H. C.; Datta, Kalikinkar—*An Advanced History of India*, Macmillan & Co., London, 1953, p. 786.
49 *loc. cit.* 47, p. 258
50 *loc. cit.* 41, p. 17
51 Mitra, A.—*The Tribes and Castes of West Bengal*, "Census of 1951: West Bengal," Government of West Bengal, Calcutta, 1953, p. 8.
52 Farquhar, J. N.—*Modern Religious Movements in India*, Macmillan, New York, 1919, pp. 8—12
53 *loc. cit.* 39, p. 286
54 Altekar, A. S.—*The Position of Women in Hindu Civilisation*, The Culture Publishing House, Benares Hindu University, 1938, p. 165.
55 Zeh, Lucie—*Zur Frage der Kinderheirat in der indischen Gesellschaft in moderner Zeit*, Thesis submitted for the Degree Examination in Indology in Humboldt University, Berlin, in 1956.

(The study is based on the following publications:—Blunt, E. A. H.—*The Caste System of Northern India*, Madras 1931; *Census of India, 1931*; *Census of India, 1951*; Crooke, W.—*The Tribes and Castes of Northwestern Provinces and Oudh* (4 Vols.), Calcutta, 1896; Hutton, J. H.—*Caste in India*, Oxford, 1951; Haas—*Die Heiratsgebräuche der alten Inder* (im 5. Bd. von Weber's *Indischen Studien*); Ibbetson—*Punjab Castes*, 1891; Jolly, Julius—*Recht und Sitte*, II. Bd., 8. Heft (im Grundriß der indo-arischen Philologie und Altertumskunde); Mayo, Katherine—*Mutter Indien*, Frankfurt, 1928; Mitter, Dwarka Nath—*Position of Women in Hindu Law*, Calcutta, 1913; Nesfield, John C.—*A Brief View of the Caste System of the North-Western Provinces and Oudh*, Allahabad, 1885; Oldenberg, Hermann—*Zur Geschichte des indischen Kastenwesens*, ZDMG, Leipzig, 1897; Rai, Lajpat—*Unhappy India*, Calcutta, 1928; Risley, H. H.—*The Tribes and Castes of Bengal* (2 Vols.), Calcutta, 1891; Russell, R. V.—*The Tribes and Castes of Central Provinces of India* (4 Vols.), London, 1916; Thurston—*Castes and Tribes of Southern India*, (7 Vols.), 1909; Weber,

Albrecht—*Indische Studien*, Berlin, 1862, Bd. 5; Winternitz, Moritz—*Die Frau in den indischen Religionen*, Leipzig, 1920; Winternitz, Moritz—*Das altindische Hochzeitsrituell*, Denkschriften der Wiener Akad. der Wissenschaften, Phil.-Hist. Klasse, 40. Bd., Wien, 1892; Bhandarkar, R. G.—*History of Child-Marriage*, ZDMG, 1893.

The absolute figures from which the percentages of "castes and tribes" have been worked out in the text of the present study are 209 for child-marriage only, 176 for child and adult marriages, and 175 for adult marriage only.)

56 The absolute figures from which the percentages in the text have been derived are as follows:—

"Castes and Tribes"	Child marriage only	Child & adult marriages	Adult marriage only	Total
(1)	(2)	(3)	(4)	(5)
High-castes or Caste-Hindus	162	99	57	318
Low-castes (details as in the text)	43	71	110	224
Total	205	170	167	542

57 *loc. cit.* 54, pp. 73—74

58 *loc. cit.* 39, p. 286

59 *loc. cit.* 54, p. 186

60 *loc. cit.* 41, pp. 61—66

61 Lyall, Alfred—*Asiatic Studies*, London, 1882, p. 102.

62 Elwin, Verrier—*The Aboriginals*, Oxford University Press, 1943, Chapter entitled "A Loss of Nerve".

63 Anonymous—*The Fifth Report from the Select Committee on the Affairs of the East India Company, ordered by the House of Commons to be printed, 28 July 1812*, British Parliamentary Papers, London, 1812, p. 13.

64 *ibid.*, pp. 18—19

65 *ibid.*, p. 47

66 See, for instance, any standard work dealing with the agrarian question or the economic problems of India, such as M. B. Nanavati and J. J. Anjaria's *The Indian Rural Problem*, The Indian Society of Agricultural Economics, Bombay, 1953; P. A. Wadia and K. T. Merchant's *Our Economic Problems*, New Book Company, Bombay, 1946; etc. One may also consult *loc. cit.* 2, Part III, for a coincise account of the agrarian crisis that developed in India during British rule.

67 Quoted by R. C. Dutt in *The Economic History of India in the Victorian Age*, Routledge and Kegan Paul Ltd., London, 1950, p. 114.

68 For Bengal such a situation as noted in the text has been shown in a publication of the writer entitled *The Dynamics of a Rural Society: A Study of the Economic Structure in Bengal Villages*, Akademie-Verlag, Berlin, 1957. Direct or

indirect hints and descriptions to such a state of affairs in other parts of India as found for Bengal are available in the studies of Indian "castes and tribes" as referred to in *loc. cit.* 55 as well as in many other publications, such as, *loc. cit.* 62, *loc. cit.* 66, P. N. Driver's *Problems of Zamindari and Land Revenue Reconstruction in India*, New Book Company, Bombay, 1949; G. S. Ghurye's *The Aborigines—"So-called"—and Their Future*, Ghokale Institute of Politics and Economics Publication No. 11, Poona, 1943; Radha Kamal Mukherjee's *Land Problems of India*, Longmans, Green & Co., London, 1933; Mohinder Singh's *The Depressed Classes: Their Economic and Social Condition*, Hind Kitabs, Bombay, 1947; etc.

69 O'Malley, L. S. S.—*Indian Caste Customs*, Cambridge University Press, 1932, pp. 180—181.

70 Marx, Karl—*The British Rule in India*, New York Daily Tribune, June 25, 1853.

71 *ibid.*

72 *loc. cit.* 63, p. 18

73 Quoted in *loc. cit.* 2, p. 218.

74 Quoted in *loc. cit.* 2, p. 219.

75 *loc. cit.* 66. It may be of interest to note that the point made in the text is clearly supported by the *Report of the Congress Agrarian Reforms Committee*, published by the All-India Congress Committee, New Delhi, 1951.

76 Cf. *The Report of the Indian Statutory Commission*, Government of India Publication, 1930, Vol. I, p. 15.

77 Anonymous—*India 1955: Annual Review*, Information Service of India, Government of India publication, London, 1956, pp. 193—194.

78 *loc. cit.* 41, p. 335

79 *loc. cit.* 2, p. 272

80 *loc. cit.* 1

81 *loc. cit.* 70

82 *ibid.*

83 *loc. cit.* 16, p. 27

84 *loc. cit.* 7; quoted in *loc. cit.* 16, p. 27

85 Smith, Adam—*An Inquiry into the Nature and Causes of the Wealth of Nations*, Everyman's Library, J. M. Dent & Sons, Ltd., London, 1927, Vol. 2, pp. 131—132.

86 *loc. cit.* 67, p. 105

87 *ibid.*, p. 112

88 Quoted in *loc. cit.* 2, p. 115.

89 *loc. cit.* 16, p. 100

90 Quoted in *loc. cit.* 16, pp. 105—106.

91 *loc. cit.* 67, p. 106

92 Quoted in *loc. cit.* 2, p. 193.

93 *loc. cit.* 70

94 Quoted in *loc. cit.* 2, p. 100.

95 Emerson, G.—*Voiceless Millions*, 1931, pp. 140—141; quoted in *loc. cit.* 2, pp. 201—202.

96 *loc. cit.* 16, pp. 197—200, etc.

97 Calculated from Karl Marx's *India Bill (b): Sir Charles Wood's Apologia*, New York Daily Tribune, June 9, 1853.
98 *loc. cit.* 2, p. 119
99 Quoted in *loc. cit.* 16, p. 51.
100 Quoted in *loc. cit.* 16, pp. 49—50.
101 *loc. cit.* 1
102 *ibid.*
103 Cf. *Clive, in the House of Commons*, March 30, 1772; quoted in *loc. cit.* 2, p. 100.
104 Parliamentary Papers—*The Third Report of the Committee of Secrecy Appointed by the House of Commons on the State of the East India Company*, London, 1773, p. 311.
105 *loc. cit.* 2, p. 101
106 Parliamentary Papers—*The First Report of the Committee of Secrecy Appointed by the House of Commons on the State of the East India Company*, London, 1773, p. 148.
107 *loc. cit.* 16, p. 33
108 Macaulay, T. B.—*Lord Clive*, "Critical and Historican Essays" contributed to the Edinburgh Review, Tauchnitz, Leipzig, Vol. No. CLXXXVIII, 1850, 88—89.
109 *loc. cit.* 47, pp. 230—231
110 *loc. cit.* 104, p. 311
111 *ibid.*, p. 311
112 *ibid.*, p. 311
113 *loc. cit.* 108, p. 63
114 *ibid.*, p. 64
115 *ibid.*, p. 64
116 Scrafton, L.—*Reflections on the Government of Indostan*, London, 1763; quoted in *loc. cit.* 2, pp. 101—102.
117 *loc. cit.* 2, p. 101
118 Marx, Karl, and Engels, Frederick—*Selected Correspondence: 1846—1895*, Lawrence & Wishart, London, 1943, p. 117.
119 *loc. cit.* 104, App. 391—398
120 Parliamentary Papers—*The Fourth Report of the Committee of Secrecy Appointed by the House of Commons on the State of the East India Company*, London, 1773, p. 535.
121 Verelst, Harry—*View of the Rise, etc., of the English Government in Bengal*, London, 1772, App. 177; quoted in *loc. cit.* 16, p. 47.
122 *loc. cit.* 16, pp. 51—52
123 Quoted in *loc. cit.* 16, p. 52.
124 Hunter, W. W.—*Annals of Rural Bengal*, p. 381; quoted in *loc. cit.* 16, p. 53.
125 *loc. cit.* 16, p. 42
126 Quoted in *loc. cit.* 16, p. 43.
127 *loc. cit.* 121, p. 70; quoted in *loc. cit.* 16, p. 44
128 *loc. cit.* 16, p. 58
129 Torrens, W. M.—*Empire in Asia—How We came by It: A Book of Confessions*, Trübner & Co., London, 1872, p. 76.

130 *loc. cit.* 16, p. 61
131 *loc. cit.* 129, p. 199
132 *loc. cit.* 16, pp. 61—68
133 *ibid.*, pp. 69, 85, 92
134 Parliamentary Papers—*The Ninth Report of the Committee of Secrecy Appointed by the House of Commons on the State of the East India Company*, London, 1773, p. 55.
135 *ibid.*, p. 55
136 Parliamentary Papers—*The Fifth Report of the Committee of Secrecy Appointed by the House of Commons on the State of the East India Company*, London, 1773; quoted in *loc. cit.* 16, p. 90.
137 *loc. cit.* 16, pp. 69—72
138 *ibid.*, pp. 73—77
139 *ibid.*, p. 175
140 *ibid.*, p. 176
141 *ibid.*, p. 188
142 *ibid.*, p. 405
143 *ibid.*, p. 405
144 Dutt, R. C.—*The Economic History of India in the Victorian Age*, Routledge & Kegan Paul Ltd., London, 1950, p. 46.
145 *ibid.*, p. 46
146 *loc. cit.* 16, pp. 98—101
147 Quoted in *loc. cit.* 16, pp. 101—102.
148 *loc. cit.* 16, p. 102, n 1
149 *ibid.*, pp. 103—104
150 *ibid.*, pp. 104—105
151 *ibid.*, pp. 107—108
152 *ibid.*, p. 109
153 *ibid.*, pp. 113—114
154 Quoted by James Mill in *The History of British India*, James Madden, London, 1858, Vol. V, pp. 22—24.
155 *loc. cit.* 16, p. 115
156 *ibid.*, p. 111, n 2
157 *ibid.*, p. 111
158 *ibid.*, p. 112
159 *ibid.*, p. 113
160 *ibid.*, pp. 399—400
161 *ibid.*, p. 400
162 *ibid.*, p. 113
163 *The Minute*, dated 15th August, 1821; quoted in *loc. cit.* 16, p. 353.
164 *loc. cit.* 16, pp. 353—354
165 *ibid.*, p. 354
166 *ibid.*, p. 357
167 *ibid.*, p. 357
168 *loc. cit.* 144, p. 65
169 *Bombay Administration Report*, 1872, p. 41; quoted in *loc. cit.* 16, p. 375.

170 *loc. cit.* 16, p. 377
171 *ibid.*, p. 380
172 Quoted by L. Natarajan in *Peasant Uprisings in India: 1850—1900*, People's Publishing House, Bombay, 1953, p. 53.
173 Quoted in *loc. cit.* 16, p. 381.
174 *ibid.*, pp. 402—405
175 *loc. cit.* 144, pp. 18—19
176 *ibid.*, pp. 90—92
177 *ibid.*, pp. 90—91
178 Malcolm, Sir John—*A Memoir of Central India, including Malwa and Adjoining Provinces*, Parbury, Allen & Co., London, 1832, Vol. II, Appendix XII.
179 Quoted in *loc. cit.* 16, p. 369.
180 *ibid.*, p. 370
181 Calculated from the data supplied in *loc. cit.* 144, pp. 158—160.
182 *ibid.*, pp. 158—160
183 Martin, Montgomery—*Eastern India*, London, 1838, *Introduction* to the Third Volume.
184 *loc. cit.* 144, p. 215
185 *ibid.*, pp. 216—218
186 *ibid.*, p. xv
187 *ibid.*, p. 5
188 *ibid.*, pp. 115, 212
189 *loc. cit.* 183, *Introduction* to the First Volume
190 *loc. cit.* 144, pp. 115, 158—160, 212
191 Calculated from the data supplied in *loc. cit.* 144, pp. 115, 158—160, 212.
192 *loc. cit.* 70
193 *ibid.*
194 Quoted in *loc. cit.* 144, p. 222.

CHAPTER 6

THE LAST STAGE

1. Company and Parliamentary Influence

The English merchants estimated that Europe's annual consumption in 1612 of pepper (6 million lbs.), raw silk (1 million lbs.), cloves (450,000 lbs.), nutmegs (400,000 lbs.), indigo (350,000 lbs.) and mace (150,000 lbs.) used to cost "in the old way, from Aleppo, £ 1,465,000, but by being purchased from India direct, cost only £ 511,458."[1] For 1670 it was estimated that after consuming saltpetre, pepper, indigo, calicoes and drugs to the amount of £ 165,000, England "exported pepper, cowries, calicoes, chintz to the amount of £ 250,000, which returned six times as much specie as the Company exported to India."[2] Evidently, the trade of the Old East India Company, or the London Company, was thriving in those days. Therefore, as described previously, grave unrest was caused among those sections of the English mercantile bourgeoisie which were deprived of this lucrative commerce, and eventually they brought parliamentary influence to bear upon the privileged section in order to achieve their end. The upshot was that the amalgamation of the Old and the New East India Companies took place in 1708–09, thereby silencing that section of the English merchant-bourgeoisie which did not previously have the legal opportunity and also the necessary facilities to exploit the oriental countries.

Some discontent within the class of merchant bourgeoisie, however, still remained. Therefore, "efforts were made at every epoch of the renewal of the Charter, by the merchants of London, Liverpool and Bristol, to break down the commercial monopoly of the Company, and to participate in that commerce estimated to be a true mine of gold."[3] But placed more securely in its position the Company could successfully parry such attacks by its traditional method of offering "presents" and "loans" to the government as well as bribes to the influential persons in England. Marx wrote:[4]

> "The union between the Constitutional Monarchy and the monopolizing moneyed interest, between the Company of East India and the glorious revolution of 1688 was fostered by the same force by which the liberal interests and a liberal dynasty have at all times and in all countries met and combined, by the force of corruption, that first and last moving power of Constitutional Monarchy, the guardian angel of William III, and the fatal demon of Louis Phillippe. As early as 1693, it appeared from parliamentary enquiries that the annual expenditure of the East India Company, under the head of 'gifts' to men in power, which had rarely amounted to above £ 1,200 before the Revolution, reached the sum of £ 90,000. The Duke of Leeds was impeached for a bribe of £ 5,000, and the virtuous king himself convicted of having received £ 10,000. Besides these direct briberies, rival companies were thrown out by tempting the Government with loans of enormous sums at the lowest interest and by buying off rival Directors.
>
> The power that the East India Company had obtained by bringing (bribing?—RKM) the Government, as did the Bank of England, it was forced to maintain by bribing again as did also the Bank of England. At every epoch when its monopoly was expiring, it could only effect a renewal of its charter by offering fresh loans and fresh presents made to the Government."

Thus, when the arbitration of the Lord High Treasurer of England in 1708 provided the "United Company" with the continuation of its privileges "till three years' notice after the 25th of March, 1726," instead of terminating the period "on three years' notice after the 29th of September, 1711," the Company had to agree to the stipulation that "a sum of 1,200,000 *l.* without interest should be advanced by the United Company to government, which, being added to the former advance of 2,000,000 *l.* at 8 per cent interest, constituted a loan of 3,200,000 *l.* yielding interest at the rate of 5 per cent upon the whole."[5] Then again, when the question of renewal of the Company's charter came up in 1730, (since "in the year 1712, on the petition of the Company, the period of their exclusive trade was extended by act of parliament, from the year 1726, to which by the last regulation it stood confined, to the year 1733, with the usual allowance of three years for notice, should their privileges be withdrawn"), the Company secured the renewal of the charter until 1766 with the usual three years' notice; but, "in order to aid the parliament in coming to such a decision as the Company desired, and to counteract in some degree the impression likely to be made by the proposal of their antagonists to accept of two per cent for the whole of the loan to Government, they offered to reduce the interest from five to four per cent, and, as a premium for the renewal of their charter, to contribute a sum of £ 200,000 to the public service."[6]

Then came the period during which the Company became the master of Bengal, Bihar and Orissa, and began to penetrate farther into Indian territory as a political power. Its effect was at once felt in England; the East India Stock rose to £ 263 and dividends were paid at the rate of 12½ per cent. So, there appeared "a new enemy to the Company, no longer in the shape of rival societies, but in the shape of rival Ministers and rival people."[7] Marx wrote:[8]

> "It was alleged that the Company's territory had been conquered by the aid of British fleets and British armies, and that no British subjects could hold territorial sovereignties independent of the Crown. The Ministers of the day and the people of the day claimed their share in the 'wonderful treasures' imagined to have been won by the last conquests. The Company only saved its existence by an agreement made in 1769 that it should annually pay £ 400,000 into the National Excheqer."

But, in the following years, not only did the East India Company fail to keep its agreement and "instead of paying a tribute to the English people, appealed to the Parliament for pecuniary aid," but a new situation confronted England; viz. "the English nation having simultaneously lost their colonies in North America, the necessity of elsewhere regaining some great colonial Empire became more and more universally felt."[9] So, the year 1773 saw the first step towards the establishment of sovereignty of the British Government as the ruler of the territories conquered in India, when Lord North's Regulating Act was passed. By this Act the office of the Governor-General for India, his Council and a Supreme Court were established. By this act, the private interests of the Company bosses in England and of their employees in India were drastically curtailed. It was enacted that "no person employed in any civil or military capacity in the East Indies shall be capable of being appointed director, until such person shall have returned to and been resident in England for the space of two years; fraudulent transters of stock for voting purposes would be forbidden with severe penalties; and that "no proprietor shall be deemed qualified to vote in respect of any stock amounting to less than one thousand pounds."[10]

This was the beginning. The next was the attempt of Mr. Fox in 1783 to abolish by his India Bill the Courts of Directors and Proprietors of the Company and to vest the whole India Government in the hands of seven Commissioners appointed by Parliament. Failure of this Bill, "by the personal influence of the imbecile king over the House of Lords," was made "the instrument of breaking down the then Coalition Government of Fox and Lord North, and of placing the famous Pitt at the head of the Government."[11] What followed then has been well summed-up by Marx as follows:

> "Pitt carried in 1784 a bill through both Houses, which directed the establishment of the Board of Control, consisting of six members of the Privy Council, who were 'to check, superintend, and control all acts, operations, and concerns which in any wise related to civil and military Government, or revenues of the territories and possessions of the East India Company'. On this head, Mill, the historian says: 'In passing that law two objectives were pursued.' To avoid the imputation of what was represented as the heinous object of Mr. Fox's Bill, it was necessary that the principal part of the power should *appear* to remain in the hands of the Directors. For Ministerial advantage, it was necessary that it should in reality be all taken away. Mr. Pitt's Bill professed to differ from that of his rival chiefly in this very point, that while the onc destroyed the power of the Directors, the other left it almost entire. Under the Act of Mr. Fox, the powers of Ministers would have been avowedly held. Under the Act of Mr. Pitt, they were held in secret and by fraud. The Bill of Fox transferred the power of the Company to Commissioners appointed by Parliament. The Bill of Mr. Pitt transferred them to Commissioners appointed by the King."[12]

2. Company and the British Industrialists

In this trend for control of the Company by Parliament there was the growing influence of the industrial bourgeoisie of England, who were making themselves felt with the Industrial Revolution accomplished in England in the second half of the eighteenth century.

As noted before, the governing object of the East India Company with the typical aim of the monopolist companies of Merchant Capital had been "not the hunt for a market for British manufactures." So, from the beginning, the British manufacturers were opposed to such a policy. For instance, in 1670, the "wear of muslins was first introduced in England instead of cambrics, lawns, and other linens from Flanders and Germany;" and in 1673 complaints were made that the wear of Indian silks, chintz, etc. tended to lessen the demand for the home manufacture.[13] Afterwards, on the 23rd of February, 1676, the printing of calicoes was first undertaken in England; and in 1681 the "weavers of Spitelfields" complained that they sustained injuries by the importation of the East India Company of wrought silk and other fashionable articles of wear.[14] The Turkey Company also protested against the East India Company, stating that the importation of silk by the latter interfered with its concern as it lessened the demand for woollens.[15] Shortly, the anger of the British manufacturers was raised to such a pitch that "the silk weavers," who were more and more displeased with the preference given to the wear of Indian wrought silks, attacked the India House in London in 1697.[16]

In this and other ways, skirmishes went on between the growing industrial bourgeoisie and the well-established mercantile bourgeoisie of England; but until the industrial revolution had been fully accomplished, they were not strong enough completely to curtail the privileges of the Company. Yet they continued to agitate against the basic policy of the Company, and obtained some redress to their "grievances." At the end of the seventeenth century, John Pollexfen lamented over "England and India inconsistent in their manufactures;"[17] and by 1720 the British manufacturers "had succeeded in securing the complete prohibition of the import of Indian silks and printed calicoes into England, and increasingly heavy duties were imposed on all Indian manufactured cotton goods."[18] On the other hand, for the first time in 1728, the Company tried to trade in grains and salt in Bengal, duty free.[19]

Continuing the process, during the reign of William III, the wearing of wrought silk and of printed and dyed calicoes from India, Persia and China was prohibited by law, and it was further enforced that anybody found to possess or wear these articles would be fined £ 200. Similar laws were enacted during the rule of George I, George II and George III, "in consequence of the repeated lamentations of the afterwards so 'enlightened' British manufacturers."[20] Henceforth, the Company could import these goods from the East only for re-export to the Continent.

Meanwhile, the full flowering of the role of British merchant capital (after the Company began to usurp political power in India from 1757) contributed significantly to the industrial revolution in Britain, as the immense wealth of the subcontinent—wrenched away from the Indians in the forms of taxes, tributes, "presents" from the *nawabs*, and sometimes simple appropriation of what the artisans, peasants and traders possessed (and which they had to submit to the Company's officials and other private English traders)—began to pour into England. Brooks Adams stated:[21]

"Very soon after Plassey, the Bengal plunder began to arrive in London, and the effect appears to have been instantaneous; for all the authorities agree that the 'industrial revolution,' the event which has divided the nineteenth century from all antecedent time, began with the year 1760. Prior to 1760, according to Baines, the machinery used for spinning cotton in Lancashire was almost as simple as in India; while about 1750 the English iron industry was in full decline because of the destruction of the forests for fuel. At that time four-fifths of the iron used in the kingdom came from Sweden.

Plassey was fought in 1757, and probably nothing has ever equalled in rapidity of the change which followed. In 1760 the flying shuttle appeared, and coal began to replace wood in smelting. In 1764 Hargreaves invented the spinning jenny, in 1776 Crompton contrived the mule, in 1785 Cartwright patented the powerloom, and, chief of all, in 1768 Watt matured the steam engine, the most perfect of all vents of centralising energy. But, though these machines served as outlets for the accelerating movement of the time, they did not cause that acceleration. In themselves inventions are passive, many of the most important having lain dormant for centuries, waiting for a sufficient store of force to have accumulated to set them working. That store must always take the shape of money, and money not hoarded, but in motion. Before the influx of the Indian treasure, and the expansion of credit which followed, no force sufficient for this purpose existed; and had Watt lived fifty years earlier, he and his invention must have perished together. Possible since the world began, no investment has ever yielded the profit reaped from the Indian plunder, because for nearly fifty years Great Britain stood without a competitor. From 1694 to Plassey (1757) the growth had been relatively slow. Between 1760 and 1815 the growth was very rapid and prodigious."

Thereafter the industrial bourgeoisie of England became a formidable force and the strongest enemy of the Company's monopoly. Their rapidly mounting manufactures needed a suitable outlet, and to this the Company was then the greatest hindrance. As Engels wrote:[22]

"The conquest of India by the Portuguese, Dutch and English between 1500 and 1800 had *imports from* India as its object—nobody dreamt of exporting anything there. And yet what a colossal reaction these discoveries and conquests, solely conditioned by the interests of trade, had upon industry: they first created the need for *export to* these countries and developed large-scale industry."

What was necessary, therefore, was

"... a revolution in the economic system, from the principles of mercantile capitalism to the principles of free-trade capitalism. And this in turn involved a corresponding complete change in the methods of the colonial system.

The new needs required the creation of a free market in India in place of the previous monopoly. It became necessary to transform India from an exporter of cotton goods to the whole world into an importer of cotton goods. This meant a revolution in the economy of India. It meant at the same time a complete change-over from the whole previous system of the East India Company. A transformation had to be carried through in the methods of exploitation of India, and a transformation would have to be fought through against the strenuous opposition of the vested interests of the Company's monopoly....

It was obvious that, in the interests of effective exploitation, the wholesale anarchic and destructive methods of spoliation pursued by the East India Company and its servants could not continue without some change. The stupid and reckless rapacity of the Company and its servants was destroying the basis of exploitation, just as in England a few years later the unbounded greed of the Lancashire manufacturers was to devour nine generations of the people in one. And just as the greed of the manufacturers had to be curbed by the action of the State on behalf of the capitalist class as a whole, in the interests of future exploitation (the attack being led by their economic rivals, the landed interests), so in the last quarter of the eighteenth century the central organs of the State had to be invoked to regulate the operations of the Company in India. Here also the attack was led by the rival interests. All the numerous interests opposed to the exclusive monopoly of the East India Company combined to organise a powerful offensive against it. ...

This offensive, which had the support, not only of the rising English manufacturing interests, but of the powerful trading interests excluded from the monopoly of the East India Company, was the precursor of the new developing industrial capitalism, with its demand for free entry into India as a market, and for the removal of all obstacles, through individual corruption and spoliation, to the effective exploitation of that market."[23]

The first tangible result of the offensive was felt in 1769, when along with the first introduction of Parliamentary interference it was stipulated that "the Company should, during each year of the term, export British merchandise, exclusive of naval and military stores, to the amount of 380,837 *l*."[24] This role of the British industrial bourgeoisie and their growing influence on the Company's rule in India is also revealed by the following polite commentary by R. C. Dutt on the situation in India in 1769.

"British weavers had begun to be jealous of the Bengal weavers, whose silk fabrics were imported into England, and a deliberate endeavour was now made to use the political power obtained by the Company to discourage the manufactures of Bengal in order to promote the manufactures of England. In their general letter to Bengal, dated 17th March 1769, the Company desired that the manufacture of raw silk should be encouraged in Bengal, and that of manufactured silk fabrics should be discouraged. And they also recommended that the silk-winders should be forced to work in the Company's factories, and prohibited from working in their own homes.

'This regulation seems to have been productive of very good effects, particularly in bringing over the winders, who were formerly so employed, to work in the factories. Should this practice (the winders working in their own homes) through inattention have been suffered to take place again, it will be proper to put a stop to it, which may now be more effectually done, by an absolute prohibition under severe penalties, by the authority of the Government.'

'This letter,' as the Select Committee justly remarked, 'contains a perfect plan of policy, both of compulsion and encouragement, which must in a very considerable degree operate destructively to the manufactures of Bengal. Its effects must be (so far as it could operate without being eluded) to change the whole face of that industrial country, in order to render it a field of the produce of crude materials subservient to the manufactures of Great Britain.'"[25]

While British industries were being promoted at the expense of the Indians, an ideological offensive against the Company was launched by Adam Smith, "the father of the classical economy of free-trade manufacturing capitalism, and precursor of the new era."[26] In his celebrated work, *An Inquiry into the Nature and Causes of the Wealth of Nations*, which came out in 1776, Adam Smith mercilessly attacked the entire basis of the exclusive companies and concretely cited the East India Company as a harmful relic of the past. Referring to the English and the Dutch East India Companies he noted:[27]

"Such exclusive companies, therefore, are nuisances in every respect; always more or less inconvenient to the countries in which they are established, and destructive to those which have the misfortune to fall under their government."

He further expanded his views on this point elsewhere in his book as follows:[28]

"When a company of merchants undertake, at their own risk and expense, to establish a new trade with some remote and barbarous nation, it may not be unreasonable to incorporate them into a joint stock company, and to grant them, in case of their success, a monopoly of the trade for a certain number of years. It is the easiest and most natural way in which the state can recompense them for hazarding a dangerous and expensive experiment, of which the public is afterwards to reap the benefit. A temporary monopoly of this kind may be vindicated upon the same principles upon which a like monopoly of a new machine is granted to its inventor, and that of a new book to its author. But upon the expiration of the term, the monopoly ought certainly to determine; the forts and garrisons, if it was found necessary to establish any, to be taken into the hands of government, their value to be paid to the company, and the trade to be laid open to all subjects of the state. By a perpetual monopoly, all the other subjects of the state are taxed very absurdly in two different ways: first, by the high price of goods, which, in the case of a free trade, they could buy much cheaper; and, secondly, by their total exclusion from a branch of business which it might be both convenient and profitable for many of them to carry on. It is for the most worthless of all purposes, too, that they are taxed in this manner. It is merely to enable the company to support the negligence, profusion, and malversation of their own servants, whose disorderly conduct seldom allows the dividend of the company to exceed the ordinary rate of profit in trades which are altogether free, and very frequently makes it fall even a good deal short of that rate. ... The East India Company, upon the redemption of their funds, and the expiration of their exclusive privilege, have a right, by act of parliament, to continue a corporation with a joint stock, and to trade in their corporate capacity to the East Indies in common with the rest of their fellow subjects. But in this situation, the superior vigilence and attention of private adventurers would, in all probability, soon make them weary of the trade."

"Here," as Palme Dutt remarked, "we have the voice of the rising manufacturers' opposition to the mercantile basis of the East India Company, and the prelude to the victory of the industrial capitalists over the old system."[29]

The results of such onslaughts from the industrial bourgeoisie and their spokesmen were as expected. British manufactures were forced into India through the agency of the Governor-General and Commercial Residents, while Indian manufactures were shut out from England by prohibitive tariffs. From the evidence of John Ranking, a merchant examined by the Committee of the House of Commons in 1813, it was found that coloured piece-goods were prohibited from being imported into England; for importing muslins and calicoes to the same destination the merchant had to pay a duty before 1813 of a little over 27 and 68 per cent, respectively; and for importing these goods for Europe, that is, only for re-exportation, they had to pay a duty of 10 per cent on muslins and a little over 3 per cent on calicoes and coloured goods.[30] The consequence of such discrimination was obvious. From the return to an Order of House of Commons, dated 4th May 1813, it is seen that the value of cotton goods alone sent out from England to ports east of the Cape of Good

Hope (mainly to India) increased from £ 156 in 1794 to £ 108,824 in 1813, that is, nearly 700 times within a period of only twenty years.[31]

Yet neither had the industrial bourgeoisie of England obtained full power, nor was India fully de-industrialized. So the decisive stage came in 1813 when, on the one hand, industrial capital was solidly established in England, and, on the other, there were no more overshadowing world issues of the French Revolution "which ended the reforming period of Pitt's administration and revealed the role of the English bourgeoisie as the leader of world counter-revolution."[32] "Till then," as Marx wrote, "the interests of the British moneyocracy which had converted India into its landed estates and of the oligarchy who had conquered it by their armies, and of the millocracy who had inundated it with their fabrics, had gone hand in hand;" but "the manufacturers, conscious of their ascendency in England, ask now for the annihilation of these antagonistic powers in India, for the destruction of the whole ancient fabric of Indian government, and for the final eclipse of the East India Company."[33] There was also the point that since Napoleon Bonaparte had excluded British manufactures from the continental ports, there was a greater demand to have the "freedom" to dump English goods in India. Hence, when the charter of the Company was renewed in 1813, its monopoly of trade with India was abolished, and thus the industrial bourgeoisie of Britain obtained a free outlet for their manufactures into the great field of India.

But there remained one thing to be done, and that was to crush completely India's industrial power. Severe onslaughts had been made until 1813 into India's industrial sphere; yet it remained in some ways superior to that of the British, especially in textile manufacture, which had become, on the other hand, one of the primary industries of Britain. In 1813, when the Company's charter was renewed but its monopoly in trade with India was abolished, an inquiry was made in the House of Commons to ascertain how Indian manufactures could be replaced by British manufactures and how British industries could be promoted at the expense of Indian industries. And this was done at a time when India had suffered from repeated famines in the preceding half-century, a famine was desolating Bombay in that very year, and industries and manufactures of India, according to all witnesses, had declined in Bengal and Madras. But the British Government had greater interests to look after than mere survival of the robbed and poverty-stricken Indians. As R. C. Dutt remarked:[34]

> "... it was not in human nature that they should concern themselves much with the welfare of Indian manufacture."

Of the many witnesses called before the Committee, there were Warren Hastings and Thomas Munro, both of whom had spent long years in India as top-grade officials of the Company and were thus fully acquainted with the situation there. Both of them declared that there was not a great scope for British manufactures in India, firstly, because of the poor financial position of the mass of the people, and, secondly, because Indian manufactures, especially textiles, were still superior to British manufactures.[35] So, to promote British industries in India and finally to destroy Indian industries, that session of British Parliament put a new duty of 20 per cent on the consolidated duties whereby the duties on calicoes and muslins for home consumption were raised to a little over 78 and 31 per cent, respectively. Wilson remarked in this connection in his continuation to Mill's *History of British India*:[36]

> "It was stated in evidence, tnat the cotton and silk goods of India up to this period could be sold for a profit in the British market, at a price from fifty to sixty per cent lower than those fabricated in England. It consequently became necessary to protect the latter by duties of seventy and eighty per cent on their value, or by positive prohibition. Had this not been the case, had not such prohibitory duties and decrees existed, the mills of Paisley and of Manchester would have been stopped in their outset and could scarcely have been again set in motion, even by the powers of steam. They were created by the sacrifice of the Indian manufacture. Had India been independent, she would have retaliated; would have imposed preventive duties upon British goods, and would thus have preserved her own productive industry from annihilation. This act of self-defence was not permitted her; she was at the mercy of the stranger. British goods were forced upon

her without paying any duty; and the foreign manufacturer employed the arm of political injustice to keep down and ultimately strangle a competitor with whom he could not have contended on equal terms."

Results were soon forthcoming from such a policy. Between 1818 and 1836 the export of cotton twists from Great Britain to India rose in the proportion of 1 to 5,200; and, while in 1824 the export of British muslins to India hardly amounted to 1 million yards, in 1837, it exceeded 64 million yards.[37] Simultaneously, the process of extinction of Indian manufactures went on under the new arrangement. In 1813 Calcutta exported to London 2 million sterling worth of cotton goods; in 1830, Calcutta imported 2 million sterling of British cotton manufactures. The first import of British cotton twist into India was in 1823; before that India had her own. But in 1824 it was of 121,000 lbs., in 1828 it rose to 4,000,000 lbs. Woollen goods, copper, lead, iron, glass and earthenware were also imported. British manufactures were imported into Calcutta on payment of a duty of 2½ per cent, while the import of Indian manufactures into England was discouraged by heavy duties ranging up to 400 per cent on their value![38] And all along British private trade with India went on swelling in bulk; "the average value of the whole private trade for fifteen years subsequently to 1814–15 was more than seventeen crores or seventeen millions sterling per annum, being an advance of nearly four millions a year."[39] Marx wrote in 1853:[40]

"Till 1813, India had been chiefly an exporting country, while it now became an importing one; and in such a quick progression that already in 1823 the rate of exchange which had generally been 2s. 6d. per Rupee, sank down to 2s. per Rupee. India, the great workshop of cotton manufacture for the world since immemorial times, became now inundated with English twists and cotton stuffs. After its own produce had been excluded from England, or only admitted on the most cruel terms, British manufactures were poured into it at a small or merely nominal duty, to the ruin of the native cotton fabrics once so celebrated. In 1780, the value of the British produce and manufactures amounted only to £ 386,152, the bullion exported during the same year to £ 15,041, the total value of exports during 1780 being £ 12,648,616. So that India trade amounted to only 1—32nd of the entire foreign trade. In 1850, the total exports to India from Great Britain and Ireland were £ 8,024,000 of which the cotton goods alone amounted to £ 5,220,000, so that it reached more than 1/4 of the foreign cotton trade. But, the cotton manufacture also employed now 1/8 of the population of Britain and contributed 1—12th of the whole national revenue. After each commercial crisis, the East Indian trade grew of more paramount importance for the British cotton manufacturers, and the East India Continent became actually their best market."

3. British Industrial Capital and "Reforms" in India

Simultaneously with this liquidation of Indian industries and her reduction to an "agricultural farm of England," as Montgomery Martin so forcefully described,[41] went the introduction of "reform measures" in order to prepare India for exploitation by British industrial capital. For a government with a long-term perspective of profiting from the colony as a supplier of raw materials to British industries and a consumer of British manufactures, it was an indispensable demand of British industrial capital that Indian society should be brought on to a stable footing, economically and socially, so far as the "reforms" did not affect the basic policy of the foreign rulers. It will be remembered that, as described in the last chapter, Warren Hastings had earlier felt the need for some "reforms" in order to establish a stable basis for British rule in India, and he was rightly characterized as having "laid the real foundations of the British power in India." But so long as British merchant capital dominated over India, a long-term arrangement was not necessarily within the purview of the ruling power and a drastic change in the socio-economic organization of India was not deliberately called for. Whereas, the need of British industrial capital to find a regular and a sustained market for British goods in India and for the constant supply of raw materials for British industries from the subcontinent demanded the orientation of India's socio-economic life to that end; and, therefore, relevant "reform measures" now became urgent.

As a result, while some social reforms were also hesitantly introduced in this period (such as the abolition of *sati* in 1829, during the Governor-Generalship of Lord William Cavendish-Bentinck) in order to pacify the insistent demand of the growing Indian intelligentsia, the principal "reforms" were made in the direction of gearing India's life to the direct needs of the British industrial bourgeoisie. It was felt that indiscriminate extraction of India's wealth and resources should be stopped completely and the method of utilizing the colony in the interests of British industrial capital should be properly planned. It was found necessary for the same purpose to introduce efficient means of transport and communication as well as a properly organized civil administration. And it was also found useful to produce cheap-priced clerks and low-grade functionaries from the native population in order to run the government machinery as well as the business organizations at a lower cost than would be entailed if even such routine duties as entrusted to these categories of office workers were to be handled by compatriots brought over from Britain.

Hence, firstly, under the Governor-Generalship of Lord Cornwallis (1786–1793, and 1805), the administration of India was reorganized, and in place of individual corruption and pillage by the British employees of the Company the foundations were laid for the system of well-paid civil servants.

Secondly, to check the unplanned acquisition of India's resources as happened in the first phase of the Company's rule, some definite forms of land-tenure were introduced in different parts of India which brought the collection of land-revenues into systematic order while keeping the way open to increase land-tax whenever demanded. The only exception to this arrangement was in the areas under the Permanent Zemindari Settlement of Land, according to which the collection of land-revenues was permanently vested in a number of landlords created, as has been described in the previous chapter, out of the previous revenue-farmers and loyal agents (*baniyans* and *gomosthas*) of the Company and its officials.[42] Thereby the revenue-demand of the Government was fixed permanently, and it could not be enhanced so easily as it was in other areas. Henceforth, provided they paid to the government treasury the stipulated sums every year, the landlords were made in all essentials free to collect, legally or illegally, as much as they liked from the peasantry; so much so that the noted sociologist Radha Kamal Mukherjee estimated that by the end of the nineteenth century the peasants were paying "30 times more to the zemindars than their due for the collection of revenue."[43]

The Permanent Zemindari Settlement of Land was, no doubt, a set-back to the principle of the ruling power of collecting ever-increasing land-tax for themselves only. But considering the spread of political discontent and recurrent mass uprisings in the Subah of Bengal in the later half of the eighteenth century, the wise Governor-General, Lord Cornwallis, apparently found it wiser to abide by the old Indian saying that "in case of disaster the wise man leaves the half." Therefore, while sustaining some economic loss, the Company created another wall of defence between the foreign government and the Indian people (besides the creation of "Native States") by planting landlords among them. This particular usefulness of the system was quite candidly declared in an official speech by Lord Bentinck, the Governor-General of India during 1828–35, who became famous for his "social reforms." Before he became the Governor-General, Bentinck had recorded in a *Minute*, dated 29th April, 1806, that: "I am satisfied that the creation of zemindars, is a measure incompatible with the true interest of the government, and of the community at large."[44] But, as a Governor-General, he came to the viewpoint on the 8th of November, 1829:[45]

> "If security was wanting against extensive popular tumult or revolution, I should say that the Permanent Settlement, though a failure in many other respects and in most important essentials, has this great advantage at least of having created a vast body of rich landed proprietors deeply interested in the continuance of the British Dominion and having complete command over the mass of the people."

This form of land settlement was, however, introduced mainly in the Province of Bengal (the States of Bengal, Bihar and Orissa of today), and it spread to some small regions in other parts of the subcontinent. In the remaining parts of India primarily three other systems of land-tenure were established which bore uniformity in that the land-tax was not permanently fixed and it was generally enhanced at every settlement operation. For once tiding over the immediate political difficulty in the worst-affected part of India, namely Bengal, the Company was no more willing to give up even a part of its basic course of extraction in other areas.

All over South India and some parts of Bombay there prevailed the system of land-tenure known as the Ryotwari System, under which the peasants paid their land-tax directly to the State and the tax was revised at each new settlement when, on the assumption that the agrarian economy had improved in the meantime, it was usually enhanced.

In northern India the predominant system of land-tenure was called the Mahalwari System, whereby *mahals* or estates were created in the inhabited parts of the country, and the "proprietors" of a *mahal* (these being held individually or by several "proprietors" conjointly) were made "responsible in their persons and property for the payment of the sum assessed by the Government on the Mahal."[46] As in the Ryotwari area, the land-tax of course could be altered with each new settlement operation; and, except in this respect, this system was thus similar to the Permanent Zemindari Settlement of Bengal.

Lastly, in the Punjab was introduced the Village System, according to which the community of peasants living in a village was forced through its headman or representative to pay every year a stipulated total sum of land-tax to the State, raised by assessments on individual peasants belonging to the "brotherhood;" and as in other places, the tax levied on the village was liable to be increased at every successive settlement operation. This system to some extent resembled the traditional arrangement between the village community and the State, but with the profound differences that, firstly, private property right in land was established along with the introduction of this system, as it was done with all other systems, and thus worked against the very basis of the ancient village community system; and, secondly, the so-called headman or representative of the village became, in fact, the spokesman of the foreign government instead of the "brotherhood" in the village. However, probably for two main reasons the

Company retained the form of the village community in the Punjab. One of them was that here it was most apparent, for the Punjab was one of the last regions to fall prey to British rule and therefore the traditional institution was maintained to the greatest measure when a systematic land-tenure was demanded by the British bourgeoisie. And the other reason was that, having been only recently conquered, the Punjab still maintained a level of militancy which the foreign rulers would not like to disturb by introducing a completely different system of extracting land revenue.

In all essentials, however, the content of the ancient village community system in the Punjab was drained off; and, just as with the other systems of land-tenure introduced in the remaining parts of India, its purpose was to establish an economic system for a well-ordered exploitation of the Indian people as producers of raw materials for the British industrialists and as consumers of British merchandise. A new economic system was thus ushered in, "without its redeeming advantages" to India; for it was to subscribe first and foremost to the needs of the British industrial bourgeoisie. As has been stated with reference to this transition in India's economy in an authoritative study of the Indian rural problems:[47]

"... whereas economic life in India in the eighteenth century was static, India had evolved a socio-economic structure quite capable of maintaining some kind of a static equilibrium. Population growth was slow; the pressure on land was not yet felt; Indian agriculture had settled down to a customary routine based on the practical experience of generations of shrewd, though not educated, farmers; in the Indian caste system, everyone and everything had a place, however humble; and, above all, the old village economy, based on the idea of self-sufficiency was a veritable asset for the masses who could remain largely unaffected by political cataclysms. Not that the standard of life was high, but it was not unsatisfactory, not so uncertain as to lead to physical deterioration and moral decay. India had a fame in the outside world for her handicrafts and artistic products; her ships crossed the far-off seas; she had a well-developed industrial structure integrated with her agricultural economy. ... The advent of modern industrialism destroyed the self-sufficiency of the village; the old towns, the centres of handicrafts and manufactures, decayed; the old order based on status and custom gave place to a new one based on contract and the cash nexus with a centralised system of administration; the old stereo-typed social system received a severe battering in the process. The economic transition in India, as our economists have always emphasized, had features of early capitalism, without its redeeming advantages. While the old system had to crumble, nothing new could be put into its place, mainly because of the policy of drift into which the government of the country had landed itself."

Henceforth, the incentives for production were (i) the constantly increasing land-tax appropriated by the State as well as the landlords; (ii) the introduction of a money economy in the villages with the determined destruction of Indian industries (both pertaining to the village community system and the urban economy) and the forceful circulation of British merchandise all over India replace them; and (iii) the establishment of private property-right in land by means of all these systems of land-tenure, which Marx recorded as "the greatest *desideratum* of Asiatic Society,"[48] for hereby the fundamental basis of the village community system was lost for ever and with it went the subsistence character of Indian rural economy. On the other hand, all over India, with the final destruction of the village community system, the introduction of a money economy of commodity production, and the establishment of private property in land, even in those areas where landlords were not directly created by the Permanent Zemindari Settlement of Land there arose "a new landlord class as the social basis of British rule" out of the money-lenders and such anti-social elements as *baniyans* of the Company and its agents. As Gadgil noted, referring to this transition in Indian economy:[49]

"The institution of the village community, no doubt, is one which was once common almost all over Europe and Asia. The form which it took in India was, however, peculiar—being found all over the country except in the eastern portion of Bengal and in Assam. Inasmuch as nearly 90 per cent of the population lived in villages the constitution of the village was the most important factor in India's social structure. . . .

Though the contact and commerce of India with the West had been going on for many centuries, this had not affected India's economic structure at all till the nineteenth century. It was only after the series of inventions that led to the application of mechanical power to manufacture on a large scale that the English industrialist gained a considerable advantage over the Indian artisan. It was at about the same time that England acquired a large portion of India, and that new administrative and judicial systems were introduced into the land. These latter had in many parts the effect of depressing the condition of the people, or of undermining old institutions like the village community as a self-contained administrative unit. . . .

The first event, in the western world, to act on India suddenly and to have a very important economic effect was the American Civil War. It was now shown for the first time how very near to the markets of the West India had been brought. This also was the first important event to force upon the notice of the cultivator the important fact of the existence of these markets.

The history of cotton cultivation in India is a long one; but, though the cultivation of cotton in India was practised from very early times, the export of raw cotton from India is a comparatively new thing. Before the nineteenth century India was chiefly famous 'for exporting her elegant fabrics to the most civilized nations in the world.' The inventions of machinery for spinning and weaving and the consequent competition of cheap goods had considerably diminished the exports of these 'elegant fabrics,' and also at the same time revealed the possibilities of India as a supplier of raw cotton. Though, as late as 1780, America as a producer of raw cotton was quite insignificant, her progress since that date had been remarkable, especially after the discovery of Whitney's new saw-gin; and by 1830 she became the principal supplier of cotton to the growing English industry. At this date India's exports of raw cotton were very small. . . . But already the British cotton manufacturers had their attention drawn to India as a possible source of supply of the raw material for their industry. A failure of the cotton crop in America in 1846 showed to them the instability of this source, and they were busy finding an alternative in case of emergency. . . . But many causes, notably the short staple of the Indian cotton, the enormous admixture of dirt in the cotton, the difficulty of communications and also the want of a stable export market, had prevented the exports of raw cotton from India from rising hitherto to great height. Then came the American Civil War; the ports of the south were closed and there was a cotton famine in Lancashire. Naturally the English manufacturers turned to India. The effects of this creation of a sudden demand for Indian cotton were truly enormous. The Government undoubtedly exerted itself vigorously in the matter by the appointment of Cotton Commissioners for Bombay and the Central Provinces, by pushing forward construction of roads and railways and other measures; but the cultivators also were very quick to seize the opportunity of making extra profit. The price of cotton had risen greatly and the growing of cotton became suddenly very paying. . . .

But the real importance, in the economic sphere, to India lay not so much in raising the price of cotton and thus bringing about a temporary period of prosperity, but rather in bringing home to the cultivator the fact that causes other than local needs were beginning to govern the nature and extent of the crops he sowed. Briefly, it was the event that most clearly and dramatically revealed a break in the economic isolation of India. . . .

The prices of food-grains and other products in India fluctuated enormously in all parts of the country during the first fifty years of the nineteenth century; but through all these fluctuations there was one common tendency, and that was of the prices to fall. The common, and generally accepted, explanation of this phenomenon was the introduction of money economy in the country, especially the introduction of cash payments of Government assessments. India never produced any large amount of the precious metals, and so the quantity of bullion in currency at the beginning of the nineteenth century was very small. But this small amount was found quite enough for the purpose of the trade, inasmuch as most transactions were conducted by barter, and the volume of trade transacted with metallic currency was extremely small. With the introduction of the system of paying Government assessments in cash, the demand for money, especially just after harvest time, increased greatly. Thus the 'duty' thrown on the amount of currency in the country largely increased, and the prices of all commodities began to fall. This general fall in prices continued till about the middle of the century, when a reverse tendency began to operate. It was about this time that the discovery of gold mines in Australia and California and of silver in Mexico suddenly increased the world's supply of precious metals; and it was about this time that the foreign trade of India was increasing by leaps and bounds. A large quantity of these precious metals, therefore, necessarily found their way to India and set up a general movement towards an increase in prices. . . .

The rise in the price of cotton, consequent on the American Civil War, was a source of profit to all the cultivators of all the cotton-growing tracts, and so also in a smaller degree to cultivators of all parts. . . . [Therefore:] As soon as America resumed its export of cotton the demand for Indian cotton fell sharply and at the same time there was a general dislocation of trade in Bombay and the failure of many prominent merchants followed. The peasant also had generally failed to profit by the spell of prosperity that he had enjoyed; he had in most cases spent the money he gained recklessly. In some cases indeed, the cultivators on account of their increased credits had actually increased their liabilities. Thus with the slump in the cotton market the position of the cultivator became suddenly very bad.

At the same time the assessments began to fall heavily on the cultivator, especially in the south. It so happened that the period of the revision of assessments here coincided with the temporary period of prosperity enjoyed by the cultivator during the sixties. The revenue officers, taking the profits of cultivation then obtaining as the standard, raised the assessments generally a great deal. But when the period of prosperity had passed away the peasant naturally found it very difficult to pay his assessment and was further forced into borrowing largely.

Then again there was a general depression of trade all over the country and some of the industries especially felt the effects of the Franco-German War. The prices of food-grains which had been constantly rising through the previous decade became either stationary or—excepting in famine times—began slightly to fall. The State was still spending large sums of money on public works but this was not the only purpose for which it was now spending money. With Lord Northbrook's resignation in 1875 the Government of India entered on a policy which entailed more and more expenditure in military expeditions and establishments. Consequently the burden of taxation was pressing more and more heavily on the mass of the people.

All the above causes, combined with a succession of severe famines, produced a measure of distress which had not been felt by the people for many years. A very significant occurrence produced by this distress was the riot of the peasants in certain Deccan districts. . . . The disturbance was put down with ease but the Committee which inquired into the causes of it found that it was due to some very deep-seated evils. It is a well-known fact that agriculturists all over the world become involved in debt with fatal ease. It was particularly the case in India where farming on a large scale is unknown to any great extent. But before the advent of the British this process was checked a good deal by the many restrictions on the transfers of land; and also in some parts, by the State refusing to give any help to money-lenders to recover their debts.

The British had given rights of free transfer and absolute ownership—especially in the 'ryotwari' tracts—to the cultivators which they had never possessed before. Again the judicial system which had been adopted gave the money-lender a great power over his debtor, and finally the Limitation Act, making the renewal of the debt-bond in short periods compulsory, made the position of the debtor much worse. Thus, though there was nothing in the nature of a peculiar hardship in the mere fact of an agriculturist being indebted, these other causes acting in concert had reduced the debtor, in many cases, to the position of a virtual serf. The process of a general trade expansion, and the fact that the crops of the cultivator had begun, all over the country, to acquire a distinct market value, had expanded the credit of the cultivator. The ease with which the money could be recovered through the courts had made the money-lender more ready to lend. The process had gone on during the period of prosperity and the cultivator was quite oblivious of where he was going, but as soon as the reaction came and the money-lender began to tighten his grip on the cultivator's land, his real position was brought home suddenly to the cultivator.

The above applied with certain reservations, substantially to all parts of India. The causes given above and their effects are very important; for in this decade was thus started the movement of a gradual transference of land from the hands of the original cultivators to—in most cases—the money-lenders. The process can be termed beneficial, if at all, only in cases in which the land thus transferred was acquired by the land-owning classes or others who were careful agriculturists; but in most parts of the country this was not the case. In the Deccan, for example, the Marwari never wanted to take possession of the land; in many cases he did not have the land transferred to himself legally, but it was still allowed to remain in the old cultivator's name; the Marwari merely appropriated to himself entire profits of cultivation by virtue of the large number of debt-bonds that he held. The cultivator had to toil hard each year and at the end of it his mere subsistence was dependent on the clemency and reasonableness of the Marwari. Thus was a great portion of the Deccan peasant class reduced to virtual serfdom."

In this way, in course of time, everywhere absentee landlordism thriving on rack-renting the peasantry became the scourge of the Indian people, and the blessing of the foreign rulers, as described in the last chapter. On the other hand, the mere possibility of survival of the mass of the people and whatever chances there remained slightly to better their conditions of living were tied to the growing demand of the foreign rulers to supply the British industrialists with raw materials and to consume the British goods dumped in India, where a market for them existed from now on both in the towns and in the villages.

Such was the real character of the land-reforms introduced in India in the last phase of the Company's rule, when the British industrial bourgeoisie were gaining an upper hand in the mother country and were enforcing "reforms" in the colony in order to alter the economic basis of India in their particular interest and not necessarily in the interest of the Indians. As Marx wrote referring to these land-reforms:

"The obstacles presented by the internal solidity and articulation of precapitalistic, national, modes of production to the corrosive influence of commerce is strikingly shown in the intercourse of the English with India and China. The broad basis of the mode of production is here formed by the unity of small agriculture and domestic industry, to which is added in India the form of communes resting upon the common ownership of the land, which, by the way, was likewise the original form in China. In India the English exerted simultaneously their direct political and economic power as rulers and landlords for the purpose of disrupting these small economic organisations. The English commerce exerts a revolutionary influence on these organisations and tears them apart only to the extent that it destroys by the low prices of its goods the spinning and weaving industries, which soil into a caricature of itself."[51]

"If any nation's history, then it is the history of the English management of India which is a string of unsuccessful and really absurd (and in practice infamous) experiments in economics. In Bengal they created a caricature of English-landed property on a large-scale; in southeastern India a caricature of small allotment of property; in the North-west they transformed to the utmost of their ability the Indian commune with common ownership of the soil into a caricature of itself."[51]

Also, for the purpose of drawing more efficiently the raw materials out of India as well as bringing every corner of the subcontinent into the market for British goods, considerable attention was paid in the last days of the Company's rule to the building of roads and railways in India. Gadgil wrote while discussing the condition of the "Agriculturists, 1860–80:"[52]

"The rapidity with which the demand for cotton from England was met by India was only made possible by the many measures of improvement, which had been undertaken in India during the past decade. Chief among these was the extension of roads and railways. The appalling state of communications before 1850 has already been described. Till about 1845 very little had been done to forward road construction in India. In the Madras Presidency after this date a certain amount of expenditure towards the construction of roads was sanctioned. Though this money was spent, the construction of roads was but little advanced till after the Report of the Commissioners (1852). A road to Agra from Bombay was commenced in 1840; while in the Presidency itself, except for the road over the Bhor Ghat to Poona, little had been accomplished. The trunk road in the north was only from Calcutta to Benares, and even this was in a bad state. About 1850 the extension of this trunk road to Delhi was undertaken and the work was completed by 1853. But the real progress in road-building was begun under the vigorous Governor-Generalship of Lord Dalhousie by the newly formed Public Works Department. The trunk road to Delhi was completed and its further extension to Peshawar was vigorously begun.

Road-building thus really began in the fifties. After 1857 the necessity of roads for military purposes and also as feeders for the great railway trunk lines was realized and the next decade saw a rapid extension of roads in India.

But this work was now overshadowed by the even more important work of railway extension. The question of railway building in India was broached as early as 1845. But when private companies were formed capital was not forthcoming. Then ensued the long series of negotiations between the companies and the East India Company on the question of a state guarantee. These did not bear much fruit until the time of Lord Dalhousie's Governor-Generalship. Lord Dalhousie interested himself in the extension of railways in India and wrote two very able minutes on the subject, in one of which he sketched routes which trunk lines in India should take. An experimental line had already been undertaken near Calcutta in 1849; and in 1854 the first line of railway in India—from Bombay to Thana—was opened for traffic. From this date the work was pushed on vigorously until 1857, when it was temporarily checked. The ten years following saw a remarkable growth of railways in India; the work was carried on continuously and the length of miles open for traffic had been increased from 432 miles in 1859 to 5,015 miles in 1869.

It is not necessary here to discuss the system of guarantee and control by which railway construction was inaugurated in India. The first obvious effect of railways was, of course, that of making communication quicker, and for long journeys much cheaper. This was very important, at it was the extension of railways and roads that made possible the carriage of cotton in large quantities from the fields to the sea-ports."

Again, it is evident that this "reform" also was demanded by the British industrialists, and for this reason it started in the last days of the Company's rule and increasingly gathered momentum in the second half of the nineteenth century when all vestiges of obstruction to the full play of British industrial capital in the colony were destroyed with the disappearance of the East India Company in 1858. As Gadgil noted:[53]

"During the regime of the East India Company the number of big public works had been comparatively small; but the number of such works undertaken after the formation of the Public Works Department by Lord Dalhousie and especially after 1859 was very remarkable."

In addition to the construction of roads and railways, a quicker means of communication was introduced by the telegraphic system. This was, no doubt, ancillary to building efficient administrative and transport systems over the whole of India. Over and above that, it was also of strategic and military value, as became evident for the first time in 1857 when it had an important role to play in the quick suppression of what was called the "Sepoy Mutiny."[54]

Furthermore, there was another significant reform introduced in this period, namely, to give encouragement to the spread of English education in India after an Education Act was passed in 1813, and to make English the chief medium of instruction in the "State system of education in India," when, in 1835, after T. B. Macaulay's remarkable discovery that "a single shelf of a good European library was worth the whole native literature of India and Arabia,"[55] Lord William Bentinck, "acting under the advice of Mr. Macaulay and Sir Charles Trevelyan, determined to withdraw the Government support from the Sanscrit and Arabic Institutions, and to appropriate all the funds which were at its disposal exclusively to English education."[56]

The spread of English education in India had undoubtedly a beneficial role to play in society, but there is also hardly any doubt that this reform also was called for by some pressing needs of the British industrial bourgeoisie. In the earlier phase of the Company's rule, along with the policy of supporting the decadent forces in Indian society, the majority viewpoint of the representatives of the Company was to oppose the introduction of English education in India. As Marshman stated in this regard:[57]

"For a considerable time after the British Government had been established in India, there was great opposition to any system of instruction for the Natives. The feelings of the public authorities in this country were first tested upon the subject in the year 1792, when Mr. Wilberforce proposed to add two clauses to the Charter Act of that year, for sending out school masters to India; this encountered the greatest opposition in the Court of Proprietors, and it was found necessary to withdraw the clauses. That proposal gave rise to a very memorable debate, in which, for the first time, the views of the Court of Directors upon the subject of education, after we had obtained possession of the country, were developed. On that occasion one of the Directors stated that we had just lost America from our folly, in having allowed the establishment of schools and colleges, and that it would not do for us to repeat the same act of folly in regard to India; and that if the Natives required anything in the way of education, they must come to England for it. For 20 years after that period, down to the year 1813, the same feeling of opposition to the education of the Natives continued to prevail among the ruling authorities in this country."

In those days, even the necessity of the College of Fort William in Calcutta, where the officials of the Company were trained in Indian languages and affairs so that they could rule India properly, was disputed. The Court of Directors were of the opinion that it should be closed down by the end of 1803; but for reasons stated below Lord Wellesley felt so strongly against this decision that he wrote a Minute to the Court of Directors, sent its copies to Mr. Pitt and Mr. Dundas, and further wrote to Lord Dartmouth:[58]

"So convinced am I of the necessity of this institution, that I am determined to devote the remainder of my political life to the object of establishing it, as the greatest benefit which can be imparted to the public services in India, and as the best security which can be provided for the welfare of our native subjects. ... Without such a system of discipline and study in the early education of the civil service, it will be utterly impossible to maintain our extensive empire in India. The College must stand or the empire must fall."

The situation, however, was changing. One of the Directors of the Company, Charles Grant, had already written during 1792–97 in his *Observations on the state of Society among the Asiatic Subjects of Great Britain, particularly with respect to Morals; and on the means of Improving it* that besides curing the Indian people from their "want of veracity," "betrayal of confidence," "venality of the natives of India in the distribution of justice," "selfishness and avarice," "cunning and hypocritical obsequiousness, mutual discord, malice, calumnies etc.," "absence of patriotism," etc., English education would help to run the British administration satisfactorily and promote the import of British merchandise in India.[59] Referring to the introduction of the Persian language by the Muhammedan conquerors as "an obvious means of assimilating a conquered people to them," Grant wrote:[60]

"It would have been our interest to have followed their example; and had we done so, on the assumption of the *Dewannee*, or some years afterwards, the English language would now have been spoken and studied by multitudes of Hindoos throughout our provinces. The details of the revenue would, from the beginning, have been open to our inspection; and by facility of examination on our part, and difficulty of fabrication on that of the natives, manifold impositions of a gross nature, which have been practiced upon us, would have been precluded. ... We were long held in the dark, both in India and in Europe, by the use of a technical Revenue language; and a man of considerable judgement, who was a member of the Bengal Administration near twenty years since, publicly animadverted on the absurdity of our submitting to employ the unknown jargon of a conquered people. It is certain, that the Hindoos would easily have conformed to the use of English; and they would still be glad to possess the language of their masters, the language which always gives weight and consequence to the Natives who have any acquaintance with it, and which would enable every Native to make his own representation directly to the Governor-General himself, who, it may be presumed, will not commonly, henceforth, be chosen from the line of the Company's servants; and therefore, may not speak the dialects of the country. Of what importance it might be to the public interest, that a man in that station should not be obliged to depend on a medium with which he is unacquainted, may readily be conceived."

The main objection as raised by his compatriots to Grant's scheme of spreading English education in India was that it was fraught with political danger. It was stated:[61]

"If the English language, if English opinions, and improvements, are introduced in our Asiatic possessions, into Bengal, for instance; if Christianity, especially, is established in that quarter; and if, together with these changes, many Englishmen colonize there, will not the people learn to desire English liberty and the English form of Government, a share in the legislation of their own country, and commissions in the army maintained in that country? Will not the army thence become, in time, wholly provincial, officered by natives of India, without attachment to the Sovereign State? Will not the people at length come to think it a hardship to be subject, and to pay tribute, to a foreign country? And finally, will they not cast off that subjection, and assert their independence?"

Grant had no intention to undermine the relevance of the above objection—"the last and most material of the objections which are foreseen against the proposed scheme;" but still he maintained that "for every great purpose of the proposed scheme, the introduction and use of that [English] language would be most effectual; and the exclusion of it, the loss of unspeakable benefits, and a just subject of extreme regret."[62] Moreover, he pointed out:[63]

"In every progressive step of this work, we shall also serve the original design with which we visited India, that design still so important to this country—the extension of our commerce. Why is it that so few of our manufactures and commodities are vended there? Not merely because the taste of the people is not generally formed to the use of them, but because they have not the means of purchasing them. The proposed improvements would introduce both. As it is, our woollens, our manufactures in iron, copper, and steel; our clocks, watches, and toys of different kinds; our glass-ware, and various other articles are admired there, and would sell in great quantities if the people were rich enough to buy them. Let invention be once awakened among them, let them be roused to improvements at home, let them be led by industry to multiply, as they may exceedingly, the exchangeable productions of their country; let them acquire a relish for the ingenious exertions of the human mind in Europe, for the beauties and refinements, endlessly diversified, of European art and science, and we shall hence obtain for ourselves the supply of four-and-twenty millions of distant subjects. How greatly will our country be thus aided in rising still superior to all her difficulties; and how stable, as well as unrivalled, may we hope our commerce will be, when we thus rear it on right principles, and make it the means of their extension! It might be too sanguine to form into a wish, an idea most pleasing and desirable in itself, that our religion and our knowledge might be diffused over other dark portions of the globe, where Nature has been more kind than human institutions. This is the noblest species of conquest, and wherever, we may venture to say, our principles and language are introduced, our commerce will follow."

The efforts of the English philanthropists and statesmen like Grant, Macaulay and others, who had a better appreciation at that time of what Britain needed from India and what she should give to them, increasingly attained success.

"In the year 1813, Parliament, for the first time, ordered that the sum of £ 10,000 should be appropriated to the education of the Natives, at all the three Presidencies. In 1817, Lord Hastings, after he had broken the power of the Mahrattas, for the first time, announced that the Government of India did not consider it necessary to keep the Natives in a state of ignorance, in order to retain its own power: consequent on this announcement, the Calcutta School-book Society and the Hindu College were immediately founded. Lord Hastings also gave the largest encouragement to Vernacular Education, and even to the establishment of Native newspapers; but those who at that time, and for a considerable time after, enjoyed the confidence of the Government in India, were entirely in favour of confining the assistance given to education to the encouragement of Sanscrit and Arabic Literature. This state of things continued down to the year 1835, when Lord William Bentinck, acting under the advice of Mr. Macaulay and Sir Charles Trevelyan, determined to withdraw the Government support from the Sanscrit and Arabic Institutions, and to appropriate all the funds which were at its disposal exclusively to English education."[64]

The upshot was that the new educational reform began to produce, according to requirement, a "Baboo Class" out of the upper stratum of Indian society in order to supply the government and the commercial organizations with cheap-priced clerks to continue routine work, for which if British officials were to be imported the cost would have been considerable and their work also would not have been so efficient because of language difficulty, etc., as pointed out by Grant. Also a new incentive was thus given to the propagation of British merchandise in India, as visualized by Grant.

From all aspects it appears, therefore, that the force effecting the above-mentioned "reforms" in India was that of the British industrial bourgeoisie, primarily for whose interest a drastic change in the socio-economic life of the colony was called for. As Palme Dutt remarked:[65]

"All these measures were intended as reforms. In reality, they were the necessary measures to clear the ground for the more scientific exploitation of India in the interests of the capitalist class as a whole. They prepared the

way for the new stage of exploitation by industrial capital, which was to work far deeper havoc on the whole economy of India than the previous haphazard plunder."

4. "Regenerating" Mission of Britain in India

It should however also be forgotten that although while introducing the above "reforms" the British bourgeoisie were concerned only with their own profits, by these measures Britain, as an unconscious tool of history, could not but lay down the material basis for the future emancipation of India and for a fundamental change in the social development of her people. Firstly, it should be noted that by bringing the whole of the subcontinent under one government and a single system dominating the life of all people, viz. the colonial system, the foreign rulers effected an unity of the Indian people which was to have far-reaching consequences in India's future course of changes. For, as the people all over India suffered under one system of bondage and all of them faced the greatest stumbling block in the form of colonial domination against the progressive development of their society, henceforth mass energy could be released on a much wider scale than it had ever happened before in order to achieve their freedom, prosperity and progress. As Marx wrote as early as in 1853:[66]

> "The Political unity of India, more consolidated and extending farther than it ever did under the Great Moguls, was the first condition of its regeneration. That unity, imposed by the British sword, will now be strengthened and perpetuated by the electric telegraph."

Secondly, it should be borne in mind that although the foreign rulers ushered in a colonial economy in India, with "features of early capitalism" but "without its redeeming advantages" to the Indian people, the fact remains that with the final destruction of the village community system (which the progressive forces in Indian society were also leading to before India came under British rule), the way was paved for a future progressive evolution of India's socio-economic life. As Marx noted in this connection:

"Now, sickening as it must be to human feeling to witness those myriads of industrious patriarchal and inoffensive social organisations disorganised and dissolved into their units, thrown into a sea of woes, and their individual members losing at the same time their ancient form of civilisation, and their hereditary means of subsistence, we must not forget that these idyllic village communities, inoffensive though they may appear, had always been the solid foundation of Oriental despotism, that they restrained the human mind within the smallest possible compass, making it the unresisting tool of superstition, enslaving it beneath traditional rules, depriving it of all grandeur and historical energies. We must not forget the barbarian egotism which, concentrating on some miserable patch of land, had quietly witnessed the ruin of empires, the perpetration of unspeakable cruelties, the massacre of the population of large towns with no other consideration bestowed upon them than on natural events, itself the helpless prey of any aggressor who deigned to notice it at all. We must not forget that this undignified, stagnatory, and vegetative life, that this passive sort of existence evoked on the other part, in contradistinction, wild, aimless, unbounded forces of destruction and rendered murder itself a religious rite in Hindustan. We must not forget that these little communities were contaminated by distinctions of caste and by slavery, that they subjugated man to external circumstances, instead of elevating man the sovereign of circumstances, that they transformed a self-developing social state into never changing natural destiny, and thus brought about a brutalising worship of nature, exhibiting its degradation in the fact that man, the sovereign of nature, fell down on his knees in adoration of *Hanuman*, the monkey, and Sabbala the cow.

England, it is true, in causing a social revolution in Hindustan, was actuated only by the vilest interests, and was stupid in her manner of enforcing them. But that is not the question. The question is, can mankind fulfil its destiny without a fundamental revolution in the social state of Asia? If not, whatever may have been the crime of England she was the unconscious took of history in bringing about that revolution."[67]

"The Zamindar and Ryotwar themselves, abominable as they are, involve two distinct forms of private property in land—the greatest *desideratum* of Asiatic society."[68]

Thirdly, while under British rule an efficient system of transport and communication was destined to serve the interests of the British bourgeoisie to drain India's wealth and resources out of the subcontinent and to dump British goods therein, in a free India it could serve the interests of the Indian people in nation-building, in the evolution of a progressive and prosperous socio-economic life. Marx noted in 1853 on this point:[69]

> "Steam has brought India into regular and rapid communication with Europe, has connected its chief ports with those of the whole south-eastern ocean, and has revindicated it from the isolated position which was the prime law of its stagnation. The day is not far distant when, by a combination of railways and steam vessels, the distance between England and India, measured by time, will be shortened to eight days, and when that once fabulous country will thus be actually annexed to the Western World.
>
> The ruling classes of Great Britain have had, till now but an accidental, transitory and exceptional interest in the progress of India. The aristocracy wanted to conquer it, the moneyocracy to plunder it and the millocracy to undersell it. But now the tables are turned. The millocracy have discovered that the transformation of India into a reproductive country has become of vital importance to them, and that, to that end, it is necessary above all to gift her with means of irrigation and of internal communication. They intend now drawing a net of railroads over India. And they will do it. The results must be inappreciable.
>
> It is notorious that the productive powers of India are paralysed by the utter want of means for conveyance and exchanging its various produce. ... The introduction of railroads may be easily made to subserve agricultural purposes... Railways will afford the means of diminishing the amount and the cost of the military establishments...
>
> We know that the municipal organisation and the economical basis of the village communities has been broken up, but their worst feature, the dissolution of society into stereotyped and disconnected atoms, has survived their vitality. The village isolation produced the absence of roads in India, and the absence of roads perpetuated the village isolation. On this plan a community existed with a given scale of low conveniences, almost without intercourse with other villages, without the desires and efforts indispensable to social advance. The British having broken up this self-sufficient *inertia* of the villages, railways will provide the new want of communication and intercourse. ...
>
> I know that the English millocracy intend to endow India with railways with the exclusive view of extracting at diminished expense the cotton and other raw materials for their manufactures. But when you have once introduced machinery into locomotion of a country, which possesses iron and coal, you are unable to withold it from its fabrication. ... The railway system will therefore become, in India, truly the forerunner of modern industry. This

is the more certain as the Hindus are allowed by British authorities themselves to possess particular aptitude for accommodating themselves to entirely new labour, and acquiring the requisite knowledge of machinery. ... Modern industry, resulting from the railway system will dissolve the hereditary divisions of labour, upon which rest the Indian castes, those decisive impediments to Indian progress and Indian power."

Fourthly, even if English education was first introduced into India in order to produce primarily office workers for the colonial administration and business organizations serving foreign interests, it could not but open a door to the Indians to the developed sciences in the West in the period of its progressive capitalist development. Thereby, as it so happened, a new intelligentsia could develop in India synthesising their socio-cultural heritage with the progress made in the West, and eventually have a dominant say in the future course of progressive development of the Indian society. As Marx had noted in 1853: "From the Indian natives, reluctantly and sparingly educated at Calcutta, under English superintendence, a fresh class is springing, endowed with the requirements for government and imbued with European science."[70]

The above features of British rule in India, characterized by the rule of British industrial bourgeoisie in India, were hailed by Marx as indicating the "regenerating" mission of Britain in India. But, as Marx had noted at the same time and as subsequent events made it clear, it could not be supposed that the British bourgeoisie were by themselves leading the Indian society to future progress. The support given to religious orthodoxies and landlordism throughout the British rule, the disbandment of the "native army" after the Revolt of 1857, the increasing controls imposed upon the Press beginning with the Press Act of 1873, and several other measures taken subsequently as the freedom movement of India gathered momentum, left no shadow of doubt that the foreign rulers were bent upon making the colony serve their interests instead of leading it conscientiously and deliberately towards future prosperity, progress and freedom.

It is worthy of note in this connection that while in 1853 Marx had found in the "native army, organised and trained by the British drill-sergeant," the "*sine qua non* of Indian self-emancipation, and of India ceasing to be the prey of the first foreign intruder,"[71] after the Revolt of 1857, as a result of "the consequent deliberate strengthening of British forces to one-third of the whole, and the strengthening of British military control,"[72] this progressive feature in British rule in India was thrown over-board. Indian soldiers were recruited thenceforth only from particular areas on the basis of spreading the myth of so-called "martial races" of India, thereby developing virtually a "caste" of Indian soldiers having as their only mission in life service to the foreign rulers. Similarly, Marx had noted in 1853 that the "free press, introduced for the first time into Asiatic society, and managed principally by the common offspring of Hindus and Europeans, is a new and powerful agent of reconstruction."[73] But this progressive measure also, inaugurated with the announcement of the freedom of the press in India in 1835, was soon curtailed by a series of Press Acts, beginning in 1873.

Indeed, throughout the colonial rule, India was kept in such a state that recounting his eighty years of life the famous Indian poet Rabindranath Tagore declared in 1941:[74]

"There came a time when perforce I had to snatch myself away from the mere appreciation of literature. As I emerged into the stark light of bare facts, the sight of the dire poverty of the Indian masses rent my heart. Rudely shaken out of my dreams, I began to realise that perhaps in no other modern state was there such hopeless dearth of the most elementary needs of existence. And yet it was this country whose resources had fed for so long the wealth and magnificence of the British people. While I was lost in the contemplation of the great world of civilization, I could never remotely imagine that the great ideals of humanity would end in such ruthless travesty. But to-day a glaring example of it stares me in the face in the utter and contemptuous indifference of a so-called civilized race to the well-being of crores of Indian people.

That mastery over the machine, by which the British have consolidated their sovereignty over their vast empire, has been kept a sealed book, to which due access has been denied to this helpless country. ...

In India the misfortune of being governed by a foreign race is daily brought home to us not only in the callous neglect of such minimum necessities of life as adequate provision for food, clothing, educational and medical facilities for the people, but in an even unhappier form in the way the blame is laid at the door of our own society. So frightful a culmination of the history of our people would never have been possible but for the encouragement it has received from secret influences emanating from high places. ...

We know what we have been deprived of. That which was truly best in their own civilization, the upholding of the dignity of human relationship, has no place in the British administration of this country. If in its place they have established, baton in hand, a reign of 'law and order,' in other words a policeman's rule, such a mockery of civilization can claim no respect from us. ... In India, so long as no personal injury is inflicted upon any member of the ruling race, this barbarism seems to be assured of perpetuity, making us ashamed to live under such an administration. ...

The wheels of Fate will some day compel the English to give up their Indian Empire. But what kind of India will they leave behind, what stark misery? When the stream of their two centuries' administration runs dry at last, what a waste of mud and filth they will leave behind them!"

In 1942, Pandit Jawaharlal Nehru wrote:[75]

"We have endured for long the painful burden of European domination in Asia. Britain may believe and proclaim that she has done good to India and other Asian countries, but the people of India and other Asian lands think otherwise, and it is after all what we believe that matters now. It is a terribly difficult business to wipe out this past of bitterness and conflict, yet it can be done if there is a complete break from it and the present is made entirely different. ...

We cannot develop our industries, even though war-time requirements shout out for such development, because British interests disapprove and fear that Indian industry may come in their way later. Industrial growth ultimately depends on the growth of the heavy and basic industries. It is just these that are prevented from taking root and being developed in India. For years past Indian industrialists have tried to develop an automobile industry, aeroplane manufacture and shipbuilding—the very industries most required in war-time. The way these have been successfully obstructed is an astonishing story. The Eastern Group Conference has not even attempted to develop a single basic industry in India and seems to have deliberately avoided encouraging any industrial growth which might compete in later years with British industry. ...

Our principal problem is after all not the Hindu-Moslem problem, but the planned growth of industry, greater production, more just destribution, higher standards of living, and thus the elimination of the appalling poverty that crushes our people. ...

One thing stands out clearly: that the present state of affairs in India is deplorable. The Government lacks not only popular support, but also efficiency. The people who control India from Whitehall and New Delhi are incapable of understanding what is happening, still less of dealing with events. ...

We have many internal problems which come in the way of our growth. Some of them are of our own making, some of British creation. But whoever may be responsible for them, we have to solve them. One of these problems, so often talked about, is the Hindu-Moslem problem. It is often forgotten that Moslems, like Hindus, also demand independence for India. ... So long as there is a third party to intervene and encourage intransigent elements of either group, there will be no solution. A free India will face the problem in an entirely different setting and will, I have no doubt, solve it. ...

One thing is certain: whatever the outcome of this war, India is going to resist every attempt at domination, and a peace which has not solved the problem of India will not endure for long. Primarily this is Britain's responsibility, but the consequences are world-wide and they affect this war itself vitally. No country can therefore ignore India's present and her future."

And, also Marx, when he was writing his articles on India in 1853 and had commented upon the "regenerating" mission of British rule in India, noted at the same time in a letter to Engels, dated June, 14, 1853, that while in his article "the destruction of the native industry by England is described as *revolutionary*," it should be borne in mind that: "For the rest the whole rule of Britain in India was swinish and is to this day."[76]

Yet it cannot be denied that what the British bourgeoisie could not help doing was "to lay down the material premises" for a progressive development of the Indian society in future, in a free and sovereign country. As Marx had stated in 1853:[77]

"All the English bourgeoisie may be forced to do will neither emancipate nor materially mend the social condition of the mass of the people, depending not only on the development of the productive power, but of their appropriation by the people. But what they will not fail to do is to lay down the material premises for both. Has the bourgeoisie ever done more? Has it ever effected a progress without dragging individuals and people through blood and dirt, through misery and degradation?

The Indians will not reap the fruits of the new elements of society scattered among them by the British bourgeoisie, till in Great Britain itself the now ruling classes shall have been supplanted by the industrial proletariat, or till the Hindus themselves shall have grown strong enough to throw off the English yoke altogether."

5. "Finis der East India Co., Indien"

Such then was the character of changes taking place in India in the last days of the Company's rule. The increasing control exercised by the Home Government (which was more and more subscribing to the demands of the British industrialists) on the administration of India and the affairs of the East India Company, the transformation of India into the "agricultural farm of England" with the destruction of her industries, and the introduction of the above-mentioned "reform measures" indicated that the force of British merchant capital was ebbing away and it was being supplanted by the new vigour of British industrial capital.

As a result, by 1813, the final limit was placed on the scope of British merchant capital in India and the path was cleared and new avenues were opened for the successful penetration of British industrial capital in the colony. Merchant capital could no more keep pace with the march of time; it was therefore laid aside. Its monopoly was abolished, and it was thus deprived of its real strength. As has been remarked: "The distinctive economic role of the Company was brought to an end with the ending of its monopoly in 1813 (except for its monopoly of the China trade, which was ended in 1833)."[78]

The actual demise of the East India Company was effected, however, in easy stages. After 1813, the shell of this ablest representative of British merchant capital lingered on for a while; but it was a spent force. The British Government went on "fighting under the Company's name, ... till at last the natural limits of India were reached."[79] By 1849, British rule spread over India from the Himalayas to the southern tip of the subcontinent, and from the Arabian Sea to the Bay of Bengal; so that, "all the native states now became surrounded by British possessions subject to British suzerainty under various forms and cut off from the sea coast, with the sole exception of Gujarat and Scinde."[80] And, while "during all this time the parties in England have connived in silence, even those which had resolved to become the loudest with their hypocritical peace-cant after the *arrondissement* of the one Indian Empire should have been completed,"[81] all of them now became very vocal about bringing India under the British Crown. Finally, the Revolt of 1857 exposed the complete bankruptcy and obsolete character of the East India Company. The next year, therefore, India passed under the rule of the British Crown and exploitation by British industrial capital. Marx recorded:[82]

> "*December 1857: Palmerston Indian Bill*; (fällt durch,) *first reading passiert,* trotz solemn protest *des Board of Directors in Februar 1858,* aber liberal ministry replaced durch Tory.
>
> *19 Februar 1858: Disraeli's India Bill* fällt durch.
>
> *2-nd August 1858 passiert Lord Stanley's India* Bill und damit *finis der East India Co.* Indien — eine *Provinz des Empire der 'graussen' Victoria!*"

The most powerful monopolist company of British merchant capital thus died a natural death. Dominating the government in their mother country, British industrial bourgeoisie had now full sway over India. The "First Architects" of the "new civilization" in England disappeared completely from the scene.

Notes and References

1 Anonymous—*Historical Sketch on the Taxes on the English Commerce in Bengal from 1633 until 1820,* Mss. Eur. D. 283 in the Commonwealth Office Library, London, p. 2.
2 *ibid.*, p. 4
3 Marx, Karl—*The East India Company,* New York Daily Tribune, July 11, 1853.
4 *ibid.*
5 Mill, James—*The History of British India,* James Madden, London, 1858, Vol. I, p. 105.
6 *ibid.*, Vol. III, pp. 33—34
7 *loc. cit.* 3
8 *ibid.*
9 *ibid.*

10 Muir. Ramsay—*The Making of British India: 1765—1858*, Manchester at the University Press, 1917, p. 133.
11 *loc. cit.* 3
12 *ibid.*
13 *loc. cit.* 1, pp. 4—5
14 *ibid.*, pp. 5—6
15 *ibid.*, p. 6
16 *ibid.*, p. 11
17 Title of the book published in London in 1697, and referred in *loc. cit.* 3.
18 Dutt, R. P.—*India Today*, People's Publishing House, Bombay, 1949, p. 109.
19 *loc. cit.* 1, p. 16
20 *loc. cit.* 3
21 Brooks, Adams—*The Law of Civilisation and Decay*, pp. 259—260, 263—264; quoted in *loc. cit.* 18, p. 107.
22 Marx, Karl, and Engels, Frederick—*Selected Correspondence: 1846—1895*, Lawrence & Wishart, London, 1943, p. 479.
23 *loc. cit.* 18, pp. 108—109
24 *loc. cit.* 5, Vol. III, p. 337
25 Dutt, R. C.—*The Economic History of India under Early British Rule*, Routledge & Kegan Paul, London, 1950, p. 45.
26 *loc. cit.* 18, p. 109
27 Smith, Adam—*An Inquiry into the Nature and Causes of the Wealth of Nations*, Everyman's Library, London and New York, 1910, Vol. 2, p. 137.
28 *ibid.*, Vol. 2, pp. 241—242
29 *loc. cit.* 18, p. 110
30 See, for instance, the *Minutes of Evidence, etc., on the Affairs of the East India Company*, Parliamentary Papers, London, 1813, pp. 463 and 467; *loc. cit.* 25, p. 261; etc.
31 *loc. cit.* 25, p. 257
32 *loc. cit.* 18, p. 111
33 *loc. cit.* 3
34 *loc. cit.* 25, p. 269
35 *ibid.*, pp. 257—260
36 *loc. cit.* 5, Vol. VII, p. 385
37 Marx, Karl—*The British Rule in India*, New York Daily Tribune, June 25, 1853.
38 For details, see, for instance, *loc. cit.* 25, Chapter XVI.
39 Cf. Lord's Committee, 1830, App. B. 5, and C. 40; quoted in *loc. cit.* 5, Vol. VII, p. 412.
40 *loc. cit.* 3
41 Quoted in R. C. Dutt's *The Economic History of India in the Victorian Age*, Routledge & Kegan Paul, London, 1950, p. 114.
42 For some details on this process of change in Bengal, which was the classical area for the elaboration of the Permanent Zemindari Settlement, see, for instance, the writer's *The Dynamics of a Rural Society: A Study of the Economic Structure in Bengal Villages*, Akademie-Verlag, Berlin, 1957, Chapter 1.

43 Mukherjee, Radha Kamal—*Land Problems in India*, Longmans, Green & Co., London, 1933, p. 305.
44 Anonymous—*The Fifth Report from the Select Committee on the Affairs of the East India Company, ordered by the House of Commons to be printed, 28 July, 1812*, British Parliamentary Papers, London, 1812, p. 160.
45 Keith, A. B.—*Speeches and Documents on Indian Policy: 1750—1921*, Vol. I, p. 215, Lord Bentinck's speech on November 8, 1829; quoted in *loc. cit.* 18, p. 218.
46 From the *Return to an Order of the House of Commons*, dated June 9, 1857, submitted by the India House, London; quoted in *loc. cit.* 41, pp. 93—94.
47 Nanavati, M. B., and Anjaria, J. J.—*Indian Rural Problem*, The Indian Society of Agricultural Economics, Bombay, 1944, pp. 74—75.
48 Marx, Karl—*The Future Results of British Rule in India*, New York Daily Tribune, August 8, 1853.
49 Gadgil, D. R.—*The Industrial Evolution of India*, Geoffrey Cumberlege, Oxford University Press, 1950, pp. 8—9, 12, 13—15, 17, 19—20, 22, 26—29.
50 Marx, Karl—*Capital: A Critique of Political Economy*, Charles H. Kerr & Co., Chicago, 1909, Vol. III, p. 392.
51 *ibid.*, p. 392, n 51
52 *loc. cit.* 49, pp. 17—18
53 *ibid.*, p. 18
54 See, for instance, R. C. Majumdar, H. C. Raychaudhuri and Kalikinkar Datta's *An Advanced History of India*, Macmillan, London, 1953, p. 780.
55 Quoted in *loc. cit.* 10, p. 299.
56 Cf. John Clarke Marshman's statement before the Select Committee of the House of Lords, British Parliament, *Parliamentary Papers: The Second Report of the Select Committee of the House of Lords on Indian Territories*, London, 1852—53, p. 113.
57 *ibid.*, p. 113
58 Quoted by John Clarke Marshman in *The Life and Times of Carey, Marshman, and Ward*, Longman, Brown, Green, Longmans, & Roberts, London, 1859, Vol. I, p. 170.
59 Mahmood, Syed—*A History of English Education in India*, M. A.—O. College, Aligarh, 1895, Chapters II and III.
60 Cf. *Parliamentary Papers relating to the affairs of India: General*, Appendix I, *Public*, London, 1832, pp. 3—89; quoted in *loc. cit.* 59, p. 12.
61 Quoted in *loc. cit.* 59, p. 14.
62 *ibid.*, pp. 14—15
63 *ibid.*, p. 17
64 *loc. cit.* 56, p. 113
65 *loc. cit.* 18, p. 112
66 *loc. cit.* 48
67 *loc. cit.* 37
68 *loc. cit.* 48
69 *ibid.*
70 *ibid.*
71 *ibid.*

72 *loc. cit.* 18, p. 90
73 *loc. cit.* 48
74 Tagore, Rabindranath—*Crisis in Civilization*, Visva-Bharati, Calcutta, 1950, pp. 6—7, 12—13, 13—14, 16—17.
75 Nehru, Jawaharlal—*What India Wants*, The India League, London, 1942, pp. 8, 9—10, 11, 12, 15.
76 *loc. cit.* 22, p. 70
77 *loc. cit.* 48
78 *loc.* cit. 18, p. 96
79 *loc. cit.* 3
80 *ibid.*
81 *ibid.*
82 Marx, Karl — *Chronologische Auszüge über Ostindien* (Chronological Notes on India), Photo-copy of the original manuscript in the Institute for Marxism-Leninism, Berlin, p. 150. (All underlined words in the manuscript are italicized in the extract.)

INDEX